THE "TRUTH" OF THE BIBLE

LONDON AGENTS
SIMPKIN MARSHALL LTD

The "Truth" of the Bible

By

STANLEY A. COOK, Litt.D.

*Hon.D.D., Aberdeen; F.B.A.; Regius Professor of Hebrew
in the University of Cambridge*

CAMBRIDGE
W. HEFFER & SONS LTD
LONDON
SOCIETY FOR PROMOTING CHRISTIAN KNOWLEDGE
NORTHUMBERLAND AVENUE, W.C.2
NEW YORK
THE MACMILLAN COMPANY

First Published 1938

4 1488

PRINTED AND BOUND IN GREAT BRITAIN
AT THE WORKS OF
W. HEFFER AND SONS LTD
CAMBRIDGE, ENGLAND

TO THE
UNIVERSITY OF ABERDEEN
AND TO THE MEMORY OF
WILLIAM ROBERTSON SMITH
(1846-1894)

C

Preface

THE concluding chapters which give their title to this book will explain its scope. The unusual device of placing the word "Truth" in inverted commas is to provoke attention to four questions which have constantly been before me: What is the Truth we expect or desire to gain from the Bible? What true things, important for us to-day, emerge from the modern critical study of the Bible? What is the process whereby we reach a position where we are able to say that so-and-so is true? And finally, what is there that, just because it is true, must be made real and must be manifested in life and thought? Accordingly, although the "Truth of the Bible" might sound a somewhat hackneyed subject, there are some fundamental questions which we should ask ourselves, questions which it is easier to ask than to answer.

For an age of stern events, an age of change and of choice, the Bible is of unique significance. Not only has it been of incalculable influence—hitherto at least—upon Western culture, but also the story of its growth and of its interpretation testify to developments so fundamental that we have everything to gain from a fuller knowledge of them. In these days of conflicting "-isms" and "ideologies," we have, on the Right Wing, the old, elaborate and highly systematised theology and scholastic philosophy of the Roman Church, and we are confronted on the Left, by the militant, anti-religious idealism and philosophy of Marxism and Communism. There are also "totalitarian" systems which have found the Truth they desire—or at least the way to it; but there are numerous less conspicuous movements in the world of thought, straws which show that winds are blowing strongly—but which do not as yet point in one direction. All around we see uncertainty, change and decay; and Christianity, Christendom and the West are not alone involved. There is a wide-spread feeling of impending change, and what to-day is virtually a crisis in the history of Religion means that there is a crisis in men's conceptions of what is ultimately most real, effective and true.

Three main lines of thought run through these chapters: (1) the historical view of Nature and Man; (2) History and Religion; and (3) what I have called the "Theory of Religion." Here some personal remarks may be permitted.

(1) In my most impressionable years the Bible, *Pilgrim's Progress*, and the works of Darwin, Thomas Huxley and Lyell, were equally accessible and were perused with almost equal curiosity and interest. Geology and the Bible did not seem to conflict; there was no notion that Nature and Man should be severed. In more mature years, reading of the researches into the past "history" of things, I was already prepared to take a single continuous "historical" view, passing from the story of the Universe to the dawn of life, and from prehistoric man to the events before, in and after the Bible. It did not seem that there must be an absolute gulf between the age-long processes at work in Nature and those in her offspring Man; nor could I feel that the mind when it is thinking about Nature is different from the mind when it thinks about Man. Needless to say, my debt to the great leaders in Science and Philosophy is far more complete than my references would suggest; and, venturing into a field where the untutored layman so easily goes astray, I can only hope that I have succeeded in showing that our ideas of the "history" of Nature and Man must include those periods of history where the principles and processes of development can be more readily investigated—namely in the lengthy history of the lands of the Bible.

(2) To that great Anglican Dean, Arthur Penrhyn Stanley, after whom my Nonconformist parents had named me, I came to owe—after many years—the watchword "Whatever is true History teaches true Religion" (see p. 83). He himself, more than sixty years ago, recognised that the Exilic Age and the middle centuries of the first millennium B.C. formed "one of the most strongly-marked epochs in the history of the world." Subsequent research has amply

justified the accuracy of his insight, and the period round about the sixth century B.C. holds a central position in these pages, as being scarcely less epoch-making than the rise of Christianity itself. The period is a landmark for Religion, Science and Philosophy, a turning-point in the history of human thought, only to be equalled perhaps by the present age. In Israel it was the age of the restatement or reassertion of the existence of Jehovah;[1] and the doctrine of the God of Israel, the God of the Universe, paved the way for the later doctrine of the New Israel, and God in Christ. The Old Testament may be said to turn upon a decisive mono-theistic movement, the culmination of the work of the reforming prophets, even as, a few centuries later, the New Testament turns upon the reforming movement among the Jews that led to Christianity.

(3) To-day the Bible and the world's religions are studied in a scientific spirit. In every religion are particular forms of Religion, and my own conviction that some restatement of Christianity affords the only foundation for any further progressive development of Culture[2] arises from a comparative and historical study of Religion that to some readers may appear too uncompromising. To Robertson Smith I owe what I would call the conception of the "Theory of Religion." There are many theories of the origin, content and nature of Religion, but I have in mind a general view of Religion—what it has to say for itself, what it implies, the significance for us of what men in the past have felt to be most real and true, the relation between *their* Reality and *ours*, and above all the interconnection between "religious" truth and reality and what we consider true and real in the "non-religious" realms of life and thought. Fundamental questions of course arise at once; e.g. if it be really true that "in Him we live and move and have our being," how does this bear upon our thinking processes? And again, are there really innumerable gods and spirits, such as the Comparative Study of Religions reveals to us? How are we to co-ordinate

[1] The form Yahweh is used in these pages.
[2] I use the word Culture, throughout, of civilisation, and especially its moral, spiritual and ideal aspects.

and systematise our material? Philosophical and meta-physical problems abound; and, in fact, it was in the attempt to draft chapters on the Religion and Philosophy of the Bible that the need for these preliminary studies made itself felt.

Chapter I, on the Interdependence of Religion and Research, deals especially with the interpenetration of the two spheres, or hemispheres, of the "religious" and the "non-religious."

Chapters II, III and IV are introductory and rather more popular. They are concerned with Old Testament criticism and the way in which the Pentateuch illustrates the Exilic Age; the work of the Prophets; the idea of "Righteousness"; the post-exilic Israel; and the interrelation between the changes in the Exilic Age and those in the first century A.D.

Chapter V, on the development or evolution of Religion in and behind the Bible, emphasises the uniqueness of the Book for our knowledge of processes of growth and change, and the necessity of understanding the bifurcation in the first century A.D. into Christianity and Rabbinical Judaism.

Next, Chapter VI turns to the more philosophical aspects of the changes which took place in and behind the Bible and also of the changes in our interpretation of these; the creative movements in life and thought; the emergence of new stages and the difference between the "before" and "after;" and the essential difference between the Biblical and the non-Biblical material and the various ways in which we approach and use it. Knowing, as we do, the influence of the Bible in history, we may also ask ourselves whether the critical study of the Bible will exercise a fresh influence upon theology and philosophy, more in accordance with modern thought.

Chapter VII, on ideas of Holiness and Righteousness, is of a more introductory character. The holy or sacred is not necessarily ethical, and ideas of Righteousness (Rightness), Order and Truth are interconnected. By a "God of Right(eous)ness" we mean One whose acts are sooner or later recognised to be right, true and natural; and the Holiness of God involves also the Transcendence of One

who is immanent in the Universe.   Man is no machine,
his God-granted creativeness and freedom account alike
for his evil and wrong-doing and for his goodness and
achievement: the evident processes that constantly repair,
adjust and set right what is wrong, involve our ideas
of forgiveness and atonement.   In general, we are led to
consider the principles of any successful, permanent and
progressive advance, whether we regard it as revolutionary
or evolutionary.

Chapter VIII gives a summary account of the period
round about the sixth century B.C.   The Bible is Levantine
(Palestinian) rather than Semitic or Hebrew, and the continuity in the religion of Israel is—for some reason—more
significant than the vicissitudes in other lands.   This
continuity throws into greater relief the events of the first
century A.D.; there is a "natural" interrelation between the
"spirit" of a religion and its "body" or embodiment, and the
tragic history of Palestine by the side of the rapid growth of
Christianity cannot be too earnestly heeded.

Chapter IX is an independent essay on Ethical Monotheism
and the Theory of Religion.   The former forces us to crys-
tallise our religious thoughts and sharpens the difference
between the religion of Israel and other religions.   The
latter integrally associates Man with the Universe or with
its God.   Deeper thinking reveals the organic connection
between Man and Nature, but it also makes men sons of a
Divine Father.   The unsuspected or unconscious influence
of Man's cosmic or his Divine relationship may account for
the paradoxes that arise as our thoughts pass from this real
external world in which we have to live to the point where
one may question whether, in the last analysis, there is
really any "external" world.

The last three chapters carry on and supplement the
previous nine.   Chapter X is more concerned with historical
processes, the way in which the present epoch and the two
great epochs in the Bible interpret one another, and the nature
of the processes that move history in individuals and peoples.
If we ask whether God is to be found only *here* or *there* in
Biblical history or whether He is to be seen throughout—

and, indeed, not in Biblical history alone—we distinguish between the *religious* truth that God is everywhere immanent, and the truth in *history*, that He manifests Himself anew to men and peoples at the great historical crises. In Chapter XI we find, as we go deeper into the Bible that philosophical questions arise of Truth, Order, Right and Reality. The material of history consists of events, but the ideas they manifest give "form" and meaning to it. Disorder and disorganisation give new emphasis to ideas of order and organisation, and we can pass through a transitional period from one stage or order to another. The humanism and naturalism of to-day reject too much important religious evidence; and revolutionary ideas ignore the orderly development of progressive thought. The present-day concern with "patterns" and the like is of special interest in that they link up with the Platonic "ideas" or "forms" and the ancient conception of a transcendent Wisdom, or Logos. In general, the present age is reorganising its material. And while Science has its field of sense-data, in the world of thought we work more consciously on a higher conceptual level, seeing that through the progressive development of religious and non-religious thought in human history we owe our modern investigation of the objects presented to our senses. How we come to think as we do is not less important than what it is we think about.

Finally, arising out of the deeper study of the Bible are questions that concern the further history of Culture in general. The dialectic process in history is not so much philosophical or even social-economic as religious: God creating the world and reconciling it to Himself in His Messiah the Christ. Christianity—one may say—arose out of the new consciousness at a certain period in history of a Divine Process which creates, loves its creatures, gives them freedom, and atones and repairs their errors. It was a religious Truth revealed in history, and it may require a new historical event, and a sweeping religious awakening, once more to give it renewed freshness, reality and driving power. Through the Messiah men approach the Ultimate Reality, God; but God must not be a "blank cheque"—to

use the late Canon Streeter's term—and this age may have
to reaffirm what it means by "God" and "Christ."

The Christian ideal—it must be emphasised—is that of
the normal co-existence of the "religious" and the "non-
religious," making for the fullest development of the faculties
and for life abounding. God is surely a "natural" part of
the total Universe; there is a higher "naturalness," and what
we call Nature and the world of our tested knowledge
are but a part or aspect of it. Of this Ultimate Universe we
are ignorant; of the limitations of our positive knowledge
we are painfully aware; there may even be higher psychic
powers (e.g. in telepathy) waiting to be developed; and a
complete view cannot leave out of reckoning the question
of the noble and cherished dead. But there is an orderly and
"natural" development of life and thought, and there can be
no "short cuts" to our Promised Land. Between us and the
Ultimate Reality there is a veritable hierarchy of processes
(physical, organic, psychological and, now, ideological), and
through them every creature, according to its stage of
development, gains experience, and fulness of life. The
words ideology, ideological, and the like have an ugly
sound for many of us; but these chapters culminate in the
conviction (a) that the "ideological" processes are the
"highest" while the physical are the "lowest," (b) that all
the processes can be mutually illuminative, and (c) that the
uncertainty and unrest of the present age are due to the fact
that we have not yet found the "ideology" that answers to
the world-wide awakening of consciousness. But along with
this conviction is another: that only some form of Christianity
will be able to point the way, and that in so doing it will lead
to a yet further development in Man like those in the past.

Of these chapters some have already appeared in print; for
permission to republish them (in a revised form) I have to
thank the Editors of the *Hibbert Journal* (Chapter I), the
Bible and Modern Religious Thought (Chapters II and III),
the *Modern Churchman* (Chapters V and VI), the *West
London Synagogue Association* (Chapter IX), and the
Cambridge Review (a few pages in Chapter XII); fuller
details are specified in their proper places. Certain portions

of them were originally popular addresses, but they clear the ground, and I have not re-written them. Some repetition will be found, mainly of points which I have been anxious to stress; moreover, some of the more important matters of Biblical Criticism and of Comparative Religion are not so well known as they deserve to be. On the other hand, space has often been saved by references to my earlier book, *The Old Testament, A Reinterpretation*, to which this is in many respects the sequel.[1] ,

Although I have had to handle controverted matters, the pages were not written and I hope will not be read in any controversial sprit. But I have written freely, and hope that others may share my experience of being stimulated most by those from whom they have perhaps differed most. The age is sorely in need of spiritual re-armament; the amount of human suffering that is being caused by conflicting ideologies staggers the imagination. One cannot with any complacency regard the present apparent helplessness of Christianity. The future of the world-religions is at stake; once again men's convictions of Truth and Reality are in the balance, and surely the essence of Christian conviction is that there is a Way, a Truth and a Life waiting to be re-discovered. Many are the contributions to this quest, and the fact that these essays take what to a certain extent is a line of their own may justify this addition to the number.

Of the many imperfections and gaps in these pages I am deeply conscious. That they are not worse is due to the kindness of the Rev. J. S. Boys Smith of St. John's College, Cambridge, who read the proofs and made many valuable suggestions. He has also verified the Biblical passages and has enabled me to make useful additions to the theological and philosophical references, though he is not committed to my arguments or views.

In conclusion, I dedicate this volume to the University of Aberdeen in token of gratitude for the high honour it recently bestowed upon me. With it I couple the name of one of its most distinguished *alumni*, of whom Cambridge,

[1] It is cited as *O.T.R.* For other abbreviations, see the General Index.

too, will always be proud. For over forty-five years the work of William Robertson Smith has been a constant inspiration, guiding my studies and stimulating my thoughts. I have ever been impressed by his confidence that that great step in the cultural development of the Western world which we call the Reformation has even now not fulfilled all its promise. I cannot but think that he, perhaps more than any other writer, courageously pointed the way to this end. Nor could any disciple of his, who had ever tried to catch something of his spirit, visit Aberdeen and pass through the vestibule of Marischal College without recalling that dauntless figure whose motto might well have been the quaint words with their quaint spelling inscribed thereon: *Thay haif said; Quhat say thay? Let thame say.*

The seeds sown by Robertson Smith still bear fruit, and his combination of unequalled knowledge and simple faith is as a beacon-light to those who fear that the harmonious adjustment of the claims of Religion and of Research is no longer attainable. On his tombstone in the little village of Keig are engraved the words of Psalm xxv. 14: "The secret of the Lord is with them that fear Him"—challenging words, if true, and, like the motto of his old University: *Initium Sapientiae Timor Domini*, a fine devotional sentiment to be respectfully left with those who can believe in them. . . Or can they be as objectively true for our knowledge to-day as they have repeatedly been felt to be true for the knowledge of past ages? The task is to justify one's faith that the words are simply the height of Reason.

STANLEY A. COOK.

Cambridge,
March, 1938.

Contents

xvii   B

CHAPTER I

The Interdependence of Religion[1] and Research

IT is a familiar fact that a man's reflections and inquiries outside the sphere of religion can exercise a powerful influence upon his religious convictions and his conceptions of religion; and also that his religion or theology can control his ordinary scientific and other "non-religious" thinking to such an extent that it is not rarely considered to be prejudicial to the spirit of free and fearless research. Evidently, therefore, our religious and our non-religious thoughts are not naturally contained in separate water-tight compartments; and it would seem that whatever "realities" belong to the sphere of religion, and are experienced or recognised by the men whom we call "religious," must be connected with whatever "realities" are recognised outside that sphere in such a way that our ideas about both can interact in the way they do. Indeed, the history of thought has been characterised by increasing differentiation—the separation of religious from non-religious aspects, the appearance of new departments, bodies, or, we may say, "species" (e.g. astronomy, astrophysics, biochemistry, chemistry, etc.), and the process is significant for our conceptions of objective progress. The most fundamental of inquiries is that into our own mental development, whereby we come to realise the necessity of distinguishing between the "religious" and the "non-religious," or between what is and what is not "scientific," seeing that it is this development which accounts for our present conflicting attitudes. In fact, it may be submitted that a closer examination of the dynamic and differentiating aspects of the processes of thought in the history of individuals

[1] Reprinted with revision from the *Hibbert Journal*, XVIII (July, 1920), pp. 702–713.

I

and peoples is the necessary prelude to any critical reconsideration of the implicit and explicit theologies, philosophies
or ideologies which now sever us and impede social and other
advances.

Although modern thought has become increasingly
specialistic, there are many indications of the feeling that
analysis may outstrip synthesis, and that the interrelations
of existing divisions or subdivisions cannot be neglected with
impunity.[1] Two studies, geology and geography, for
example, may be pursued independently; but from time to
time one is found to depend upon the other, and throughout
the vicissitudes of the various departments of thought there
are alternating phases of isolation and interrelation, processes
which are especially instructive when we turn to problems
of religion. For, without further ado, I wish to suggest
that the future of our progress outside the sphere of religion
depends vitally upon religion, indeed upon a further development of religion itself, and that the latter will rest upon an
advance in those realms which our science and criticism
jealously shield from religious, confessional and subjective
entanglements. In other words, the separate aspects which
we dichotomise into "religious" and "non-religious" are so
united that progressive development cannot be partial or
one-sided.

It will doubtless be agreed that the further social, political
and other development of individuals and peoples turns, to
a certain extent at least, upon their self-control, moderation,
and so forth: that is, upon their ethical and moral character.
What I submit is that we are at the stage where, if we are
to maintain our position and make a further advance—and
the two aims prove to be one—only a religious development
will stimulate and unify our research, and only an advance
in our research will bring religion into harmony with the
best thought of its day. The advance, in a word, will turn
upon a further development in man's relationship with the

[1] See, e.g. Professor J. M. Coulter on "The Evolution of Botanical
Research," in *Nature*, 29th January, 1920, pp. 581 ff. (The question
of the possibility of an analogy between evolution in the world of
life and evolution in the world of thought is to be borne in mind
throughout these pages.)

God of whom it has been said that "in Him we live, and move, and have our being" (Acts xvii. 28). For, if this is true of God—and it is the living experience of many—"God" must stand for some tremendous reality, on another plane, but inconceivably more vital, than all our other and non-religious conceptions of reality.[1] Consequently there is a fatal rift in our outlook upon life until we have made up our minds and formed some provisional Theory of Reality. Either we differ hopelessly upon a question than which there can be none more vital for every aspect of human welfare; or we do lip-service to an agreement, but our research does not at present enable us to interpret our experience and give it a real meaning. Our religion and our research thus appear to be inevitably interconnected. This at once involves the future of Christianity and the Bible.

My starting-point is the field of Biblical Criticism, the unprejudiced study of Sacred Writings in the light of all that research has to offer. As a result of past advance of thought the Church is no longer the sole interpreter of the Bible, nor does the Bible interpret itself alike to all men. Different types of scholars—conservative, moderate and radical—differ from one another, and among themselves; and such are the cross-divisions and combinations among them that they can no longer be easily labelled. Not to speak of the ethical, moral and religious problems of the Bible, the claims of textual, metrical, literary and historical criticism frequently conflict; while archaeology, anthropology, psychology and history often seem to pull in opposite directions. Consequently, not only do readers differ seriously, because of their different temperaments, preconceptions, convictions and the like, but the "secular" studies have not reached the stage where they can be so

---

[1] This is neither Pantheism nor Deism, nor that "kind of multiple deism" which has tried to introduce "God" on all the great occasions. It is not the "God" who once wound up the clock, nor the "God" who is supposed to appear at certain times and in definite acts. See B. Bavink, *Science and God* (1933), p. 122, who remarks that it is in accord with the new conceptions of physics wherein "creation" becomes equivalent to maintenance and the *creatio continua* of the old theologians. Cf. p. 273 n. 1.

co-ordinated as to preclude the extreme divergences which now hinder the progress of Biblical Criticism. Biblical Criticism can justify itself by the fact that its methods are those employed in other fields; but its progress is bound up with those fields and consequently Biblical study itself needs a methodology, not merely of the departments of research, but more especially of the distinctively "religious" and "non-religious" inquiries.

The Bible, then, will not interpret itself to ordinary readers, nor will it be interpreted by the Church in any adequately harmonious manner, until our research has reached a higher and more co-ordinated stage than at present, where all alike are hopelessly at variance. The goal, however, is no monotonous, static identity of view, but a congruence of method and a new underlying unity, so that the various problems and the departments of thought may be less out of harmony, and the road be open for the newer problems—each age has its own—now being impeded and obscured by the absence of methodological unity and the conflict between religious and other knowledge.

The really fundamental problem of the Bible is not its literary analysis—there is sufficient agreement upon essentials—but the reconstruction of the entire political and religious development of Israel to replace the traditional narrative which modern criticism cannot in any circumstance accept in all its details.[1] There are the gravest internal and external difficulties, and there is not that development during the many centuries between the Mosaic and the post-exilic ages which we are entitled to anticipate on the ground of the teaching of the religious reformers (i.e. the great prophets) and other evidence. The usual attempts to reconstruct the history in the light of our modern knowledge and of our conceptions of development

---

[1] Scholars are of course divided as to precisely what may or may not be accepted. I, myself, am frequently radical and sceptical as regards the value of the historical narratives of the Old Testament for the period with which they deal, but freely recognise their value for the light they throw upon the periods when they were written, collected and edited. This light illuminates, therefore, not the earlier periods, but later ones.

are, in general, opposed to the religious philosophy
of the old writers, with their periods of apostasy and
penitence, of decline and reform; and the fundamental
Biblical conception of a primitive revelation is replaced by
the no less impressive conception of a progressive revelation.
It is this problem of religious development, whether in the
history of a people (viz. Israel), or in the history of the race,
which now stands in need of reconsideration. The aim is
to determine, so far as may be, what really happened.

In reconstructing the outlines of the history of Israel,
insufficient attention has been paid to the vicissitudes in and
around Palestine. The problem was studied too narrowly
within the covers of the Bible.[1] Now, however, we are
gaining a broader view of the history of a small people in
a land surrounded by ancient civilisations, and our ideas
can be further enlarged by a better knowledge of the history
of the rise and vicissitudes of other religions. There we
find alternating periods of decay and revival, the latter not
infrequently associated with great political and other
movements; and at the same time there is a genetic development, such that the revival is a return of the old, but of
the old in a new form. Very subtle and rather novel
problems arise when one seeks to determine more narrowly
the distinctive features: the disappearance, reshaping, or
re-interpretation of the old, the appearance of new positive
elements, and the inauguration of new stages, cycles, or,
as one is tempted to call them, "species." The history of
religions elucidates the principles of the development of
religious and other thought; and, in forcing a reconsideration
of Biblical religion, it also brings us to the problem of the
progressive development of modern thought. The history
of transitional periods in other lands and ages now becomes
of supreme interest, and the history of Israel, in particular,
gains a new significance.

The problems of the Old Testament turn upon a few
centuries in the middle of the first millennium B.C., when

---

[1] This was largely inevitable. It was necessary to concentrate
upon the biblical evidence, and external evidence was not always
reliable or accessible.

the downfall of the Hebrew monarchies was followed by a
certain disintegration, leading to a new reconstruction which
was essentially religious. Instead of a simple evolution
from the religion of nomad Israelites in the wilderness
between Egypt and Palestine to the priestly legalism of
the post-Exilic Age, we have to understand (1) the earlier
vicissitudes after the entrance of semi-nomads into a land
of long-established culture; and (2) the later decline from
the height of the monarchies, the appearance of relatively
simple conditions, and the work of reconstruction which
produced post-exilic Judaism. In the seventh and subsequent centuries B.C. Assyria fell, and the artificial archaisa-
tion in Babylonia and Egypt led to decay; but the reconstruction of Israel, with its results so profoundly beneficent
for humanity, is a phenomenon which cannot be too carefully investigated, so suggestive is it for our own tasks of
to-day. The study of that reconstruction and our new
interpretation of the whole course of Israelite development,
down to and including the rise of Christianity, belong to
Biblical Criticism; but, involving as they do a reconsideration of the facts and theories of the development of life and
thought, the Biblical problems become essentially problems
of this age. This age will both interpret and be interpreted
by them.

If we feel we have outgrown earlier stages of religious or
other thought, nothing is better attested than the repeated
renewal or reassertion of elements in forms that are in
harmony with newer conditions. With this fusion of resemblances to and differences from the old we have analogies
in the history of successive stages in organic evolution;
and while it may be said that we of to-day are witnessing,
if not helping to introduce, a new stage in human evolution,
we have this responsibility—that our knowledge of development in the past can enable us more consciously to contribute
to the next stage. But our research has yet to investigate
critically and without prejudice the nature of the resemblances and the differences.

Tendencies in life and thought are leading to what, on
the analogy of literary, textual and historical criticism,

might be called "religious" criticism.[1] The problems of
the relation between Christianity and other or earlier
religions need more objective treatment than they usually
receive. The application of psychology to religion has also
raised new questions. Problems of the relation between
religion and magic, of religious decline and the pathology
of religion, of holy men, intermediaries, and the like, have
far-reaching implications. Even the familiar theory of the
priority of magic over religion—if it were to be substantiated—would have an unsuspected significance for our ideas
of God. The theory that religion "began" with totemism
or with ancestor-worship—to mention no other views—
bears upon that of the source of our own religious experience
to-day, and upon our convictions of God and the world.
The comparative and psychological study of varieties of
Christian experience, of non-Christian religious experience,
and of non-religious but related experience (e.g. cosmic
emotion, art, etc.), raises profound problems which are
bridging the gulf between "religious" and "non-religious"
thought. Anthropology, psychology and the study of
religions are preparing the way for a veritable science of
religion; they are leading gradually to the recognition that
our conceptions of religion must be adjusted so as not to
be out of harmony with the best thought. If only we were
agreed upon the essential nature of magic and the real
difference between magic and religion, we should have an
immeasurably firmer grasp of true and progressive religion—
and of its antithesis—than we possess at present.

While research is thus impinging upon the sphere of
religion—and to an extent to which organised religion
cannot be indifferent—another change becomes inevitable.
The problems which belong to the criticism of religion
sooner or later raise the question, How did people think
of *their* gods? what did their gods *mean* for them?[2] And

---

[1] The attempt to introduce such terms as hierography, hierology
and hierosophy seems to have failed; see Pinard de la Boullaye,
L'Étude Comparée des Religions, II (1925), pp. 11, 364 n.

[2] This method of inquiry, though commonly ignored, was that
so brilliantly expounded by Robertson Smith (*Religion of the Semites*,
3rd Ed., p. 82 f.).

here it is not difficult to see how one's personal experience both affects and is affected by one's study and treatment of the problem. When we ask ourselves what reality—and I suppose one must begin by adding "if any"—lies behind the data of religion, our research is applying itself to men's conceptions of God and Reality. Moreover, not only is the consistent thinker consciously or unconsciously developing his own personal convictions—which will be the less "subjective" as religion is studied in a scientific spirit—but to the fearlessness and sincerity demanded by the temper of science there must be added, as the ideal, a "spiritual" equipment, and character. The fact, for fact it is, is assuredly significant for our conceptions of the subject of inquiry; for what must "God" mean if our inquiries into ancient or modern, primitive or developed, religion seem to take us to our own inmost depths? Even feelings of antipathy or hatred to religion show that in some way the centre of our life is touched.

Already the psychological study of religion emphasises the "naturalness" of religion and associates "religious" truth and reality with what is open to the psychological discussion of human nature. Moreover, sociological and other students tend to admit that religious experience has *some* reality or actuality to justify it; it is the theistic interpretation and expression which is adversely criticised. Yet it is very instructive to observe the efforts to express what, if it is not "religious experience," is at least related to it—"cosmic emotion," for example—in a way that shall avoid theology or philosophy; they indicate how inextricably our distinctively "religious" experiences and modes of thought are interwoven with all the deeper experiences and thought outside the sphere of religion.[1]

[1] Thus, W. K. Clifford spoke of "the consciousness of a presence which arises within [a man] and says, as plainly as words can say, 'I am with thee and I am greater than thou'." Henry Sidgwick refers to the "emotion which is felt in regard to the Universe or sum of things viewed as a cosmos or order." More recently, Einstein has said: "I am a deeply religious man," but, as J. H. Morrison observes, this does not involve any belief in the personality of God, moral responsibility or the immortality of the soul (*Christian Faith and the Science of To-day* [1936], pp. 97, 214).

But when it is said that religious experience is "really" connected with man's social nature, or that it is the experience of the social organism of which he is part, it is difficult to see how this is to be proved or disproved. Whatever be the reality experienced so variously by theists and others, we evidently need some clearer formulation of what this reality means for our own life and thought. The question cannot be left where it is; we seem to require a more or less systematised Theory of Reality on the basis of which we can approach the rival and opposing conceptions of ultimate reality, and co-ordinate our own particular conceptions of this and any other realities we recognise.

Whatever form such a Theory of Reality may take, I suppose that one of the main differences between (a) the God of Theism, (b) the "Humanity," or other "God" of ethical and positivist cults, and (c) let us say, a mascot (which can be psychologically very effective), lies in the field of thought and action proper to each, the content of each, and the significance of each for our life and thought. Conceptions of reality are thus bound up with the efficacy of the Reality under discussion. According to our conception of it so we can use it. Now, to go back for a moment to Biblical Criticism, we find that theories, principles and the like proved imperfect or erroneous as they became less effective in their relevant field; difficulties increased, inconvenient facts had to be ignored or forced, old principles conflicted with new ones. To this we may add a growing uneasiness and dissatisfaction which was more than merely "intellectual." But in Biblical Criticism, as in other departments of research, when old theories have been replaced by new ones, the data have been more effectively handled, the relief has been more than "intellectual," and even when the new theory has been uncommonly drastic, it has really been less complex, more synthesising and unifying, and more in harmony with new tendencies, principles, or facts. The test, then, of our theories, principles and conceptions, is their efficacy in the field which they claim to cover.

The process—one that requires more careful treatment

than can here be given it—is one wherein theories and so forth are found inadequate, and are replaced by new ones which, in spite of the intervening struggle, have often, like new stages in the history of a religion, maintained continuity with their predecessors. The process of reconstruction in the world of thought has its analogy in that of the world of life, where our theories, principles and outlooks are usually less consciously held. And the analogy may be pursued; for, if our theories and views of life are imperfect and erroneous, like our theories in research they will be ineffective, do what we may to ignore or suppress inconvenient facts. We may even *feel* a certain dissatisfaction which it is difficult to specify. If we believe that there is a Moral Law in the Universe, our life and thought cannot proceed with impunity along lines contrary to it. With greater force will this principle apply to our conceptions of God. We may say with the contemporaries of Zephaniah (i. 12), that the Lord will do neither good nor evil, or we may think of God as Him in whom we live, and move, and have our being. But if men act, even unconsciously, upon wrong conceptions of what is most vitally real and true, the consequences are bound to be untoward, even though at present we are not agreed as to how far religious reality is significant. The more significant it is, the more detrimental will be our imperfect and erroneous conceptions.

In any case, it is unfortunately unnecessary to refer at length to the prevailing bewilderment, disillusion, unrest, suspicion and despair, the indications of moral, ethical and spiritual ill-health, and the many bizarre, fantastic and often veritably pathological features of the age. Psychologists emphasise the varying results of the possession of either a well-organised or a discordant or dissociated personality, of good or of bad complexes. The prevalence of what is abnormal enables one to realise what is normal; and "the psychology of insanity" leads to a "psychology of sanity."[1] Moreover, the psychology of adolescence and conversion has much to suggest for an age distracted, anxious and in

[1] Edmond Holmes, *Hibbert Journal*, XVIII (April, 1920), pp. 509–518.

search of rest, confronted with the disintegration of one system of life and thought, and the necessity of constructing another. How far may not this "ill-health" be due to erroneous ideas of life and reality, to imperfect or misleading conceptions of "God" and of the reality for which this Name stands? The answer will depend upon our conceptions of the meaning of God for man, and the relationship in which a man, consciously or unconsciously, stands to Him.

The question is much more than merely "religious"; it is not disposed of by leaving it to the theologians. The assertions and claims which recur throughout the world's religions are such that, if religion is not a stupendous illusion—and this is inconceivable—man is in some way part of the Universe more profoundly than he can understand. Science can indeed associate the human organism with the Universe of Space and Time; but the most extraordinary convictions and statements of man's place in the Universe are not only contained in "man-made" mythologies, theologies or philosophies, they are also in large measure implicit in men's activities which, as they become more earnest and fundamental, have a significance transcending our positive knowledge. Man himself is but a very recent appearance in the history of the earth, and as he becomes more conscious of himself and the whole of which he is part, the differentiating process whereby he severs Man and Nature, or distinguishes the religious and non-religious aspects, tends to obscure the earlier and more fundamental unity of experience.

Yet the way in which the individual is influenced by what we call "religious" experience, the effect of a conviction of "God" upon his life and thought, and the nature of the development of his world of ideas, combine to show that the "realities" of religion cannot be held utterly apart from those of ordinary experience, and that "God" represents a reality significant even for the individual who knows Him not. The experiences which have forced men to convictions of an existence "outside" and "beyond" this life point to a consciousness of something that "transcends" what we call "this" world of Space and Time. In a word, then, there are convictions and experiences that are unintelligible and meaningless unless they point to certain ultimate facts to which our interpretations are approximations—facts, too, such that the genetic development of individuals and of the race can lead to truer and more effective interpretations. There is a religious dialectic, a certain naturalness and orderliness in the vicissitudes of religion, and it forces the assumption of the existence of some Reality, even though it be known only through our imperfect apprehension and statement of it.

We often entertain conflicting beliefs, for example, of a bodily or non-bodily resurrection, which if pursued consistently would speedily land us in hopeless confusion. So, as regards our experience, interpretation and systematisation of whatever is real and true, if we are consciously and unconsciously proceeding in diverging directions our whole self must suffer in some measure. If, as religious experience suggests, we are normally part of a larger life, we thwart our deeper selves if we persist in thought and action that denies and excludes this.[1] If we think that Reality is only physical and confined to what is given to the senses, the more consistently and systematically we develop our ideas in all their ramifications, the more imperfect will be our personality —that is, *if* our fundamental conviction is "really" wrong. We shall be living within a closed system that thwarts our further growth. Hence, for the credit of research, it is incumbent upon men to make up their mind upon the significance—"if any"—of the religious consciousness and religious experience for scientific and other "non-religious" thought; and it is no less incumbent upon them, for the credit of religion, to utilise "non-religious" inquiries and

---

[1] I say, we "thwart," just as men are said to thwart and impede God's work. But if we agree that ultimate facts of existence (e.g. God, a life beyond the present) ultimately force themselves upon our consciousness, we seem to imply that by our nature we are (? subconsciously) one with Reality. We imply, that is, certain facts of human nature and existence which, together with much else in Comparative Theology, can be handled objectively, and are assuredly vital for our theories of knowledge.

the criticism of religion to the end that religion may have fresh life by being brought into harmonious relationship with the progress of thought.

The value of the comparative study of religious, philosophical and other conceptions of God and Reality lies in its contribution to new developments. It enlarges our ideas of God and Ultimate Reality, and in showing how, from the religious standpoint, God has revealed Himself to individuals and peoples at different levels, enables us to form some more objective estimate of these "levels" in terms of concepts, categories, knowledge and systematisation of thought. Further, this study throws light upon the dynamic processes of the mind: the consciousness of something outside ordinary experience and the effort to consolidate the ground gained in the new advance. Here we find ourselves passing between God and Man, between Human Personality and Divine, between man's convictions of Ultimate Reality and the consciousness of his own reality. Thinking of God's nature and activities man has grasped new possibilities, and reflecting upon God's rule in the Universe he has developed his own mental processes and illuminated his own nature.

There are two extremes. On the one hand there are speculations which to many appear futile—the old discussions of the movements of angels and the space they occupy, the way in which the Universe is contained in God's mind, the modes of thought of disembodied beings or of an omnipresent Being, and so on. On the other hand is that cruder rationalism and positivism which would thwart the individual's development by rigorously rejecting all that falls outside so-called rational thought. Meanwhile, however, the extension of ideas of relativity, the impetus given by mathematical and scientific speculation, and the widespread interest in psychology have broken down barriers. We are confronted with an irrationalism, an anti-intellectualism, wishful thinking, the retreat from reason, and the prominence of sections of population unable to follow specialistic thought. Perverse idealism, unwise sentimentalism and unworthy belief prevail, and there are no coherent, systematising conceptions of God, Man and the Universe to unify men and lay the basis of a new reconstruction. None the less, recent decades have seen great strides in our knowledge of the physical Universe and in our knowledge of man, his nature, and his conceptions of himself and of what he feels to be most real and most true. The age, it may be hoped, is preparing its own cure.

The more educated—whether Biblical critics, scientists, teachers, or others—have their share of the responsibility for the disintegration of life and thought; and if they refuse to take part in constructive work, destructive work will be pursued by others. Before we can educate the "masses," the "classes" need re-educating; it is their apathy and inertia which make so many impatient minds see the sole hope of the future in the "virgin soil" of the more impressionable masses. Just as we become forced to take long views in economic and political questions, so, where thought is concerned, a more dynamic outlook is needed of the mental development of individuals and peoples. We have to make up our mind touching the importance of Religion, and to find conceptions of Religion, God and Reality that shall guide us to the next stage in our development. Religion alone, without an advance of thought, would quickly tend to be magic and superstition; and theologies that form closed systems leave no room for further advance. Life and thought need a new co-ordination and re-organisation; and it is necessary to do justice alike to rival and conflicting facts and to opposing and hostile factions.

A new way of correlating the distinctively "religious" and the distinctively "non-religious" aspects of life and thought is demanded, and the work of research will proceed *pari passu* with the duty of acting justly towards the divers religions within our ambit. The reconstruction of social and political life and of religious and other thought is one task throughout. The task is, in a word, to advance to the stage where differing competing and conflicting "facts"— and some of them uncommonly noisy ones—may be treated in a way that does justice to the principles of the best thought. And if it be admitted that social and political developments are forcing a higher type of character—that is, if we are not to fall behind—certainly, if we are to maintain our intellectual level, the reconsideration of our conceptions of effective Reality will also demand, and tend to produce, a mental advance. The goal at which to aim is, in truth, another and higher stage in human evolution; and an advance to a higher conception of Ultimate Reality can only be made through a fuller consciousness of the relationship upon which this evolution depends. And the "theory" that runs through the great religions is that man cannot make this advance unaided.

Again and again men have been able to reconcile their profoundest experiences and their conceptions of the Universe. To-day the task is greater—it is to pass beyond, that is, to transcend, the accumulated experience and knowledge of past ages. We cannot ignore man's modernity or the implication of his experiences. There has been a repeated experience of the oneness of the Universe; and when St. Paul speaks of the whole creation as the object of redemption (Rom. viii. 22), modern knowledge tells us that man cannot be the sole object of cosmic evolution—this would be Nietzsche's "superman" over again! Man may be unavoidably anthropocentric; but he is infinitesimally small, and only if man is an integral part of Ultimate Reality can the anthropocentric intuitions be justified. There is something intellectually shocking and clearly "undemocratic" in the supposition that there can be any effective outlook upon life which ignores the best scientific, philosophical and other "non-religious" thought, or which does not do justice to religious and related experiences, however diverse and unusual. We need a synthesis of the conflicting interests in the worlds of life and of thought; and this involves some new advance, and a co-operation on the part of all men of good will. No more "creative" task can be imagined.

CHAPTER II

The Goal of Biblical Criticism[1]

THE aim of this chapter is to raise questions rather than to attempt complete replies. What is the goal of Biblical Criticism? Does "criticism" really make the Bible more intelligible? Is it true that the "external" evidence of archaeology and the monuments is compelling the critics to reconsider their theories? And not the least important of the many questions that arise: Who, precisely, are these "critics"?

At the outset, then, we may remember that the late Dr. James Orr, in his book *The Problem of the Old Testament* (1905), p. 9, asserts quite frankly, "the truth is, and the fact has to be faced, that no one who studies the Old Testament in the light of modern knowledge can help being, to some extent, a 'Higher Critic.'" His is perhaps the most helpful of all attacks on Old Testament criticism, and yet he recognises, as does every competent writer, that the Old Testament brings intricate problems which require *some* explanation. No serious student can refrain from being in some degree a "critic"; it is when we come to examine the views that are held and the solutions that are offered, that we perceive how widely they differ.

Certain views and theories, however, prevail as to the nature of the compositeness of the Old Testament and the remarkable variation in its religious standpoint and treatment of history. These have come to hold the field and constitute what has sometimes been called the "regnant" hypothesis of Old Testament criticism. Their effect is, briefly, to shift the emphasis from Moses and the Pentateuch to the Prophets and the Exile and the reorganisation under the Second Temple, to ascribe an exilic or post-exilic date

[1] Reprinted with revision from *The Bible and Modern Religious Thought*, IV (Dec., 1933).

to considerable portions of the Old Testament, and to illuminate what once seemed to be a blank chapter in such a way that we can pass naturally from the exilic and early post-exilic (Persian) periods to the Greek and Roman periods and the rise of Christianity. This unites the Old Testament and the New in quite a fresh way.

Now this hypothesis, as a whole, is commonly named after the German scholar Wellhausen, whose incisive treatment of the Pentateuchal problems, and especially his *Prolegomena* (1878), compelled every Old Testament scholar to reconsider his position. Because of Wellhausen, in particular, the "higher criticism" has sometimes been decried as something specifically German. But, although Biblical Criticism is profoundly indebted to German scholarship, it is well to bear in mind that the most minute treatment of the Biblical literary problems was by the Dutch scholar Kuenen (who received the honorary degree of LL.D. at Edinburgh in 1889), and that the Aberdeen professor, William Robertson Smith, wrote what was in many respects the most original and, from the religious point of view, the most persuasive exposition and justification of the "Wellhausen hypothesis."[1]

In fact, it is obvious from the history of criticism that the "critics" have not been mere copiers of Wellhausen or of any other founder of the modern stage of Old Testament criticism, but independent workers who have found the "Wellhausen hypothesis," in spite of its admitted defects, the only helpful one. Whatever the future may bring, so far, at least, no one has formulated any approach to the scholarly study of the Old Testament so comprehensive and stimulating as that which has won its way. To obtain a "true" view of the Bible one must have what offers the most "true" approach to it. It is, however, generally felt that the Biblical problems are much more complicated than they seemed to be a few decades ago. Moreover, it is necessary to remember that modern Biblical Criticism has

---

[1] It may be mentioned that two of Smith's books were translated into German, as also was S. R. Driver's classic *Introduction to the Literature of the Old Testament*.

two sides.   The one is primarily literary and more analytical, and concerns the relative dates of the Biblical documents; the other, more historical, deals with the social, political and historical development of Israel. As regards the former there is sufficient agreement among scholars.[1]   It is as regards the latter that they often differ widely, owing to the value they attach to the *contents* of the documents, their views of the religious and other vicissitudes, and the extent to which they diverge from one another in their solutions of the special problems.

Now the literary theory of the dates of the documents turns upon a certain preliminary estimate of the course of Israelite religion and history, namely, upon the significance of the great prophets.   It is a fundamental belief in criticism that these figures form a dividing-line between the "pre-prophetic" stages and the more "priestly" type of religion that subsequently—in the post-exilic age—became prominent.   The great creative prophets are earlier than the Law, the Pentateuch, *in its present form*; and we cannot even *begin* to understand the Old Testament intelligently if the Pentateuch in its present form preceded them.

But Old Testament criticism to-day is confronted by a mass of external contemporary material, the value of which cannot be over-estimated.   Much is now known of the close interrelations between Palestine, Syria and the surrounding civilised powers, whose Golden Ages mostly antedate the rise of Israel.   Palestine itself flourished long before the entry of the Israelites, and it is clear from the Amarna Letters that Palestine, round about 1400 B.C., already possessed a religious phraseology with points of contact even with relatively late parts of the Old Testament.[2] The pre-Israelite deities of Palestine were no mean deities, and tendencies to monotheism can be found.   The pre-Israelite

---

[1] Thus, the now disputed question of the relative priority of J or E, or of the precise date of D is irrelevant for our purpose.   The views of the American archaeologist, Professor W. F. Albright, *The Archaeology of Palestine and the Bible*, pp. 162f., 213f., are especially interesting for their support of the general critical position (cf. *ibid.*, p. 176f.).

[2] See the *Cambridge Ancient History*, II, pp. 336ff.; *O.T.R.*, p. 90f.

natives recognised the divinity of their Egyptian over-
lord, and traces of the "divine kingship" survive in the
Old Testament. The wonderfully dynamic concept of
"Righteousness" is also pre-Israelite.[1] The essential rites
of Israel were agricultural, as also were the Messianic ideas of
future abundance: these would be of native rather than
of outside (Israelite) origin. Finally, when we consider the
unique significance of Zion and its environs for the religious
idealism of Israel, we should observe that Jerusalem flourished
as early as about 2000 B.C., and seems to be mentioned in an
Egyptian text of the Middle Kingdom along with other
places of evident importance in the eyes of Egypt.

No doubt it may be disconcerting to find that there is
much in Old Testament belief and ritual which is native
Palestinian rather than due to Israelite invaders. Indeed,
on purely archaeological grounds, it would appear that the
distinctiveness which characterises the Old Testament as a
whole had its roots in pre-Israelite times.[2] It is not
surprising, therefore, that archaeology and the monuments
should be placing old problems in a new light; but they are
not leading scholars to return to some earlier or conservative
position. They are not disturbing the *literary* hypothesis
of the Old Testament, although it becomes evident that all
theories of the historical and religious development of Israel
must be tested anew.[3]

It is easier to determine what Palestine had to offer to
invading Israelites who had come from the Desert, than
to agree as to what beliefs and rites the Israelites brought
with them. It is very widely held that not all the tribes
of Israel had been in Egypt, and that the invaders who inter-
married with the natives (Judges iii. 6; Ezra ix. 12 f.;

[1] See p. 141.

[2] See my *Religion of Ancient Palestine in the Light of Archaeology*
(Schweich Lectures for 1925), p. 230 and n. 1.

[3] On Archaeology and Biblical Criticism, see *Journal of Biblical
Literature*, LI (1932), pp. 273 ff. Note the high estimate of Albright,
a leading archaeologist, of the work of such critics as S. R. Driver
and Eduard Meyer (*Archaeology of Palestine and the Bible*, pp. 20,
52, 108 f., 175 f.).

Ps. cvi. 35 ff.) naturally took over much that was "Palestinian" or "Canaanite." However that may be, we should not ignore the Biblical and other evidence for *later* movements by tribes from outside Palestine, when there were situations that in certain respects remind us of the earlier entrance and settlement of the Israelites.[1] The result is not a little surprising, the more especially when one takes into account the internal social and religious history of Judah and Israel (Samaria) from the fall of the Northern Kingdom to the decisive repudiation by the Judaeans of the friendly Samaritans.[2] It is here, I venture to think, rather than in the pre-monarchical or pre-prophetical periods, that Old Testament criticism will have to concentrate.

What were the internal conditions in Judah and Samaria prior to this final cleavage? According to the American scholar, J. A. Montgomery (*The Samaritans* [1907], p. 61), "both Judaism and Samaritanism go back to a common foundation in the circumstances of the age of the Exile in the sixth century." That is to say, there had been some *rapprochement*, or some union, before the divorce. Other scholars approximate to this view or develop it much further; so notably the late Professor Kennett (from 1905 onwards).[3] It must be admitted that the force of the evidence has not been generally recognised.[4] On the other hand, practically every scholar agrees that the period of the Exile was one of far-reaching developments, and that the Second Isaiah (that is, at least, Chs. xl.–lv.) illuminates certain aspects of the religious conditions. Whatever be our particular conception of the course of events from the fall, first of Samaria, and then of Jerusalem, to the rebuilding

---

[1] See the *Cambridge Ancient History*, III, pp. 366–368, 384, 393, 405 f.; VI, p. 184 f.; and cf. T. H. Robinson, *History of Israel*, I, p. 383 n.

[2] See p. 44.

[3] See the references in my introduction to the collection of his essays and studies, *The Church of Israel*, p. xlvi, n. 2.

[4] But note how Oesterley (*History of Israel*, II, pp. 142 ff.) sets the stage for the events that follow, and throws light upon that period when, *on critical grounds*, the written history of the preceding periods was beginning to reach its present form.

of the Temple, and the reorganisation described in the books of Ezra and Nehemiah, these grand chapters must find a fitting place somewhere. We of to-day can perhaps realise that the mere possession of *earlier* religious literature is not in itself enough to enable a people to pass through its crises; and although we know little enough of the history of the sixth century B.C.—and scholars differ over important questions—we can hardly fail to see in the Second Isaiah the reflection of some movement which gave Israel new hope and, as it proved, ushered in a new age.

In these chapters Old Testament prophecy finds its sublimest expression, and their pure and exalted doctrine of monotheism surpasses all that went before. It is true we are often assured of the "monotheism" of primitive man, of Babylonians, or of Sumerians; but in the interests of progressive religion we must insist that those monotheistic or monotheising beliefs or tendencies of which we have information are not to be mentioned in the same breath with that lofty spiritual teaching which is Israel's permanent contribution to mankind.[1] It is necessary to emphasise this from the purely religious point of view. Indeed, when we look more closely at the period now under discussion, we see, first, pessimism and the conviction that God had forgotten His people (Isa. xlix. 14); He could do neither good nor evil (Zeph. i. 12)—a negligible God. We then pass to those chapters in the Second Isaiah which we might perhaps call "Israel's Rediscovery of her God." We contrast this new consciousness with what had gone before, and can thenceforth appreciate more vividly the work of reconstruction, the deeper personal piety of the Psalms, and the care taken in the priestly writings to preserve the holiness of the God who was once more in the midst of His own people (cf. Ezek. xlviii. 35).[2]

This overwhelming majesty of Israel's own God meant that—to use modern terms—He was at once transcendent and immanent. Though the historical circumstances are exceedingly obscure, it is clear that we are at the zenith

[1] See p. 226.
[2] See *O.T.R.*, pp. 195 ff.

of Israelite religion—this is proved by the value we all attach to the Second Isaiah from the New Testament point of view. It is the end of one series of stages and the beginning of another which leads on to the rise of Christianity. Indeed, for ordinary purposes of teaching, it may be suggested that the Second Isaiah rather than the fall of Jerusalem or the beginning of the Exile should be the terminus of one course and at the same time the starting-point of the next.[1]

Biblical Criticism demands more than the scholar's equipment. The great creative prophets were theistic rather than social and ethical reformers; and that religious sensitiveness is surely dulled which does not appreciate the difference between their spirituality and the Pentateuch. Does this beg the question? Wellhausen, in the Introduction to his *Prolegomena* (p. 3), tells us how he felt that between the Law on the one side, and the historical and prophetical books on the other, was "all the difference that separates two wholly distinct worlds"[2]; and Robertson Smith, in his *Old Testament in the Jewish Church* (Ch. X), speaks of the different "theories" of religion in the Old Testament. Is one really justified in ascribing a unique religious value to the Second Isaiah or in speaking of it as Israel's Rediscovery of God? The question is important, for the more highly we esteem its chapters the more significant must they be for the historical development of the religion of Israel, and the incidents which gave birth to them must be of exceptional importance from a purely historical point of view. It is well-known that the age of the Second Isaiah is, broadly speaking, that of widespread religious movements, e.g. Lao-tse and Confucius, the Buddha, Zoroaster, Orphism. Of vast significance though these have proved to be for the course of human thought, we of the West cannot but attach even greater significance to the events that lie behind the Old Testament and the New. Without

---

[1] Similarly, the New Testament is the end of one development (as is recognised in Oesterley and Robinson's *Hebrew Religion*) and the commencement of another. The Old Testament should also be studied so as to understand the subsequent bifurcation into *both* Christianity and Rabbinical Judaism.

[2] The passage is cited in *A New Commentary*, Part I, p. 25.

the Old Testament we cannot conceive the rise of Christianity;
had there not been the reorganisation of Israel after the
Exile there could have been no Christian "Israel" (Gal.
vi. 16); and the "Rediscovery of God" which we find in
the Second Isaiah is followed after the lapse of centuries
by the next step—the revelation of God in Christ.

   In spite of the incompleteness of modern knowledge and
modern criticism, the history of Israel has become ever more
absorbing and fascinating.   It is part of world history, and
Israel's religion is part of the world's religion.   The whole
history becomes more realistic.   Thus, when one has read
oneself into the great creative prophets, and has sought to
grasp the essentials of their teaching, one is apt to be
conscious of a certain decline or deterioration as one passes
to the later stages.   One can certainly put one's finger
upon some decisive developments.   Israel had been condemned by her reformers, she suffers punishment; later,
she is consoled, and a new era is opened up.   She had
provoked her God to *jealousy*, but now in her plight He is
zealous on her behalf.   The older religion had been too
nationalistic; there is a period of social and political disintegration and of pronounced individualistic tendencies
But in time we come upon a new unity and a new religious
nationalism: it is the reconstruction after destruction.
The earlier prophets had placed ethical righteousness above
cult and ritual; but subsequently we observe a new emphasis
upon the rites and the festivals.   The reforming prophets,
men of remarkable personality, taught the true relationship
between God and Man; but ultimately this relationship is
mediated through the priests.   Much more could be said
along these lines.[1] We are witnessing sweeping developments
in the disintegration and redintegration of a people and
its religion; and though much is unknown—especially the
movements behind the Second Isaiah—we do gain a far
more vivid idea of the history than when we read the Old
Testament uncritically.

   We who live in an age of uncertainty and change, the issue
of which we cannot foresee, have everything to learn from

   [1] See *C.A.H.*, III, pp. 465ff.; *O.T.R.*, pp. 180ff.

a thorough-going critical study of a history which has proved to be of unique meaning for humanity. We do not take a merely European or Western view when we lay such store upon the history in and behind the Bible; for it is part of the history of Palestine, which in turn was always more or less closely connected with other lands, whose history, however, has been of less world-wide significance. In what may roughly be called the "Mosaic" Age, viz. that illustrated by the Amarna Letters and the "Hittite" tablets from Boghaz-Keui, Palestine was exposed to Iranian (Old Persian) or Indo-European influence. This was centuries before the days when it was part of the Persian Empire. The non-Semitic influences upon Palestine and Syria form a study in themselves, for not only must we place Biblical history and religion upon a vaster background of history and religion, but all the non-Israelite or non-Hebraic factors, both within Palestine and without, must be taken into account.[1] In the Mosaic Age, Varuna, the remarkable ethical god of Ancient India, was known to North Syria, and round about the time of the Second Isaiah, the Zoroastrian Ahura-Mazda, doubtless known to the Israelites, was a deity even more spiritual. And to descend later, the Bhagavad-gita, the "New Testament of Hinduism," is approximately contemporary with the early growth of Christianity. Yet the more definitely we place the Bible in the light of universal history and religion, the sounder and more objective is our estimate of its grandeur and power.

Now, in certain important respects the great creative minds of Israel were *men* rather than Israelites or Semites— even as a statesman to-day may be a good European rather than merely a nation's politician.[2] Moreover, in spite of later Oriental (Jewish and Syrian) missionaries, neither the Old Testament nor the Bible as a whole exercised much religious influence in the East. And while Judaism has flourished best in Christian lands, for the religious

[1] See pp. 132 ff.

[2] Cf. Baudissin, *Kyrios*, III (1929), p. 209, and contrast p. 237; see also *J.T.S.*, XXXII (1931), p. 244.

interpretation of the prophets of Israel we must look to the Gentiles. The West has got far more out of the Bible than ever the East has done; and "Christianity," as Dean Inge has well said, "is the least Oriental of all the great religions."[1]   Palestine and the Near East have played their part in universal history; but it by no means follows that the Western world will continue to be the best interpreter of the Bible.   Are there not those who are ready to believe or to fear that Western civilisation will in turn decline and die?   Yet, on the other hand, any survey of the past will suggest that even if our culture were to disappear—as did that of Crete, Babylonia, Egypt and other lands—some future country may one day feel that the torch has been handed to them, and our own civilisation will be simply the penultimate stage in the line of progress at the head of which they would claim to stand.

If the Jewish historian Josephus, who lived in the first century of this era, could refer to "the Britons previously unknown to history,"[2] it is conceivable—though we may perhaps prefer not to dwell upon it—that the future of civilisation will one day rest with some land or people whom we now regard with indifference.   And just as the prophetical writings of Israel, though treasured by Judaism, have been best interpreted by non-Orientals of the West, so the whole Bible, the Book of Christendom, might conceivably be better interpreted in the future by those whom "Christians" of to-day would consider the most unpromising of spiritual heirs of Israel.   In other words, criticism enables us to understand, in a less emotional and a much more reasoned way, the greatness of the Bible.   It belongs to those who can utilise its spiritual value to the fulness of their capacity; and as we become increasingly impressed by those eternal truths of which Israel's teachers were conscious, we realise more keenly that the Bible has an ultimate value, and we can be more confident of its future than we can be of the future of our own civilisation.   Indeed, we may even say

---

[1] Inge, *The Church in the World* (1932), p. 109 and Preface, p. vii.

[2] *War*, Book II, xvi. 4 (363); cf. Book III, i. 2 (4).

that the happiest future belongs to those who can carry on the progressive interpretation of the Bible.

The record of Biblical Criticism, like that of all science, is one of slow and faltering steps; criticism is still in its infancy, and the nature of the deeper problems is only slowly being recognised. This criticism is truly "constructive" as well as seemingly "destructive." Many vital spiritual truths are untouched even by the most radical criticism; and it must not be forgotten that narratives do not lose their religious value when criticism, though mistrusting their worth as history in the narrower sense, recovers the religious ideas which inspired some later writer or his circle, and thus enhances history in a wider sense. If some events of undoubtedly religious importance have lost much of their worth as history, others can be discerned which, like the "Rediscovery of God" and the reconstruction of Israel, are of pre-eminent interest, especially for this age.

Not the Exodus and the journey to the Land of Promise, but the Exile from God and a journey of another kind are the real centre of Old Testament criticism. Yet how strangely Exodus and Exile are interconnected! On the critical view, the account of the Exodus and the Wanderings in the Wilderness is now in a post-exilic form—this does not of course exclude sources of earlier origin. It is later, therefore, than those passages in the Second Isaiah which treat the Return from Exile as another Exodus (e.g. Isa. xliii. 14 ff.). The narratives, and indeed the whole Pentateuch itself, may be interpreted in the light of the great internal vicissitudes of, roughly, the eighth–fifth centuries, the age of transition from the fall of Samaria, through the Exile, to the complete and final reorganisation associated with the names of Nehemiah and Ezra.

To supplement what has already been said concerning that age, we may observe that among the various transitions —including one from a certain democratic sentiment to one more exclusive and priestly[1]—most noticeable of all is the tradition that Moses and Aaron suffer the penalty of their

[1] See below, pp. 42, 219 f.

failure to respect the Divine Holiness (Num. xx. 12).[1]
The men specially chosen to lead the people into the land
of their fathers, one of them even the "steward" of His own
house (Num. xii. 7), are, in some way, found wanting.
Surely here we have neither the history of the Mosaic
Age, nor miscellaneous though apparently meaningless
traditions; rather has the post-exilic compiler given us
something far more impressive: the majesty of Israel's
own God whom both prophet and priest—and one ventures
to add the mysterious Messianic figure Zerubbabel (p. 51)—
must reverence. What we have is not the God of the
Exodus, but the God of the Exiled; and when we look back
to the days when "the Lord could do neither good nor evil,"
may we not feel that the compiler is inspired by fundamental
truths which apply to all who have their eyes set upon a
Promised Land?

Thus it will be seen how, as we approach the Old Testament from different angles, there is much more to be done
before we have gained from it all it has to offer. Every
Biblical student knows something of the gulf between the
more popular narratives (JE) and the more priestly (P),
yet the Pentateuch contains both. Is this a compromise?
Like the Old Testament, as a whole, it does not represent
any one standpoint or tendency. In the actual history of
Israel we see ebb and flow, the individualism of prophet and
the institutionalism of priest, the retention of much that is
Palestinian or Canaanite, and the insistence upon the wall
between the true son of "Israel" and the "heathen." As
we pass through the centuries each age has its needs, its
problems and its solutions. It is a wonderful epic that is
displayed to us, and we must be thankful that in the later
stages of the growth of the Old Testament no one "party"
won the day, but that the very compositeness of the Old
Testament enables us in some measure to look behind the
scenes. From the critical point of view a veritable history
is reflected in the writing and compilation of the history,
and it is the task of criticism to proceed farther upon the
lines laid down in the past.

[1] See p. 44.

The ease with which, even on the critical view, we pass
from pre-exilic to post-exilic times, and trace a development
which spans the disasters of the Exile, shows how successfully continuity was maintained.   It is not otherwise when
we reach the New Testament and feel that, although there
is an entirely new development, there is no break with the
past—else the Bible would not strike us as a *whole* in the
way it does.   Yet Israel had shot her bolt; she was unable
to make another advance, and what was primarily a movement within the Jewish circle snapped the bonds and took
the course it did—in Christianity.   It was a "spiritual
Israel" and not an "Israel after the flesh."   The "Israel
of God" (Gal. vi. 16), as Dr. Goudge says, "has no more
lost continuity with the old than the restored Israel of
Ezra and Nehemiah had lost continuity with the Israel of
David and of Isaiah."[1]

All this may be familiar enough, but we scarcely realise
how serious are the critical problems raised by the *idea* of
"Israel."   The post-exilic "Israel after the flesh" was
Judaea, Galilee, the Diaspora—but not the Samaritans, the
people of what was once Israel, the rival of Judah.   Judah
had felt herself—as we see in Chronicles (note 2 Chron.
xiii. 4–18)—to be the true Israel, in contrast to the mixed
people of Samaria.   Yet her own population was to some
extent of semi-Edomite affinity (as can be seen from 1 Chron.
ii., iv.), and the people of Samaria, partly of the older
Israelite stock, were not repudiated by such prophets as
Jeremiah and Ezekiel.[2]   If under the monarchy Israel and
Judah were rivals, and the former sometimes the more
powerful (e.g. under the dynasty of Omri), Judah was also
an integral part of Israel, as one of its several tribes, and
again—on one critical theory—after the fall of Jerusalem
in the sixth century.[3]   Be that as it may, if we go back far
enough we recognise, as has already been observed, that
much that we call "Israelite," or associate with an Israelite
Jerusalem, was really of native or pre-Israelite origin.   Thus

[1] See *A New Commentary*, Part III, p. 416.
[2] See p. 44 n. 1.
[3] See p. 152.

Israel is an *idea*—"for they are not all Israel which are of Israel" (Rom. ix. 6)—and the idea has its cradle in ancient Palestine, however much be due to the influence of tribes of Israel from the desert; and, as such, the idea transcends secular history.[1]

History does not repeat itself mechanically; but when we consider the deeper knowledge we are gaining of the Bible and its background, we may wonder whether this age will succeed in effecting some further progressive development of the idea, or whether—like the Palestine of nineteen centuries ago—it too will have shot its bolt. The fundamental and life-giving principles that were incarnate in Israel did not depend for their existence upon the national existence of Israel; and we now seem to be at the stage where the future of the "spirit" of Christianity will depend upon the "body" that Christendom shall give it. It is at least clear from the steps in the history of the growth of our Bible that there can be no guarantee that we shall succeed, nor can there be any predetermined certainty that we shall fail. It rests with us; and it is for the thoughtful reader to consider how Biblical Criticism and the question of its goal bear upon our estimate of the age in which we live.

[1] This does not, of course, detract in the slightest from the work of the great prophets. On the higher morality of the nomad and desert tribes, see Oesterley and Robinson, *History of Israel*, I, pp. 49 f., 106 f., 169, 225; *Hebrew Religion* (2nd Ed., 1937), pp. 166 ff. On the depth and prevalence of the Canaanite and Palestinian culture in the religion of Israel, see Albright, *op. cit.*, p. 153 f., and *Journal of Biblical Literature*, LV, pp. 165 ff.; Graham and May, *Culture and Conscience : An Archaeological Study of the New Religious Past in Ancient Palestine* (1936), p. 312 f.; E. A. Leslie, *Old Testament Religion in the Light of its Canaanite Background* (1936); cf. also above, p. 63, nn. 3, 5.

CHAPTER III

The Prophets as Teachers of Righteousness[1]

It is now commonly agreed that the teachings of the prophets preserved Israel through the Exile. The monarchies of Israel and of Judah fell, Judah went into Exile, and after the Return there was a reorganisation and a reconstruction associated with the names of Nehemiah and Ezra. The period covered by these events is clearly of incalculable importance for the growth of the Old Testament, and therefore for the prelude to Christianity. The Exile was a supreme disaster, a dividing-line in the history of the people; the restoration or reconstruction was a supreme turning-point in the history of religion. This profoundly impressive achievement becomes doubly so when we look more closely at the middle centuries of the millennium B.C. For Egypt and Babylon had reached the end of their tether; there were archaising movements, but they were sterile. Only in Israel can we find an advance, in the inauguration of what we call post-exilic Judaism; it was this Judaism which the Maccabees fought to maintain, and it paved the road for Christianity.

This reconstruction is remarkable when we look at it in the light of ancient history: it gives Israel a perfectly unique position. Inevitably we contrast the age some centuries later, when a new movement arose, when Judaism was unable to make a further advance, and Christianity became a separate religion. Thus we have, first, the reconstruction of the religion—this gave us the Old Testament; and later, the failure to progress—and we witness the rise of Christianity and the growth of the New Testament. The two

[1] Reprinted with revision from *The Bible and Modern Religious Thought*, I (July, 1927).

periods are of vital interest for those who regard this present age as a turning-point in history, and a deeper study of that age of reconstruction is of immediate interest for this age; for the problems which that age brings, however academical they may appear, bear immediately upon the pressing religious problems of the day.   In other words, they unite the Bible of the "higher critic" and the Bible of the ordinary reader.

Our first task must be to understand the prophets.   They are the "acid test," the criterion of one's attitude to Biblical religion.   It makes all the difference in the world what is thought of their achievement.   If, on the old traditional view, the whole Pentateuch is truly Mosaic, and was simply re-introduced in the age of Nehemiah and Ezra, what place can we give the prophets?   But, if we accept the modern ordinary critical view, the prophets brought a new spirit into an old religion; they made what was virtually a new religion.   That is their significance in history.[1]

Were the prophets merely foretellers of the future?   The persistent popularity of the Book of Daniel shows how easily we are attracted by mere foretelling.   Were the prophets essentially social reformers?   They were more than that; they were alive to the troubles of their day, and they were convinced that they knew where the hope for the future lay. They contended against current conditions and current religion, and they are characterised—the best of them at least—by an astonishing boldness.   When they condemn, they are condemning all governing and leading classes— rulers and nobles, priests and prophets; but the whole nation is at fault.   We make a profound mistake if we suppose that they would take sides; they went below existing divisions to find the source of a new unity.

[1] In his preface to the English translation of Wellhausen's epoch-making *Prolegomena to the History of Israel* (1885), Robertson Smith writes: "The plain natural sense of the old history has constantly been distorted by the false presuppositions with which we have been accustomed to approach it—having a false idea of the legal and religious culture of the Hebrews when they first entered Canaan, we continually miss the point of the most interesting parts of the subsequent story, and above all, fail to understand the great work accomplished by the prophets in destroying Old Israel and preparing the way first for Judaism and then for the Gospel" (p. viii).

Whereas New Testament scholars will sometimes do scant justice to the Old Testament, the Old Testament student cannot confine himself to the centuries before the Christian era: the history of religion in Palestine cannot be divided in that way. We know how scholars have compared Jeremiah and Jesus—"from Jeremiah to Jesus" is a convenient phrase for gathering up the great movements in the religion of the Jews. But "from Amos to Paul" is wider and more extensive, and it gives us a better grasp of the history of the great ideas in the Bible.

The prophets of the Old Testament were first and foremost teachers of Righteousness, and it is this phase of their work which we must emphasise: *Social Righteousness* is their central theme, and what this really meant, we have to understand.

There are three things which especially strike us about the prophets: (1) Their detachment from all current social, political and religious presuppositions. They go behind all society and organisation, and behind the accepted beliefs; they are absolutely fundamental—they go back to the first principles of God and Man. (2) Their convictions of God and of His Righteousness take us to ultimate values: God is no respecter of persons; He is bound by no human demands. The prophets teach God's Righteousness: it is, in a sense, an unalterable "necessity" inherent in His own nature, and untramelled by men's confident assurances of His character and conduct. And (3), they have in view the religion of the people or nation *and* the religion of each and every individual; it is the relation between national and individual religion which constitutes their practical problem. They looked for a new Israel, a new universal religion; and the road lay through the hearts of individuals.

Amos is the first of the prophets whose writings have survived, and he strikes the note of authentic prophecy in a way that makes him stand out as the first of the great prophets, and—so far as we know—different from all his predecessors. We can paraphrase his teaching thus: your religion may be real to you, but it is futile; it does not make you better men and women; you go to Bethel and sin; you take too much for granted; you rely upon past history, upon the old-time relationship between God and your people. But God belongs equally to the Aramaeans and Philistines; and just because *you* claim a unique relationship with God, *you* shall be judged by a higher standard than other peoples who do not make such claims. . . . And so it is with the prophets in general: the self-consciousness of Israel, her self-confidence and her very assurance are a danger to her. The temple at Shiloh, the Ark, and the temple at Jerusalem—all that on which Israel relies—are broken reeds. Centuries later, in much the same strain, Paul condemns the Law. It is an impressive fact in the history of Religion that particular beliefs and rites, which at one time further the progressive development of a people, can become an impediment to further progress. They need re-shaping, reinterpretation; they have lost the spiritual value which they once possessed.

Peoples—so the prophets teach—are as clay in the potter's hands, to be thrown away if they prove useless. Or again, Yahweh, the national god of Israel, treats his own people as though they are strangers, and he lets himself be found of them that seek him not. Men must not treat their religion as a fetish, as an automatic protection. Similar is the warning, centuries later: if you boast that you have Abraham as your father, God can raise up children to Abraham from these stones (Matt. iii. 9). If you point back to a fruitful past—directly the tree brings forth no fruit it is hewn down. Or new branches could be grafted on to the old tree—but these in turn could be cut off, to be replaced by others, or the old tree could bud afresh (Rom. xi.).

Throughout, from Amos to Paul, we see one idea—true for all time. The past history of Christianity does not make our religion on that account permanent. The true followers of Christ are those known to God (Matt. xxv. 31 ff.); and however incredible it might seem, the future development of Christianity might run, let us say, in South America, or in Japan.[1] The prophets are teaching that we cannot assume that the line of evolution which we see on retrospect

[1] Cf. above, p. 25.

will take the course in the future which seems to us most
natural.   This uncompromising detachment of theirs is their
most impressive characteristic.   It is revolutionary.   Christianity, we say, is a revolutionary religion—but it does not
follow that it will take the course which this or that "revolutionary" may think it will take.[1]

When the prophets teach God's Righteousness, it is the
Law of His Being which they teach.   His chastisement of
His people—the destruction of His people—was not His
will; we remember the grief of Hosea, of Micah, and of
Jeremiah.   It was a dreadful necessity.   God is Love—but
chastening love.   He raises up a foe to discipline His people,
and when the foe boasts of its own power it is flung aside.
But when Israel returns and seeks her God, He comes to
her help.   God's Righteousness is, so to say, absolutely
neutral: of necessity His own people suffer for their sins;
of necessity, when they return to Him, He will be reconciled
with His own.   The prophets are teaching an absolute
theistic law: it would be shattering, if it were not a religious
and an ethical one, the justice of which man cannot dispute.
We talk of economic "laws," "laws" of health, and so
forth, and Rabbinical Judaism had its doctrine of "merits"
and their effects; but to ancient Israel, God is the sole
cause—they did not differentiate as we do—and this is a
fact to be remembered when we turn now to consider that
word "Righteousness."

It is perhaps the most fascinating word in the Old Testament.   It has a very wide meaning; even as the word "Holy"
meant what was set apart for God, or the gods, what belonged
to them, including even the temple prostitutes, the ḳedēshôth.
Spiritual and ethical considerations from our point of view
did not necessarily enter into the terms Holiness or Righteousness, except when the prophets taught that these aspects
were more significant than all else, and gave them an
explicitly ethical and spiritual meaning.   It is helpful for
us to think of Right, Rights, Rightfulness and Righteousness
as one word.   We say that so and so is ours "by rights";

[1] If we call it the religious counterpart of the "principle of
indeterminacy," it is qualified by the idea of a Divine Righteousness.

and if we had our "rights" our cause should win; but from the primitive standpoint our "rights" depend upon our being "righteous" and "in the right." Righteousness, Salvation and many other words which we tend to regard as purely "spiritual," had distinctly material, concrete implications for the ordinary Israelite.[1] Righteousness carried with it the concrete rewards of righteous behaviour; and Yahweh's Righteousness meant, popularly, that He did what was Right, Due and Natural where his people were concerned—He did what ought to be done "by rights."

The ordinary Israelite looked for protection and prosperity from his national god—it was only "right" that he should defend his own; the prophets destroyed this dogma by teaching that it was as "right" that Israel should suffer for her shortcomings as that she should be rewarded for her piety. This Law of Righteousness contained Israel's ruin and her restoration, it was a threat and a hope. It is a permanent law. Strip it of its specifically religious form, and it becomes a horrible law, grinding down mankind—as India found the doctrine of *karma*.

The word was widely used—what was "righteous," was right, true and proper in various ways. A loyal man was "righteous" because he behaved to his suzerain as was expected of him; and Yahweh was "righteous," as Zephaniah taught, when He was faithful to Israel in spite of her apostasy (iii. 5). But, as these examples show, it is bound up with a relationship: X acts "righteously" to Y, it is the natural and expected behaviour of X to Y. Now we are acquainted with words that express a class and class-behaviour, e.g. gentlemanly, lordly, regal, noble, *noblesse oblige*. Also, in the words *kin* and *kind* we have the connection between family bond and the natural behaviour among kin. At the earlier stage of thought at which we find the Israelites, the Hebrew root of Righteous, Righteousness, Right, Due, Proper, etc., seems to have a group-application—it is what is proper, right and natural among the members of a group, especially the kin-group. If we think of *kin* and *kind*, and give *kind* a much wider connotation,

[1] See pp. 120, 214 n. 1.

including generosity, discipline (even the chastisement of a Divine Father), and then think of *kin* as *kin-group*, we may gain some idea of what Righteousness meant. It is the due relationship among kin and all that it entailed. Abraham believed in the Lord, and it was counted to him for righteousness (Gen. xv. 6)—it was a sign of the kin relation which thenceforth subsisted between the two (Isa. xli. 8); and later tradition has well recognised this, when the Mohammedans call him *Halil*, "the friend"—God's friend. The loyal belief in God and the relationship which followed this was "Righteousness." It will be seen that we gain much fuller ideas of what the word" Righteousness" meant than if we attempted some colloquial or popular translation (e.g. Abraham "put himself in the right with the Lord"), which does not offer the same wealth of meaning.

Now to teach Righteousness the prophets must appeal to individuals. In early thought gods and men would form parts of one group—a social group; and it was taken for granted that the god of the group would be well-disposed to his people, and that his people should act as was proper towards him. "Righteousness" meant the due, natural and right relations between man and man, and between God and Man. Hence the word comes to have a legal sense—when a man is legally in the right; and one could speak of God's Righteousness, because of the underlying conviction that God was bound by what was right and natural, even though this meant the discipline of Israel.

No people felt the naturalness and inevitableness of this interrelationship between a god and the people more keenly than did Israel. The Bible illustrates the working out of the relation between Yahweh and his body of worshippers. How striking is the intimacy and confidence of Israel! Moses is pleading with Yahweh on behalf of the people: If you kill off Israel for her sin, other nations will only say that you were unable to fulfil your promise and bring them to the Promised Land, and so you slew them (Num. xiv. 15f.). And Joshua, after the defeat at Ai, bids Yahweh consider what will happen if he lets Israel be destroyed (Joshua vii. 9). We can understand the shock, therefore, when the prophets destroyed the accepted conviction of a natural inevitable bond between Israel and her God.   It was a period of social and political weakness, great changes were in the air, and the prophets seemed to complete the disintegration by undermining the very foundations of the national religion.

But they were more constructive than destructive.   They established the idea of Righteousness as a cosmic principle. The relationship, however, was not between God and Israel, but between God and those who worshipped Him in truth. It was a step towards universalism, such as we find centuries later: love thy neighbour as thyself—but who is my neighbour? (Luke x. 29).   Or again, Whosoever doeth the will of the Heavenly Father, he is the Son's brother and sister and mother (Matt. xii. 50).   It was a reciprocal relationship *de novo*: a new kinship.   What the prophets taught made for a new unity, though at first it was not a unity of the people.[1]

The righteousness of the people rested upon that of every individual, and the teaching of Jeremiah and Ezekiel is characterised by the new note of individualism.   It is a watershed in the development of thought.   Yahweh would write a New Covenant upon a man's heart (Jer. xxxi. 31ff.); It was not to be a national and collective covenant with Israel as a whole, but one with every man.   These prophets wipe out the past: henceforth no man will suffer for the sins of his fathers; and—quite logically—no one can mediate for and bear the sins of another.   Men cannot have it both ways. With corporate or group responsibility innocent men may be punished for the short-comings of others; but the innocent can also willingly suffer to help others.[2]   Individualism freed a man from the burden of the past, but it put a new and heavier responsibility upon him; and in the history of religion it comes to pass that men find the burden too heavy, and feel the need of a Saviour God.   The course of thought is not very clear, but one is struck by that sublime chapter (Isa. liii.), where the unmerited sufferings and death of the Servant have brought the conviction that Israel's sins were forgiven and that a new era had dawned.   Isa. liii.—

[1] See *O.T.R.*, pp. 184 (cf. p. 118), 210.

[2] Cf. *O.T.R.*, pp. 111f., 118.

the profoundest chapter in the Old Testament—is a landmark in the development from an old unity through
individualism to a new religious unity—even as it is a
landmark in the development of ideas of Service, Mission
and Destiny.   If we could only be quite certain of the true
interpretation of Isa. liii., we should have a clue to the New
Testament as well as the Old.

From the individualism of Jeremiah and Ezekiel we pass
over the intervening centuries until we come to the teaching
of Jesus on the value of each and every individual—the
lost sheep, the missing coin, the prodigal son . . . none
must be wanting.   But with this teaching we have to take
the Parable of the Talents (Matt. xxv. 14ff.).   We with our
five or our two talents are judged each according to his
ability; but the poor, the thoughtless, the thriftless, and
those with one talent—something is expected even of them.
We think only of the widow's mite, and not of the careless
possessor of the single talent.   But we have to understand
that the religion of democracy—and there can be no democracy unless it has its religious aspects—is no true religion
until the responsibilities of the poorest and the humblest
are as distinctly recognised as their rights.   This is especially
to be emphasised because of the striking democratic note
in the Bible.

This democratic note is marked in both the Old Testament
and the New.   In their *destructive* aspects the prophets
denounce social and other evils; but in their *constructive*
aspects they are teaching that every man has his responsibilities.   The individual must bear a yoke, which is easy,
and a burden, which is light (Matt. xi. 30).   For an earlier
parallel we must go back centuries: Israel is shortly to cross
over into the Promised Land; the commandment given to
them is not out of their reach, it is very nigh to them; it is
not up above in the skies, nor beyond the seas: "it is in
thy mouth, and in thy heart, that thou mayest do it"
(Deut. xxx. 14).   Men do not enter into their inheritance
unless they are prepared to take each his share in bearing
the burden, and Social Righteousness depends upon the
relation between individuals and their God.

We do not grasp the full meaning of the Bible unless we realise the ideological connection between the Old and New Testaments: rights and responsibility; national and individual righteousness; and choice, mission and the conditions of service. No other people like Israel worked out these ideas, and the permanent value of the Bible lies in what it contributes to our knowledge of the greatest creative movements in history which the world has known. Conscious of a destiny and of religious privileges, Israel had to learn what these entailed. To be a "chosen people" involved great responsibilities; but to fail to use one's endowments was fatal, one may not renounce one's task (cf. Jer. xx. 9 with Luke ix. 62). Israel could never throw off her extreme self-consciousness; conscious of a religious superiority, she could not learn that self-sacrifice was the price of leadership, and that he who would be first must walk last, and that he who was most conscious of self must lose that self. If we were merely dealing with chapters of ancient history we might dismiss the story of Israel; but we have in the Bible, not particular events that happened once and for all, we have instead unique examples of ideas of universal validity which the old Israel had the privilege of carrying out and developing: and if they were "true" then, they cannot be less "true" now.

CHAPTER IV

The Prophets and the Reconstruction of Israel

THE reconstruction of Israel in and after the sixth century B.C. came through the prophets' appeal to the individual; thereby a new national unity was built up. Their teaching of the supremacy of God and of His covenant with Man was essentially neutral, universal; but it led to a new stage in the development of Israel. We leave behind us social and political disintegration, extreme individual and national confusion; we pass from the age of Jeremiah and Ezekiel and in due course we find a new integration, a fresh synthesis, a reconstruction. The bond between Yahweh and His people was restored. It was an event in history the significance of which we cannot too highly estimate; the questions it brings cannot be too carefully examined.

Mark what happened. The great prophets had stressed ethical rather than ritual requirements; but we now find a new emphasis on the ritual, viz. in Malachi, the last chapters of Isaiah, and in "P," i.e. the post-exilic portions of the Pentateuch. The sacrifices, the temple, the temple services, now have a new importance, and disaster—e.g. drought—is due to the neglect of ritual.[1] Further, the prophets had made Yahweh entirely independent of the people; but now Yahweh again moves history for the sake of Israel. The supremacy of Jerusalem and its temple meant little to a Jeremiah; but now Zion and her priesthood are the centre of the religious world, and Yahweh is so holy as to be unapproachable save through the priestly classes. If there is universalism, it is under Jewish aegis; it is a "religious imperialism," like a Roman Catholicism directed from Rome, or a Universal Proletarian Brotherhood, the Church of Moscow. The world is sinful; but the post-exilic

[1] *O.T.R.*, pp. 176–184.

sacrificial system is "the divinely appointed means
for the preservation and restoration of that holiness in
virtue of which alone the theocratic community of Israel
can realise its true ideal as the people of a holy God."[1]
The prophets had taught, ethically and spiritually, the
Holiness of God and His Righteousness; we have now the
teaching applied to Israel and the world—religion is
"socialised."

As we pass from one phase to another the contrast is
impressive. We cannot say that the prophets had failed,
or that the reactionaries have won. We have to recognise
the vast difference between the more individualistic teachers
and the rank and file, between the spiritual "experts," so
to say, and the ordinary men. The latter cannot reach the
height of the specialist; or, to put it differently, the religion
of the living, working people cannot be that of the more
detached teacher and reformer. An adjustment is always
being made between the teaching of the few and the needs
of the many. The fact may be depressing to the reformer;
but developments of this sort are unavoidable, and this
apparent reaction or counter-reformation—call it what you
will—is an established fact in the modern critical view of
the Old Testament. We contrast the *prophets'* teaching of
Righteousness and Holiness with the *priests'* effort to ensure
the Divine Holiness and secure the righteousness and
holiness of the people. It is true that perhaps we pass
from one extreme to the other; but without the prophets
there would have been no reform, and without the priests
the reform could not have been made socially effective.

The priestly tendency is in many respects intelligible;
naïve, personal religion is apt to need regularising, private
cults are apt to need socialising. On the one hand, we
recall the free way in which Gideon asks for a sign that
Yahweh will help him: "how shall I know?" is the keynote of one type of popular religion, give men a sign that
they may trust Him.[2] On the other, is the Deuteronomic

---

[1] A. R. S. Kennedy, *Leviticus–Numbers* (*Century Bible*), p. 35.

[2] Moses, Exod. iii. 11 ff.; Gideon, Judges vi. 17, 36 ff.; Hezekiah,
2 Kings xx. 8, and Abraham, Gen. xv. 8 (with which contrast *v*. 6).

injunction—"thou shalt not tempt (i.e. put to the test) the Lord thy God."[1] The naïve free cross-examination is deprecated. Especially interesting is the story of Eldad and Medad (Num. xi. 26). Seventy elders are taken outside the camp into the Tent of Meeting to be consecrated; the divine spirit rests upon them, and they become prophets; but these two remained in the camp, and yet in some way they received the spirit and "prophesied." To Joshua's expostulation Moses replies: Would that all Yahweh's people were prophets! It is a grand utterance, by one who himself stood in God's council (Num. xii. 7f.). But look more carefully at the wording: even those in the tent were prophets only when the spirit came upon them; we read that "they did so no more"—the Authorised Version ("and did not cease") has entirely missed the point. This spoils the object of the narrative, which was to give Moses permanent helpers (see *v.* 16f.). Still more is this the case when we observe that Eldad and Medad are said to be "among them that were on the register." The true point of the story is surely the remark of Moses: the free gift of Yahweh's spirit of prophecy; but this is whittled away when we learn that the seventy in the tent had it on that occasion only, and that if the holy spirit rested on Eldad and Medad, who were not of the seventy, nevertheless they were, so to speak, on the books! In other words, here and elsewhere we can see the tendency to regularise religion, to organise spiritual gifts and privileges, and to mark the difference between the properly instituted priest or prophet and the layman. It is the step from a more democratic to a more hierarchical religion.[2]

On the modern critical view the Law comes *after* and not *before* the Prophets: the characteristic sacerdotalism and

[1] Deut. vi. 16; cf. Exod. xvii. 7. See Driver on Exod. xvii. 2 (*Cambridge Bible*).

[2] On the "democratic" and "rationalistic" note in Deuteronomy, see *O.T.R.*, pp. 122, 185f.; G. A. Smith, *Deuteronomy*, p. xxxvii. Cf. the history of the Montanists in the second century A.D.: on the one hand, it was necessary to curb the practice of ecstatic utterance; on the other hand, the effect was "to restrict belief in the operation of the Holy Spirit to His working in and through institutional channels." See C. E. Raven, *Evolution and the Christian Conception of God* (1936), p. 43f.

legalism are post-exilic. They are two stages in a long religious history. But they represent only one side, though a very important one, of the religious life.[1] And although legalism has always its bad side, the Psalms are proof that simple piety not only could flourish under the Law, but could be inspired by it.[2]

Further, we have to remember that we are dealing with only a few of a series of successive stages. The lessons taught by the prophets were not learnt once and for all; and although the prophets attacked an old régime and were responsible for the rise of a new one, there was no millennium. Biblical history forces us to take a very long view, and bids us not to expect that a religious reformation or reconstruction will solve all our problems. We, living in an age of disintegration, may feel the need of a new social and religious integration; but what we learn from the Bible is, not to expect the solution once and for all of all future difficulties, but the fact that every age has its own task, and that the recognition of the next step to take is more important than millennial visions. We can see how some new change can come, and can be of permanent effect; but though we know that Israel weathered her storms, we cannot trace all the steps in the process.

The old Israel passed through what we might call an age of "destructive criticism" to a new reconstruction, and just as the exilic period was vital for the process of national reconstruction, so the critical study of that period is proving vital for our reconstruction of Old Testament history and religion.

Before giving some further illustrations I must first turn aside to what may seem to be "advanced" or "destructive"

---

[1] "It would correct many false impressions about Old Testament worship if we accustomed ourselves to think of the Book of Leviticus and the Book of Psalms as written in parallel columns, for they were more or less contemporary productions" (H. Wheeler Robinson, in *Christian Worship*, ed. Micklem, p. 25).

[2] For a New Testament parallel, see Goudge, in *A New Commentary*, Part III, p. 432: "There is always the tendency of cautious teachers to clip the wings of St. Paul's theology, and bring back a certain amount of legalism."

criticism. After the fall of the Northern Kingdom we are apt to think only of "Lost Ten Tribes" and of a heathenish Samaria. But Jeremiah and Ezekiel speak sympathetically of their northern neighbours; and we have reason to believe that a new Israel was growing up.[1] With the fall of the kingdom of Judah there was a better opportunity for closer relationship between north and south; and Professor Kennett and others have argued that there was a reunion, and they place in this age the Book of Deuteronomy. In fact, Deuteronomy is actually addressed to an "all Israel," i.e. all the northern and southern elements. On the other hand, we are wont to take the attitude of the Judaean writers of history, and to associate ourselves in sympathy with the exiles who went to Babylonia and returned with reforming aims; but Biblical Criticism is also interested in the conditions in Palestine itself, and this theory of a united Israel and of the exilic date of Deuteronomy (in its present form) is extremely illuminating.[2]

Next, we may note that the return of the Davidic Zerubbabel, the Messianic prophecies of Haggai and Zechariah, and the rebuilding of the Temple, inaugurate a new era. There was a descendant of David and a new Temple; enthusiastic hopes were kindled. The new hopes would be enough to arouse the suspicions of Samaria; and in the prophecies of Zechariah we have hints of a conflict between the Messianic Zerubbabel and the priestly party. We do not know what followed. There is a blank in the history until some sixty years later, the age of Nehemiah and Ezra, when we find a picture of distress and ruin; the Messianic monarchical ideas have disappeared, and the régime is becoming a priestly one. This blank is one of the mysteries of Biblical history, but it is evident that it was a grave time for Judah and Jerusalem. Indeed, there are some hints of a fresh disaster.[3] That is to say, the age which

---

[1] Cf. *C.A.H.*, III, pp. 406f., 415 n.; VI, p. 181.

[2] See Kennett, *Church of Israel*, pp. 90ff.; cf. pp. xliiff.

[3] *C.A.H.*, VI, p. 183f.; cf. S. H. Blank, *Hebrew Union College Annual*, XI, pp. 172 (with references), 182.

seemed to be so brilliantly inaugurated by Zerubbabel collapsed—how, we can only guess; we know only that some decades later we have the reconstruction which we associate with the names of Nehemiah and Ezra. The *fact* of Israel's subsequent restoration or reconstruction is not affected; but the successive stages are more than obscure.

Now, it is probable that to the period of the Davidic Zerubbabel and the Second Temple belong the accounts of the Davidic monarchy and the First Temple, and the emphasis upon the character of a king and the permanence of the Davidic dynasty.[1] That the Book of Deuteronomy is ascribed by some scholars to the sixth century has been already mentioned; but I myself would go further and place here a larger amount of popular literature in its present form. Everyone recognises the popular democratic character of the Biblical history; the contrast with the records of Egypt, Babylonia and Assyria is most striking. The tone is simple and didactic. One has only to consider, for example, the space given to the heroic Elijah and Elisha in the history of the monarchies, and to note especially the more popular stories (e.g. 2 Kings ii. 19–24; iv.; vi. 1–7), which are not history in the modern sense, but of a sort to give the history a value to the ordinary reader. We should note also the popular didactic character of the stories of the patriarchs, and the Exodus and Invasion. They are for the simple-minded, and not for the students of history. We know something of the nature of monarchical and priestly litera-ture, of aristocratic and heroic writings; but this is not what we have in the Old Testament. On ordinary psycho-logical grounds it is clear that the popular narratives which have always appealed to the ordinary reader were written for the ordinary man of Israel. In them he had the story of his ancestors and the conquest of the land in which he lived; he learnt of his institutions and of the relations between his land, his people and his God. He found en-couragement and example, inspiration and warning, and

[1] Cf. Solomon's prayer (1 Kings viii. 47): should there be an exile, and should the people return to him, Yahweh is besought to show mercy.   See G. F. Moore, *Ency. Biblica,* "Historical Literature," § 7.

even threat—and throughout is that superb religious simplicity which would move him as it has moved us. This
popular, democratic note in the religion and religious literature of Israel is a unique phenomenon. There is nothing like
it elsewhere, and my own conviction is that as a whole it
belongs round about the sixth century—the age of reconstruction: that is to say, it is not earlier than the great
prophets as is generally believed, but after them.[1] The
canonical history sets the Law before the Prophets; modern
criticism places the Prophets before the Law; and the view
here suggested is that the great creative prophets also
precede the history in the form in which we have it. The
current criticism passes from the great reforming prophets
to the priestly and legalistic spirit of the post-Exilic Age;
whereas, on my view, the history-writing comes in
between.

How was Jeremiah's teaching of the New Covenant
between man and God to be translated into action? The
spiritual experts need their interpreters and intermediaries,
and we require a bridge between the great preaching prophets
and that age of reconstruction when the priests organise
popular religion. The prophets preached spiritual truths to
individuals; but in the popular narratives every man of
Israel found the truths enshrined in the history of his race.
It is, perhaps, not difficult for us of to-day to understand
how men might feel the need of a New Covenant. But
merely to subscribe to one is not enough. If truths are
to work themselves out in men's lives and thoughts, they
require some more concrete shape, something "historical";
and it seems not improbable that the biblical narratives
were the application of the doctrine of Jeremiah's New
Covenant to every Israelite. Do not we ourselves feel that
we require a "historical" background or framework for our
truths to render them more concrete? Similar periods
interpret each other, and the wonderfully written stories
of Yahweh's dealings with His people become immensely
more significant—both for Biblical Criticism and for this

---

[1] Cf. below, pp. 51, 152 f.

age—if we may date them in that age of destruction and
reconstruction.[1]

I will now give two illustrations to justify what I am
saying. Instead of indulging in analysis, let us take as a
whole the story of Israel's Origins and Descent into Egypt,
the Exodus and the Invasion. Instead of attempting to
distinguish early and late, we may look at the narratives,
en bloc, in the light of the Exilic and post-Exilic Age. Let
us start by thinking of to-day: the unrest and anxiety, the
absence of unity, the failure to recognise any supreme
Divine authority, the hope of a new and better age, the
desire to put behind us all that oppresses and burdens,
the longing for a happier land, a New Covenant, a new
relation between man and God. Now that, *mutatis mutandis*,
would be the situation in that far-off age. Turn, therefore,
to the story of the Exodus, and take, first of all, the purely
expository standpoint; reflect upon the escape from
Egyptian bondage, the saving acts of Yahweh, the march
into the Promised Land, and the discipline of the people.
Could not the preacher find much that is suggestive for us
in *our* journey to a Better Land?

But if this religious argument is sound, criticism will not
allow us to take the narratives as a trustworthy account of
the Mosaic Age. No doubt some tribes came out of Egypt
and invaded Palestine; but in their present form the narratives are late; they are of the Exilic Age, the age of disintegration. It was the period of the Deuteronomic law-
giving, and we know from the Second Isaiah how the return
from Exile was treated as a new Exodus.[2] There was in
more than one respect in that age of destruction and reconstruction a journey to a Promised Land and the disciplining
of a people. We may, therefore, treat the Pentateuchal
story as more or less contemporary with the hopes of the
Exilic Age and the return from Babylon to the ancestral
land. We look at the Pentateuch from this late standpoint.

---

[1] See *C.A.H.*, III, pp. 472 ff.; *J.T.S.*, XXX, pp. 304 ff.

[2] See Skinner on Isa. xl. 3 (*Cambridge Bible*, and Index, *s.v.*
Exodus").

"See," said the writers, "how your ancestors were led and disciplined when they came out of Egypt," and they rewrote the past in order to set forth teaching that was meant for the present. They taught how the people were disciplined. And more than this, they taught how the leaders were disciplined. Recall the importance of the more prophetic figure Moses and of the more priestly Aaron, the stories of rivalries, of Moses as mediator (Exod. xxxii. 32), and note that modern criticism finds the reflection of late vicissitudes in the story of Korah's revolt (Num. xvi.). Recall in particular how much the people owed to their leaders, and then observe that those very leaders were punished for not reverencing Yahweh as they should.   In Lev. x. 1–7 is the story how the eldest sons of Aaron were consumed by fire because of a *ritual* fault: Yahweh's words are quoted: "Among those that are near to me I will show myself holy, and before all the people shall I glorify myself."   But in an earlier passage (Num. xx. 12) and elsewhere, there are references to some vaguer offence: Moses and Aaron in some way did not show respect to Yahweh, and they, the chosen saviours of the people, were not permitted to bring the people into the Promised Land.[1]   It is not a ritual offence as in the later Leviticus story, but both stories are at pains to establish the supremacy, the transcendence of God.[2] Even His own chosen leaders and priests must pay the penalty; for Yahweh works, not for Israel's sake, but for His Name.[3]   It is the teaching of the prophets concerning Israel's mission.   Consciousness of mission and destiny does not entitle men to forget that they are God's servants, doing God's work; and that it is God and not Man who is behind the processes of history.[4]   That is what the great prophets taught, and it is interesting to observe that the

---

[1] See Ps. cvi. 33, and *Ency. Bib.*, "Massah and Meribah."

[2] Similarly when Israel goes forth to war, it is emphasised that it is God who gives the victory, and not the heavy battalions (Judges vii. 2, Deut. viii. 17, Ps. xliv. 3; cf. the ideas in 2 Chron. xx. 15, 17).

[3] See Davidson and Streane, *Ezekiel*, p. xliiif.; cf. Exod. ix. 16.

[4] Cf. Isa. x. 15; xxix. 16; Hab. i. 15ff.

Leviticus story, where the sons of Aaron commit a purely *ritual* offence, is due to the later post-Exilic priestly writer, and corresponds to the stress laid by the priestly school upon the importance of correct ritual.

Take this insistence upon Yahweh's absolute supremacy and co-ordinate it with the Exilic Age and with to-day. The idea of an immanent rather than a transcendent God is to the front to-day: Divine transcendence is unintelligible to an age endeavouring to be "democratic," conscious of its strength, and with that "self-sufficiency" that is at the core of so much modern thinking.[1] Many are so sure of the road to the Promised Land, and so confident that they possess the key to unlock the gates, or so persuaded that it is God's work they are doing, that we do well to mark the ideas which the ancient writers are putting forth. In the Exilic and post-Exilic Ages there was need of emphasising the ideas—not only as regards Israel and her mission, but also as regards the function and destiny of the Servant of the Lord—for here, too, the fundamental idea is that the path of the leader of Israel, the light to lighten the Gentiles, is one of sacrifice, altruism and meekness. The true servant of the Lord, as set forth in Isa. liii., was despised and rejected, the last man one would choose to save a people— to lead it into a Promised Land. There are other hints, too— the tradition of Nebuchadrezzar—which point to an age when the idea of supermen was in the air: the age of "God-given" strong men, dictators. It was an age when men had to learn the reality of Divine transcendence.[2]

Consider such ideas as these: the jealousy of the gods, the vaulting ambition that has its fall, the over-weening confidence and ambition, spiritual pride—all these ideas are familiar; and especially in the old Oriental world do we find men of extraordinary driving power and intensity. And while such men are, in a sense, often extremely "religious," their activities are at times excessively fantastic and

---

[1] Cf. Emil Brunner, *The Word and the World* (1931), pp. 90, 113, 119f.

[2] Cf. the myth in Isa. xiv., the King of Tyre in Ezek. xxviii., and Skinner (*Genesis*, p. 229) on the story of the Tower of Babel.

outrageous.[1] In Israel, more than in any other people, the extreme consciousness of mission, destiny and intimate relationship with God needed disciplining. The Oriental was conscious of the ineffable sovereignty of the Ultimate Power men call God; but at the same time there was a consciousness of a unique relationship, and with this consciousness went often the conviction that *he* knew the Divine will, *he* was the Divine vehicle, and that *he*, like his Deity, was above all law. "Religious" assurance is typically Semitic. It was against such assurance that the prophets had to contend, and not with complete success.

But now pass on to the early chapters of Genesis: Man's sin and the world-wide Deluge, the New Covenant with Noah, the new international brotherhood—all men, one speech—the attempt to build a tower unto heaven, Yahweh's descent to stop this arrogant act, and the scattering of the peoples (Gen. vi.–xi.). It is really a second disaster, and we proceed in due course to the call of Abraham; it is the dawn of the history of Israel. Again, I am not analysing, but am taking the chapters as a whole. They give us a conception of history which we might trans-late into modern terms: a devastating catastrophe, a fresh beginning when nothing seems impossible, for there is no transcendent God; man himself is remaking the world; there follows a fresh disaster, the new reconstruction has failed, and then, and only then, does true religion begin to dawn.

Again turn to the present situation. Consider our anxiety to get going after the World War:—the League of Nations, a noble internationalism, a worthy humanism, and even hopes of a single world-wide language.[2] But the religious spirit is lamentably ineffective; the Kingdom that is envisaged is often a very secular one; it is Man and not God who has all things under his feet. There are those who foresee the collapse of our civilisation and the loss of the

---

[1] A good example is afforded by that remarkable caliph, el-Ḥākim (*c.* A.D. 1000).

[2] Those acquainted with "basic English" may even translate Gen. xi. 1, "and all the earth was one tongue and a small vocabulary!"

fruits of the past. But even should this befall, there are yet those who would say that the death of Western culture will not mean the end of all progressive development: at some age and in some area there will be a new continuity, even as we can see the continuity between Palestine and Western Europe. Thus, later ages may see that the real line of progressive development has shifted to another part of the globe. All this can be easily imagined, and it helps us to understand the writer responsible for the chapters in Genesis: here and often elsewhere current conditions enable us to enter more sympathetically into the past.

Very few, I suppose, would take those chapters literally; but the ideas are surely profoundly true, and it is here suggested that their historical background lies in the Exilic and post-Exilic Age. After the fall of the monarchies come the Exilic period, the rise of a new pan-Israel, the new Davidic monarchy, the Messianic Zerubbabel and the Second Temple—it is a fresh start-off. And then, as already mentioned, we have hints of some new disaster, a scene of ruin in the days of Nehemiah and a priestly régime. In this new disaster and the inauguration of the priestly phase, have we not the key to the philosophy of history of the writer of Genesis?[1] It is precisely the old monarchical idea with the king as God's representative which, in the story of Zerubbabel, seems to fall under suspicion; we see it again in the secondary account of Saul's election (1 Sam. viii. 7; x. 19; xii. 12, 19f.); and it is precisely the priestly religion which secures the transcendent majesty of Yahweh, and becomes more ritual than ethical by the cordon of priests which severs the laity from the most holy things. Accordingly (1) we have the fundamental ideas underlying the story in Genesis of the Deluge, the Tower of Babel, the Dispersion of Mankind and the Call of Abraham; (2) these ideas are really independent of the historical value of those narratives; they are primarily of psychological, spiritual value, and (3) we can, I venture to think, find a new

[1] Kennett, too, sought to find a historical basis, though at an earlier date, viz. after the deportation of Judaeans in 586 B.C.; see his *Old Testament Essays* (1929), pp. 10, 21; and cf. *J.T.S.*, XXX (1929), p. 305, n. 4.

historical background for them if my own "advanced"
views are correct.[1] See further, pp. 153 ff.

Dean Stanley has said: "True History teaches true
religion."[2] Whether we take the Old Testament literally
or not, we all agree in recognising its permanent *spiritual*
value. No doubt we vary according to the standpoint we
adopt—the spiritual worth of the Old Testament to the
thorough-going "Fundamentalist" cannot be quite identical
with what it is to him who accepts Biblical Criticism. But
I would urge that we can find a greater and more realistic
religious gain when we are able to place the Old Testament
on a new historical background. We may all appreciate the
spiritual kernel, though we may differ as to the value of the
historical shell; but kernels are like abstract truths, the spirit
needs the letter, the soul needs the body, and spiritual
religion needs translation into the concrete. I am suggesting
that we can find a new historical "shell," a new and truer
conception of the history of Israel at a particular formative
period when the great ideas were red-hot. They have their
historical background in the age when an old order was
giving way to a new, and the old religion was being replaced
by what was virtually a new or rather a reorganised religion.

Thus, I am concentrating upon a later age, when great
history was being made. I see reason to date much literature in that age, and although of course other ages have their

---

[1] That there are no "short cuts" to the Promised Land seems to
be the idea underlying Num. xiv. 40 ff., where the Israelites attempt
to enter Palestine direct from the south, *but without the Ark*, and
suffer defeat. The narrator has omitted the rest of what was a very
significant tradition—it is of the first importance for Biblical
Criticism—for the sake of the teaching he wished to inculcate.

It may be added that points of contact have often been suggested
between Moses and the actual Servant of the Lord. In any case,
the Pentateuch was, on the critical view, assuming its shape in the
age of the Second Isaiah, Zerubbabel and the inauguration of post-
Exilic Judaism. It will be seen that whereas current criticism
regards the Pentateuch as *now* post-Exilic, though containing much
that is pre-Exilic, I am treating even the old as being *now* in the form
in which the post-Exilic compilers or editors left it. It is on the
same principle of "advanced" criticism that most scholars treat
both the Book of Isaiah and the Psalms as *now* in post-Exilic form,
though with much that is earlier; see p. 66, n. 2.

[2] *The Jewish Church*, Vol. III, Preface.

importance, for present purposes it is necessary to focus attention upon that transitional period and to recognise its supreme historical religious significance. The great prophets, and especially the Second Isaiah, are Israel's abiding glory, and Israel stands out uniquely for her achievement in undergoing reconstruction when her powerful neighbours decayed and died. Through her reconstruction we have the Old Testament; the Old Testament leads on to the New, and thenceforth the line of development has been that of the Bible, and Biblical study, and learning based upon or arising out of the Bible.

This line is surely of the most profound significance. May one not say that the future of religion depends upon the use and interpretation of the Bible? If Biblical Criticism has had its share in weakening the authority of the Bible, may one not assert that, as it proceeds, it gives newer and greater values?[1] In the history which lies behind the Bible we have the living experiences of peoples and individuals to whom are due the profoundest stages in the evolution of human life and thought. There is in it a depth which we find nowhere else. We can appreciate the overpowering influence of supreme experiences in shaping the lives of men and peoples. Such experiences are of absolute objective authority, they invite explanation, they demand expression, they determine the future. They are an inspiration, a new birth, a new starting-point. We recognise an event or series of events of this sort in the history of Israel, especially in the steps leading up to the reconstruction of her religion. Similar creative events in the rise of Christianity, in the Reformation, and also in other religions elsewhere, enable us to perceive the tremendous driving-power that a new religious spirit, an awakening of the religious consciousness, would have upon *us*, in taking *us* away from the past and in heralding a new future. The

[1] Cf. Bacon's words: "It is true that a little philosophy inclineth men's minds to atheism; but depth in philosophy bringeth men's minds about to religion: for while the mind of man looketh upon second causes scattered, it may sometimes rest in them, and go no farther; but when it beholdeth the chain of them confederate and linked together, it must needs fly to Providence and Deity."

effect of such spiritually creative and constructive ages in the past helps us to realise what could recur to-day; and I am convinced that a new stage in the history of religion, with the reinterpretation of the Bible as its foundation, is what is needed and what may come to pass.

Let me now notice a few points arising out of this suggestion. Note, first of all, the attitude to the land in Lev. xxv. We are at the beginning of a new era. The land now belongs to Yahweh (*v.* 23), and the people belong to Yahweh; and when offerings of first-fruits and firstlings are made to Him, men give Him what is already His own. Observe the implications of such ideas. To say that the land belongs to the people is a misleading half-truth; whereas the Hebraic idea—also to be traced in Islām— places land and property, ownership and usufruct on a theistic basis. Like the prophecies of a return of the Jews to the Holy Land, the ideas are fundamentally theistic and have no substance otherwise.

If we grasped the fundamental idea of Righteousness, and sincerely believed that there was a real sense in which the Universe is God's, and that we are His, we should have the framework of a new religious, social and political platform, immensely more powerful than any of the regulative ideas that are current to-day. Just as in Israel religious, social and political ideas were interconnected—and the prophets were, in a sense, national reformers—so it is in every way likely that a new movement based on a reinterpretation of the Bible would have much more than a merely religious significance.

Further, all ideas of brotherhood, commonwealth, and especially of a League of Nations, require for their stability an ultimate authority before whom all are on equal terms. Here the great prophets of Israel come to our aid, for we can see how their doctrine of Divine Transcendence—God's absolute impartiality, regardless of individuals and nations, and also of religions—is above all social, economic, political and national differences. If the idea of Divine Transcendence and Immanence were truly grasped, and not emasculated and sterilised as it so often is, men would see behind their essential differences a still more essential unity, and gain a truer conception of their place in the Divine Order and of their responsibility for Human Order.

Again, in the history of thought there is a typical transition from religion to philosophy. Men reflect upon experience and seek to rationalise it; men pass from the rare heights of an intense spirituality to a calmer synthesis of knowledge, spiritual and secular. In ancient times we can pass from the religion of Israel to the "Wisdom" or philosophy of the Greek age, from Christian religion and theology to Christian philosophy. To-day our philosophy, such as it is, is doubly imperfect, for either it excludes the data of religious experience, an intolerable and indefensible omission, or even when it is religious or Christian, it does not, in the opinion of many, do justice to the pre-Christian and non-Christian religions. There is much more to be said about the nature of religion in general before we can get the philosophy, and even the theology, that modern knowledge requires; and it may be urged that the new knowledge we are gaining of the Bible and of its background, and of other religions, is pointing the way to a new stage in our treatment of theological and philosophical problems.

Our forefathers, with the Bible behind them as the basis of their knowledge, had an at least implicit philosophy of religion and history. Can this be restated? To understand the Bible aright we have to follow a stream of history, a series of great vicissitudes, varying depths of experience, a rise and fall of hopes, periods of decay and of rebirth of religion. We observe the varying importance of prophets and priests, of reformers and organisers, destruction and construction, revolution and evolution. We see how national ideas are carried over and applied to individuals— e.g. the resurrection of the nation and, later, of the individual; the worth and destiny of "Israel" and so of every man of "Israel." Ideas of individuals are applied to nations—the suffering Servant, the suffering Israel. And as we endeavour to understand the fluctuation and development of thought in the course of the centuries, we gain a veritable philosophy of history, or rather of evolution, far more real than any that can be gained from the scientific study of the Universe of Space–Time. Modern Biblical Criticism has sometimes been condemned as the offspring of Hegel's philosophy; it would be more true to say that the newer study of the Bible may force us to a conception of the development of thought of the utmost significance, not only for philosophy, but for the history of thought in general.

The inner connection between the Old Testament and the New is only natural when we consider historically the inter-connected centuries during which the Bible took its rise. There are earlier and later forms of ideas; ideas become more mature, or are worked out, or reshaped; the implicit becomes explicit. Here the old-fashioned typology had right on its side when it discovered some essential connection between the earlier and later forms of ideas— whether the ideas are set forth in teaching, or inform persons, events or institutions. To-day we have what we call the "comparative method," and it enables us to go further in tracing continuity beneath discontinuity, and similarity underlying difference. The development from the Old Testament to the New is towards a greater fulness; and it is in this sense that the New Testament, from the more critical point of view, can be said to "fulfil" the Old. But this "fulfilment" has not ceased. The effect of Biblical research has been to recover and restate the great pregnant ideas, and in this sense later ages may be said to "fulfil" the Bible. As the New Testament "fulfils" the Old, so may we not say that the Bible is to be "fulfilled" by this or some later age? In our interpretation of the Bible, in our efforts to effect a readjustment between the Bible and the age, we are, in a certain sense, "fulfilling" it. And one ventures to think that such "fulfilment," resting as it must upon active co-operation and labour, is a far more "spiritual" one than the somewhat passive expectation that "fulfilment" will take the form of a Second Coming, of an actual millennium,[1] or than the notion that a Kingdom of Heaven can be introduced by violence.

The experiences of this age enable us to understand and

[1] See, on this, pp. 99, 124.

interpret the Bible in a way that our fathers could not. At the same time, the Bible is being ever more closely bound up with non-Biblical, non-religious studies. Biblical study is simply one part of the entire field of scientific or critical research. This, too, is significant for the future. The Bible certainly does not interpret itself as it did. But it is no less certain that the Church of to-day does not interpret it as it merits. We may say that the truly progressive Church of the future will be that which has the best interpretation of the Bible. But this will depend upon our growing knowledge of ancient history and religion, and their significance for the present. It will depend upon so many interests in the world of thought that the ultimate authority, as I take it, will be neither Church nor State, still less will it be a university or even some syndicate of studies; but it will be the *explicit* recognition of the essential fundamental interrelation of all the interests, studies and spheres of research with which the Bible is bound up.

In former days the Bible was the touchstone, the criterion of all sound knowledge; but to-day we are placing the Bible, viewed in the light of criticism, against the new background of thought. Its permanent spiritual and religious value, will, I cannot but think, become ever more clear and more sure; and I believe that there will be a new interrelation between the Bible and the non-Biblical world of study. But this new synthesis which may be anticipated is vastly different from mediaevalism. It is no deliberate return to old positions, no reintroduction of scholasticism—no "Neo-Thomism." Contrast the advance of Israel in the middle of the first millennium B.C. with the decline and decay of the old empires of Egypt, Assyria and Babylon. Contrast the reconstruction of Israel with the futile archaising in Egypt and Babylon. History does not repeat itself literally or mechanically; but we must take warning, as well as encouragement, from the past. Certain periods stand out with startling vividness, e.g. (*a*) the reconstruction of Israel in and about the Exilic period, (*b*) the tragic failure of Israel to advance at the rise of Christianity, and (*c*) the Reformation. This age is no whit less significant for human

history, and from the creative periods of the past we have
to turn to the creative aspirations of to-day. If we look
back over the past, it is to take it up and carry it forward;
and in that sense we "fulfil" the promise of the past. So,
as I venture to urge, we can take our stand upon the history
of Israel, upon the Bible, by elucidating the new meaning
that the Bible has for this age, its profound historical and
religious meaning, its extraordinarily *real* value. May one
not say that in a certain sense we are gaining a new Bible?
We get (1) the new history in which we are placing the
Bible, (2) the great ideas that make it of permanent value,
and (3) the fact that these ideas were incarnated in individuals and events.

They were ideas which made history and shaped the
world. In the Middle Ages, most men found only dead
history in the Bible. It was Luther's complaint that his
opponents looked upon Biblical history simply as things
that had taken place and no longer concerned men. They
were unable to understand the great pregnant, history-
making ideas in the Old Testament; they had no clear
sense of the organic connection between Old Testament
and New, because they had lost the historical significance
of the Bible. But the Reformers had a new way of looking
at the Bible. They vindicated for the Bible a new use and
a living interest which made it impossible that the Bible
should be neglected. That, as I conceive it, was one of the
outstanding factors of the Reformation of which we are the
sons and heirs.

CHAPTER V

The "Evolution" of Biblical Religion[1]

THE modern way of viewing Biblical religion along evolutionary lines has become so firmly established that no one who has once discovered how it has enabled him to understand the religious history of Israel will want or, indeed, be able to return to any earlier outlook. This evolutionary approach is the offspring of a tendency rather than of any philosophical or other school. It can be traced back to such pre-Darwinians as Reuss and the Hegelian Vatke (1833–35); but modern Old Testament criticism regards as its founders Kuenen (1869–70), Wellhausen (1878) and Robertson Smith (1881), none of whom could be called Hegelians or Darwinians.[2] More recently, however, the theory of "evolution" has been reconsidered. Mendelism, the Great War and the collapse of the belief in a continuous advance, along with new developments in Biblical research, have combined to threaten the "moderate critical" way of treating the history and religion of Israel. It is, of course, agreed by all Old Testament scholars that there has been some sort of religious development, and even extremely conservative attitudes, including some found among Roman Catholics,[3] are no longer what they once were. But the problem of "evolution" has become increasingly urgent, and these pages are offered as a preliminary contribution to the subject.

[1] Reprinted with revision from *The Modern Churchman*, XXIV (Nov., 1934), pp. 471 ff.

[2] Cheyne (*Founders of Old Testament Criticism* [1893], pp. 137 ff.) points out that Vatke's thesis does not depend upon his abstruse philosophy; if anything, as G. B. Gray observes, it retarded criticism (*Ency. Brit.*, 11th Ed., "Bible," III, p. 863a).

[3] It must be admitted that an attitude so favourable to Biblical Criticism as that of the late Baron Friedrich von Hügel is rare among them; see his *Essays and Addresses*, I, pp. 72 ff.

In fact, I wish to suggest that whether Old Testament scholars use such terms as "development," or "evolution"—even with marks of quotation—the task is to frame as adequate a view as possible of the broad outlines of the whole course of Biblical religion. Whether it will deserve to be called an "evolutionary" one is really a secondary matter. Such have been the unique processes in and behind the Bible—the foundation of our civilisation—that we have to examine them without any presupposition that what holds good in the scientist's world may also hold good for us. After all, it is not impossible that a fuller knowledge of the processes in the history of religious thought may prove more suggestive for the understanding of those in the specialist fields of history and science than conversely.[1]

Our notions of Old Testament religion and history generally begin, not with the patriarchs and the descent of Jacob's children into Egypt, but with the Exodus of the "children of Israel"—the sons having become tribes and clans—and their conquest of the land of their fathers. On interrogation, scholars are found to differ widely as to the value of the book of Genesis for our knowledge of pre-Israelite conditions. It is commonly agreed that of those people whom we call Israelites only a section had been in Egypt; consequently it must have been only in course of time that the original Mosaic tradition, whatever its content, became the canonical tradition of all Israelites, whether their ancestors had been in Egypt or not.[2]   Many reconstructions have been proposed; and special mention may be made of that of Burney, who was convinced (in 1908) that Babylonian and other "external" evidence would revolutionise our

---

[1] Specially suggestive in this connection are F. J. Teggart's *Processes of History* (New Haven, 1918) and his earlier *Prolegomena to History : the Relation of History to Literature, Philosophy and Science* (1916).

[2] Two references will suffice: N. Baynes (*Israel Amongst the Nations*, published by the Student Christian Movement, p. 201) writes, "only a part of the Israelites went down into Egypt"; and W. F. Albright, the American archaeologist and Orientalist, says, "it is now quite certain that a large part, perhaps more than half, of the Hebrew people remained in Palestine, and did not enter Egypt at all" (*The Archaeology of Palestine and the Bible*, p. 148).

views of early Israelite religion.[1] He argued that those tribes of Israel who remained behind in Cannaan practised a "Canaanite Yahwism", and that only after a long struggle, did their kinsmen who descended into Egypt and returned along with North Arabian (Kenite) clans succeed in replacing a Yahwism more in harmony with ordinary Semitic religion by their own purer faith. Burney thus implied that Old Testament religion was indebted both to Israelite immigrants from Egypt and to an earlier pre-Mosaic or pre-Israelite Palestinian source.

As to the content of Mosaism and the history of the early period, there is no agreement whatever among scholars. On the other hand, of the contemporary religious and other conditions in and around Canaan or Palestine much is known. There were deities not deficient in admirable traits, and tendencies to henotheism or monolatry of a monarchial type. The Egyptian suzerain was freely recognised as divine, and the phraseology of the Palestinian and other letters (found at el-Amarna), not only sometimes recalls even late passages of the Old Testament, but indicates how men could have addressed their native gods. Jerusalem was already powerful by about 2000 B.C., and its religious *milieu*— Anathoth, Valley of Hinnom, Beth-Shemesh, etc.—scarcely derives from Israelite invaders, but reminds us of the tradition of the half-Amorite, half-Hittite ancestry of this "Canaanite" city (Ezek. xvi. 2f.). It is a tradition which archaeology and the contemporary records confirm and supplement.[2]

Thus, to enquire what Palestine could offer the Israelites from Egypt is far more practicable than the admittedly speculative reconstruction of Mosaism from the Old Testament; and although the evidence does bring perplexing problems, all who study the history and religion of Israel are bound, sooner or later, to take this enquiry more seriously than at present, and to adjust their conceptions of the

[1] *J.T.S.* (1908), IX, pp. 321–352. His article attracted considerable attention at the time.

[2] Jirku (*Journ. of Bibl. Lit.*, 1933, pp. 108ff.) finds in the Amarna letters fragments of "Canaanite Psalms." For the Amarna evidence, see pp. 18, n. 2, 140 ff, and *Ency. Brit.*, 14th Ed., "Hebrew Religion."

"evolution" to the facts. The age round about the
fourteenth century B.C.—we may call it the "Mosaic Age"—
is singularly well illuminated. It is a landmark in history
and religion. The monism of the Egyptian "heretic" king
Amenhotep IV, Ikhnaton, was, on the most moderate
estimate, an extraordinary phenomenon, as Breasted has
repeatedly urged.[1] Not less remarkable is the presence in
and to the north of Syria of Indian or Indo-Iranian groups
who worshipped Mitra (Mithras), Varuna, Indra and other
deities well known in the Rig-Veda. Here again, it is no
exaggeration to say that the great ethical god Varuna
was regarded as "a holy god, omniscient, the punisher
of sin," and that to the Christian reader passages in
the hymns to Varuna "inevitably suggest verses from the
Psalms and Job"; the thought "approximates as rarely
elsewhere to the moral sublimity of Hebraism."[2] No doubt
the existence of such lofty religious speculative thought
in the environs of Palestine—with traces in Palestine itself
—may be more than a surprise; but only when one has
frankly and discerningly realised the situation in the Mosaic
Age is one entitled to go on and contrast the sequels—the
decline of Egypt, the tragic fall of Varuna, and the
continuity and progressive development of religion in
Palestine.[3]

Only in Palestine can there be traced such a development:
for example, the ancient ideas of "sanctity" or "holiness"
(the goddess Kadesh) and of "righteousness," which were
non-Israelite and pre-Israelite, received their distinctively
ethical and spiritual stamp in the days of the prophets of

[1] *The Dawn of Conscience* (1934), pp. 291 ff., 367 ff. The late
Dr. H. R. Hall wrote: "We see in his heresy . . . the highest
development of religious ideas before the days of the Hebrew
prophets" (*Ancient History of the Near East*, p. 300).

[2] S. Cave, *Redemption Hindu and Christian* (1919), p. 26. The
exalted conceptions of Varuna have even led to the conjecture—an
untenable one, as G. F. Moore observes—that the religion of this
god was adopted from a Semitic people (*History of Religions*, I,
p. 250 f.). See further *O.T.R.*, pp. 93–95, and below, pp. 110, 144.

[3] The cult of Varuna was replaced in India by that of the more
nationalistic Indra, who was also known in the Near East; but the
later Iranian Ahura-Mazda carries on and develops the old religious
and ethical idealism.

Israel.[1] The soil of Palestine—as its archaeology also
suggests—had a cultural individuality of its own even in
pre-Israelite times and independently of Israelites entering
from outside.[2] In fact, it is being increasingly recognised
that the religion of Yahweh must have been far more
Canaanite than ever imagined.[3] Yahwism, one might
almost say, was, apart from its name, a Canaanite religion
which was profoundly spiritualised and ethicised, and it
owed its permanent value both to the prophets and to
influences—rather Puritanical, if not fanatical—from the
desert.[4] Some such conclusion as this—the best formula
may not yet have been found—is being forced upon us by
the fruits of "Archaeology and the Monuments."

But archaeology and the monuments have not made
it easier to trace the early religious history of Israel.
Not until the days of the great creative prophets is
there any definite reforming movement, and then its
effect was such that the religious conditions of the
preceding centuries before and after Moses can hardly be
recovered from our sources. If the reader will consider
carefully the conditions implied in the measures ascribed
to Josiah (2 Kings xxiii.), and in the allusions of Jeremiah
and Ezekiel to the contemporary idolatry, he will have
some notion of the task that confronts Old Testament
scholars when they proceed to sketch the course of post-
Mosaic religion.[5] But let him pass on to the sixth century,

[1] See *Religion of Ancient Palestine in the Light of Archaeology*,
p. 106.

[2] See *Rel. of Anc. Pal.*, p. 229f., and cf. Hempel, *Orient. Lit.-
zeitung*, 1936, col. 373.

[3] Cf. Dussaud, *Les Origines Cananéennes du Sacrifice Israélite*
(1921), pp. 66–70; Eissfeldt, *Theologische Blätter*, Oct., 1934, col. 280;
Vincent, *Canaan d'après l'Exploration Récente* (1907), p. 463; and
p. 29, n. 1 above.

[4] See p. 155, and n. 2.

[5] Note the persistence of the cult of the Queen of Heaven (Jer.
xliv. 16–19) and of human sacrifice. The agricultural rites would
naturally be more Canaanite than Israelite, and Powis Smith (*The
Prophets and their Times*, 1925, p. 61), commenting on Hosea,
observes that even in the eighth century B.C. Northern Israel had
not yet come to think of Yahweh as the God of the soil and its
products. See also *Rev. de l'Hist. et de Philosophie Rel.*, IX (1929),
pp. 308ff.

the Exile, the Second Isaiah and the "Servant Songs."
He will find himself breathing another air. The lofty convictions in Isa. xl.ff. are familiar to all: Yahweh's thoughts
transcend man's (lv. 8f.); Heaven is his throne and earth
his footstool (lxvi. 1). And this One and Only God of the
Universe is Israel's own God—the relationship is vital—and
is raising up His own people. We are in the midst of real
history. We have left behind us the blank scepticism and
indifference of Zephaniah's day (i. 12), and the despair as
the ruin of Jerusalem draws near. The Second Isaiah,
commonly regarded as the height of Hebrew prophecy, and
the culmination of Israelite religion, comes between the
fall of the monarchies and the new reorganisation described
in the books of Ezra and Nehemiah.

This new emphasis upon the supremacy and transcendence
of Israel's God enables us to understand the post-Exilic age
and the priests' insistence upon His supreme holiness. It
is the new consciousness of His nearness (cf. Ezekiel's vision,
xlviii. 35) which so naturally explains the profounder sense
of sin, the elaborate sacrificial system, and the intervening
wall of Levites, even as the new relationship, more on the
lines of Jeremiah (xxxi. 33f.) than of Ezekiel, deepens
individual piety as we find it in the Psalms. Thus a new
era is opened up. The Reformers, as is usual, "dig
themselves in," and, in due course, we notice what strikes
us as a decline. There is the old egotism, though in a new
context (Isa. lx.); and, archaeologically speaking, the
nationalistic Yahweh of Isa. lxiii. reminds one of the old
storm and war-god Hadad, and the aged god of Daniel's
vision (vii. 9) recalls the elderly gods depicted at Beth-Shan
and elsewhere. The Temple still has a sort of "magical"
significance (e.g. Zech. xiv. 17);[1] and, in general, the post-
Exilic religion presents many strange features which help
one to imagine what the old cultus would have been in
pre-Exilic and pre-prophetic days.

As the centuries pass we come to the "Wisdom" Literature,
with its humanism and shrewdness; it is instructive to contrast, for example, the words of the sage on the risks of

[1] See *O.T.R.*, p. 151.

adultery (Prov. vi. 32 ff.) with the anguish of the Psalmist
(Ps. li. 4). Descending further, we find ourselves on the
threshold of Christianity. In spite of the gaps there is a
fairly intelligible narrative from the fall of the kingship,
down through the prominence of high-priests and Has-
monaeans, to the appearance of the Messiah. After the
new Yahwism of the Second Isaiah and the "Servant,"
the facts of spiritual decline and of adjustment or compromise are the stuff that religious history is made of. Nor
is it without a parallel when the next wave of religious
creativeness does not carry on the religious thought of
contemporary Jews in Palestine or Alexandria—indebted
though it is to both—but rather enhances the spiritual
wealth of the movement which in the sixth century had
given new life to Israel. The line from Israel's re-discovery
and re-statement of her God to the doctrine of the Messiah,
the Son of God, is of such unique significance that our
conception of the inner history of Biblical religion, as a
whole, must be based upon a thorough understanding of
the vicissitudes.

Now, when we attempt to go back before the sixth century
B.C. or the prophets our most serious difficulties begin.
Mosaism and the introduction of Yahweh by Israelite
invaders would undoubtedly be a new religious and ethical
movement; and consequently it is instructive to observe
the downfall of the ethical god Varuna in India and the
destruction of Ikhnaton's monistic cult in Egypt. But
Biblical history has been written to emphasise Israel's
separateness from the Canaanites, and Judah's separateness
from (North) Israel;[1] and we have to allow for what a
Roman Catholic scholar has called the *Lehrbuchcharakter* of
the Old Testament.[2] Moreover, it is "orthodox" criticism
that JE—J on "evolutionary" grounds is earlier than E[3]—
is anterior to D in its present form; but while scholars usually

---

[1] See *O.T.R.*, pp. 52 ff.

[2] Riessler, cited by his pupil, T. F. Stier, *Gott und sein Engel im
Alten Testament* (1934), p. 158. See further *Mélanges Cumont*, II
(1936), pp. 539 ff.

[3] Some dissentient voices place E before J.

begin by carrying back the contents of JE to as early a date as possible, the literary-critical theory of J, E, D, P really implies that it is now in the form in which the post-Exilic editors left it.[1] This is a sound method, already applied by S. R. Driver to the Psalms and by G. B. Gray to Isaiah.[2]

It is necessary to remember that the Wellhausen *literary* theory of J, E, D, P is not to be confused with the reconstructions of history and religion based thereon by Wellhausen himself or others. Some are conservative, others radical, and others again are by no means "evolutionary." In fact, the weakness of the ordinary "evolutionary" views of the religion has become ever more clearly manifested as external evidence accumulated.[3] After all, we scarcely realise that our current conceptions of J, E, D and P ignore North Israel after about 721 B.C., pass over the Second Isaiah, and rely upon the books of Ezra and Nehemiah, which are part of the "Chronicler's" work, which, where it can be tested by comparison with the books of Kings, is relatively untrustworthy. Whether the Old Testament is viewed through conservative or through "moderate critical" spectacles, behind it are the gravest historical changes and discontinuities—the passage from Canaanite or pre-Israelite to Israelite religion, the sweeping events in the seventh to fifth centuries B.C., and, ultimately, the transition from an "Israel after the flesh" (a mixed Judah that claimed to be the true Israel) to an "Israel of the spirit."[4] Indeed, when we consider the profoundly significant "Israel idea" which Christendom inherited and developed, there is a sense

---

[1] For this now post-Exilic JE, cf. *J.T.S.*, XII (1911), p. 468. Joh. Pedersen, the author of *Israel*, a brilliant study of Hebrew mentality, is of a similar opinion (*Zeit. f. Alttest. Wiss.*, 1931, p. 178).

[2] Driver, *Lit. of the O.T.*, p. 386; G. B. Gray, *Isaiah*, pp. xxxii, 227. Their emphatic statement of their principles should be carefully read.

[3] The most impressive attack was, perhaps, Hugo Winckler's forceful though rather too polemical pamphlet, *Religionsgeschichtler und geschichtlicher Orient* (Leipzig, 1906).

[4] Whatever be thought of Kennett's theories of the eighth and following centuries B.C., he does not stand alone; see his *Church of Israel*, pp. xlvi, n. 2, xlvii, n. 2.

in which "Israel" is throughout an "idea" rather than a continuous, stable, national stock. What will be the future of this "Israel"?[1]

Any development or evolution which impresses us will be more accurately apprehended if we go below the surface and perceive the actual historical circumstances underlying it. Thus, we may look back to "Dark" or "Middle" Ages, and to Greece and Rome, and the Bible; but our retrospect becomes more helpful when we remember that our Western civilisation is really a very young one, and that it is an adolescent and acutely self-conscious age that is now scrutinising the heritage handed down from the past. We must be realists, and must remember that whereas ordinary views of the Bible usually refer to a *book*, we have really to do with the literature of a *people*, in a land within an area of whose history we know far more than was suspected by Wellhausen, Robertson Smith, and other founders of the modern literary critical position.

To-day we are placing the Bible in the midst of world-history and world-religion, and at the same time world-wide problems of current history and religion are both urgent and disquieting. The evolutionary view of J, E, D, P leaves off in the middle of the history; and even if our view of the Old Testament extends to the New Testament, as the culmination of the Old, it runs the risk of stopping there, 1900 years ago, and remaining out of touch with real history. Organic evolution may have ceased with the appearance of Man, as many years ago as scientists decide; but any "evolutionary" theory in which Religion and the relation between God and Man are concerned must not be indifferent to those processes in the very midst of which we are living. An evolutionary view that is to be of any use to-day must cover the whole Bible, and it must go from the Bible of the past to the interpretation of it to-day; it must be a view of the past that has a meaning for our future.

Old Testament criticism cannot stop at a Maccabaean Daniel, or sever Hebrew prophecy and apocalyptic from the New Testament. In a sense, the New Testament is the

[1] Cf. above, p. 28 f.

dénouement of the old Yahwism, and its last book the last chapter of Hebrew religion.[1] Like the Second Isaiah, the New Testament is the culmination of one series of stages and the inauguration of another. Moreover, we can look back upon (a) the Mosaic Age with its Egyptian and Indo-Iranian movements; (b) the Second Isaiah, the age (broadly) of Zoroaster, Buddha, Lao-Tse, and others; and (c) the rise of Christianity, with the contemporary Stoicism and Bhagavad-gita. In brief, the whole development which Christians value for its uniqueness was part of a far-reaching series of stages, and it would be a dangerously narrow interpretation that ignored the total environment in which our religion has grown up and now finds itself.

Coming from the Palestine of the Old Testament to that of the New, one receives an impression that may seem strange to the theologian. Something is now known of the deities of the Near East in Old Testament times: deities old and young, deities who are fathers, brothers or sons; kings who stand in an immediate relationship with their god or who have an intermediary god or goddess; kings subordinate to their gods, but yet at times hardly distinguishable from them. The world of the Palestine of the New Testament age is not an entirely new one. Archaeology and mythology testify to the persistence of many ancient features, though in a new dress. We observe the prominence of Baal, and Hadad, and Mithras—all already known about 1400 B.C. There are solar cults and tendencies to solar monotheism; solar gods and emperor cults; youthful gods and gods of an Apolline type are especially noteworthy; and the nature of the various deities and the relations between them imply a rich and complicated mythology.[2]

[1] Thus, the *History of Israel* by W. O. E. Oesterley and T. H. Robinson, and their *Hebrew Religion*, both go down into the first century A.D. and the beginnings of Rabbinical Judaism.

[2] Some material will be found in my *Religion of Ancient Palestine in the Light of Archaeology*, Ch. III. Quite recently it has been shown that the Phoenician cosmogony of the Hellenistic Age goes back, in part, to the thirteenth century B.C. (in the Ras Shamra tablets from North Syria); cf. Eissfeldt, *Zeit. d. Morgenländ. Gesell.*, XIII (1934), pp. 181 ff.; Graham and May, *Culture and Conscience* (1936), p. 153; E. A. Leslie, *Old Testament Religion* (1936), p. 45 f.

The deities, too, as in the past, are not without some attractive features; they are "answering," "compassionate," and "rewarding": Jewish influence need not be suspected.[1] It is interesting to find a Marna(s), "Our Lord," and a deity Phanebal, "Face (or Presence) of Baal"; the latter recalls the fact that, while it is the title of the goddess Tanit among the Phoenicians, Judaism had always to fight against tendencies to treat the Name or the Face (or Presence) of Yahweh, the Shechinah, and the Memra (Word), as personal entities.[2] In brief, we find ourselves in a world which must have provoked speculation—mythological, theological and philosophical—as to the relations between the gods and between them and men.[3] To be sure, all this was outside orthodox Judaism, whose monotheism, however, was far from simple; but when Judaism itself could include men like Philo and Josephus, it is obvious that the rise of Christianity must be studied in the light of the heterogeneity of belief from Antioch to Alexandria.

Whether or no Josephus and "Luke" (Luke–Acts), writing for Romans, were ignorant of one another, the former shows how internal anarchy, "false" prophets, and religious fanaticism proved the undoing of the unhappy Jews.[4] On the other hand, the Christian writers stress the political innocuousness of the new sect (Mark xii. 17)—how naturally the populace preferred Barabbas, a member of the insurrectionary movement which seemed to offer far better prospects of a release from Rome![5] It was an age of diverse individualistic and extremist tendencies, and

[1] Or at least the Jews were unorthodox; see C. Moss, *Quart. Stat. of the Palest. Explor. Fund* (1928), p. 103.

[2] See G. H. Box, *Jew. Quart. Rev.*, XXIII, pp. 103–119, on the idea of intermediation in Jewish theology.

[3] On this see n. 2, p. 68, the works of Cumont, and also H. Seyrig, *Syria*, X, pp. 340 ff.

[4] Josephus throws valuable light upon the Jewish mentality of his day. He considers that the disastrous famine was one of the main causes of the revolts that led to the fall of Jerusalem (*Ant.*, XVIII, i, 1). Among many incidental details of interest is the fact that of three of his acquaintances who were crucified, but on his entreaties taken down, only one recovered. (*Vita*, § 75.)

[5] See p. 156, n. 2.

"builders" rejected the One who was to become the corner-
stone (Acts iv. 11); one is reminded of the "Servant" in
Isa. liii.   The extent of the movement for which John the
Baptist stood can be gathered, not only from the case of
Apollos of Alexandria and the men of Ephesus (Acts xviii. 25;
xix. 3), but from the prominence so pointedly given to him
in Luke i. and John i., and from the significant emphasis upon
the vital difference between the Baptist's mission and the
humblest member of the movement which was to supersede
him (Luke vii. 28).[1] Had it not been for Jesus of Nazareth
there would have been no Christianity; but the content of
the new religion was not derived from its Founder alone—
again one thinks of the Servant.[2] The heterogeneity of
life and thought *before*, and the different nuances *after*
(e.g. 1 Cor. i. 11f.), will seem entirely natural to anyone
who has traced the history of new movements; one may
even recall the situation in Old Testament criticism before
and after its chief founders: divergence, convergence, and
again tendencies among the disciples to divergence upon
the new foundations their masters had laid.

The Palestinian Old Testament led to the bifurcation
into Rabbinical Judaism and Christianity; and while the
former can hardly be said to have carried on the creative
spirit of its Sacred Book, the latter was certainly not
indebted for its content to the Old Testament alone.   To
the student of religion, the world-wide recognition of a God
is overwhelmingly impressive, but far more important is
the question of the effectiveness of the content of each
God-idea and its ideological setting.   Israel owed an
incalculable debt to the events behind the Second Isaiah;
but they have been blotted out, and the central figure is
lost to human knowledge—like the reforming movement
that produced the wonderful ethical god Varuna.   By
harking back to Moses and to Abraham, Judaism became

---

[1] Cf. also M. Kiddle, "The Teaching of John the Baptist," *Expository Times*, June, 1937, pp. 396ff.

[2] Cf. *C.A.H.*, III, pp. 490–498.   The study of the Servant (individual, Israel whole or part) and that of Christ (Jesus, the Christian
body, the ideal Church) cannot be isolated one from the other.   Cf.
H. Wheeler Robinson, *The Cross of the Servant* (1926), pp. 64ff.

an ossified system, a sort of stereotyped nationalism which, in spite of its many fine theistic and ethical elements, had a conception of God which necessarily differed from Christianity, which had a larger field of history to cover. To this may be due the failure of Judaism to contribute to the further religious interpretation of the prophets in the way in which those Christian interpreters have who have once *felt* the advance from the Old Testament to the New. But to-day we feel the necessity of a further advance in the synthetic interpretation of the whole Bible, and Christianity itself is now on trial.

The Jew found his God through the mediation of a divinely-given Law and a divinely-directed history; whereas Christianity tended to break down the old tribal, national or historical limits of an "Israel of the flesh"—limits, as criticism now shows, not historically justified.[1] The Old Testament prepared the way for Christ; but the Messiah is the culmination and sublimation of earlier ideas of divine kings, high-priests, "son" gods and intermediaries. Christianity is in the line of old primitive religion when it takes the conception of a Person and then spiritualises it. But when Christ is ultimately to hand the sovereignty over to God (1 Cor. xv. 24), St. Paul, as Edward Caird once said, looks to the end "in a way that almost carries him beyond Christianity."[2] To St. Paul, the Jew, God was first and last and above all things, as in the Second Isaiah (xli. 4; xlviii. 12); Christian experience was the road to a fuller experience of God, and the Apostle did not feel that the Jew was precluded from reaching it (Rom. x.f.). One has only to look at the history of religion in general, and, in particular, at the conditions in the Palestinian area in the first century A.D., to see that Christianity was the first successful effort to solve a problem fundamental wherever there are religious experiences differing in quality, content and environment. But Christianity must not repeat the mistake of the Judaism of the first century A.D. The God of Israel was not Israel's alone, nor was the Son of God

[1] See pp. 28, 44, 136.

[2] *Hibbert Journal*, II, p. 18. See p. 178.

for those alone who used His name (Matt. vii. 21ff.). Consequently, when we come back to the present day, our
religion, and the interpretation of the Bible upon which
it is based, should not ignore the religious conditions in
other lands where "men feel the presence of His Spirit
even though they do not call upon His name."[1]

I am urging that our knowledge of the Mosaic Age, quite
apart from the internal criticism of the Old Testament,
compels a fresh reconsideration of our ideas of the development or evolution of the religion of Israel. Whatever be
the best "reconstruction" of the history and religion of
the centuries that followed, the events of the sixth century
B.C. and the Second Isaiah force us to co-ordinate our views
of the earlier period with the age that extends to the first
century A.D. and the rise of Christianity. We have to take
a wider survey of the environment of Biblical religion from
beginning to end, and to pay heed both to the religious
conditions when Christianity began to dawn and to all that
contributed to its content. The Bible is our first source
for understanding certain great forward steps in the past:
the successful reconstruction of Israel in and about the
sixth century B.C. and the fresh advance a few centuries
later, when Christianity, it can be said, continued the curve
of development and Judaism flew off at a tangent.[2]   The

---

[1] From the University Sermon preached by the Lord Bishop of
Birmingham at Cambridge, 14th October, 1934 (*The Modern Churchman*, XXIV [1934], pp. 484–489).

[2] In spite of a friendly protest I retain the last seven words.
Certainly one must not fall into the common error of being a victim
of one's phraseology; but there is a difference between a further
positive development of a religion (as in Christianity) and an
intensive development. F. C. Burkitt (*The Modern Churchman*,
XXIV [1934], p. 345) wrote: "Judaism, admirable as it is in many
ways, is not evolutionary in the modern sense. The mind of God,
according to Jewish theory, is expressed once for all in the Law . . . .
The Christian theory is different . . . . We put the New Testament
side by side with the Old, and there are some things in the New
Testament which are not in the Old, and which embolden us to say
that parts of the Old are now antiquated and of no more authority.
Surely this is an Evolutionary theory. Yet it is something to which
the Fundamentalist and the Modernist, the traditionalist and the
critic will all subscribe . . . ." But, as I have already indicated,
it is the question of the future of Christianity that is now at issue.

more adequately we can understand the course of history, the more adequate will be our conception of the development or evolution of religion in, behind and outside the Bible. But we cannot isolate our research from the needs of our age. We live at a time which, once again, seems to be the culmination of the past and a prelude to a new future. Those who come after us will assuredly have a far better conception of progressive development than we who are making the road along which they will look back. And to see the sort of task that lies before one, the sort of questions that have to be asked, and to descry, however dimly, the road to take—all this shows that Progress, progress in the re-statement of the relations between Man, God and His universe, is no illusion.

Ancient history becomes ultimately of purely antiquarian significance unless Biblical history forms an integral part of it; and the Bible runs the risk of being merely an object of emotional or superstitious veneration unless it is re-interpreted as part of a history which reaches to our own age. The vicissitudes of Christianity have turned upon the interpretation of the Bible; and the Bible itself may be said to turn upon the two periods in the past when great steps were taken. At the rise of Christianity, what could have seemed more inspiring for the world than the noble ethical monotheism of Judaism! But it was not in touch with the growth of consciousness and the movement of thought —and therein is a warning for us to-day. And if the vigour, confidence and independence of the new sect must have distressed the devout sons of Israel, in like manner, some centuries earlier, men must have been shocked when a prophet like Jeremiah was pointing the way to what was to be a new and permanent advance.

At such times ordinary remedies are unavailing (cf. Jer. viii. 11); but the cataclysmic expectations, at both periods, did not bear fruit as did the internal spiritual renewals. At such times men must know that they may no longer speak or think as children, or do after the things they then do (Deut. xii. 8); the ages of ignorance are past (Acts xvii. 30), and a higher type of righteousness is

imperative (cf. Matt. v. 20). The individual must know his
responsibility for his "talents" (cf. p. 118): there is a Law,
but it is near at hand; a yoke, but it is light (Deut. xxx.
11–14; Matt. xi. 30). So to-day one must take heed lest
the "Word of God" become as much a fetish as was the
"Temple of the Lord" in the days of the prophet
(Jer. vii. 3ff.). A people may be looking back on the past,
to the story of what God has done in the past, and not
forward to a God waiting to manifest Himself (Jer. xxiii. 7f.).
And though in difficult times men may feel that they are
in exile and away from all symbols of Religion, God reveals
Himself in men's hearts, and the permanent essentials of
Religion are found *there* and not within the man-made
institutions which from time to time need renewal
(Jer. xxxi. 31ff.). The course of Biblical history is of far
more than ordinary "religious" importance: it is a unique
example of an "evolution" that has made us what we are;
and the Renaissance and Reformation will not have borne
their fruits until modern research has placed Biblical
history and religion within the framework of our increasing
knowledge of our Universe.

CHAPTER VI

Biblical Criticism and the Interpretation of History[1]

TO-DAY we can look back upon the growth of the Old Testament, the complete Bible, the Early Church, Mediaeval Catholicism and the developments during the last four or five centuries. We pass from the Bible to Christian Theology and Philosophy, and to Western Christianity. We should agree that the Bible has had an incalculable influence upon the course of Western thought. But with the progress of Biblical Criticism inherited ideas of the Bible have been shaken and are now being reshaped. Hence we may well ask ourselves whether we suppose that the changes will affect the theology and philosophy of the future, and in any way shape the future course of Western thought. Biblical Criticism has sometimes been held to be at least partly responsible for modern scepticism, loss of faith and moral decay; although, on the other hand, there are those who testify that it has lessened or removed their doubts and difficulties. But we may attempt a wider survey and, confining ourselves mainly to Old Testament history, consider the bearing of Biblical Criticism on present history. It will be convenient to number the main points.

(1) That the value and authority of Religion are directly or indirectly involved in the urgent problems of to-day will scarcely be denied: the current social, political and national difficulties have a moral or spiritual "aspect"—though some readers would probably prefer to say that "root" is the correct word. In any case we cannot be indifferent to the question of the future of the Bible. To-day it is possible—as in Communism—to aim at an idealism that is anti-Biblical, or rather, decisively anti-religious. Also, there

[1] Reprinted with revision from *The Modern Churchman*, XXVI (June, July, 1936).

are those who are definitely hostile to the Old Testament,
and not solely on "anti-Semitic" grounds. Again, it seems
possible to combine the sincerest recognition of the supreme
importance of Religion with actions against Jews, or against
political opponents, or against an external enemy, which are
widely felt to be incompatible with civilised ideals.   Moreover, the Churches in general, and the Roman Church in
particular, are on trial; nor are they unaware of their own
internal fundamental difficulties.   Such is the anxiety of
men, their distress and their impatience, that no one can
foretell the outcome.   We can only feel sure that, in so far
as religious questions are involved, the significance, value
and authority of the Bible are at stake.   We cannot look
for speedy or easy solutions—this is my first point; the
present situation in the whole world of thought has grown
up irresistibly and in all good faith out of the past, and it
behoves us to take a wide, candid and deliberate view of
things in the light of all that will help us to understand our
own position.

(2) Meanwhile, Biblical Criticism is impinging upon
matters increasingly delicate and controversial.   In some
quarters, it is true, there is a complacent feeling that it
has shot its bolt: have not archaeology and the monuments
established the substantial truth and accuracy of the
Bible?   It is as though all that men needed was to be
assured of the accuracy of the Pentateuch and other portions
of the Old Testament.   The consequence is that there are
sincere men actuated by the best of intentions who are,
however unwittingly, leading people away from the really
important facts of the Bible and concentrating their attention upon relatively secondary matters.   But, on the other
hand, the comparative, psychological and historical study
of religions is emphasising the profoundly different qualities
or grades of Religion.   In our endeavour to estimate these,
our present religious standpoints are involved, and we are
often forced to test and reconsider our deepest personal
convictions.   Everywhere the blend of good and evil in the
world's religions arouses us to the fact that the facile
dichotomy of the "religious" and the "non-religious"

spheres of life and thought is not enough.   The differences
in Religion itself have shaped history, and Biblical Criticism
has now to face questions immensely more complex and far-
reaching than the historicity or credibility of this event or
that narrative.   The Bible means one thing to a Biblical
Criticism that is seeking to *understand* the Book, and
another to those who are concerned mainly to defend it
or prove its accuracy; for the aim of criticism is to determine
the objective significance of the Bible for world history and
religion.

(3) Biblical Criticism has a specially important place in
modern thought.   Because the Bible is studied from various
"non-religious" points of view—history, psychology, anthropology and the rest—the principles and methods must be
not less objective and penetrating than those in "secular"
research.   There is something in the Bible that has made
it play a unique part in the past, and our conclusions must
do justice to this fact.   Similarly, the Comparative Study
of Religions must combine a perfectly free and unprejudiced
attitude to all the tested evidence, with a whole-hearted
recognition of its impressiveness for men and of all that
Religion has achieved.   In both fields of study there must
be some reasonable combination of Biblical and non-
Biblical lines of research, and of Christian and non-Christian
ideas.   Accordingly, if there was once a day when all
thought was subordinated to the Bible, the present tendencies are towards giving the Bible and Christianity—
viewed in the light of modern knowledge—a new place in
the midst of human culture.   Such a position must be a
natural and a rational one, recognising the persistence and
intensity of men's religious convictions, and co-ordinating—
less imperfectly than does the average man—the two
diverse "hemispheres" of our life.   The ideal goal is a
working harmony between the "religious" and the "non-
religious" categories, between the "real" life of practical
experience and the not less but more "real" experiences
of the religious consciousness.

The Bible is our sole authority for some of the profoundest
creative movements in man's history.   If it no longer seems

to have the supreme value so often attached to it in the past as a living force in history, we should remember that the story of its actual growth is one of ebb and flow, of decay and of fresh life. Biblical Criticism aims at a reasonable synthesis of "religious" and "non-religious" thought; and consequently it has a scope which is not possessed by those studies or enquiries whose aim is more restricted. Taking a thoroughly historical survey of the streams of thought in the past, it cannot treat the present world-situation as other than transitional, and it is therefore obliged to look beyond the present state of culture and the present condition of Biblical studies.

(4) Biblical scholars are, as such, free and independent "arm-chair" students, under no compulsion to "close the ranks" against some common foe. But were this unfortunately necessary, it might of course be possible to draw up a programme, to set up a banner under which all could unite. For example, it would be very generally agreed that the Pentateuch, the Psalms and the Book of Isaiah were not by Moses, David and Isaiah respectively;[1] and that the Fourth Gospel has not the historical value of the Synoptists. But behind our agreement there might be very serious differences; and these might hamper our progress, since to emphasise them would only embarrass our "party" and prejudice our cause.[2] Yet among our opponents we should find much that we could and should readily adopt, were it not that we might seem to "sell the pass" and play into the hands of the "enemy." Hence our unity might at one time further our cause, but at another it might impede the free play of thought among ourselves; what might on one occasion clarify the vital differences between ourselves and our opponents might, on another, sever us from those from whom we might otherwise have much to learn; at one time our activity must be "intensive," at another we gain everything by extending our environment and going "outside."

[1] The reference is, of course, to the books in their present form.

[2] I refrain from crossing *t*'s and dotting *i*'s; readers *au courant* with the history of Biblical Criticism will recall the "dangerous" men and the "suspicious" characters: *Non tali auxilio?*

Similarly, in the world of affairs an anxiety for "reunion" against a common "enemy" can paralyse growth. In religion the enemy will be said to be Modernism, Unitarianism or Materialism, or the current attacks upon Christianity. But however intelligible may be the desire to close the ranks and present a common front, the consequences can be detrimental both to the cause and to the progressive development of thought. A survey of the past will persuade us that the age-long movement of thought is more impressive than the kaleidoscope of shifting scenes and changing "policies." Just as Biblical Criticism has gained by intensiveness and a narrow specialism at one time, but at another has suffered and has been forced to widen its horizon, so in the world of affairs the corresponding phases of particularism or nationalism have been powerful factors, now in advancing the march of thought and now in restricting it. Indeed, one of the most impressive results of Biblical Criticism is (1) the picture we are gaining of the manifold phases, both in the actual growth of the Bible itself and in the subsequent interpretation and criticism of its contents; and (2) the difficulty of estimating their relative value.

There are processes extending over many centuries which give the Bible a universal and world-historical significance that is not realised when we fasten our eyes upon and estimate the particular circumstances at any one date. The more proportionate our survey of the past, the more judicially can we understand the present, and appreciate the difference between a given situation and the inconspicuous factors that are helping to shape the future. Thus, to-day certain relatively weak movements that might well influence subsequent events can be recognised, not only in lands dominated by Communist, Fascist or National-Socialist systems, but also in Religion and in Biblical Criticism. Moreover, there is an immense output of literature to warn us that our religion cannot remain where it is. Accordingly, the point to be made here is the importance of the historical study of the processes of thought in ancient and modern times, in the light of which we can more competently apply ourselves to the ancient or modern problems under consideration.

(5) To-day the Bible is being set in the field of history and religion: the early chapters of Genesis, the knowledge of the old writers, are being replaced by our own knowledge of the beginnings of things. The age of Abraham already finds Palestine an integral part of the Ancient Near East; and we have history and religion in the lands of the Old Testament long before we can utilise its contents and place them in our new picture.[1] The age of Moses is already brilliantly illuminated; and our horizon widens as we reach the age of the reconstruction of Israel in the Exilic Age, i.e. in and about the sixth century B.C., and the rise of Christianity some six centuries later. Accordingly, the Bible is now placed upon a vaster canvas, and we can more truly apprehend the essential difference between the growth of Biblical religion in Palestine and the vicissitudes of religion and history elsewhere, even as we best appreciate the distinctiveness of *homo sapiens* or *homo faber* when he is placed among the other primates.

Now, in this wider history Israel's Exilic period becomes extraordinarily interesting. Let the reader follow the Old Testament narrative from the last days of the Judaean monarchy, through the Exile, to the books of Ezra and Nehemiah. Here he has to find a place for the monotheistic idealism of the Second Isaiah, a teaching so sublime from the Christian standpoint that we are forced to conclude that it must have some definite historical background. There must have been some distinctive religious movement

[1] The consequences are scarcely recognised. Any significant theory based upon or involving the Old Testament must take a wide view of the relevant fields. (a) It is precarious to enlarge upon an absolute transition from nomad or pastoral life to settled agricultural conditions forgetful of the chequered ethnical and political fortunes of the land. (b) It is no less precarious to trace an orderly (evolutionary) development of literary types (*Formgeschichte*) in such pages of the past as happen to be preserved out of what was once, as we can tell, a considerably larger body of literature. Finally, (c) neither a history of Old Testament religion nor an Old Testament theology can be safely based upon that Book alone: it simply does not give the material for a proportionate or systematic view. The consequences for the New Testament are rather different, cf. p. 68 f.

that paved the way for the reconstruction of Israel and for the centuries that were to be the prelude to the rise of Christianity.[1] The reader will more vividly appreciate that age if he turns to the outside world upon which the history and religion of Israel are to be placed. He can follow the history of the surrounding powers and pass from an old Oriental epoch to that of Persia, Greece and Rome.[2] He can read of the great epoch-making changes in the history of religious and other thought from China to Greece. In this way the Second Isaiah holds a pre-eminent place in a mighty transitional act, and the reader may not unnaturally be tempted to associate Israel's new convictions of Divine Reality and the Greek theories of Reality in the world of space and time.[3]

The story of these events has hardly become familiar to us, but they undoubtedly enable us to understand anew the Biblical history.[4] Israel's monotheistic impulse comes after the fall of the kingdom and before the inauguration of post-Exilic Judaism. It is at the close of one series of stages and at the beginning of another. From Israel's rediscovery and restatement of the relationship between herself and her God we pass at length to the time when the approach to God is to come, not through Israel and her Torah, but through a Person and a new Israel. Upon two great creative periods turn the Old Testament and the New,

[1] See above, pp. 20 ff, 153 f.

[2] Arthur Penrhyn Stanley, sixty years ago, spoke of three vast periods, two of which have already passed away: "they may be called, in general terms, Primaeval History, Classical History and Modern History." The Exilic Age divides the first from the second. See *The Jewish Church* (6th Ed., 1876), III, Ch. XLII.

[3] See p. 144 f.

[4] See Oesterley and Robinson, *Israel*, I, p. 13 n.; *C.A.H.*, III, pp. 489, 499, and the Synchronistic Table. F. Weinrich, *Rel.-utop. Charakter d. prophet. Politik* (Giessen, 1932), p. 8 and n. 6, gives references to German literature (e.g. Deussen, *Allgem. Geschichte d. Philosophie*, I, 3, p. 116). H. G. Wells (*Short History of the World*, Ch. XXIII, end) remarks on the importance of the sixth century B.C. in the history of humanity: Greek philosophers were "beginning the research for clear ideas about this universe and man's place in it," and the Second Isaiah was "carrying Jewish prophecy to its sublimest levels." "From Athens to the Pacific the human mind was astir." See further, Ch. VIII.

and if we are to understand the Bible *historically* we cannot know too much of their background.

But how meagre is the Biblical treatment of the history of the Exilic period! What is given to us in Kings, Chronicles, Ezra and Nehemiah is of the slightest, though it is undoubtedly important, from the standpoint of post-Exilic Israel. The written history—which brings exceedingly intricate problems—emphasises the continuity between pre-Exilic and post-Exilic times, but it utterly obscures, or rather, it ignores the part played by the great reforming prophets and the Second Isaiah. It depicts the reintroduction and the re-establishment of a Mosaism of many centuries earlier—of the far-off Amarna Age, now so well known to us; and it has been left for modern criticism to go behind the imperfect record and recover a far more inspiring story—a truer story—of what was surely the most vital factor in the reconstruction of Israel.

For better or for worse Israel forgot the secret of her spiritual progress. Post-Exilic Judaism was instituted, and it served its purpose; Israel's new ideology preserved her—until the rise of Christianity. So it was that a religion, a history and an ideology which distinguished the Jews from all other peoples of the earth and gave Israel a pre-eminence in world history carried her through the centuries until another irresistible movement left her behind, depriving her of her old creative and impregnating power.[1] A written history, an interpretation of history, may serve as a stimulus and an inspiration; but Israel became the victim of a tradition so inadequate and imperfect as to be misleading. Christianity was the fruit of the next regenerative movement, and the Christian very naturally recalls the Second Isaiah and the Servant of the Lord. But it is not enough to think of these as an anticipation, a foreshadowing; rather have we two distinct but comparable events of the sixth century B.C. and of the first century A.D., the second of which had tragic consequences for the old Israel.[2]

Christian Biblical Criticism is finding beneath or behind

[1] See p. 72.

[2] See pp. 164 ff.

the Bible events the more inspiring, indeed the more sobering, the more historically they are examined. Our better knowledge is warning us that our own conceptions of Biblical history may in turn be so imperfect as to be misleading and "untrue." What we know of the reformed Israel of the Exilic Age and of the "Israel" of the rise of Christianity brings us to a new stage in our own history which affects the future outlook of both Christianity and Judaism. Hence, for the fifth point, I cannot do better than quote the striking words of Dean Stanley: "Whatever is true History teaches true Religion, and every attempt to reproduce the ages which immediately preceded or which accompanied the advent of Christianity, is a contribution, however humble, to the understanding of Christianity itself."[1] True history makes for true religion and true theology and true philosophy.[2]

(6) Next, let us glance for a moment at the Maccabaean Age. As we read of the brave struggles of Israel, her repudiation of Hellenism, and her fight to preserve her national religious genius, we must surely realise that had she failed, had she lost all that gave her her distinctiveness, there would have been no Judaism, no Christianity. To us it is clear that the Jews, however unconsciously, were fighting the world's battles.[3] Of course there is much to be said against Antiochus Epiphanes; but, after all, his policy "had a sane purpose."[4] Yet Israel's rebellion was justified, even though she stood for rites that to some

[1] *Op. cit.*, Vol III, p. xxii.

[2] "History," writes Tennant, "is not a department of knowledge, ancillary to philosophy, it is rather the source and the determinant of philosophy" (*Philosophy of the Sciences, or the Relations between the Departments of Knowledge* [1932], p. 94 f.). Entirely characteristic of the trend of thought is, not the comparative method (cf. Acton, *A Lecture on the Study of History* [1905], n. 55), but the historical: this co-ordinates the immense "history" of the Universe itself up to the present day with the successive physical, chemical, ideological and all other processes in Nature and in Man. Cf. also above, p. 280.

[3] Cf. Edwyn Bevan, *C.A.H.*, VIII, p. 514: "of all that was happening in the kingdom of Antiochus, the events of Judaea were by far the most important in their consequences for the mind of man in ages to come."

[4] *Op. cit.*, p. 499.

must have seemed unimportant: "the Maccabees," as Israel Abrahams said, "have an interest for the history of culture."[1] However, the years pass, and we experience a certain feeling of disappointment. It is only too easy to comment upon the narrowness of her religion and the worldliness and ruthlessness of her internal politics.[2] But this is not without analogy: the Second Isaiah had stirred a dispirited Israel by the tidings that she had a part to play in God's world; but later, a by no means pleasing particularism marred the idealism of the Jews. Nor can we ignore the contrast between the fine conception of the Servant of the Lord and the later gloating of the "servants" over the faithless (Isa. lxv. 13 f.).

We must take no narrow or one-sided view of the stream of events in Israel's history. The stubborn and fiery spirit that upheld her in the Maccabaean Age had its darker side, and the sturdy confidence in her own Yahweh which sustained her in her fight against "apostates" also made her disown the sect that became Christianity. The history of peoples, like that of men, has its lights and shades; indifference and enthusiasm; tragic mistakes and glorious heroism; despair, confidence—and then, over-confidence. A movement starts with enthusiasm—or fanaticism—and it ends in necessary compromise, opportunism, and what looks like hypocrisy. Of such stuff is history made; and any excessive laudation of ancient Israel is as misleading—and unfair to the Jew of to-day—as a determination to see only the faults and errors. It takes a valet to "debunk" a hero, whereas by patience and sympathy we may see, from within, the achievements of men of the past who, confronted by the difficulties of their own age, were scarcely less honest than their judges of to-day. And thereby may we see more wisely, albeit more humbly, what lies before us in an age which in its turn may be called upon to be true to itself, if not rather to become conscious of that to which it is called upon to be true.

[1] *Campaigns in Palestine from Alexander the Great* (1927), p. 4.

[2] Edwyn Bevan, *C.A.H.*, VIII, p. 533. Cf. also Oesterley and Robinson, *Israel*, II, p. 281 f.

Men and nations can have the defects of their qualities; it is no less true of religious and other systems of thought. We read our Biblical history, we can pass from the Exilic Age to the rise of Christianity, we can survey the wide diversity of thought and action—and the more candidly we can understand the heights and depths that perpetually confront us in the lives of men and nations, the more insistent is the problem of *Geschehen* and *Geschichte*: the vital difference between successive happenings and what makes great history, between the "letter" and the life-giving "spirit" of peoples and of individuals.[1]

(7) Thanks to archaeology, comparative religion and the internal criticism of the Bible, we are gaining profounder conceptions of the great creative and history-making ages that can be recognised in and behind its contents. But the traditional way of regarding the Old Testament and that of Biblical Criticism are poles asunder. On the one view, the Pentateuch stands at the beginning of Israelite national history: Mosaism is something once and for all delivered to the saints of Israel; after several centuries it was, so to speak, endorsed by the prophets and at last reaffirmed by Ezra. But however this view be expressed—and it is not easy to determine what its exponents hold—it is opposed absolutely by the other, which claims to follow the evidence and to be in harmony with usual historical processes. The familiar difference of opinion is an exceedingly important one. From time to time we may read of a "return" to Primitive Christianity, to pre-Reformation Catholicism, to Mediaeval Scholasticism, to Kant, or what not. Yet the only "return" of any significance that could be cited as a precedent or a parallel would be the old traditional view of a post-Exilic "return" to Mosaism—if it were authentic. The critical "evolutionary" view is admittedly incomplete; but Biblical scholars are confident that there was no "return" in the Exilic Age to the Mosaism of eight, nine or ten centuries previously. On the other hand, reassertion and restatement

---

[1] Cf. Artur Weiser in *Werden und Wesen des Alten Testaments* (ed. Hempel, 1936), p. 218, and his highly stimulating study, *Glaube und Geschichte im Alten Testament* (1931).

are everyday occurrences: the old will constantly reappear
in a new system or body; and those who in any way think
of a "return" or who maintain the traditional view of
Mosaism and Ezra should make clear what it is they really
have in mind.

On the critical view, certain sweeping changes occurred in
and about the sixth century B.C., though when it comes to
details there is considerable difference of opinion. While
everyone recognises the historical significance of the first
century A.D., that of the earlier prophetic movement should
rank among the outstanding discoveries of modern research.[1]
Both ages should be considered together, as far as possible,
for their bearing upon the present age, which might usher
in some new forward-reaching movement, or might haply
witness a development as unsuspected as that when Christianity arose at the tragic end of the Jewish state in Palestine
and in due course found a new field elsewhere.[2]

With this question of a "return" or a "reassertion" are
bound up questions of "origins" and the search after
"nature" and the "primitive."[3] Throughout we have to
do with questions of evolution and of revolution, new movements, and the "reassertion" of the old in some new form.
And the point to be stressed is that the Bible is a unique
source for the examination of the profoundest (r)evolu-
tionary processes known to us. Of the majestic evolution
of the Universe we are learning something; but more
immediately remarkable is that evolution of the human
mind that could discover it, and that must now find a
place for the Bible in its scheme of things.

(8) Christianity did not evolve naturally out of the
thought of its age. It came "from outside," as it were,
taking and transforming what it needed, and inaugurating

---

[1] The recognition of the Exilic background of Isa. xl.–lxvi.
dates from 1775, but the first notable step was taken by Gesenius
(1820–21).

[2] See p. 158, and, for the three ages, p. 211 f.

[3] On "origins," see below on "primitive monotheism," p. 226 f.
We do not discover absolute origins, but creative ideas (see *Rel.
Sem.*, pp. xlix, 497) and initiating stages (below, p. 101, n. 2).

a new line of development.[1] Like the prophets, their predecessors, there were men in opposition to their age, men who, like Amos (vii. 14), disclaimed kinship with its accredited representatives. Christianity was no ordinary synthesis of existing tendencies; there was no round-table conference. Nor can we describe the post-Exilic reorganisation of Israel as a synthesis of current trends of thought. Typical of the introduction of some new stage is not the judicious "*in medio tutissimus ibis*," but "*this* is the way, walk ye in it." The adjustments, combinations and compromises come later, as, e.g. when JE and D and P are woven together in one book, the Pentateuch—much lies behind that!—or when the Canon is definitely fixed.[2] But, typically, a choice has to be made, even as when Wellhausen by his famous *Prolegomena* (1878) forced all serious students to take up their stand "for or against," and a veritable revolutionary *volte-face*—as regards the position of P's narratives—became an "evolutionary" process.[3]

A comparative study of the inauguration and early course of strikingly new movements or transformations in thought proves helpful in many ways. We may think of the pioneers, the voices crying in the wilderness, the heterodoxies of one day which often rightly remained the heterodoxies of the morrow, and at last, in the fulness of time, the successful inaugurator or inaugurators. There are the occasions when the least adherent of the new order is greater than the greatest of the rival, and the worst enemy of the cause is

[1] Roman Catholic and other writers opposed to modern Biblical Criticism are so far in harmony with Marxists that they recognise, instead of ordinary "evolutionary" processes, the effects of transforming rather than reforming factors, and of discontinuities as well as continuities. Cf. below on Darwin and Mendel, p. 88 f, and see the Appended Note on the *Originality of Christianity* (pp. 99 ff).

[2] See p. 221. There are evident cases of compromise also in the history of the post-Exilic priesthood.

[3] It is difficult for us to realise how revolutionary the step seemed to those outside the ranks. Orr speaks of Graf's "somersault," and of the "development, if that can be termed development, which is more properly *revolution*" (*Problem of the Old Testament* [1905], p. 199).

he who—to the outsider at least—seems to be of the same household. There are the usual misunderstandings and the premature compromises, the fear of "reaction," and that apparent "reaction" which is a legitimate and necessary reassertion of the old, a *bona-fide* adjustment of the old and the new "vertebra," the old kernel in a new "shell." Throughout, wherever there is (r)evolution in thought, in research, in social-political crises, or in the history of religion, we deal with comparable processes, and it is found that what occurs in one field will often prove helpful and suggestive when we consider another.

(9) Let us pursue further the comparison of movements in history and in research. (*a*) The successful movement requires its appropriate environment. The Second Isaiah is of the same general period as Jeremiah, Ezekiel and Deuteronomy; the rise of Christianity is illuminated by Philo, the Psalms of Solomon and other writings; ideas of evolution were in the air before Darwin; and there were tendencies towards the present Old Testament literary-critical position before Wellhausen wrote in 1878. There are the difficult situations in social, political or intellectual fields when men "heal the hurt too lightly" (Jer. vi. 14); their solutions are premature, inadequate or impermanent, they cannot be accepted by the circle to which they appeal. But yet (*b*) when once some new movement has started, it may be too individualistic; it rests upon too narrow a basis, and is more suited for a specialised group than for the community as a whole.[1] As the movement progresses, the earliest stages may be superseded; like Astruc's theory of J and E, they have played their part.[2] So it will pass over into a new phase, as when Mendelism becomes the successor of Darwinism, and transformations, mutations and discontinuities become regular phenomena in (r)evolution. Interesting and not dissimilar questions arise, also, when we consider those who carry on any "tradition":

[1] Cf. the difference between the two types of Buddhism, the more "ethical" Hīnayāna and the more "catholic" Mahāyāna. On the difference between the reforming individualistic prophets and post-exilic Judaism as a social-religious organism, see pp. 41, 219 f.

[2] See *O.T.R.*, p. 46.

Marx and his successors, orthodox and unorthodox; the relation between the age of Wellhausen and the Biblical critics of this century; and the vicissitudes of doctrinal and ecclesiastical development.[1]

Now (c) when a movement has a broader basis and appeals to a wider circle, the needs of less detached and less specialised minds must be satisfied. Elements of the old and now superseded order will re-enter, though in a new form, as part of an entirely new system or organism. In Biblical Criticism the earlier and wider point of view of Ewald, Stanley and other writers was followed by the narrower, more intensive and indispensable work of literary-historical criticism. It has proved to be a necessary stage, and the present tendency to extend our survey makes the *post*-Wellhausen stage in certain respects recall the *pre*-Wellhausen stage, with the vastly important difference that, thanks to the Wellhausen stage with its literary criticism and to the general progress of thought, we can see things in a way that Ewald, Stanley and their age could never have foreseen.[2] In fact, one now finds that one can often gain hints from the earlier if not "pre-critical" writers on the Old Testament, and it is even useful to ask whether some thoroughly antiquated phase, e.g. the importance formerly attached to typology, belongs wholly to the past or is only an antiquated form of something that can and should be reinterpreted.[3] Earlier intuitions, phases or tendencies of thought may often be worth reconsidering.

Here the point I am making is the way in which in the course of development a new stage rejects elements which

[1] Not without analogy, too, is the fact that the second phase does not come at once. For example, Mendel published his experiments in 1865, but the significance of his work was not recognised by biologists until 1900, eighteen years after his death.

[2] See Stanley, *Jewish Church*, III, Preface, p. xvii, and especially Chs. XLVf., where, in his survey of the Exilic period, he glances at Zoroaster, China, India and Greece, and devotes several pages to Socrates. With this compare R. Kittel's *Geschichte d. Volkes Israel*, III (1929), Section 56.

[3] Here I would only refer interested readers to A. B. Davidson, *Old Testament Prophecy*, Ch. XIII ("Typology in Nature and Revelation"); see p. 307, n.

it finds irrelevant but which later on may prove to have a new or another value. For example, Mediaeval Scholasticism represents the mentality of a bygone and pre-Reformation age, but there are in it certain features which, though ignored by the new Protestantism, can be reinterpreted and restated. It represents genuine and necessary thinking —this is often forgotten—but the particular questions we ask, and the sort of answers that would alone satisfy modern knowledge, will make a gulf between the Scholasticism of the past and any new and more comprehensive system that may replace it.[1]

(d) A new movement is a force that requires a field, an environment. It may create it by forceful proselytising, by ruthless suppression of antagonistic influences, or by capturing the hearts of the young and the impressionable. Even if it creates its environment the varied needs of its members are not necessarily satisfied.[2] There may be fallow ground to be broken up (Jer. iv. 3). In Israel the Exilic period was one of ethnical, political and social changes, fitted for the breaking down of an old order and the introduction of a new one. Also the rise of Christianity was, as the pages of Josephus testify, at a time of grave internal crises. But the new religion could not find a lasting environment in Palestine or in the East; and now the West, after becoming Christianised, has to face the problem of a new adjustment between some form of Christianity and some stable environment. Here, as in other spheres of energy, both the "force" and the "field" are necessary; and the question: Which comes first? is one that is raised in the world of science as in that of thought.

(e) A new movement needs new clothes; it looks with suspicion upon new patches on old garments. The actual results are interesting when one considers early Jewish or Palestinian as distinct from Gentile Christianity, or the distrust of the thorough-going Communist for the *bourgeois*

[1] The question of the prospects of Roman Catholic Neo-Scholasticism is therefore an interesting one; see further, below, pp. 284, 291.

[2] Does Communism satisfy the religious needs of its members? Communists themselves are in two minds over the cult of Lenin.

and "tame" Socialist. Here the question of "short circuits" is particularly instructive, for the men who "pick up" a new body of thought without "going through the mill" often know neither the *rationale* nor the strength or weakness of their position.   Their knowledge is "patchy"; it is unsystematised.   There are many who know something about J, E, D and P, but scarcely understand the implications of the literary-critical hypothesis they have accepted. In like manner, are there not those who genuinely hold religious beliefs, though of an isolated and rather miscellaneous character, and do not realise the implications of their convictions?   In both cases there is the need of cohering and systematising principles that shall unite men and give them stability without standardising them; failing that, there are apt to be all sorts of promiscuous combinations, "syncretisms" devoid of root and power of growth.   Here Biblical Criticism has undoubtedly a very important part to play,[1] partly because it is gradually treading upon the ground which concerns the theologian rather than the Biblical critic as such, and partly because it raises questions which come first, before a theological synthesis can be attempted.

(*f*) As a new movement progresses men forget the factors that inaugurated it and gave it driving power. Thus, as regards Biblical Criticism, there is a tendency to forget that the uniqueness of Hebrew prophecy was the clue to the theory of the priority of the reforming prophets over the priestly ritual of the Pentateuch. Men ignore or belittle the work of the prophets themselves, and fail to see the necessity of the conflict between prophet and priest in old Israel, or of St. Paul's anti-Jewish stand, or of the Protestant Reformation. The subsequent adjustments and "reassertions" of the old in the new movement may even allow

---

[1] Cf. A. B. Davidson, *Theology of the Old Testament*, p. 5: "Criticism or Introduction must precede any attempt at a scientific Old Testament Theology."   This is naturally even more necessary as regards the restatement of Biblical Theology. The failure to recognise that religious principles must be systematised "theologically," even as the data of science must be systematised "scientifically," is characteristic of the modern "retreat from reason."

the impression that earlier uncompromising attitudes were uncalled for! In this way men will feel that their own inherited conservative or traditional attitude is being justified, or that the movement will somehow arrive at or lead to the rehabilitation of their own position. Like Mephibosheth of old, they cherish the hope that the fresh unstable conditions are going to restore to them the kingdom of Saul (2 Sam. xvi. 3). And sometimes it does look like it! After all, post-Exilic Judaism did contain many elements that had a pre-prophetic ancestry, and Christianity includes elements—too many for some people!—that are pre-Christian or non-Christian.

These are typical changes in (r)evolutionary movements such as are found in ancient and modern history, in the vicissitudes of religion, and in the chequered progress of diverse lines of research. They need far more competent treatment than ever this pen could give them, for they are important for our estimate of the great problems that lie in and behind the Bible, for the history that is now being made, and for the highly technical study of mental processes of all kinds. Criticism in this way unites the study of the development of thought in the Bible with the principles of development in general, and links together Biblical studies, practical problems of religion, and important types of research in mental science. In this way it may claim to be contributing to a new stage in culture. This cultural and philosophical significance of Biblical Criticism should not be overlooked.[1]

(10) A very brief reference to certain concrete Old Testament problems will perhaps give definiteness to what has just been said. (a) How shall we estimate the great reforming prophets? Were they such iconoclasts as is usually thought?[2] Opinions differ; but events in Russia have illustrated the passage from an initial revolutionary iconoclasm to subsequent adjustments and compromises.

[1] See pp. 279 ff.

[2] Might not the prophets have been "social nuisances" (Burkitt, *A New Commentary*, I, p. 430)? Bishop Gore points out how Jesus "refused all compromise; He was not conciliatory" (*ibid.*, III, p. 288). Cf. Dr. Goudge's observation, cited above, p. 43, n. 2.

(*b*) There are always inveterate religious needs to be satisfied, and our estimate of the work of Israelite reformers will be incomplete if we ignore this. For example, local cults are so persistent, even to the present day, that it is difficult to suppose that the "high places" ever entirely disappeared. Hence the question arises, are the local sanctuaries of JE of the age before the reformers, or—as I think—later?[1] (*c*) Religion must be practical, and the magical or magico-religious ideas which are to be found in the post-Exilic priestly religion of Jerusalem would certainly not be weaker in pre-prophetic times.[2] That is to say, from the *reformed* religion in post-Exilic times we can, with due caution, consider what it was at an earlier stage prior to the reforms; and this is true of any stage after a (r)evolution.

(*d*) Sacred beings must be accessible and able to perform their functions; hence the numerous angels of the post-Exilic period can probably be best explained as the late representatives of the earlier gods.[3]   (*e*) Finally, when the older religion was "reformed," the evidence goes to suggest that crude and "heathenish" ideas of an existence after death were killed by ethical monotheism.[4] Fellowship with God was the *summum bonum*: it constituted a bond which was not broken by death. On this, A. B. Davidson has some important remarks which deserve careful attention because of their general validity. The reason why ideas of immortality occur only in late sources is because there was something in the old religion which had made them unnecessary; but as men's ways of thinking changed and their former modes of thinking were modified, their spiritual needs must be satisfied afresh.[5] What we have expressed in our own words is the fact that earlier beliefs and practices which *implied* a relationship with Israel's Yahweh were broken down, and that subsequently there arose new

[1] See p. 129, and *O.T.R.*, pp. 147 ff.

[2] See *O.T.R.*, p. 151f.

[3] *Op. cit.*, p. 159.

[4] *Op. cit.*, p. 134. See T. H. Sprott, *Inspiration and the Old Testament* (1909), p. 157f.

[5] Based on his *Theology of the Old Testament*, p. 405f.

H

explicit convictions of resurrection and another life. The "great object" of revelation, he says, "was to enable men in each age practically to live unto God; . . . at all times it gave them light sufficient for this." This is true; the comparative study of religions does indeed show how men of different ages and types of culture have beliefs and practices which evidently enable them to live out their lives; but from time to time there come the great changes, shattering one system of life and thought and replacing it by another (cf. p. 271, n. 2).

The chief problems of Biblical Criticism turn upon the nature, the depth, and the results of profound religious changes in the history of lands, peoples and individuals. New movements and reforming measures are apt to destroy the good with the bad, to set aside or ignore earlier tendencies which will subsequently come to the front again; in their anxiety to blaze the new track, they often fail to satisfy genuine needs and aspirations. The conflicts between Religion and Science, the insistence of the Fundamentalist upon certain primary values which Biblical Criticism seems (to him) to destroy, and the heresies of all ages—whether justified or not—are recurring processes as important for our own interpretation of the Biblical history as for our thoughts concerning the future of our culture.

(11) When we turn from the steps in the development of religion to the creative factors, we may refer, first, to the new interest in the question of Primitive Monotheism. All that need be said here is that there is abundant evidence for religious experience—*of sorts*, and for the recognition of high gods, creators, fathers, etc. But although genuine religious experience, sometimes of a relatively profound nature, is a world-wide phenomenon, we are obliged to treat the evidence critically, and ascertain, as far as may be, the significance of the experience or the religious conviction for the history of the individual, tribe or people. Invariably every new religious factor works upon the existing conditions whether we are dealing with the familiar evidence for the effects of religious conversion upon the individual or, let us say, the effects of the ethical monotheism of the Second

Isaiah upon the thought of his age.   Whether a "religious" experience or conviction is rightly so styled will depend upon its content and effects; and of course among very rudimentary or prehistoric tribes the content would be extremely primitive.   Religious and mystical experiences differ markedly in character and in value, and, not in Palestine alone, some of them—for whatever reason—have been enormously more genetically significant than others.[1]

There is genuine religious feeling in Philo, the pseudepigraphical literature, and above all in Jewish piety; but it was not the ethical monotheism of Judaism, it was a new religious enthusiasm with fresh driving power that determined the next stage in history.   And if we go back to the Exilic period, the religion of Deuteronomy is not precisely that of Ezekiel or of the Second Isaiah; and while Deuteronomy is humanistic, rationalistic and programmatic, it is the religious intensity of the Second Isaiah that did most for the reconstruction of Israel.[2]   Amos and Hosea live in times of impending or existing danger, but they tell of Divine Righteousness and Love; the rise of Christianity was at a time of narrow nationalism, class-feeling and fanaticism, but it was the teaching of the relationship between God and Man that introduced the new historical epoch.   That is why the Exilic period is so exceedingly interesting: Deuteronomy has so many attractive features, and yet there is a mystery about the history of a book which subsequently has to take a second place.[3]   With all its social idealism it is narrow, and in its antipathy to the non-Israelite it is fanatical.   This was not the spirit of the Second Isaiah, and P, too, manifests a greater tolerance. To us, to-day, when a fanatical Marxism or Communism seems to its followers to hold out the only hope of a new world, certain problems of Biblical Criticism have an almost

[1] See further, p. 180.

[2] On D as a brave but unsuccessful effort to stem the decline of Israel, see Causse, *Acts of the Congress of the History of Religions at Lund* (1929), p. 286 f.; cf. also *O.T.R.*, p. 185 f.

[3] Cf. Welch, *Deuteronomy, the Framework to the Code* (1932), pp. 66, 183 f. and especially p. 209; *Post-Exilic Judaism* (1935), p. 283.

topical value; and in some oft-quoted words of Marx himself we may find a truth which he certainly could never have realised: *Die Kritik der Religion ist die Voraussetzung aller Kritik.* The challenge is to be accepted and all its consequences. Is the fear of the Lord *really* the beginning of Wisdom?

(12) To conclude. Biblical Criticism aims primarily at recovering, as fully as may be, the history and religion of Israel and at depicting it upon the background of universal history and religion. But in the life-histories of both individuals and peoples—as also of lines of thought—there is a difference between *Geschehen* and *Geschichte*.[1] Every incident will have its own appropriate relevance and value; but guiding principles are necessary to help us to distinguish between tested "facts," which as such are "true," and those essential "truths" which give meaning and continuity to all that can be treated historically. Similarly the data of religion have their own "truth"; but we have to distinguish between the phenomenology of the subject and what we feel to be essential for the "truth" of religion. In either case the task is no antiquarian or academic scrutiny of what happened or was believed long ago, although this scrutiny is a necessary preliminary step; we have in view the future, and seek a starting-point for a better handling of the whole field by ourselves and others. Moreover, conceptions of Biblical religion cannot rest upon the Bible alone, a much wider field is required; and, in like manner, a Biblical theology must seriously consider the extent of the environment it hopes to inform, and the faiths it desires to purify.

In addition to this, the intense religious realism of the outstanding portions of the Bible illustrates the difference between (*a*) a supernaturalism which is in contrast to the "natural" world, and (*b*) the theism of the prophets, which may be said to place the "supernatural" within the "natural." To the prophets Yahweh was in an effective relationship with all who did His will; and if their "realism" might appear to lay undue stress upon the Immanence of

[1] See above, p. 85, n. 1.

God in this world, no one felt His Transcendence more truly than did the Israelite at his best.   But the Hebrews were not philosophers,[1] and Christianity, among many permanent debts to Greek thought, owes also the more ambiguous and dangerous dualism of body and spirit, against which there is to-day a certain reaction.[2]   Whatever attacks upon Christianity from outside there may be to-day, it cannot be too earnestly taken to heart that there is much heart-searching within, and a widespread recognition of the necessity of an entire re-thinking of its most fundamental tenets.   So, Biblical Criticism, starting from very obvious and pressing enquiries, raises vital questions *which come first*, and which have priority over any premature synthesis or systematising.   The "hurt" of the people cannot be lightly healed.

Past history tells of men who aimed at a millennium: the aim has guided their steps, but what has been reached has been another stage, or the inauguration of a new series of stages.   Men have concentrated upon their immediate goal; but what they felt to be irrelevant, secondary or superseded has later "returned" or reasserted itself.   If there has been what might seem to be "reaction," the men who lived in the new movement, members of a new organism, did not necessarily feel it as such.   There has been progressive development because of men intuitively aware of what should come first, men who concentrated their attention upon the next stage, and not upon the precise stages which might or might not follow.   There are men who in all honesty cannot find a place in their minds for certain elements which do in fact reassert themselves—

[1] Professor D. B. Macdonald, *The Hebrew Philosophical Genius: A Vindication* (1936), does not, as far as I can see, show that this genius dates from before the Greek period.   On the other hand, the religion had immense implications for philosophy.

[2] In this connection it is worth remembering that Davidson (*op. cit.*, pp. 250, 412f.) thought that we may have diverged from Hebrew theism, "not indeed in fundamental faith but practically further than was necessary."   Schweitzer (*Decay and Restoration of Civilisation* [1932], p. 68) remarks upon the retention in our religion of outgrown Greek and Oriental conceptions which are making us bleed to death.

though in a new form—and they are fearful of the subsequent return or reassertion of that against which they or their ancestors fought. But any analysis of past creative movements will show how much detailed history has been forgotten, how many and varied are the minds that have contributed, and how readily—too readily—we telescope the past and ignore the prolonged toil and anxiety that went to the success of those movements which we can survey in fewer moments than it took years to effect.[1]

First things come first, and Biblical Criticism tells us of (r)evolutionary movements which ultimately made Western civilisation what it is. It opens up questions of Biblical history itself, of the *rationale* of progressive development— and so of progressive revelation. It brings vital questions of the processes of thought in the individual—who is the atom—and in our knowledge of the Cosmos itself; for the evolution of the Cosmos and of Man, and his increasing consciousness of all that has gone before, are parts of one and the same process. Everything turns upon problems of Divine Reality; and if first things come first, we need to rediscover for ourselves that reality of God which the prophets of the Old and New Testaments so keenly felt. And if so, forthwith men will need the conception of a *personal* approach to God; and a new synthesis of the Old Testament and the New Testament will unite both the reality of God and of the Person through whom He is approached.

To some of us it seems certain that if Christianity is to have a future, the first task is not so much to "bring souls to Christ" as to understand Who it is to whom it is the function of the Christ to bring men. A new comprehension of the spirit of the Old Testament will give a fresh meaning to the New. And *if* we can imagine a renewal of the passion for Ethical Monotheism—the belief in a One and Only Righteous God—and the Spirit of Christ, and *if* we can imagine a new movement inaugurating a new series of stages in the history of Religion, then indeed a future age, reading and interpreting its Bible in the light of its new

[1] See pp. 220 ff.

religious experience, may look back and say, "So there was a Second Coming after all." But this is to television the future as we already telescope the past.

APPENDED NOTE ON THE "ORIGINALITY OF CHRISTIANITY"

WHEN this chapter first was published, a correspondent[1] commented on the phrase "from outside" (p. 86), in these terms: "Surely one of the important results of Biblical Criticism and archaeology is a realisation of the fact that the originality of Christianity lay in its new selection of truths already half-realised, its change of emphasis within accepted systems of thought. Granted that, having first acted as a broadening influence within the safe limits of sub-prophetic Judaism, in the sphere of Hellenism it 'took and transformed' (and inevitably narrowed), but wherein did it innovate, and where in this history do we find anything other than 'natural' in its evolution?"

This raises intricate questions. Were one asked where to draw the line between "outside" and "inside," between "transforming" and "reforming," and between "discontinuities" and "continuities," one would at once be in the midst of extremely difficult but fascinating problems which are constantly arising in the fields of religious and secular thought. Are we to consider as normal and natural the intense experiences of mysticism, conversion, revivalism and the like? We have further to recognise that the crudest examples of what we should call "supernaturalism" were evidently perfectly "natural" to some people, while to the prophets of old the God of the Universe was assuredly "natural," even though His thoughts were not men's thoughts. Is one not entitled, if not compelled, to speak of that which comes "'from outside,' as it were"—the very wording is apologetic!—in order to mark the *qualitative* difference between all ordinary religious and other experience and those highly special occasions when a new force and authority gives new impetus to the whole life? If we find ourselves speaking of the "other" world, or a life "beyond," or the "wholly other," is it not that we human beings in this world of space and time are compelled to give this distinctiveness to certain intuitions, experiences and convictions which we regard, not as normal,

[1] *The Modern Churchman*, XXVI (Nov., 1936), p. 460f.

nor as ab- or sub-normal, but as super-normal? May one not think that St. Paul, St. Augustine and Luther—to name no others—felt that something had come from "outside," even though "normal psychological processes" were involved?[1] In the same way, love itself is as "natural" as ordinary human affection, but we should agree that there is a vast *qualitative* difference between X's affection for Y and the overwhelming, soul-filling passion which inaugurates a new stage in his life.

One may say that what we call "God" is no part of the "natural" world of the physical sciences, but an integral part of the larger universe of the scientist *qua* human being, whether he be conscious of this or not. Thus there is the "natural" world of space and time—Nature, and there is the "natural" world of those to whom all their religious truths, though transcendent, are also "natural"; and a great deal of confusion is caused because we think partly as occupants of this smaller world and partly as conscious or unconscious members of the ultimate universe of which the sciences give us only a very partial and imperfect knowledge.[2] And we have to maintain that "God" is transcendent, not only because a merely immanent God soon loses all distinctiveness and is felt not to be so real as the Self, but also because in the history of religions men constantly feel a new life-giving power coming from "outside" their accustomed world of life and thought: it is an expression of the recurrent discovery that our whole psychical development is incomplete, and it justifies the conception of a "revelation."

Among the first Christians there were of course "normal psychological processes." But the consciousness of a new illumination at a new stage, or a new start-off, is not confined to religion; and it is an exceedingly interesting task throughout to compare the "before" and "after," to see what is new and what is old, and to appraise the psychological and ideological processes involved. Christianity, it seems to me, gave a force and content to the conception of the Fatherhood of God which it had never possessed before. The Body of Christ and the mystical relation between Christ and this "body," indeed the new approach to God, are as little Jewish as the new and peculiarly pregnant treatment of the old conception of Wisdom-Logos.

[1] The writer had asked whether I was implying that the minds of the first Christians were exempt from normal psychological processes.

[2] If this be granted, its philosophical and metaphysical significance will be recognised.

It was a time when not only men but also ideas and conceptions and bodies of thought were being "born again." We have to understand the bifurcation, in the first century A.D., into (1) a Judaism which was continuous with the past and a natural part of the thought of its age, and (2) a Christianity which took over and respiritualised ideas (e.g. pre-existence, the idea of being first-born), so that thenceforth the two religions went different ways.[1] There is no record whatever of any other historical person of that age so significant as Jesus, and Christ as ἀρχή (Col. i. 18) was regarded as an originator or initiator.[2]

So the question of the "originality" of Christianity raises the question as to what really constitutes true, persisting and helpful "originality" in all life and thought. It is more than a "new selection of truths already half realised"; even as the work of a Newton or an Einstein is more than a rearrangement of letters and symbols—it is something pervasive and impelling. There is a "life" that issues from all men of personal worth such that we assimilate not only the new ideas they give us, but something of the "spirit" that gave and still gives them vital and pregnant power.

After all, we shall understand the New Testament better when we can more vividly realise the feeling that an entirely new age was dawning: of this the early Christians were assured. We ourselves hear enough of the end of this age and the like;[3] and presumably many Fascists and Communists are perfectly assured that they are witnessing the dawn of a new age. But does it grow "naturally" out of the thought of modern Europe? Is it not rather a reaction against it? For my part I am struck to-day by the two diverging tendencies: one towards a drastic social revolution, the other towards a religious reformation: both are of world-wide import. Should the latter materialise—as I believe it will—then indeed we, or another generation, shall see in what sense a new age can "evolve naturally," or is due to impulse "'from outside,' as it were." When, for example, Streeter (*Buddha and the Christ*, 1932) says "this is a day of promise and of hope" and speaks of "a fresh start," the last words clearly imply something other than an ordinary development or growth. The very argument among Marxists that the

[1] Cf. above, pp. 70, 72.

[2] See Lightfoot's note; also J. L. Myres, *The Political Ideas of the Greeks* (1927), Index, s. Arkhe; and W. R. Smith, *Religion of the Semites*, 3rd Ed., pp. xlix, 584, n. 3.

[3] E.g. N. Berdyaev, *The End of our Time* (1933).

dialectical process leads to a new social-economic creation in their hoped-for Communist society really enforces the fact that it leads more obviously to a much-needed religious Reformation.

But, throughout, technical questions of psychological and ideological processes are involved, and underlying this chapter are the two convictions, the one that the interpretation of the great creative ages to which we owe the Old and New Testaments and the historical process in which we are now living to-day cannot be dissociated; the other that the whole world of thought is involved, seeing that a living and progressive religion depends for its vitality and appeal upon an entirely "rational" relation between its essential truths and the principles which are accepted as essential in all departments of research. Christianity is not only a life to be lived; it is an experience to be thought out.

CHAPTER VII

Holiness and Righteousness

FREQUENT reference has been made to the idea of Righteousness, but the idea, on closer examination, is found to involve that of Holiness. The two ideas are mutually supplementary. The reverse of Holiness and Righteousness is unrighteousness, wrong, evil, sin; and the remedying of these and the restoration of Righteousness or Rightness involve ideas of Forgiveness, Reconciliation and Atonement. Ideas of Holiness take us to those of Transcendence and the supernormal; and ideas of Righteousness and its reverse take us to actions, outlooks, views of life that are not right but are wrong; and the task of setting right aught that is wrong takes us to the processes of making good. In this way these two great fundamental ideas of the Bible involve questions of general cultural significance.

Holiness or sanctity is the attribute of Yahweh, the God of Israel, and of other gods and supernatural beings. The underlying notion of the Hebrew root (k–d–sh) appears to be that of separation, distinctiveness and qualitative "otherness." Men must "sanctify" ($kiddēsh$) God, and treat Him and all that belongs to Him as sacred or holy ($kādōsh$). By sending judgments upon Sidon Yahweh gets himself treated with honour and is sanctified (Ezek. xxviii. 22); and an obscure story tells how Moses and Aaron in some way failed to respect his holiness, and he showed himself holy, or vindicated his holiness (Num. xx. 13). When the two eldest sons of Aaron, in offering up incense, broke some ritual law, Yahweh sent down fire and destroyed them in order to manifest his holiness and glory (Lev. x. 3). War was "holy"; and, indeed, when men approached their "holy" God, they, too, must be "holy" (cf., e.g. Exod. xix. 10). Where the sacred is concerned men must be heedful; offenders will suffer, and in the familiar story of

103

Uzzah this unfortunate man was destroyed by Yahweh because he, a layman, had taken hold of the sacred ark (2 Sam. vi.).

Now the idea of sacred or holy is a generic one, and in itself does not necessarily have any ethical implications. Neither Aaron's sons nor Uzzah transgressed ethical or spiritual demands. In fact, it is convenient to distinguish the general term "sacred" (Latin *sacer*) and the specifically ethical and spiritual term "holy." But this is not enough. Robertson Smith, Frazer, Marett and many others have shown that all the world over are tabus, some foolish, many socially effective; and it proves more than difficult for us to separate the tabu, the sacred and the holy into three distinct compartments.[1] There are things you may not name, look at, or touch; and natives have been known to pine away or die because they ate tabu food or were solemnly cursed for some misdemeanour. "No man can see God and live"; but constantly there are sacred objects (e.g. the bull-roarer) at which the uninitiated must not and dare not gaze. It is dangerous to treat the tabu lightly and disregard it; and from the psychological point of view the evidence for the effective working of the tabu is as impressive as the more "spiritual" teaching of the Bible. Throughout the world's religions whatever is sacred or holy must be treated as such. In the Book of Proverbs (xxviii. 9) the prayer of the man who disregards the Law of God is an abomination; the Sermon on the Mount impels us to ask whether God will receive our offering if we are at enmity with our brethren (Matt. v. 23–6); and I need only refer in passing to St. Paul's warning in 1 Cor. xi. on guilty participation in the Lord's Supper. To put it quite generally, men find that there are things so delicate, so sacred and so holy, that they must be handled with heed and caution: the crudest of native cults and the highest religions have this feeling in common.

---

[1] See W. R. Smith, *Rel. Sem.*, Index, *s.v.* "Holiness"; Sir J. G. Frazer, *The Golden Bough*, Part II, "Taboo, the Perils of the Soul" (1911); R. R. Marett, *Sacraments of Simple Folk* (1933), cf. above, p. 34.

The general idea has a psychical basis. Any given example is not as such necessarily religious; and even if it is, the ethical value (e.g. of treating certain foods as tabu) may not be high. The idea involves the consciousness of "otherness." In like manner, genius impresses us; but there is perverse, if not diabolical genius; the dramatist or novelist moves us—but in what direction? His may be mere emotional force, without reason or guidance. We are impressed by mysticism, but its content and value vary enormously; and how easily it can become mere eroticism![1]

When I say "*this* is holy, or sacred, or tabu," it may be that I have been taught to share this feeling; but when there has been a real, living experience, the feeling has a fresh personal, psychical basis; it has its inherent absolute authority. But how do I gain such an experience? Men have resorted to various devices to gain the experience of what seems to be another sphere of existence. So a distinction may be drawn between the experiences that come unsought; those that are engendered, it may be by a devotional exercise (e.g. prayer) or by some technique, and those produced by such external means as drugs or liquor.[2] The enquiry into the Holy, the Sacred and the Tabu has precisely the same perplexing and embarrassing character as when we study Prophecy, and pass from the greatest of super-normal prophets, through the diviner to the lunatic or madman so readily regarded in the East as inspired. Thus questions arise which concern not Religion alone, but the place and content of Religion in its cultural environment, and in its relation to all that is outside the normal.[3]

But it is with the higher phenomena of Religion that this chapter is concerned. The history of religion is not merely that of the transmission or survival of beliefs and practices: the vitality of religion depends upon vivid personal experiences, choosing, testing, verifying and purifying the

[1] Illustrated in aspects of Tantrism and Taoism in India and China respectively.

[2] See *Rel. Sem.*, p. 575. Cf. *Testament of Judah*, xvi, 4 (dated round about 100 B.C.): "wine revealeth the mysteries of God and men."

[3] See *O.T.R.*, pp. 167 ff.

religious heritage. Nowhere as in religion is there so intense a consciousness of the truths of God, Man and the Universe, truths which prove fundamental for both religious and non-religious thought. But in our analysis we must always distinguish between (1) the bare consciousness or experience as such, (2) its content, and (3) the value of the content.

The Ionian Xenophanes (sixth cent. B.C.) remarked that Ethiopians and Thracians fancied that their deities, like themselves, had black skins and blue eyes, and he went on to say that if oxen or lions had hands and could paint they too would make gods in their own image. Like people, like gods; or is it, like gods, like people? (Hos. ix. 10). Each is true in its time! In Assyria the atrocities of warfare were to appease the hearts of the angry gods. The Psalmist declares that with the merciful God shows Himself merciful, with the pure He is pure, and with the froward He is froward (Ps. xviii. 24ff.).[1] And finally, John Smith, the Cambridge Platonist, said, "such as men themselves are, such will God Himself seem to be."[2] Ye are my witnesses," declares the Second Isaiah (xliii. 10), and men do implicitly and unwittingly testify to their convictions of God or of Reality, and all that to them is most real and true. The study of religions proves that men's conceptions of Deity are so manifold that the subjective belief in "God," however sincere, is not enough; it may be misleading or dangerous—everything turns on what men think of His nature. Men's ideas of God are like the air they breathe—the purer the ideas the more healthy their spiritual, moral and intellectual lives.

The problem of "God"—what is this Reality? When the prophet declares that His thoughts and ways are not man's thoughts and ways (Is. lv. 8) he is affirming the transcendence of an *immanent* Being, that is, not one

---

[1] D. B. Macdonald (*The Hebrew Philosophical Genius* [1936], p. 18), citing this passage, remarks: "The fact that Jehovah becomes all things to all men could not be put more clearly; they are personalities who have become what they have become by their own free working, but Jehovah meets them in all their becomings."

[2] *Select Discourses* (1660), p. 5.

unknown or inaccessible, but one so much within human consciousness that this absolute "otherness" is vividly felt. Such a God is terribly near—He is dangerous, as in the post-Exilic priestly religion; but He is also preciously at hand, as in the Psalms. This utter nearness and utter otherness are distinctive of the higher conceptions of God; but indeed the paradox of proximity and distance characterises even the lowest religions.[1] After all, any new and vivid experience of Divine Reality is not an addition to knowledge, as when one learns a new language or visits another land; it is not additive, but transforming; and I should like to suggest that real religious experience may be called "transubstantiating."[2] Moreover, this Divine Reality of which men become conscious was already part of their ordinary psychical environment, part of the "field" in which they lived. It comes, as it were, "from outside"; but men find that it was part of their ultimate environment: "In Him we live and move and have our being."[3]

We cannot express the basic facts of religion in terms of space and time, when—in these rarer experiences—men "go outside" the normal life. On the other hand, the data of religion force us to realise that on going far "outside" ordinary life men do not necessarily reach or even approach the super-normal. What takes a man "out of himself" has only too often been supposed to take him into a super-sensuous and sacred realm. The conviction of Divine Reality must be guided and disciplined; and nowhere as in the old Oriental religions is there that religious assurance which can be mere self-assurance and antinomianism: there is a tremendously powerful God, and He is *my own* God![4]

The Study of Religion is also the study of our deepest selves (see p. 182). Unless men's lives and thoughts move

---

[1] Mana (Power) and Tabu (Precaution) are complementary; see *Rel. Sem.*, p. 552 f.

[2] Cf. also Judges vi. 34, where Gideon becomes, as it were, the incarnation of the Spirit.

[3] See pp. 3, 99ff.

[4] See *O.T.R.*, p. 104, and Bamberger, "Fear and Love of God in the Old Testament," *Hebrew Union College Annual*, VI, pp. 39–53.

along channels that are intellectually, ethically and spiritually valuable, the overpowering non-normal experiences can be harmful and degrading; they are abnormal not super-normal. Confronted by true and false prophets, true and false Messiahs, Christ and anti-Christ, we cannot understand the nature of what we call "religion" unless we realise that there are grades of religion, and that the differences make and mar men and peoples. The story of the Old Testament is one of the conflict of qualities of religion; and behind the New Testament is the tragedy of a noble religion, admirable in ethical and spiritual possibilities, one indeed that has preserved its followers for nineteen centuries, yet one that did not meet the needs of the age. The course of religious history in the first century A.D. is a fact that cannot be explained away; but the enquiry into the conflicts of Christians and Jews in the distant past is not so important as the question of the possibilities of Christianity in the future.

We must not exaggerate the psychological aspects of the holy, sacred and tabu. In the Old Testament, especially from the time of Isaiah, "holiness" acquires an explicitly ethical significance.[1] The Book of Leviticus, and especially the "Code of Holiness" (xvii.–xxv.), combines ritual and sacrificial laws, social morality and humanitarianism. "Be ye holy as I am holy": do not touch unclean food (xi. 44f.); show yourself a "separated" people by repudiating heathen customs (xx. 7, 24–26); and the very Code that so definitely emphasises Yahweh's holiness includes the injunction "thou shalt love thy neighbour as thyself" (xix. 18).

Moreover, the great prophets declare that God is near to the merciful, the just and the righteous.[2] That is to say, in a religious exercise one may vividly *feel* the nearness, the holiness of the Divine; but there is already a relation between God and Man when one succours the helpless or does good to the least of His children (Matt. xxv. 40), that is, in other words, when one manifests the qualities which otherwise are attributed to *Him* (cf. Deut. x. 18; Ps. lxviii. 5).

[1] Earlier, ethical principles are *implicit* in all cults that are for the welfare of a social group. See *Rel. Sem.*, *s.v.* "Ethical Ideas."

[2] *O.T.R.*, p. 187f.

Consequently, Religion really implies a stupendous "theory" of God, Man and the Universe, a theory that has more than a solely "religious" bearing. To this I now turn.

What is practised or tolerated under the aegis of Religion —e.g. human sacrifice—may become as abhorrent as what is sometimes done in the name of Liberty and the Brotherhood of Man (cf. Is. xxix. 13). On the other hand, much that belongs to normal, unpretentious, kindly social intercourse may have the profoundest ultimate meaning. In a word, when we consider the range of the ideas of tabu, sacred and holy we perceive that true Holiness involves Righteousness; and, as we must also recognise, true Righteousness involves Holiness. Religion without ethics or morality is a *force*—it may be superstition or fanaticism—it is not necessarily a force for good; and the conception of Righteousness has so wide a range that by itself it is apt to lose all its distinctive value. Holiness, it has been said, is a personal relationship, Righteousness is a principle of activity.

The Hebrew root of the latter word is found in the names Zadok, Melchizedek, etc. It connotes what is true, what is as it should be, natural, fit, and the like; and Sir George Adam Smith has described righteousness as the state in which a thing is all right.[1] The notion is thoroughly primitive, neutral and dynamic; it involves the recognition of a norm or standard, of what is natural, of correspondence with what is to be expected, and of a standard to which to adhere. In Arabic the adjective is used of a "trusty" spear that is as it should be. It will be useful to keep in mind the wide range of nuances: "Righteousness" is being "right," our "rights" are what are "righteously" due to us, and ideas of the Right, the Effective and the True are closely interwoven. The idea is thoroughly dynamic, for from time to time a higher standard is demanded, e.g. "righteousness" came to connote "almsgiving," and the Sermon on the Mount calls for a righteousness higher than that of its day (Matt. v. 20).

---

[1] See *Rel. Sem.*, pp. 655 ff.; and the articles on the subject by J. Skinner and G. B. Stevens in Hastings' *Dictionary of the Bible*. See also pp. 34 f., 244.

I

In the Old Testament, the Holy and Righteous God is God of the Universe, and all that He does is "right": He is true to His nature, and, in Isaiah's words, the Holy God through His righteous judgments compels men to recognise His divinity (Is. v. 16). Now, as far back as the Mosaic Age we find—outside Palestine—the belief in a universal order or right-ness, social and cosmic, under the care of the ethical god Varuna.[1] That is to say, in the one case there is a wholly righteous God of the Universe, in the other universal order is guaranteed, as it were, by God. These are the prototypes of Religion, Ethics and Science, for either we can reflect upon *our* God and the relationship between Him and us, or we can reflect upon the cosmic or the social order apart from the question of a divine guarantor. In the one case there is the personal God, in and by Himself, whatever His function in the world; in the other is the outside world, the world in which we live, as apart from God.[2]

If we believe that there is really a natural law, or order, or "rightness" in this Universe, it may be for one or more of three reasons: (a) because the evidence of the sciences points that way; (b) more fundamentally, because only if there is order can we organise our minds; for any fundamental disorder, irregularity or absence of system in the physical universe betokens our inability to systematise such knowledge as we have; and (c) because our belief in God holds such a place in our minds that we say that the Universe of a Righteous God must necessarily be one of order.

If we ask whether there is really a Righteous God, as the old prophets testified, our answer will depend upon what we consider to be God's function in the world around us,

---

[1] See p. 62. Representations of the Egyptian goddess *Maat*, who personifies a cognate idea, have been unearthed in Palestine; see p. 141, n. 1.

[2] This differentiation is more clearly seen in and about the Exilic Age, see pp. 151 f, 244. Again, at the Renaissance and Luther's Reformation there is, on the one side, a new consciousness of the outside world and a new humanism, and, on the other, an enhanced conviction of the Reality of God (see G. S. Hendry, *God the Creator* [1937], pp. 76 ff.).

and upon what precisely we mean by "righteous." We must bear in mind that "righteous" is not a static term. In the history of religion we find inferior, bad and helpless gods who were far from "righteous." Everyone will recall the criticisms passed by the Greeks themselves upon the gods of Olympus. The gods of Moab and of Syria, as certain personal names prove, were regarded as "righteous," but the Israelites, especially the prophets, doubtless attributed a higher "righteousness" to their own Yahweh. In Palestine itself the concept is an old one—it occurs in the Amarna Tablets in a letter from a king of Jerusalem—but we can trace a development of ideas, as, for example, when it is questioned whether Yahweh really demanded the sacrifice of the first-born.[1] Nor must we forget how the ethical monotheism of Israel was later challenged by the Christian ideas of God. In a word, from time to time men heighten the current or inherited ideas of God (or the gods) and their righteousness. Moreover, we recall the faith of the three youths in Daniel (iii. 17 ff.): God may deliver us, but even if He cannot, we will not serve the heathen gods. God may seem to be weak and negligible; but human faith is strong. Job is convinced that, although God seems to be acting unjustly, there is a Divine Righteousness behind and above all the evil which God seems to allow;[2] and in Greek tragedy Aeschylus is confident that in the long run the gods will be found to be just and benevolent.

So, at times when men are conscious of a higher truth and of standards higher than the current conditions tolerate or represent, they must testify to ultimate principles which seem to have been forgotten or shattered. Just as we say "Honesty is the best policy" in spite of periodical appearances to the contrary, and proceed to make it true, so, likewise, there may be principles which are not being manifested, but we intend to make them true, to incarnate them in individual or national deeds. This creation and main-tenance of "Truth"—not by Society, but by the conscious

---

[1] *O.T.R.*, p. 154.

[2] An excellent passage from the Jewish philosopher Maimonides (twelfth century) is quoted in *A New Commentary*, I, p. 313.

few—is a vital aspect of our conception of Truth.[1] "Truth" is both recognised and re-created, and history is constantly testing and re-stating men's convictions of the ultimate truths of Divine personal reality and of impersonal principles. But there are changing ideas of the character, attributes and demands of God, of the nature of the Universe, and of the meaning of Right and Righteousness. Consequently, the subject is by no means solely a "religious" one.

Faith in Divine Righteousness justifies itself. Let us look at history through the eyes of Israel's monotheism: Our God is a One and Only God, but He is not our own private God, the God of one party or people; He has no favourites. He is bound by a universal Right-ness. He is not arbitrary or changeable as men are; and should He change, there will be an intelligible reason for it, simply because He is righteous. Accordingly, there may be disaster, or exile, God's holy city Jerusalem may be destroyed, His first-born Israel may be scattered and almost annihilated, His only begotten Son may be crucified. But God is not unrighteous, weak or indifferent: a convenient dualism, blank scepticism and atheism only cut the knots and lead to chaos. So did men gain a fuller conviction of Divine Reality and reach the fundamental conviction—the very difficult one—that absolute righteousness meant a universal love.[2] At such crises men are faced by disruption and chaos or by a real advance in life and thought.[3]

[1] Here it is appropriate to note the fallacy in one of Marx's principles when he says: "It is not the consciousness of men which determines their existence, but on the contrary, their social existence determines their consciousness" (from *Aspects of Dialectical Materialism*, by H. Levy and others, p. 78 f.). This overlooks the part played by the individuals who stand up against some aspect of the current conditions.

[2] Jeremiah protests that Yahweh was as a deceitful brook (xv. 18); that is, the very reverse of reliable or "righteous." Perhaps nowhere as in the Book of Jeremiah do we witness what a prophet's path may mean.

[3] Kennett points out that though the conception of righteousness might differ in different ages and among various sections of Israel, all were convinced that their actions must be those that Yahweh puts into their hearts (*The People and the Book*, p. 389, ed. Peake, in the course of an essay on the contribution of the Old Testament

The author of the Book of Wisdom explains that God has tolerated evil because all men are His; His spirit is in all things (xi. 25 ff.). And the seer in the Second Book of Esdras, in the Apocrypha, rent by the overwhelming catastrophe of his people, is assured that he cannot love his people better than does their Creator (v. 33; viii. 4).[1] The late Bishop Gore once said, "I have always thought that the only very difficult dogma of the Church was the dogma that God is love."[2] But it is the only doctrine that does justice to all the facts, even as in ordinary research what might seem to be the harder and more difficult hypothesis may cover the widest field of facts and prove to be the simplest in the long run.[3]

I have already observed that the conception of Holiness has profound implications outside Religion. We have next to see that the "religious" theory of Divine Love and Righteousness has a more than "religious" application. It implies, in effect, that everything has a certain right or justification.[4] Everything is rational and intelligible considering the circumstances; it is what the old schoolmen called *bonum.* Neither earthquakes nor diseases are other than "natural"; and Nature's "redness in tooth and claw" and man's cruelty and utter selfishness cannot be severed from the question of "freedom," which means freedom to do good or evil, to act justly or to do wrong. If, e.g., a man diligently devotes his energies to crime it would be an unreliable and unjust universe if he did not get some measure of success—there is *something* that does help those who

to the Religious Development of Mankind). This implies that the relationship between God and Man can have a direct meaning for a man's intellectual as well as his emotional—or devotional—life. See further below, p. 185 f.

[1] See, in this connection, Montefiore's interesting booklet, *IV Ezra : A Study in the Development of Universalism* (1929). Cf. *O.T.R.*, p. 214.

[2] Cited from J. H. Morrison, *Christian Faith and the Science of To-day* (1936), p. 208.

[3] Whether uncomfortable "facts" are living people or dead data, the easiest way is not necessarily to ignore them, render them harmless, or otherwise save oneself the trouble of finding a place for them in one's world.

[4] Cf. Gen. i. 31; Eccles. iii. 11; Ecclus. xxxix. 16, 33.

help themselves—and still more unreliable if his reward
was not subsequently capped by what we should consider
ethically just. Men reap what they sow, and even the
"hypocrites"[1] of old get their reward (Matt. vi. 2). A disease
like cancer is, as the schoolmen would say, *bonum sibi*,
not *bonum alteri*, it is in accord with its own specific nature;
and the standing example from St. Thomas Aquinas is
fornication as a *bonum*—a *bonum quoddam temporale*, but
incompatible with the superior *bonum* which the sinner
ignores.[2] The *bonum* is as neutral as the "survival of
the fittest," as neutral as the idea of the sacred or the
tabu; and in all neutral processes the good or evil lies in
the use men make of them. We do not echo Pope's words
"whatever is is right," but whatever is, has had its right, its
justification—which is not necessarily an argument for
preserving it. Things have "the law of their being," that
is what *we* discover; but the law, the higher law of our own
being, is not so readily discerned.

A consistent monotheistic doctrine requires us to recognise
that throughout creation God has granted growth and
liberty and freedom—but within limits; each has freedom
within the law of its being. Men are always discovering
that there are limits to their rebellious wills and that there
are lower and higher grades of what is Right. "Sin" is
the misuse of freedom. The earthly father who loves his
creatures, his children, and gives them all the liberty he
can in order to help them to express themselves and partici-
pate in his life, must run the risk that they will do much
that is selfish, harmful and evil, much that will grieve him
and thwart his purposes. Everywhere, growth in life and
thought does bring with it the possibility of divergence,
error, even grave error, and this will demand correction,
rectification. All progressive evolution carries with it the
potentiality of a subtler evil, and a higher process is needed
to remedy the un-righteousness of him who has had freedom
to go his own way. A world of exact requital, even if

[1] See on this term, p. 167, n. 1.
[2] See A. E. Taylor, *Faith of a Moralist*, II, p. 427; Sheen, *Religion
without God*, p. 324 f. (cf. *ibid.*, p. 266 on what is perfect or true at
an earlier stage but is no longer so).

devoid of wrongdoing, would also be devoid of personal liberty or freedom; it would be un-human.[1]

If, now, we say that even an earthly father will continue to have faith in the child he loves, how much more should men abide in faith in their Heavenly Father.[2] Biblical history tells of the tragedies of man's blindness and rebellion; but also of the re-discovery of God's righteousness, and the new life it gave. Men must maintain their faith, their steadfastness, even as in research tested principles must be maintained. If we really believed that our tested regulative principles of life and of thought would sooner or later prove misleading, we could have no hope for the future. To believe in some ultimate indeterminacy, irrationalism or un-reason, or unchecked liberty would be to open the door to utter tyrannical arbitrariness and a lowering of aims and ideals.[3] Any failure of our hypotheses of life and of thought is a call for a better one that rises above the one that has proved imperfect or misleading.[4]

[1] See D. S. Cairns, *The Riddle of the World* (1937), p. 296, on the sort of world that some "humanists" would seem to prefer.

[2] Isa. vii. 9, see the commentaries. The Hebrew word translated "truth" means, rather, faithfulness, continuance.

[3] Science, observes Max Planck, is compelled to start with the general assumption that a general rule of law dominates throughout Nature (*The Universe in the Light of Modern Physics* [1931], p. 59); and he points out that there is no rhythmical swing of the pendulum in the history of physics, but more or less steady progress in a definite direction, by adding to the content of the world of sense and giving us a firmer grasp of it (p. 13).

[4] Exceedingly interesting and not dissimilar questions arise when we consider the connection between an earlier hypothesis and one that supersedes it. (1) In physics, Bavink, *Science and God* (1933), p. 56f., finds a certain continuity, which however, does not appear to be recognised by some other physicists. (2) In Biblical Criticism, N. Baynes, *Israel Among the Nations* (1927), p. 7f., speaks of the Wellhausen literary hypothesis (see above, p. 17f) as one which "the historical student must at any moment be prepared to abandon" (but see above, p. 19, n. 3); none the less there is no sign of any alternative hypothesis that offers as satisfactory an approach to the Biblical problems. Also, Sir Charles Marston, *The Bible is True* (1934), p. 264, cites some pessimistic words of Sir James Jeans on the insecurity of modern physics as a warning to Biblical critics. On the other hand (3), that there is a fundamental continuity behind the profound discontinuities in the development of Biblical religion is self-evident. It is in the light of considerations such as these that one should approach the question of the future of Religion and the Bible.

The conviction that our God is a *transcendent* God of Love and Righteousness makes our faith in Him entirely rational; for it is perfectly rational to trust that there will be continued growth of experience and knowledge, and higher conceptions—better, and not wholly other convictions—of the interrelation between God, Man and the Universe.   If it is difficult to-day to look round and maintain that there is such a God, a God of Love and Righteousness, it is because the world-conditions have not as yet led us to higher conceptions of Divine Reality such as were reached by the prophets in their day.[1]   Have we such a religious interpretation of history as we find in Israel, one that would guide our steps in the future?   If Israel found God in their own history, was He not also to be found in the history of other peoples (Amos. ix. 7), and in a people's troubles as well as in their prosperity?[2]   There is a loss of an *effective* faith in God, for God is not the world-proletariat, or the Totalitarian state, or the Soul of a nation, or even the Visible Church.   If the world has lost hold of some great embracing principles, regulating life and thought, it has certainly not yet found new ones to meet the altered conditions in which it lives.

Men have freedom and liberty to live and to think, but they have also to understand that with freedom and liberty there is always the possibility of proceeding along wrong lines, and that there is constant need for reconciling, atoning and forgiving.[3]   "Sin" is the abuse of freedom.   Accordingly there arises the question of Individual Responsibility. Men readily feel that they have some responsibility for the maintenance of *social* order—*social* righteousness; but at earlier stages of thought they were often convinced that

[1] It is tragic how "God is Love" has been degraded from the most profound of spiritual truths into a sentimental platitude (Christopher Dawson, *Enquiries into Religion and Culture* [1933], p. 298).

[2] See Cairns, *op. cit.*, pp. 288, 291. The very evils which make some doubt or deny the existence of God are to others a proof of the absolute Right-ness that rules in the Universe. It is perhaps a sign of the breakdown of current philosophy that this is not more generally recognised.

[3] Cf. Phil. ii. 12f.; I Cor. iii. 9, on the conjoining of "human" and "divine" activity.

the order of nature, cosmic order, and all that at higher levels of thought was in the care of gods or spirits, was directly or indirectly bound up with their lives. In particular, the failure of crops or lack of sunshine or rain might be laid to the charge of a chief, a rain-maker or a divine king. In the Old Testament national welfare in general depended upon Israel's integrity, and monotheistic belief regarded her successes and disasters as a divinely sent reward or punishment. It has, in fact, been a widespread fundamental notion that men—or certain men—may have more or less cosmic powers and cosmic responsibilities. Perhaps this is not so strange when we consider some fundamental ideas in Religion. One of them is excellently set forth in the old Indian doctrine that the soul of man is ultimately identical with the soul of the Universe (*tat tvam asi*); which, if really true, would mean that we must be in some respects one with the Universe itself (see p. 182). The other, in contrast to this pantheism, is theistic and implies, as in the Bible, that there is a direct actual or potential relationship between Man and the Supreme God of the Universe. In this case, men are not one with the Universe, but through God as the middle term there is some real contact between Man and the Universe over which He has given him dominion (Gen i. 26). In either case the "religious" idea should have the profoundest implications for our "non-religious" thought.

We have to deal with some world-wide types of belief, varying in content and value, like the ideas of the Holy and the Sacred. Are we in any way one with the Cosmos?[1] Consider the beliefs seriously, remembering that they were as real to those who held them as our own positive knowledge is to us. Consider the prevalence of "magical" ideas, man's apparent control of nature, the many daring convictions of man's destiny, the tremendous and sometimes megalomaniac pretensions of Israel and Judaism. If we treat the evidence realistically, we shall agree that, taken as a whole, it implies an extraordinary "theory" of Man, God and the Universe. But in the Bible the old Israel

[1] See pp. 182 ff, 287, n. 2.

and the new "Israel of God" are being trained and disciplined. The old Israel was not blamed for her conviction
of a unique relationship between God and herself, but she
was warned. She was the instrument of a Divine Process;
and the oft-quoted warning of Amos (iii. 2) means that
the nearer one feels that one approaches Divine Holiness
and Righteousness the more fatal are one's shortcomings.
God Himself, because He is the absolute supreme Personal
Being, must be absolutely Holy and Righteous; and Israel,
with her conviction of the otherness and the nearness of
God, is judged by a higher standard. Just as Isaiah in
his inaugural vision (Ch. vi.) became conscious both of God's
Holiness and of his own impurity, so it is precisely the
religion of Israel which, *at its best*, combines Divine Holiness
and Man's unworthiness, Divine Righteousness and Man's
departure from it, Man's tremendous destiny (Ps. viii.) and
the completest dependence of the creature upon the
Creator.[1]

> And they who fain would serve Thee best
> Are conscious most of wrong within.

Primitive belief readily attributed to certain men cosmic
powers and responsibilities, and in Israel the Deuteronomic
law laid upon the Israelite a responsibility otherwise set
upon kings, priests and the like.[2] At the great religious epochs
the responsibilities of the individual are stated afresh. In
Deuteronomy the Law is not inaccessible—it is near at
hand, it is *here;* and in Christianity there is a yoke, a burden
—but it is light, when not borne by man alone (see p. 74).
In the Parable of the Talents there is what I would venture
to call the Law of Religious Relativity. If X has five talents
and Y has one, X is not five times better off than Y—from
each according to his endowments and opportunities. It
is in this way that men can be said to be equal in God's

---

[1] Cf. St. Peter's words, when he recognises the divinity of his
Master (Luke v. 8); and note that when Robertson Smith connects
holiness and kinship it is the consciousness of intimacy which
intensifies the gulf between the human and the divine (see *Rel. Sem.*,
pp. 289, 400, 549).

[2] Cf. *Rev. d'histoire et de Philosophie Relig.*, IX (1929), p. 307;
and Causse, *ibid.*, XIII (1933), p. 296.

sight. It is not what they have, but the use they make of
their selves that counts. So, whereas there is a tendency
to-day to submerge the individual in the community and
for the individual to reject responsibility, in the great crises
God and the human soul are alone, and the man in his
solitariness is in the presence of his Creator : the immense
worth of the individual—in the sight of God—and, equally,
his immense responsibility! A man is much more worthful
than he thinks he is—or, perhaps, than he wants to be;
the burden is too great. Man's freedom to work out his
own self and his inability *not* to err—"there but for the
grace of God goes . . ."—no wonder that in Religion we
pass from this dignity *and* responsibility of the individual
to the means to strengthen and support him.[1]

In primitive religion there is the clearest recognition of
wrongdoing and unrighteousness. Sin is judged from the
standpoint of the clan, tribe or group. This is public
wrongdoing, inimical to social or national welfare. But
there is also the private wrongdoing that may never become
public, although confession—especially of sexual misdeeds—
is not uncommon on critical occasions (e.g. men on fighting
or hunting expeditions, women at childbirth). A distinction
can be drawn between (1) the confession of admitted wrongdoing and (2) any evil, harm or suffering which the victim
feels has been inflicted upon him. In the Old Testament
evil (*ra'ah*) is properly any affliction, e.g. such as that which
befell Job, and which could have come from God.[2] But it
is also moral wrong, which is repugnant to God and to the
human conscience, and this God does seem to tolerate:
"O Lord, how long!" is the cry (Hab. i. 2, cf. *v*. 13; Ps.
lxxiv. 10).

There is an advance of thought when cosmic ills and
disasters cease to be regarded as supernatural punishments.
Thus, God will no longer destroy man and beast as he did
at the Flood (Gen. viii. 21; cf. Is. liv. 9); the rain falls alike

---

[1] Cf., eg. the part taken in Buddhism by Amitābha (Amida);
see p. 318 f.

[2] ii. 10: "shall we receive good at the hand of God, and shall we
not also receive evil?" Cf. Amos iii. 6; 1 Sam. vi. 9, and see *O.T.R.*,
p. 153.

on the just and the unjust (Matt. v. 45).[1] It might seem as
though man could now sin with impunity once the fear
of such a catastrophe is removed, but there is a tacit appeal
to man's conscience: sin is an offence against a personal
God and not a mere destructive power. In searching for
the cause of some affliction or disaster the way lay open for
gross superstition, for witch-hunting, and for the discovery
of the identity of the offended supernatural being; for
typically every evil was supposed to have ultimately some
supernatural cause. But the road was also open for the
search after what we should call "natural" causes. Similarly when it is a case of conscience, there may be excessive
introspection and morbidity. But Job suffering external
physical ills of body and estate was not conscious of sin;
and he reached profounder conceptions of God than if he
had been conscience-stricken, or had no belief in a God,
or believed in natural causation. Every departure from
the normal, the natural or the right has acted as a stimulus,
and, in the long run, has made for a true progressive
development.[2]

Ideas of sin and evil and of forgiveness and salvation have
been typically practical, material or external.[3] Sterility,
loss of goods, drought, defeat—these were recognised
evidences of divine or supernatural wrath, or of man's
misdeeds, or of both, and removal of these ills was a sign
of forgiveness, and of the renewal of friendly relations between
man and his God, that is, of at-one-ment.[4] The primitive
mind exteriorises, and once the misfortune has passed it
readily forgets—"the Devil was ill, the Devil a saint would
be. . . ." If a man's conscience does not smite him and

[1] For Rabbinic parallels to the latter, see H. Loewe, *Judaism and
Christianity*, I, p. 127. Contrast Hag. i. 11; Mal. iii. 10; Zech.
xiv. 16f. (see *Rel. Sem.*, p. 582).

[2] The tendency seems to have been to look for an explanation
of the abnormal, and the like, and only secondarily for an immanent
or for an extrinsic factor to uphold order, see *Rel. Sem.*, pp. 550ff. (on
Mana, etc.), 657ff. (on Order).

[3] W. R. Smith, *The Old Test. in the Jewish Church*, pp. 306f., 441;
A. B. Davidson, *Theol. of the Old Testament*, p. 388; Kennett, *Church
of Israel*, p. 167f.

[4] See *Rel. Sem.*, pp. 645ff.

things are all "right," does it mean that he is "righteous" and that he has the reward of his "righteousness"? Primitive thought is easily satisfied. On the other hand, when men suffer and, in spite of their prayers and searching, gain no relief, they may be led to face their trials and surmount their difficulties; faith and character are strengthened; the mountains are not removed, but they become as mole-hills. In general, the point to be made is that when we consider the vicissitudes of ideas of sin, evil and unrighteousness, and of forgiveness, salvation and reconciliation, we observe how there can be an advance in personal character, in the relationship between Man and God, and in the knowledge of His Universe. We must not sever the ideas of Man, God and the Universe. "Against Thee only have I sinned" (Ps. li. 4) is the climax of Old Testament teaching, for it means that in the last analysis only God makes right all that from which we have suffered or for which our conscience holds us responsible.[1]

When we consider the ideas of forgiveness, atonement and the like, we notice how commonly from primitive religion upwards there are ritual ways of removing sins (e.g. washing, fumigating); and on ordinary psychological grounds we can understand that they were felt to be effective.[2] But if a man has done wrong and feels forgiven, is this feeling of relief or of forgiveness enough? The Old Testament concentrates upon the relation between Man and God: divine anger terrifies a man, divine grief or sorrow tames him. There are ideas of the "return" to God, or of a new spirit or heart in man (Ezek. xi. 19; xxxvi. 26); and in later Judaism repentance virtually leads to a new divine indwelling in man.[3] The Old Testament has its stories of inevitable divine retribution: Samson, David and Bathsheba, Ahab and Jezebel; but the story of Joseph tells how evil was turned into good (Gen. xlv. 7f.; l. 20). It is the same with ourselves

[1] Cf. in this connection Matthew Arnold's familiar dictum, cited below, p. 200, n. 1.

[2] See *Rel. Sem.*, p. 646f.

[3] *Rel. Sem.*, p. 604, citing Abelson, *Immanence of God in Rabb. Lit.*, p. 140.

when we have not been dealt with after our sins, or when good has in some way come out of evil. The glory of God manifests itself when good comes out of evil and He vindicates Himself—i.e. His Name, as Ezekiel has it; but men must not do evil that good may come (Rom. iii. 8; vi. 1), and it is for men to be disciplined, to "accept chastisement," i.e. to acknowledge that He is righteous.[1]

How is unrighteousness turned into righteousness; what is it to "make right"? A normal healthy man may suffer from a perfectly normal illness; it is removed by medical treatment which acts in its own perfectly natural way: it counteracts what is harmful, destroys or removes the evil, gives new vigour to the weakened body.[2] Any higher process will subjugate and dominate the lower, deciding what to remedy or eradicate, what to destroy and what to introduce. In like manner the will of a man may be controlled by his higher self or by another personality to whom he submits himself. Or again, take some outlook in life or in thought that is genuinely held but is imperfect or misleading; as such it is not "right," it is a departure from "right(eous)ness." There is need of a better outlook, even as in research it may become necessary to replace an inadequate, repressive or harmful hypothesis by one that offers a better treatment of the field. In this way we can perhaps see how the question of righteousness and unrighteousness, of good and evil, of sin and of salvation involves the consideration of all the reconciling processes in life and in thought by no means confined to the sphere of religion. We have to consider how a lower process is replaced by a higher, how the sick soul requires accessory treatment as well as healing medicine and the removal of the mischief, and how even an outlook, a theory of life, may be harmful,

---

[1] Ps. li. 4 and Rom. iii. 4 show how efforts were made to develop the monotheistic view of good and evil (see the commentaries).

[2] A Buddhist parallel is worthy of notice. "Buddha, as a healer of the soul, habitually sums up his doctrine under four heads corresponding to the formula in which the task of the physician is defined by Indian medical authorities: the nature of the disease, its aetiology, the removal of the cause, the remedy" (G. F. Moore, *History of Religions*, I, p. 285).

because it is preventing the acceptance of a better one. Post-Exilic Judaism proved to have fatal imperfections, else it had never been challenged and superseded by Christianity; it was not sufficiently "right" or "true" for its day; and to-day all the great religions are suffering from some inherent weakness, which makes them less "right" and "true" than when they were living, effective powers.

The question of sin and forgiveness raises an important point which I must briefly indicate. The Old Testament concentrates upon the relation between God and Man and does not speculate upon existence after death.[1] Our age-long ideas of heaven and hell are foreign to it; and though they have considerably weakened, nothing appears to be taking their place. It is perhaps remarkable that, although we may be interested in ancient history, the authorship of the Pentateuch, the mysterious Universe, and so forth, we do not speculate whether we ourselves shall ever know whether we have worked along right lines. As individuals we die and depart into the Unknown; whereas our environment which we have helped to make or to mar goes on its way. But if God were what we think Him to be we might, in a future existence, see some of the secrets of Man and the Universe with which we have been wrestling. We might even perceive the fruits of our good and of our bad deeds. And if so, how readily we can imagine the possibility of a Heaven and Hell far more realistic, and more intelligible than many of the ideas that have prevailed in the past.

We say, God may forgive but Nature cannot forget. God may and does forgive; but were men to see the consequences of their deeds, the anguish and evil they may have caused, or even the way in which their evil had been turned into good, we can conceive the possibility of humiliation, suffering and penitence more intelligible, more just and righteous perhaps, than the eternal physical torments of the Hell of old-time popular belief. Light-hearted speculation is to be deprecated, but at a time like the present when men—

---

[1] The belief in immortality begins and ends with God; cf. Davidson, *Theology of the Old Testament*, p. 416; Inge, *God and the Astronomers*, pp. 276, 297f. (with quotations from Jowett and von Hügel).

doubtless with the best of intentions—are laying up a sorry heritage for their children, one wonders what a God of Righteousness can do!

As it is, weakened conceptions of the All-Merciful, the God of Love, encourage the belief that a man's wrongdoing after all concerns himself alone: *Dieu pardonnera, c'est son métier*. But remorse, which no philosophy of the world can shake off, is the signature of a man's knowledge that he has had freedom, and has made the wrong choice; and the attempt to place the blame upon the social environment ignores the extent to which a man is the creator and not the creature of his real world of life and thought—his spiritual environment—although it is the social environment which he has helped to mar that remains the scene of the processes which are to turn "wrong" into "right."

In other words, genuine feelings of forgiveness, reconciliation and atonement which men may experience do not necessarily in themselves remove the consequences of the mistakes of the offender or the sufferings of his victims. Quite apart from the question how "wrong" is made "right," we have, in fact, to understand that forgiveness, reconciliation and the like are not the finale, but the prelude to another stage, even as the "rediscovery of God" in the Exilic Age and the rise of Christianity mark each the end of one period and the beginning of another. This is true of all powerful experiences, they close one chapter and open another.

Now if this be so, there are important consequences. The ideas of a Day of the Lord, a Millennium, a Kingdom of Heaven or a Messianic Kingdom are not those of static blessedness, but of a higher righteousness. Here a distinction must be drawn between the old conception of an age upon earth of perfect justice and the later apocalyptic fancies where the scenes are transferred to a heaven. All eschatological topics are excessively difficult, and it is necessary to bear in mind that according to one old typical belief God with all His holy ones dwelt in the sky, but was effectively upon earth and had His abode among men.[1] Ideas

---

[1] See *O.T.R.*, pp. 126 ff., and cf. especially Kennett, *Church of Israel*, pp. 176 ff. and the Introduction, p. xxviif.

of a better régime upon earth or of some abode in realms above become exceedingly complicated. The beliefs and rites had reached an advanced state of development before the age of the prophets, and neither the reformed religion of the Exilic Age nor Christianity could start upon an unwritten page. Consequently, we have inherited a medley of beliefs from bygone ages, reflecting diverse types of thought. It is important, therefore, to observe how our various religious ideas have grown up, how to the prophets the God of the Universe was, as we should say, "natural," and how the "natural" and the "supernatural"—to use *our* terms—were within one sphere and were not, as we might say, worlds apart.

There were far-reaching developments in thought round about the Exilic Age, and these divide us with our classical categories from the great creative prophets of Israel.[1] Consequently it is very difficult for us to grasp clearly the Biblical ideas of a better world, whether on earth or in the sky. They blend genuine religious experience and secondary speculation; and the ages for which they were "true" and "natural" have gone. Indeed, the task that lies before those who reflect upon the future of Religion is essentially philosophical, cultural, and of a sort unprecedented in human history. It is not some eclecticism that is needed, but a re-thinking of the fundamental conceptions —*ab ovo*, as it were—such as is now taking place in Science.[2] The task does not concern Christianity alone, although it is in and through the Bible that the profoundest developments among all the world's religions have taken place.

Once more, in considering ideas of unrighteousness, sin, and the like, we may notice three main types: (1) the external evils (e.g. drought), which were commonly—and sometimes rightly[3]—regarded as the fruit of man's folly; (2) all that for which man's conscience might prick him;

---

[1] See pp. 113 ff, 216 f.

[2] Cairns, *op. cit.*, p. 53, compares the "calibration," the periodical overhauling of scientific apparatus.

[3] E.g. in the case of disease, or failure of crops due to negligence of irrigation. Modern parallels may haply be found in excessive deforestation and in upsetting the "balance of Nature."

K

and (3) a vague *malaise*. By the last I mean the feeling
of missing the mark, falling short of the right. The familiar
Hebrew word (*ḥāṭā*) means to miss the mark, to blunder;
and the point is that there is a state of mind when it is not
clear *what* the goal is, or *where* it is—a sense of frustration
and feeling that things are not "right," and that ours is
but an imperfect and incomplete self. Of course we hardly
call this "sin." But "sins" are so often reckoned by
reference to the Decalogue that one forgets the New
Testament teaching of all that severs man from God and His
Righteousness. Even in Babylonia we find among the
recognised offences, estranging relatives, neglecting parents,
false weights, saying yes for no and no for yes, having a
frank mouth but a false heart; and in the "Declaration of
Innocence," in the Egyptian Book of the Dead, are included
such faults as stirring up strife, deceit, avarice, bad temper,
etc. We should enlarge our conceptions of both
"right(eous)ness" and "sin," and remember that "salvation"
and to be "saved" meant something more actual and
practical than a "spiritual" state of mind.[1] If to-day there
is no explicit feeling of guilt or sin, is it not, partly at least,
because of our ignorance of the "righteousness" at which
we should aim? For even a genuine desire to do the
"right" fails, if the righteousness, as in New Testament
times, does not exceed that of the day. It fails, even as,
when we turn from the world of life to the world of thought,
the honest effort to give the best treatment of a problem
fails if it does not cover the field.

But the mere consciousness of failure, frustration, or of
a vague *malaise* is significant. We have only to recall some
notable words: Augustine's "Thou hast made us for Thyself
and our heart is restless till it finds rest in Thee"; or the
words of Pascal, "Thou wouldst not seek me hadst thou not
found Me";[2] or the Mohammedan Sufi poem, "your calling
'Allah' was my 'here am I'."[3] Quotations need not

---

[1] See Pedersen, *Israel* (1926), pp. 311 ff.

[2] *Pensées* (ed. of 1905), vii. 555.

[3] See R. A. Nicholson, *Mathnawi*, iv. 15. (He inform me that
the preceding lines, which are sometimes quoted with the above,
are found only in late and largely interpolated MSS.)

be multiplied. They combine to represent the climax of men's convictions of the relation between the Supreme Reality and himself: the relation already subsists, it is one which God is waiting and wanting to renew.[1] He is not outside man's environment: He stands at the door and knocks (Rev. iii. 20). Indeed the point I am really making is this: If the Supreme Being of the Universe is all that Religion asserts, is there not likely to be a tension if men have not found that peace and confidence which follow upon a restoration of the relationship between God and Man? If it is true that in Him we live and move and have our being, does this not account for all *malaise*? Our "theory of Reality" (p. 9 above), our "theory of God"— if the phrase be allowed—must do justice to convictions which have so often been tested and found not to be illusory.

In life as in thought we may feel that we are in a *cul-de-sac* or enclosed in a vicious circle of circumstances. Yet when escape is found, we start off afresh, and in both life and thought there is a new creature, a new power, a forward look. We see this re-creation in the Exilic Age after the "exodus" from an actual Babylon, viz., in the new monotheism of Israel; and again at the birth of Christianity when, as St. Paul says, in Christ a man is a new creation (2 Cor. v. 17). It is what we find in any new sweeping hypothesis that gives us a new prospect of dealing with troublesome facts.[2]

In these pages I am attempting to suggest how we should combine a modern outlook upon the Bible with our outlook upon the present age. In research as in life it sometimes

[1] This relation (on which cf. below, p. 184 and n. 2) is also implied when in the Mission Field natives are able to respond to the Christian message. Cairns (*op. cit.*, p. 366) quotes "a very successful and much honoured missionary" as saying: "I never yet preached the Gospel to a heathen audience, but I found that the Spirit of God had been there before me." Cf. p. 250 n.

[2] The Psalmist in li. 10 prays to Yahweh to "create" a clean heart and to make a new spirit (cf. cii. 18). In all the great changes in life and thought the new stage does not arise directly out of the old, and the old conditions do not wholly disappear. We say that the change comes "from outside," but it is a question of the spiritual and psychical environment of the individuals; see pp. 99 ff, 298 f.

becomes necessary to reconsider even the greatest of hypotheses, and I am suggesting that the interpretation of the Bible and the interpretation of Life are really one and the same problem. We approach the Bible to enquire what really happened. We place its history and its religion on a world-wide plane. The mathematician by assuming that parallel lines meet makes significant discoveries; and we, if we might assume that the world's religions do contain some truth, do thereby widen our horizon: we gain new knowledge of what men have felt to be most real and true, and acquire new ideas touching the relations between God, Man and the Universe. Moreover, just as we can conceive of geometries other than Euclid's, so we can consider the theoretical possibility of building up a religious system upon Mohammedan, Hindu or Buddhist foundations: the progressive development of Christianity is by no means to be taken for granted. On the other hand, in the Bible we encounter epoch-making developments, periods of decline and of rebirth, periods of growth and decay, so that, even on the most rationalistic of grounds, we learn far more from our efforts to interpret it than from any other Sacred Book. Western culture has so closely grown up from it that it is more than difficult to believe that it can continue apart from it.[1]

The Marxist or Communist has concentrated upon the problem of making a successful revolution. That is our problem, in the sense that we hope for a successful transformation, one that starts, not from the social-economic conditions, but from those principles which have given new life and growth in the past. The critique of Religion is indeed the presupposition of all criticism,[2] for the great religious movements that we find in and behind the Bible are but the outstanding examples of the lesser thought-provoking occasions of ordinary life, and the problem of religious restatement is only part of the larger cultural problem of the reorganisation of thought in general. After all, Christianity does claim to be a revolutionary force.

[1] See above, p. 77.

[2] On Marx's maxim, see above, p. 96.

The Bible takes us full circle—decay and growth, growth and decay; the anticipation of a change and the reassertion of the old in a new form. It is the gamut of processes. We may work for a better age, but a later age may have the old battles to fight over again; we may systematise, but the system will subsequently cramp further growth. "In its prime every system is a triumphant success; in its decay it is an obstinate nuisance."[1] We may pull down heathen altars, but in the Old Testament the local cults were not destroyed but purified; and although the prophets repudiated the cult of the Queen of Heaven, later centuries replaced her by the Virgin Mother. Indeed, to the gods of a polytheistic régime we owe, in some measure, our angels. That is the stuff that history is made of. The processes of history are transhuman, and men and women are unknown soldiers, who bring about the changes which they cannot foresee; in being true to themselves, they brought the changes from which we benefit.[2] History may make us cynical—what does it matter? *plus ça change!* Or History impels us to maintain the old faith in Divine Righteousness, the freedom that is given to men, the limits they must not transgress, and the Divine Power that transmutes evil into good. Only as instruments of a Higher Purpose striving to act up to their highest ideals—but always failing—men build better than they know, through the Holy Power that forgives, reconciles and sets right their departures from all that is "right."

To-day we are confronted by conflicting doctrines and ideologies. It is no time to take sides. Any non- or anti-religious doctrine is inevitably defective; but a distinctively religious one may be so gravely imperfect as to be ineffective and lifeless. Our trouble to-day—as I see it—is our religious disarmament. We can see much "right" on all the contending sides, and also much "wrong"; but have we anything better to offer? We may wish to recall the people to Religion: but precisely *what* Religion, what is

---

[1] Whitehead, cited by J. H. Morrison, *Christian Faith and the Science of To-day* (1936), p. 76.

[2] See pp. 221 ff.

its content, what is the cultural value of the Religion to which we would recall them? Not Christianity alone is interested in the future of Religion. Religion consists both of what we do and what we think. If God is known by His attributes men are His witnesses. If to love God is to tend his flock (John xxi. 15-17), God's love for men must be repaid by men saving others from themselves even as we feel that we too have been saved from the worst consequences of our follies. And if a God who loves His creatures desires the true liberty of *all*, and therefore shows no favouritism to *one*, this in turn must be man's action. If God, the eternal Ultimate Reality of the Universe, is really "righteous," mankind will never cease to learn what this "rightness" means. If our interpretation of the Bible throws light upon the Divine Process in history, *that* is the Process with which men must work in harmony. If certain things are true, their truth must be maintained; we prove them by acting up to them.

In this way we come to realise human weakness, our inability to act up to what we know to be true. Such knowledge condemns us, and we understand St. Paul's attitude to the Torah: for the knowledge of all truth convicts those who fall away from it, as certainly as any new and better outlook in life or in thought reveals the weakness of the old one. If God is altogether absolutely Righteous, if He turns men's follies into good, and is thwarted by men's rebellious and lower ideas of liberty, then are men convicted of unrighteousness, of wrong doing, and of falling away from the mark. But that same God who in His love for His creatures has given them freedom, knows their weakness and their self-seeking. Men can only escape by fleeing from a lower to a higher process, from a lower self-centred freedom to that larger personal freedom which is found in obedience to a higher Will.

We speak of the Old Testament as fulfilled in the New. The central problem of the Old Testament is the growth of men's conceptions of God in the course of historical change. Only by reasserting the reality of God and of His attributes was the road laid for the New Testament,

and God revealed in Christ.   But to-day it is only too easy
to have imperfect conceptions both of God and of Christ;
and if Religion is to be the power that we know it ought
to be, we must go back to the fountain-head and restate
what we mean by "God"—and this involves not only our
religion but our non-religious and scientific thought.
Thereby do we manifest our convictions of the "Truth"
of the Bible; for the Bible is true, as long as we find in it
the things that are true; it is inspired, as long as it continues
to inspire us.

The ideas of Holiness and Righteousness circle around
the conception of a universal "right," the attribute of
a transcendent God.   In the course of man's mental
development there have grown up explicit differentiations of
the varied sorts of right, order, law, and the like in both
Nature and Man.   In the two following chapters something
has to be said on this differentiation: on the significance
of profound changes in and about the sixth century B.C.
and on the difficult conception of a One and Only Ultimate
Reality.[1]

[1] The general argument is continued on pp. 158ff.

CHAPTER VIII

The Exilic Age and its Significance

THE aim of this chapter is to emphasise the importance of the middle of the first millennium B.C. for the development of universal history and religion. The Exilic Age was one when a new Palestine was taking shape, and at this, as also at certain other great periods, external and non-Palestinian influences were especially prominent. The student of the New Testament has long been familiar with the discussion of the relative depth of Hebrew or Jewish, and of Hellenistic or Greek influences. There are various ideas and modes of thought which do not seem to be in the direct line of the Old Testament tradition. Is the Bible really "Hebraic" or "Jewish"? Some writers are of the opinion that the influence of Greek speculative thought has obscured the fundamental principles of Hebrew theism.[1] On the other hand, the tendencies of Barth and Brunner and their followers are sometimes felt to be too "Hebraic," too austere. The discussions of to-day go back essentially to the Exilic Age of about twenty-five centuries ago—which is roughly about mid-way between ourselves and the rise of the First Dynasty of Ur (c. 3000 B.C.), the city so familiar to those who have followed the excavations in Babylonia. This Exilic Age may be said to form a definite watershed between a very old world and one that is now coming to an end, and the following pages will be devoted to a separate and necessarily brief statement of the main facts to be borne in mind and their bearing upon the rise of Christianity.

First, as regards the new Palestine. It is generally agreed that the fall of Jerusalem in 586 B.C. and the Exile had a

[1] See pp. 97 n., 157, n. 2, 218.

profound effect upon the development of Israel. In fact, the terms "pre-Exilic" and "post-Exilic" are among the commonest in modern Old Testament study, for the Exile is regarded as a landmark on account of the differences between pre-Exilic and post-Exilic thought. The chief events are familiar. The Chaldaeans laid waste Judah and Jerusalem, and destroyed the Temple (586 B.C.)[1]; many Judaeans were carried into exile, and numbers of them returned later, in the days of Cyrus, Darius and Artaxerxes; the Temple was rebuilt (516), and the religion of Israel was in due course re-established. These events were, of course, of far-reaching significance; but they do not sufficiently explain the differences between the pre-Exilic and the post-Exilic thought of Israel.

Although the Exile itself belongs to the sixth century B.C., it will be convenient not to limit ourselves to that century, but to think of the longer period from the fall of the Northern Kingdom in 721 B.C. to the times of Nehemiah and Ezra. The Biblical sources are abundant, and include Jeremiah, Ezekiel, Lamentations, Second Isaiah, Haggai, Zechariah. We have writings, either in existence or coming into existence. Thus, if the Pentateuch is substantially Mosaic, it was evidently already in existence; but if portions are Exilic or later, it was coming into existence. This applies also to the books Joshua–Kings, so that even if there is difference of opinion on questions of literary criticism, we may agree that there was a very great variety of literature in process of *either* being *or* becoming.

From non-Biblical sources much is known of the great historical changes in the Near East during the period under discussion.[2] In the middle of the seventh century B.C. Egypt opened a new chapter of history. Egypt and Greece were again resuming relations, just as, long before, Egypt had been in contact with Crete and the Aegean. The

---

[1] Albright, *The Archaeology of Palestine and the Bible*, p. 171, claims that archaeological evidence in the shape of deserted cities in South Judaea can be found.

[2] See *C.A.H.*, III and the Synchronistic Table at the end; also *ib*. VI, Ch. VII.

"Dark Age" of Greece is over.[1] Egypt was taking a new interest in North Syria, just as she had done in the eighteenth and nineteenth dynasties; although at this time she was faced, not by the empire of the Hatti (Hittites), but by Assyria. New factors appear—Scythians, Medians and Chaldaeans. Egypt, the Levant and South-West Asia were brought into close contact, even as they had been six or more centuries previously. When the Assyrian empire fell, Egypt hoped to be its heir; but the Battle of Carchemish in 605 B.C. gave the sovereignty to Nebuchadrezzar. The Chaldaean or Neo-Babylonian empire which he established was as short-lived as was the power of the Medes. In 555 Median power passed to Cyrus the Persian; and his series of rapid successes culminated in the capture of Babylon in 539. This new Achaemenid or Persian empire inherited the claims of Egypt, Assyria, Babylonia, Media and Lydia. It was an empire that was to last for over two hundred years, until Alexander the Great brought East and West together in a new way. Thus, there were vast historical changes over a very large area. We pass from the old Oriental epoch of Sumerians, Minoans, Hittites and the rest, to the prominence and the dominance of Persia, of Greece, and finally of Rome. East and West have met, the centre of gravity is beginning to pass westwards, and, through the intermedium of the Roman empire, the new epoch has continued down to the present day.

In these changes Palestine, Judah and Jerusalem were inevitably involved; the Exile and the restoration of Israel formed only a very small part of greater events. To the Biblical student the Biblical events are invariably of epoch-making importance; to the historian Israel seems a very insignificant actor in a mighty drama. Similarly, in the Maccabaean revolt the Jews were fighting the world's battles, though to the historian it was only one of many revolts. And again in the first century A.D. the historian places on a more extensive background the events that will always be of prime interest to Jews and Christians.

Accordingly, from the Biblical sources we can perceive

[1] *C.A.H.*, III, pp. 527, 635.

the permanent importance of what was happening in Palestine; at the same time we should take a larger survey and understand something of the great world-movements that enable us to place Biblical history in a real historical perspective.

Turning from secular history to religion, we know that there were widespread religious movements: Taoism and Confucianism in China, Jainism and Buddhism in India, Orphism and mystic cults in Greece, and the rise of Ionian speculation. In Palestine, the individualism of Jeremiah and Ezekiel, and the lofty idealism of the Second Isaiah, were among Israel's contributions to the history of religious thought. All these great movements in religion and in history were introducing the new epoch,[1] one of not less significance than the rise of Christianity itself. It was an age of widespread revival, by no means confined to Palestine alone. In Egypt there were remarkable archaising tendencies in art, dress and thought. The Egyptologist, the late Dr. Hall, has spoken of them as an archaising crusade, as though we in England were to go back to the Anglo-Saxon period for our inspiration and imitate it in every way. In Babylonia, both Nebuchadrezzar and Nabonidus were zealously restoring old cults. The latter spent some time at Tema, a site well-known to the Israelites, and re-established the moon cult at Ḥarran (Haran), the place so closely associated in tradition with the ancestors of Israel. As for Palestine itself, it was not until Cyrus became king that the Persians actively encouraged the Jews; and the rebuilding of the Temple in the reign of Darius (516 B.C.), and the subsequent work of reorganisation by Nehemiah and Ezra were indebted to Persian patronage. It was an age of awakening, and from the purely historical point of view it is important to consider carefully the activity in Greece, Egypt, Babylonia and Palestine, and to contrast the results: the permanent fruits of the reorganisation of Israel and of

[1] Cf. Stanley (p. 81, n. 2 above) and Dilthey (p. 216, n. 2 below). G. F. Moore speaks of "a maximum in the tides of religion (*Hist. of Rel.*, i, p. ix), and Galloway notes this "era of prophetic religion" and comments on the "growth of the personal and prophetic spirit" (*Philosophy of Rel.* [1914], 133ff.). Cf. p. 81, n. 4.

the awakening of Greece, and the decline of Egypt and Babylonia.[1]

Throughout the whole period under discussion there were many social and ethnical changes in and around Palestine itself. A new Palestine was being formed. Arabia became more prominent, and the Arab tribes in Transjordania gave Assyria considerable trouble. The unrest continued. Nabataeans pressed upon Edom, and Edom pressed upon Judah. The desert tribes to the east and south of Palestine were always ready to invade the land; and sometimes they succeeded. Centuries before, the Israelite invasion had led to a permanent settlement; but in the days of Gideon a great Midianite invasion was repulsed (Judges vii.). The tribe of Judah, as can be seen from the names in 1 Chronicles ii. and iv., was largely composed of South Palestinian clans. In Samaria, after the fall of the North Kingdom, Sargon introduced various Arabian peoples, including the Tamud (a well-known name) and the Hayapa (probably the same as the Midianite Ephah of Gen. xxv. 4). Midian, Edom and other desert peoples were sometimes hostile, but at other times settlers in Palestine. The Biblical writers tell how Ammon, Moab and Edom took advantage of the calamities of Israel during the Exile (Jer. xlix. 1; Ezek. xxxv. 10; xxxvi. 2, 5). Consequently there was a considerable infiltration of desert blood. Moreover, in 700 B.C. Sennacherib claims that he carried off from Judah 200,150 men, and transferred western territory to the cities of Ekron, Ashdod and Gaza. The evidence will suffice to show how drastic must have been the changes due to the Assyrian conquests, the removal of portions of the native population, the settlement of colonists, and the entrance of tribes from the desert.[2]

The Biblical history, it is true, emphasises the changes in Samaria: the northern tribes were carried off, and Judah

---

[1] See H. R. Hall, *C.A.H.*, III, pp. 300ff., and his *Ancient History of the Near East*, Ch. XI. He contrasts the "artificial revivification of an old Egypt long passed away" with the "natural reflorescence of civilisation," a "true re-birth" of Greece, though in a shape very different from that of the Aegean culture of earlier days.

[2] *C.A.H.*, III, pp. 383ff.; VI, pp. 184ff.

is the sole representative of the original Israel. On the other hand, not all the northern Israelites were exiled: we are told that the religion of Samaria was syncretistic—the people worshipped Yahweh together with other gods. Moreover, isolated references prove that they continued to be interested in the Temple at Jerusalem, some of the prophets still speak of the people as Israelite, and Samaritanism itself was essentially an Israelite sect.

Although the Old Testament history tells us little or nothing of the situation in Samaria after 721, and in Judah after 586, we already know how vital and important the period was, and scholars are paying increased attention to the problems of the period.[1] There was considerable fluidity in the religious conditions. Jeremiah protested that in Israel there were as many gods as cities, and in Jerusalem itself the women maintained the cult of the Queen of Heaven. The Elephantine papyri afford a good example of Jewish syncretism even in the fifth century; they belong to colonists who worship Yahu, god of heaven, they possess a temple and temple ceremonial, and although they write Aramaic, they use some Hebrew terms.[2] Many of the personal names have a familiar stamp (e.g. Zephaniah, Isaiah, Azariah, Nathan); and relations were maintained with Judah and Samaria. But these Jews are henotheistic rather than monotheistic, and recognise two attendant and probably female deities besides Yahu. We find a similar fluidity at other times, e.g. at the Maccabaean revolt, when the upholders of the stricter Yahwism were as much opposed to their Hellenistic brethren as to Antiochus Epiphanes himself. Indeed, this was only to be expected in an age when the internal conditions were so disturbed in consequence of the movements which have been mentioned.

Palestine was an ancient land. It lay open, not only to the tribes of the desert, but also to the surrounding "non-Semitic" peoples. Long before the Persian and Greek periods it had been exposed to Sumerian, Aegean,

---

[1] See pp. 20, 28, 44.

[2] "Righteousness" (or "merit"); offering (minḥah), frankincense (lebōnah).

Hittite and Indo-Iranian influences, and it is an interesting question whether these influences had any results. It is well known that at a much later period the thought of Islam was deeply influenced by the Persians, so that its theology and philosophy became a blend of native Arabian and of foreign Persian and Greek thought. To what extent post-Exilic Judaism was affected by Persian and Greek influence has frequently been discussed. The powerful Hellenistic tendencies in the Maccabaean age deeply influenced one party of the Jews, but it also forced other Jews to reassert their nationalistic monotheism. Even in the Wisdom literature, in the Book of Wisdom itself, where we can perceive that the Jews were certainly stimulated through contact with Greek philosophy, they were not mere borrowers of an alien thought.

Hence we may expect that, in addition to the influence of the more primitive desert tribes, Palestine was both directly and indirectly affected by contact with alien and non-Semitic peoples: directly, in that it adopted certain alien ideas and ways of thought, even as the Hellenistic Jews did later; and indirectly, in that it was stimulated to reassert its older thought, even as the Maccabees were aroused by the threat to their national religion. In this way we can account for the variety of thought in Palestine in the middle and latter part of the first millennium B.C.: internal disturbed conditions making for greater individuality of thought, extreme tendencies, and the influence of desert and non-Semitic factors.

From this account of the internal developments within Palestine we turn to a more particular statement of the changes in thought. When we speak of the Old Testament as "Hebraic" or "Jewish" we use terms that are as convenient as when we speak of "Semites." The *languages* spoken by Hebrews, Aramaeans, Assyrians and Arabs formed a single well-defined group, and these can be called "Semitic"; but the people of that part of South-West Asia who spoke those languages were not of a single ethnic type, and among them are various cultural differences due to intercourse with their neighbours of Egypt, the Aegean, Asia Minor and Persia. Tentative efforts have been made to distinguish between the Sumerian and the Semitic culture of Babylonia,[1] and they justify the belief that they may be extended further by comparison with Egyptian, Indo-European and other peoples.[2]

For example, it is recognised that the Abbāsid Age at Baghdad (A.D. 750–1258) owed its brilliance to the Persians who were settled among the Mohammedans, and lived in amity with them. The acute Arab writer, Ibn Khaldūn, of Tunis (fourteenth century A.D.), records that the most eminent of the early Mohammedan grammarians and theologians, as well as those learned in the principles of Law and in the interpretation of the Koran, were Persians by race or education.[3] Is this fusion at all typical? When we go back to the Achaemenid or Persian period the question of Persian or Zoroastrian influence upon the Jews has been frequently mooted. Thus, the eminent historian, Eduard Meyer, stresses the Persian reputation for love of truth, the abhorrence of falsehood, and their rationalising temper;[4] and the probability of continued influence upon Palestine during the age of the Parthians, and later of the Sassanians, must also be borne in mind.

Morris Jastrow, the Assyriologist, suggested that Persian or rather Zoroastrian influence can be seen in Babylonia in the notion of a reign of law, inscrutable and inexorable law, and in the recognition of one great spirit (Ahura-Mazda) presiding over the Universe, instead of a multiplicity of divine power. The Persians brought a clearer conception of a universal divine order, and this paved the way for the transition from astrology, the study of the stars in their

---

[1] e.g. L. W. King, *History of Sumer and Akkad* (1910), p. 348.

[2] On the "Semites," see *C.A.H.*, I, Ch. V. For a good characterisation of the Babylonians, see Sidney Smith, *Early History of Assyria* (1928), pp. 337 ff.

[3] R. A. Nicholson, *Literary History of the Arabs* (1907), pp. xxviii, 278.

[4] See *Geschichte des Altertums*, I, § 477; *Ursprung des Christentums*, II, pp. 64 f., 75.

relations to gods and men, to astronomy, the detached and impersonal study of the stars in and for themselves.[1]

Hence it is not surprising that writers have endeavoured to specify the typical differences between the Semite, the Iranian or Persian, the Indian and the Egyptian. The conception of a world-order, an eternal law in nature, and the reign of moral powers, is felt to be Indo-European rather than Semitic, and certainly there is a marked difference between the Hebrew attitude to Nature and what we owe to the Greeks.[2] There was much in Zoroastrianism and in the conception of its god Ahura-Mazda with which the Israelite could sympathise; but the rationalising tendencies of the Persians would be repellent to his stricter nationalistic theism. The theism of the Israelite is not that of the philosopher who denies that God may be circumscribed by human attributes and asserts that He can only be defined by negatives, but that of the fervent patriot unable to allow his God to be confused and still less identified with the god of any other people, whether Marduk, or Khnum, or Zeus.

Now, the Persian Age was not the first in which Indo-European or rather Indo-Iranian influence came into direct contact with the Semitic area. Centuries earlier, namely in the Amarna Age (c. fourteenth century), powerful Indo-Iranian elements can be traced in Mitanni (North Syria) and even in Palestine.[3] The famous Indian gods Varuna, Indra and Mitra were known to the Hurrians of Mitanni and the Hatti (Hittites) of Anatolia. The god Varuna, forerunner of the later Ahura-Mazda, was the guardian of universal or cosmic order (rita), and this concept (as arta) is found in Mitannian and other names of the Amarna period, as also in the much later familiar name Arta-xerxes. The conception is thus vouched for at an age which is, roughly, that of Moses, and also that of the monotheistic or monistic religious zeal of the reforming Pharaoh, Amenhotep IV (Ikhnaton), whose wife Nerfertiti,

---

[1] *Religious Beliefs in Babylonia and Assyria* (1911), pp. 60ff., 252.
[2] Cf. G. F. Moore, *History of Religions*, I, p. 359f.; Bertholet and Lehmann, *Lehrbuch der Religionsgeschichte*, II, pp. 18ff., 201; Ed. Meyer, *Gesch. d. Alt.*, I, § 589ff.
[3] Cf. *inter alia*, S. Smith, *op. cit.*, pp. 213, 385.

and successor Tut-ankh-amon, are perhaps more widely known. In Egypt itself the old concept of Truth, Righteousness or Order (*maat*) is prominent in the thought of that ill-fated reformer, and the goddess of Truth herself, daughter of the Sun-god Re, has been found represented upon plaques, etc., unearthed in Palestine.[1]

Consequently, when Palestine in the Amarna or Mosaic Age was a small part of a world uniting Egypt, the Levant and South-West Asia, we have evidence, not only for Indo-Iranian influences, but also for the presence of the interrelated ideas of Order, Truth, and the like. Moreover, Ikhnaton, laying claim to universal dominion, called himself "Living-in-Truth," and named his new capital (the modern Amarna) the "Seat of Truth."[2] In like manner Jerusalem was known as the "City of Righteousness" (Isa. i. 26); and this Hebrew concept is especially associated with the old sacred city in such names as Melchizedek, Zadok and Jehozadek. It corresponds most closely to the Egyptian *maat* and the Indo-Iranian *rita* (*arta*); it is used by a king of Jerusalem in one of the Amarna tablets in the sense of dependable, loyal—even as it is applied, centuries later, to Yahweh (Zeph. iii. 5; Ps. cxlv. 17, etc.), and it already occurs in an old Amorite name of many centuries earlier. It is a pre-Israelite concept, even as Jerusalem itself is an ancient foundation.[3] So, too, the general religious *milieu* of Jerusalem points to old Canaanite or pre-Israelite times rather than to invaders from the desert, such as the Israelites were, hostile to the land and its culture.

We thus find (*a*) points of contact between Egypt,

[1] See *C.A.H.*, II, pp. 397 ff.; *O.T.R.*, pp. 93 ff.; and *Quart. Statement of the Palest. Explor. Fund* (1928), pp. 201 ff.   For *maat*, see Breasted, *The Dawn of Conscience* (1934), Index, *s.v.*; especially pp. 142 ff., 369. *Maat* at first meant "right," just as we use the word in a mathematical and in an ethical sense; it came to mean national and moral order, and was associated with the rule of the Pharaoh.   For the Palestinian representations, see *Quart. Statement.*, 1933, p. 15, and cf. Moret in *Comptes-Rendus* of the *Académie des Inscr.*, Jan., 1936, p. 19 f. (he asks whether the Egyptian ideas of *maat* had any influence on Palestinian thought).

[2] Breasted, *op. cit.*, p. 299 f.

[3] Cf. Albright, *Journ. of the Palest. Oriental Society*, VIII (1928), p. 247 f., and above p. 61.

L

Palestine and the North, (b) a series of interconnected ideas of Truth, Right, Order, etc., and (c) a Jerusalem culturally of pre-Israelite origin.

Palestine was always more or less in touch with Syria and the North, and we have next to notice some of the historical links between the Amarna Age and the Persian. The old Ḥatti and Mitannian cultures left their heirs in the shape of sundry Iranian names, reaching down to the days of the rise of Medes and Persians.[1] Of special interest is the prominence of the kingdom of Urartu (Ararat) during its prolonged struggle with Assyria (ninth–eighth century), when Palestine and its neighbours were intimately affected by the changing political situations. Palestine was, as usual, torn between her relations with Egypt in the south and the northern *bloc* of petty states stretching into Asia Minor and Armenia. This northern connection is note-worthy, for although we are wont to associate Palestine and the Semites in general with the Arabian desert, we should not overlook the fact that in the genealogies of "Shem"—whence the term "Semite" was taken—one tradition makes his "sons" extend from Lud or Lydia to Asshur (Assyria) and Elam, with an off-shoot running down towards Arabia (Gen. x. 22 ff.). This is perfectly intelligible in view of the old trade-route from Sardes in Lydia to Susa, the control of which was necessarily always of the utmost importance for economic and political reasons.

Not only are there these connections with the North, the ancestral traditions are interested in Ararat (Urartu), and the district of Haran (Harran) which lies in the old Mitanni. This Harranian cycle of tradition relating to Abraham and the Israelite ancestors must be taken seriously, for the early belief that Ur of the Chaldees was some Khaldian or Armenian Ur still finds its supporters.[2] The addition "of

---

[1] See Ed. Meyer, *Gesch. d. Alt.*, II (1926), Ch. 1, p. 34; II (1931), Ch. 2, pp. 363 ff., 393 ff., 420 (note p. 370 the names Kundaspi and Kustaspi); R. Kittel, *Gesch. d. Volkes Israel*, III, p. 265 f, cf. pp. 733 n., 746 f (on the possible antiquity of Indo-Iranian influence on Palestine).

[2] See Kittel, *Gesch. d. Volkes Israel*, I, p. 443 f.; Lods, *Israel*, I (1932), pp. 163 ff. Skinner (*Genesis*, p. 237) points out that although the evidence for the Babylonian Ur is very strong, "serious misgiving" is caused by the prevalent tradition in Genesis of the northern home.

the Chaldees" may suggest that others were known; and it is possible that only later tradition replaced a Khaldian Ur by an Ur of the Kasdim.   But, quite apart from this, there are in any case indubitable connecting links between Palestine and the North.

Further, the rise of the prophet Amos in the middle of the eighth century may have been stimulated by the Urartian and Assyrian conflicts.[1]   Amos is another landmark in the religion of Israel by reason of his teaching of Yahweh's universality and ethical righteousness.   No similar prophet comes between him and the Mosaic Age; he is the first whose writings have survived, and he stands at the head of a succession of prophets.   His uncompromising words will find a parallel later when the still grander teaching of the Second Isaiah will insist afresh upon the omnipotence of a supreme and righteous God.   It need not be supposed that Amos was actually or directly influenced by Aryan or Iranian ideas of world-order, though he is well acquainted with the outside world; but, like his contemporary Hesiod, he stands out as a striking figure for his age.   The precise date of Zoroaster is disputed, but great movements are about to stir up the Medes, and bring about a new international age; and Amos would be the last person to say that he represented the conventional thought of his day (vii. 14).

The great events in Biblical history are not to be treated in isolation; and both the history and the religion gain in impressiveness when we pay heed to the ebb and flow of life and thought over the larger area of which Palestine was an organic part.   When we come down to the age of the Second Isaiah we are admittedly in the very midst of stirring vicissitudes, and the rise of the Persian empire is more or less contemporary with the unnamed prophet with his conceptions of Yahweh as a supreme, cosmic, righteous power.[2]   In that age of widespread awakening, it is

---

[1] See, on the events, R. S. Cripps, *Comment. on Amos* (1929), pp. 4, 36 f.

[2] Was the Second Isaiah familiar with Persian religion?   See Simcox, *Journ. of the American Oriental Society*, LVII (1937), pp. 158–171.   Literary parallels with Babylonian inscriptions have long been known, see Stummer, *Journ. of Bibl. Lit.*, XLV (1926), pp. 171 ff., and, more recently, Gadd, *Hist. and Monuments of Ur* (1929), p. 250.

particularly interesting to set, side by side, the strongly ethical note of Zoroastrianism and of Yahwism, together with their markedly different fortunes, and the rationalising, naturalistic thought of the Ionian philosophers.

If we look back at the Amarna Age we see in the ethical god Varuna the guarantor of cosmic order—nature and society; he is the upholder, not the personification. That the conception of this god with all his lofty attributes became so uninfluential is the supreme tragedy of India's religious history.[1] It was easy to sever this *personal* god from the conception of an impersonal *principle*; and while this meant a loss on the religious side, it facilitated the development of ideas of order in Nature, quite apart from religious, mystical or supernaturalistic considerations. Also in Zoroastrianism, where Ahura-Mazda replaced Varuna and the concept *asha* (*arta*) became more definitely ethical, it was possible to consider Man as apart from God and Nature, and we find what we may call the germs of psychology and ethics.[2] It is the passage from a more "undifferentiated" stage to a more "differentiated" one.

To revert to Varuna and the Hatti empire, with its centre at Boghaz-Keui (Pteria). While traces of the earlier culture have been suspected or detected to the east of the old empire, in the west Ionia claims attention for the possibility that links may be found between it and the conditions of the Amarna Age. Ionia presents an extremely intriguing problem. It naturally was vastly indebted to its "constant contact with the great powers of Asia and Egypt," and thus escaped "the narrow provincialism of the European Greeks." As the same writer observes, "the Ionian was generally

---

[1] Sidney Cave, *Redemption Hindu and Christian*, pp. 26 ff.; cf. J. Farquhar, *The Crown of Hinduism*, p. 71: "the group of noble conceptions with which he is connected is the one segment of Rig Vedic theology which is not carried forward and used in the great culmination of Indian thought."

[2] Plutarch translated *asha* by "truth" ('Αλήθεια), and Diodorus Siculus similarly identified the Egyptian *maat*. Ahura-Mazda has six ministers, the *Amesha Spentas*; they are attributes of God, ideals of human character, personified qualities; that is to say, instead of a supreme deity with his subordinates, there is a more psychological conception of human (and divine) qualities.

concerned either with the whole universe or with his own individual soul."[1] It is no exaggeration to say that "the scientific tendency is Ionian in origin";[2] and although something of the true scientific spirit may be seen earlier, e.g. in Egyptian medicine, it is to Ionia that we have to look for the beginning of the "scientific idea."[3]

Now, Ionia had a certain independence of its own, and its ability to resist Greek encroachment has been ascribed to its possession of a comparatively high culture which had survived the fall of the Hatti power.[4] In any case, "the intellectual and artistic output of the Asiatic Hellenes in the eighth and seventh centuries has so little contemporary counterpart in European Greece that typical European Humanism may justly be said to have originally been developed in the cities of Asia."[5] Definite links between Ionia and the old empire of Boghaz-Keui are, it is true, wanting; but enough remains to justify the belief that the brilliant spiritual activity of the Amarna Age had among its fruits in the Hittite realm the dawn of the scientific mind in Ionia and the love of scientific truth.[6]

Thus, the centuries from the Mosaic or Amarna Age to the Exilic Age present many features of intense interest. The powerful Hittite empire fell, and we look, and not in vain, for its political and cultural traces of the past. Egypt passed its zenith after the eighteenth dynasty, and Ikhnaton's reforming zeal represents the last of its creative impulses. The god Varuna loses his position, and is replaced in India

---

[1] P. N. Ure, C.A.H., IV, p. 121.

[2] F. M. Cornford, *From Religion to Philosophy : A Study in the Origins of Western Speculation* (1912), p. 143; in *C.A.H.*, IV, p. 538 f. he speaks of the Ionian cities as the heirs of the old Cretan civilisation.

[3] C. Singer, in *Science, Religion and Reality* (ed. Needham, 1925), p. 92; cf. W. B. Halliday, in *Universal History of the World* (ed. Hammerton), II, p. 1004. J. Burnet, *Greek Philosophy: Thales to Plato* (1920), p.4, observes: "rational science is the creation of the Greeks, and we know when it began. We do not count as philosophy anything anterior to that."

[4] Cf. Hogarth, *C.A.H.*, II, pp. 548 ff.; III, p. 502.

[5] *Op. cit.*, II, p. 550.

[6] Cf. for some details, Sir William Ramsay, *Asianic Elements in Greek Civilization* (1927); E. O. Forrer, in *Mélanges Cumont*, II (1936), pp. 710 ff.

by Indra (also known earlier in Palestine), and in Zoro-astrianism by Ahura-Mazda. Israel arose with other independent states towards the close of the eleventh century B.C., and we contrast the creative work of Israel and the fight for the distinctiveness of Yahweh with the fortunes of her neighbours. Yahweh became supreme over the other great deities of pre-Israelite Palestine; but there was a constant struggle, both to avoid confusing him with the Baals of the land, and to purify the beliefs and cults which threatened to sap the life-blood of Yahwism. The actual course of history and religion is obscure where light is most needed; but the Exilic Age stands out for the restatement of the reality of Israel's God and the new emphasis upon His "righteousness." But did this concept mean what it did of old?

The Egyptian concept of truth, order and right (*maat*), the old Indo-Iranian (*rita, arta,* later *asha*) and the Hebrew *sedek* (and other forms of the root) connote a large range of closely interlocked ideas, and have many analogies else-where. They involve the implicit or explicit consciousness of what is right, just, natural, and therefore of whatever deviates from it. In the study of the history of Religion we commonly pay more attention to animism, animatism, and the like, or to ideas of power, or spirit; but twenty years ago Rhys Davids made the very fertile suggestion that the concept of Norm, Standard or Right and its opposites is of fundamental value as a starting-point.[1] It will be evident that it takes us to what is normal, natural and true in life and in thought: it covers the true and the untrue, the normal, supernormal and abnormal—in other words, it involves our ideas of Righteousness and of Holiness (Chap. vii.). Un-fortunately his suggestion has not received that attention it deserved, although it is self-evident that it helps us to reconsider the interconnection between Science, Morality and Religion.

Now in the Amarna Age in Egypt, besides the prominence of the concept of *maat*, the art is naturalistic. It is also

[1] T. W. Rhys Davids, "Cosmic Law in Ancient Thought," *Proceedings of the British Academy*, VIII.

utterly unconventional, and the domestic life of Ikhnaton
"living in truth" is freely displayed.[1] Egyptian realism
started from *this* world of space-time; whereas characteristically Israelite is the reality of an imageless Yahweh
and of all that belongs to Yahweh. The numinous or
religious realism of the Hebrews—and indeed of most
primitive peoples—distinguishes Israelite thought from
that more familiar to us. It explains that earnestness,
grimness and fanaticism; it accounts for the co-existence of
heights and depths, and the strange paradoxes that puzzle
the Western mind when it turns to the ancient Semites.
There is an extreme subjectivity which, however, at its
best—and only then—produces the finest of treasures.[2]
Yahweh became the god of Israel, of the Universe, and of
universal order; he was the cause and mainstay of all that
whereby men live and flourish. Israel depended for her
entire welfare, financial included (Deut. xxviii. 12 f.), upon
her submission to Yahweh's will as set forth in the customary
beliefs and rites (e.g. Isa. i. 19). But what is here essentially
the responsibility of the people is elsewhere more intimately
part of the burden of the more outstanding individuals—
the prophets (as in Ezek.xxxiii. 1–9), the priests, and the
rulers or kings. This superior function of particular
individuals is well-known in early religions; it is the form
the ideas take in Israel that here concerns us.

Ideas of a chosen people, a priestly people, a people of
supreme importance for the world take a variety of
"spiritual" forms with which we are familiar. But at
earlier stages of thought these functions and privileges
have a more material, practical or realistic form; and there
are individuals freely believed to be of veritable cosmic
importance as givers of rain, crops, and the like. There is

[1] Breasted, *C.A.H.*, II, p. 120; Hall, *ibid.*, p. 412.

[2] Söderblom, *The Living God* (1933), p. 316, quotes from Wellhausen, one of the most gifted of Biblical scholars: Yahweh com-
municates his will through the prophet apart from whom there
can be no revelation, "it dwells in the human Ego, a synthesis of
apparent contradictions arises in consequence: the subjective in
the highest sense of the word, raised above all rules is the truly
objective, the divine."

much in the "spiritual" religion of the Hebrews or Israelites which represents a special ethical or spiritual form of what was once, to our modern ways of thinking, more crude or magical. The lofty ideas associated with Jerusalem, the old "city of righteousness," the centre of the world (Ezek. xxxviii. 12), the religious capital (Isa. ii. 2, 4), cannot be severed from the conviction that it was the abode of Yahweh (Jer. iii. 17), whose king sat on the god's throne (2 Chron. ix. 8).

The "magical" ideas of Brahmanism are well-known,[1] and the immense importance attached to the Temple of Jerusalem and its sacrificial rites admits of a reasonable explanation when we explain them, along the lines of primitive religion, as intended to maintain all those processes upon which mankind depends.[2] What the "righteous" through their "merits" are able to achieve, unites the highest religion with the crudest magic; and scattered *late* allusions to the real importance of the Temple cult afford an insight into the sort of beliefs that prevailed before the old religion was reformed.[3] Even the popular reputation of the modern Zaddikim, the strange "righteous" of Jewry, illustrates the tendency to expect from men who pursue the "right" way very tangible proofs of their miraculous powers. The decline from the "spiritual" ideas of Baal Shem, the founder, to the powers and functions ascribed to the "righteous" by the devotees is typical;[4] for when we go back to ancient Palestine, positive knowledge as a whole was at that stage where "naturalistic" ideas of the world were still elementary, and primitive

---

[1] G. F. Moore, *Hist. of Rel.*, I, pp. 265, 269; S. Dasgupta, *Hist. of Indian Philosophy*, I (1922), pp. 21f., 208; Eggeling, *Ency. Brit.*, 11th Ed., IV, p. 380 d.

[2] Cf. the *later* forms: Israel possesses the true knowledge of the true God; for Israel's sake the world was created and other nations, are as nought (2 Esdras vi. 55f; vii. 11), and through Israel the earth has rain; see Marmorstein, *Doctrine of Merits* (1920), pp. 71, 90, 128, 130; cf. Abelson, *Immanence of God* (1912), p. 298f.

[3] *O.T.R.*, p. 151f.

[4] G. F. Moore, *Hist. of Rel.*, II, pp. 98ff. (see Schechter, *Studies in Judaism*, pp. 20ff.); *Jewish Encyclopaedia*, "Hasidim." Israel is the centre of creation and the Zaddikim are the foundations of the world.

ideas prevailed as to what gods and men needed of one another, and how this relationship could be maintained.

The Jerusalem of which the Israelite Yahweh became the god had been in closest touch with Egypt;[1] and although the earlier great deities, the sun-god Shamash, and the rain- and storm-god Hadad (Addu) were superseded, an old solar cult still persisted.[2] The district itself was fitted to direct the trend of "numinous" imagination. The wealth and fertility of Jericho, the Dead Sea, and the wilds and the oases of eastern Judah combined to suggest a "garden of the Lord," to arouse the sense of living next door to doom, and to breed "an austere and fanatic temper."[3] Before gods were gods of human events they were associated more generally with cosmic events; and the sun and rain, life-giving, but also devastating in their effects, were enough to suggest extremes of good and evil, which were likely to be intensified in such an environment as that of Jerusalem. Job's question (ii. 10) could have been asked of a Palestinian nature-god no less than of a spiritual power supreme over Man and Nature (as in Ch. xxxviii. ff.).

Not only do men appeal to their gods for the means of life—or by their rites hope to have their needs satisfied— but precious things readily become the centre of religious beliefs and practices.[4] Hence it may be useful to recall the economic importance of salt. Salt and incense were valuable economic products, and it is perhaps a point of some interest that in Ezekiel's vision of the healing stream that issues from the Temple and sweetens the Dead Sea the local salt marshes are to be left untouched (xlvii. 17).[5]

[1] In the Amarna Age, the Pharaoh, who was regarded as a divine being, had set his name upon the city; cf. Yahweh in Deut. xii. 11.

[2] Cf. the horses of the sun, 2 Kings xxiii. 11; see Morgenstern, "the Gates of Righteousness" in *Heb. Union Coll. Annual*, VI (1930), pp. 1–37; and Hollis and other writers in *Myth and Ritual* (ed. Hooke, 1933).

[3] Sir G. A. Smith, *Hist. Geog. of the Holy Land*, pp. 266, 269f., 314, 316, 504; cf. also Breasted, *op. cit.*, pp. 416ff.

[4] Cf., e.g. the cults at the turquoise mines at Serabit el-Khadim where the "proto-Semitic" inscriptions were found.

[5] Cf. J. Herrmann (in his commentary) on the "nüchterner Realismus" of the prophet.

In Assyria salt was regarded as divine;[1] and when a Phoenician myth states that the use of salt was discovered by Suduk and Misōr, i.e. "righteousness" and "uprightness," the reference may be to the use of salt in covenant ceremonies. And salt too, like the old nature-deities, suggested ideas of preservation (Num. xviii. 19) and of destruction (Judges ix. 45).[2]

In any event, the old "city of righteousness" involved practical ideas such that the warning in the late passage, Zech. xiv. 17 (that those who do not go up to Jerusalem at the Feast of Tabernacles shall have no rain), is an interesting indication of the sort of beliefs that would have been more prevalent in pre-Reformation Yahwism. Babylonia affords many illuminating examples of the fusion of elevated ideas with "magical" beliefs, and the Palestine of pre-Exilic times was not what it became after the Reformation. The impression that the study of the history of Yahwism makes upon unprejudiced scholars is well exemplified in F. C. Burkitt's words:

> "The religious progress of Israel was not from a ritualistic to a 'spiritual' (i.e. an emotional) worship, but from a ritualistic worship that was magical and idolatrous in intention and mixed with practices that were heartless and immoral, to a ritualistic worship, not so very different in its outward form, which nevertheless was in intention the service of the One God, whose Name and Law denoted to the Jews everything that was holy and just and good."[3]

It is, however, very necessary to remember that in the old cults there were many conceptions that *in themselves* were good, and could later be re-embodied in higher forms; and that what strike us as "magical" are often the ideas that fuse Man and Nature in an undifferentiated manner, and ascribe to men an influence over Nature (or some aspect of it) either directly, or indirectly through the gods or

[1] Sidney Smith, *op. cit.*, p. 42.

[2] See *Rel. Sem.*, pp. 270 and 594 f.

[3] *A New Commentary*, Part I, p. 429.

spirits that control Nature.   If Israel was to be a "blessing"
to others, men living at an early stage of the development
of thought would not be without some extremely realistic
ideas of the way in which this would be shown.[1]

How shall one get life, full life?   One must live or act
in accordance with the nature of things, one must imitate
realistically the process, or the god or patron of the process;
and obviously even at the earliest stage of thought men
were quick to recognise whether things were as they should
be, and to learn how to make "right" what was "wrong."[2]
In all this we are really dealing with the stage where,
needless to say, there was no theory of knowledge!   There
are some earlier types of thought that elude us because they
have not our categories.[3]   They represent ways of thinking,
familiar to readers of Lévy-Bruhl's researches, that come to
the front again under a numinous or religious impulse; and
modern theories of knowledge are inadequate if they confine
themselves too much to the higher stages of thought and
fail to see the steps through which these have passed.   The
Hebrews were neither philosophers nor scientists; their
realism expressed itself in practical affairs and in their
lofty ideals of social right.   In the Exilic Age, at the
parting of the roads, the idea of right and order led more
decisively to the division between the Hebrew and the
Greek ways of thinking; and we are the heirs of the results.
The force of the historical evidence will be realised when
we add that nearly half a century ago Robertson Smith
could already perceive in the sweeping events, from the
Assyrian conquests onwards, changes that were about to

[1] See Pedersen, *Israel*, pp. 182 ff., on the conception which we tend
to interpret as solely "spiritual."

[2] One of the most interesting of Hebrew terms is *tūshiyyah*,
effective insight or knowledge; it is used of the state or action that
corresponds to the idea, and of the thought when it corresponds
with reality.   See both Davidson and Driver on Job v. 12; Pedersen,
Israel, p. 518.

[3] Cf. Cassirer, *Die Begriffsform im mythischen Denken* (1922),
p. 50 f.; Stauffer, *Grundbegriffe einer Morphologie des neutestament-
lichen Denkens* (1929); Lévy-Bruhl, *The "soul" of the Primitive* (1928),
Le surnaturel et la nature dans la mentalité primitive (1931), and his
other works.

sever the course of Hebrew thought from that of other lands.[1]

If it is surprising that we cannot trace the changes in Yahwism less imperfectly, we must remember that our sources have come through hands which have given them a colour such that the whole of the Old Testament seems to the ordinary reader to be *uno tenore*. Yet there are indications of a rationalising and sceptical trend; and the forthright question of Manoah's wife represents a spirit widely different from the usual impressive religious idealism and supernaturalism.[2] After the fall of Samaria in 721, men from Hamath and the North were settled in the land (2 Kings xvii. 24), and we have to take into account the presence of colonists from places less under the influence of the "Semitic" temperament, and also of men from the desert (above, p. 136). It is gradually being recognised that we cannot leave out of account the conditions north of Judah during the centuries when the history-writers of Kings and Chronicles ignore them, under the influence of the anti-Samaritan notion that the genuine Israelites— the Ten Tribes—had been carried away. The question has therefore arisen whether the new population of Samaria, who—in spite of the prejudice—were often regarded as Israelites, not only accepted the traditions of Israel (as the Samaritan woman in John iv. 12 had done), but possessed a religious literature. This has been answered in the affirmative, though differently.[3] A new pan-Israel was growing up, and since attention has been drawn to the "didactic" character of the popular narratives of the Old

---

[1] Cf. *Rel. Sem.*, pp. 35, 65, 77 ff., 358.   See below, p. 216.

[2] Can man see God and live?   Contrast Gideon in Judges vi. 23 with the woman in xiii. 23: if Yahweh had wished to kill us he would not have led us on as he has done—a verse that those who mistrust Biblical Criticism might bear in mind!   For another contrast, cf. the reasons for keeping the Sabbath, Deut. v. 15 and Exod. xx. 11.   See, on the "rationalistic" treatment of history, Ed. Meyer and B. Luther, *Die Israeliten und ihre Nachbarstämme* (1906), pp. 481 f., 484 f.

[3] See Kennett, *Old Test. Essays* (1928), p. 80 f.; *Church of Israel*, pp. 30 ff.; and A. C. Welch, *Deuteronomy* (1932), pp. 43, 79 f., 137, 139 f., 204 f.

Testament, it seems reasonable to associate this with the conditions after 721 B.C.[1] That is to say, they answer to the specific situations after the fall of Samaria, and the fall of Jerusalem in 586.

As a matter of fact, when we come down to the post-Exilic sources, we have writings of so distinctive a character that they have sometimes given the impression that what we here encounter is new and wholly Exilic or post-Exilic. It was an erroneous view; but it testifies to the differences between the post-Exilic and the earlier material.[2] Yet pre-Exilic Israel had its Temple, temple-singers and cultus; and the sounder view is that in the post-Exilic literature we have post-Exilic traditions and conditions, and also much that is earlier, though how much is a matter for careful enquiry. Much is undoubtedly early, but we must start from the present form of our sources. It is at least noteworthy that in the priestly writings we have many archaic, primitive ideas, and that in Chronicles—as against Kings—we have the old conception that the king sits on the throne of *Yahweh*.[3] The theism of post-Exilic prophecy, too, recalls the gods of old rather than the Yahweh of the didactic narratives. Finally, whereas the Book of Deuteronomy aims at the social righteousness of a people Israel, and is anti-Canaanite, the post-Exilic spirit is more universal, and in spite of its defects—from the point of view of the spirit of the prophets—it made Yahwism a social life in a way that Deuteronomy could not have done.

With this in mind it is helpful to look again at the Second Isaiah. The chapters fill the gap between (*a*) the stage of disintegration, indifference and despair: Yahweh had forsaken Jerusalem (Isa. xlix. 14), and (*b*) the subsequent career of post-Exilic Judaism. They point to a fresh start; we are not given novelties, but the restatement and reassertion of some old conceptions: God, Israel, a new Exodus, a new

---

[1] See *Mélanges Cumont*, II, pp. 546 ff; cf. above, p. 51.

[2] Cf. Bousset-Gressmann, *Die Religion des Judentums* (1926), pp. 469 ff.; Causse, *Les Dispersés d'Israel* (1929), p. 161.

[3] 1 Chron. xxix. 23 (contrast 1 Kings ii. 12, the throne of his *father*): 2 Chron. ix. 8 (but 1 Kings x. 9, the throne of *Israel*).

creation.[1] The regeneration of Israel does not spring from the social order, but from the cosmic; and God, Israel and the Universe are united. It is necessary to insist upon this point. The idea of God has not its roots in the social order but in the cosmic; it is the characteristic note of the great prophets that ideas of a cosmic process, a divine righteousness or world order, inspired their efforts. They were not led into an enquiry into the physical universe—that had to come later among the Greeks—but "they insisted that cosmic authority underlay their demands for social harmony, and looked upon social experience as part of a cosmic revelation."[2] We here lay our finger on the fatal flaw in all our present reforming and transforming schemes, and must go back and grasp the spirit of the Bible to discover the cause of their failure. Social reform depends upon the reality of God, the God of the Universe, Nature and Man—there can be no reconstruction that does not do justice to the religious needs and our knowledge of man and of his world: the religious view of the Universe and the scientific cannot long be held apart.

Scholars have often contrasted pre-Exilic and post-Exilic religion. They have contrasted the rich variety of the post-Exilic world with the pre-Exilic writings; and they have looked for an explanation. This chapter suggests that it is due, not merely to the Exile, or to the circumstances of the Persian empire, but to the circumstances of the entire period and the restricted character of our Biblical material. It is due, first, to the internal and external conditions during the great changes in and about the whole period, say, from 700 to 400 B.C.; and second, to the fact that the Biblical evidence represents only partial views of the history and of the thought of Palestine. A great deal of the old pre-Exilic literature has been lost. If we follow Hoonacker and other scholars, we should place Ezra's visit to Jerusalem after Nehemiah, and in the seventh year of Artaxerxes II, i.e. 397 B.C. That is to say, about one hundred and forty

---

[1] See Baudissin, *Kyrios*, III (1929), pp. 214, 232, 677; cf. *J.T.S.*, XXXII (1931), p. 242.

[2] Graham and May, *Culture and Conscience* (1936), p. 257.

years intervene between the first year of Cyrus and the return of Jewish exiles (538 B.C.) and Ezra's steps for the reorganisation of the Jewish Church. They were years of the profoundest significance for the development of Israel, yet how extremely slight is our knowledge of the events!

Palestine was not narrowly Hebraic or Israelite, and it would seem that from time to time powerful external influences forced the land to assert its spiritual independence. Even on archaeological grounds alone it can be urged that the land has a certain individuality of its own, in spite of its indebtedness to its neighbours.[1] We can imagine that a Jerusalem, even of the Amarna Age, would give its conception of "righteousness" a nuance different from that of the Egyptian *maat* or the Indo-Iranian *arta*. It was an ancient city, and Yahwism contained much more that was of Canaanite or Palestinian origin than has been suspected. But the Israelite and desert influences are naturally not to be overlooked.

Palestine was fed from the desert. If the desert peoples brought driving power and a *moral* enthusiasm, they have also a reputation for fanatical reforming zeal, and there are also curious traces of hostility towards them.[2] There are two main lines of tradition: the one goes back to pre-Mosaic, pre-Israelite times, the other dates the national religion from the Exodus and the invading Israelites.[3] The latter is exclusive and anti-Canaanite; although Josephus did not hesitate to say that the Temple was originally founded by a Canaanite chief called "Righteous King" (i.e. Melchizedek), the first to officiate as priest of God.[4] "The roots of the Christian religion," it has been rightly said, "will be found to lie more deeply in the Hebrew and Canaanite ideology than is commonly supposed by many

---

[1] See p. 63, n. 2.

[2] The Levites (Exod. xxxii. 27f.); Rechabites (2 Kings x. 15ff.; contrast Hos. i. 4); Simeon and Levi (Gen. xlix. 5f.), also Elijah at Horeb (1 Kings xix. 17), and the spirit of Deut. ii. 34; vii. 2, etc.; even Moses and Aaron did not "sanctify" Yahweh as they ought (Num. xx. 12); see p. 48.

[3] *O.T.R.*, pp. 57ff.

[4] *War*, VI. 10, 1 (§ 438).

who seek them elsewhere."[1]   It would, however, be very difficult to decide how far the deep-lying conflict between the various native, desert and other external influences can be traced.

The slow death of the Jewish State at the rise of Christianity was accompanied by many ominous signs, and it is difficult not to see in the widespread risings and in the massacres and counter-massacres, the consciousness among the Jews that the end was near, and that the Kingdom of Heaven, as they anticipated it and strove for it, was not to be introduced in *their* way.   This is the real tragedy of the Jews of the first century A.D., that the people who more than any other gave the world the permanent and pregnant ideas of Ethical Monotheism, who owed to its prophets the purer conceptions of God which have made the Old Testament of lasting value, were the victims of false ideas of the process of Divine Righteousness.[2]

Whatever the fairest estimate of ancient Palestine, we have only to look farther afield, to the Semites of Carthage. It was the stronghold of the old realistic eschatology and of millennarian ideas, grim, repellent, immensely efficient, but savage and superstitious from Greek and Roman standpoints.[3]   So Carthage fell, leaving scarcely a trace; while in Palestine, Christianity was the swan-song of a land which was destined to have the last traces of her age-long culture washed away, and the way left open for a new monotheism.

Islam, in spite of its late appearance in world-history, was a reversion to type in its tribal and national spirit;[4] and just as Arabic enables us to understand what is genuinely

[1] Graham and May, *op. cit.*, p. 312.

[2] "The responsibility for the disastrous war which ruined the Jewish nation lay in the dangerous doctrine of the intervention of God who would deliver his people from the sacrilegious foreigner. By keeping the masses in a feverish state of expectancy, that doctrine made pacification impossible.   Worst of all, it lent itself to abuse by all sorts of cranks and rascals"; V. M. Scramuzza on the Roman policy towards Judaism, in *The Beginnings of Christianity* (ed. Jackson and Lake, 1933), V, p. 287.

[3] See Christopher Dawson, *Enquiries into Religion and Culture* (1933), p. 234; M. P. Charlesworth, *C.A.H.*, VIII (1930), pp. 491 ff.

[4] See Baudissin, *Kyrios*, III, p. 691 f.

"Semitic" in the Semitic languages, so the clan or tribal
spirit may suggest where we should look for the genuine
Semitic *psyche*. One finds among the Semites a virility
and intensity, and an efficiency which is far from being
necessarily directed along "good" lines; nor is it necessarily
patient. The antithesis "Hebraism *versus* Hellenism" is
too easy, although it contains a great deal of truth. We
must agree with the writer who has said that "the doctrine
of the living God is so strongly asserted [in the Old Testa-
ment] that it is far in advance of the faith of the Christian
Church at the present day, which has been misled by
scholastic dogmaticians into abstract conceptions of God."[1]
And again, when another points out that Luther de-
hellenised the mediaeval synthesis which was an amalgam
of Hebrew and Greek thought, we must agree that the old
problem of the relation between religious experience and
the intellect is the clamant one of the day.[2] Christians and
non-Christians can hardly avoid approaching it from
different angles.

Allowance must obviously be made for the fundamental
difference among thinkers when men have grown up *in*—
or perhaps *away from*—in the one case, the specifically
Jewish religious conceptions of God, the Torah and a
chosen Israel, and in the other, the specifically Christian
conception of the Son of God. The debt to Hebrews,
Israelites or Jews has not ceased with the Bible. But it has
been said that the Jews who have contributed most, not to
Judaism itself, but to the general progress of the world's
thought, have been those who renounced their religion,
were expelled, or were not orthodox members of their
community.[3] This in itself is of no little interest. Also,
the survey of the evidence collected by a loyal member[4]

[1] C. A. Briggs, *General Introduction to the Study of Holy Scripture*
(1899), p. 646.

[2] G. S. Hendry, *God the Creator* (1937), cf. Edwyn Bevan in *The
Legacy of Israel* (1927), p. 42.

[3] J. Feibleman, *Christianity, Communism and the Ideal Society*
(1937), pp. 407ff.: he names Spinoza, Marx, Freud, Einstein,
Michelson and others.

[4] Leon Roth, in *The Legacy of Israel*, pp. 433ff.

M

does suggest—rightly or wrongly—that the God of Righteousness, the Supreme Reality in the Universe, has become more
of a purely immanent God than the transcendent One whom
the prophets of Israel proclaimed when they reformed an old
religion which would otherwise have died out. And this,
too, if well-founded, is significant.

These pages have brought us to a series of fundamental
questions.[1] The Exilic Age was marked by the new monotheism of Israel and her consciousness of mission; the
centuries that followed led up to Rabbinical Judaism and
Christianity; and a land that proved to be a dying one
witnessed the fall of Jerusalem, the death of the Jewish
State and the dawn of a new religion. When, accordingly,
one considers the vicissitudes carefully, taking into account
St. Paul's chapters on the election and fate of the old
Israel and the election of the new Israel (Rom. ix.–xi.), we
should ask ourselves how we are to regard the historical
process as a whole.

Both religions left the land of their origin and, in spite of
missionary enterprise in Asia, they moved from the eastern
part of the Roman empire, ultimately to flourish in the
West rather than in the East.[2] Is this fortuitous? Palestine itself, as has been seen, was never isolated; it was no
purely "Hebraic" or "Semitic" land. It lay as a "bridge"
between Africa and Asia; it belonged to the Levant and the
Mediterranean rather than to Asia; and there is no doubt
that geographical and physical factors "fitted" the little land
to play the part it did in world history and religion. It is
necessary to bear in mind the diversity of physical conditions
as regards Palestine, Greece, Egypt and Babylonia, Persia
and India, for this diversity undoubtedly goes far to explain
the diversity of history. But it is also very instructive to
observe—so far as the evidence allows—the diversity of
cultural development before and after the Exilic Age in

---

[1] The argument in Chap. vii is here resumed.

[2] Inge remarks that Christianity has been "the most European
and the least Asiatic of religions," in *Science, Religion and Reality*
(ed. Needham, 1925), p. 387.

general in each of these lands, and to take note of the varying phenomena of stagnation, decay and different sorts of continuity. In this way we are struck by the differences between the rise and development of religion in and behind the Bible and the vicissitudes elsewhere.[1]

Now if we say that Palestine was "destined" to give the world the Bible, we no sooner speak of destiny, election, selection and the like than we must ask whether, in true Biblical fashion, we are fusing together consequences and purposes.[2] The present age tends to suspect any claim to mission and consciousness of destiny, or at least would treat it as a purely "natural" phenomenon, psychologically intelligible; and if we were to ask—especially in view of St. Paul's chapters—whether the historical process in the Bible is "natural" or "divine," our fundamental difficulty would be that what we might call "divine" or "supernatural" might also be perfectly "natural," in that to Israel all that the God of the Universe did was "natural."

The whole historical process that gave us the Bible is on no small scale. Besides the "natural" geographical and physical factors in the history, what shall be said of the biological and racial? The influence of the Arab of the desert can never be ignored. It is easy for us, according to our predilection, to speak of "Jewishness," or of "Aryan," "Nordic," or "Anglo-Saxon" racial qualities; but when all has been said it is probable that "true" membership is determined by cultural criteria. In other words, "they are not all Israel which are of Israel" (Rom. ix. 6, cf. ii. 28f.); although there are the periods when the criterion is regional or blood relationship, or both.[3]

Everywhere are to be found temperamental differences and differences of reaction to one and the same environment. But environmental conditions—which are everywhere and

[1] There is a very striking difference even between the development of "Biblical" religion and that of Palestine itself (see p. 68).

[2] Cf. *O.T.R.*, p. 108f.

[3] Perhaps nowhere has purity of race been more keenly maintained *as an ideal* than among the Arabs and Jews, as their genealogical zeal testifies. But the ancient genealogies require careful scrutiny.

always variable—are not everything; and there are individuals who are by no means representative of any one period, place, race or culture, because they go behind the accidents of their day. Great writers have this universal appeal. In Christianity the "Son of Man" is "*the* Man," *par excellence*. But besides the outstanding names in history there are the many less conspicuous souls, each in his or her own way manifesting something of the "substance" of humanity and not its relatively fleeting "accidents." And as such they are creators of their private environment, and not the victims of the particular environment in which they are born.

We are powerfully impressed by the historical fitness of the appearance of the *outstanding* figures: the Second Isaiah, Jesus, Paul, Buddha, Mohammed. . . . "At the fullness of time" the Age has produced the Man (Gal. iv. 4, Eph. i. 10, Heb. i. 2); and while Christian thought sees therein the hand of God, we must not—in all fairness—overlook the conception of the Avatar, the god in the Bhagavad-Gita who issues forth when "religion is in danger and iniquity triumphs," or the Buddha who declares himself when the world is in travail, or the reformer of the Moslem faith who is to appear periodically.[1] Nor is the fundamental conviction solely a "religious" one. There are repeatedly the special occasions when at the psychologically appropriate moment the right man is found. And if we were to take a wide view we should range from the conspicuous occasions when we tend to descry some purposeful or meaningful process— whether "divine" or "natural"—to the far more ordinary occasions which scarcely attract our attention. Nor can we refuse to regard it as, in itself, a "neutral" process, seeing that it would be very easy to find in some religious sect, party or movement which we repudiated the figures who in their own circles were regarded as saviours, founders, leaders and guides. It is a collective process, and not a conglomeration of chance events, that we have constantly to recognise, and if we seem to aggravate our problem unnecessarily by

---

[1] With the "Buddha" foretold by the dying Gautama, cf. the promises of a successor (or successors) to Moses (Deut. xviii.15), and the Paraclete (John xiv. 16).

casting our net so far afield, to take too narrow a view is to obscure it.

Whatever the future may have in store it is certain, on all analogy, that among the manifold sequels some will seem more "natural," others more "predestined." Behind the outstanding names will be the innumerable "unknown soldiers" (cf. p. 221). The changes are not likely to be less striking than those we find round about the Exilic Age—and they were among the most sweeping of which we have knowledge. Moreover, on all analogy, there will be the "natural" diverse effects of the various temperamental, environmental, racial and geographical differences among men. All this seems self-evident. This being so, the present tendencies towards collectivism, internationalism and universalism are "naturally" confronted by the more separatist, exclusivist and nationalist trends. The former will—one may hope—succeed in establishing a convergence of fundamental principles, the common recognition of unifying ideas; but there is no reason whatever to presume that mankind, as at present constituted, will ever form a single cultural species or genus, with a single religion. It would be generally agreed that our aim should be to give the individual opportunity for self-realisation and self-expression, not inimical to the progress of the social group of which he wished to be accounted a worthy member. No political, ecclesiastical or other suppression endures for long; and continued cultural "in-breeding" proves sterile. But meanwhile this age well illustrates the way in which human society moves between the two extremes of those who clearly need and demand leadership and those who impose their own system upon others from above.

When there are "worthless shepherds" (Zech. xi. 17) and "blind leaders of the blind" (Matt. xv. 14) one can the better appreciate the social significance of the conception of the "New Covenant" of the Exilic Age. To quote A. S. Peake, it "implies an inner principle which can deal with each case of conscience sympathetically as it arises, and can ensure the fulfilment of its behests, because it has brought the inner life into perfect harmony with itself. The heart, and thus the whole life, has the engraving of the law upon it, itself become new. The heart embraces not only the emotional and ethical but also the intellectual life. And thus, by being transformed from a foreign ruler into a native and inward impulse, the law gains the power of self-fulfilment."[1] Thus it is not purely "immanent": for if it were, each man soon becomes his own judge; nor is it purely "transcendent," for then it would not be his own. But the New Covenant is both immanent and transcendent; and as the characteristic conception, both of the troubled Exilic Age and of the Age of Christianity, it has everything to suggest to those who reflect upon this age.[2] For the conception is not merely moral or ethical: the unifying principle is theistic, and the members of the new group are united by the relation between them and their God.

At periods of extreme change and disintegration there are diverse groupings, loyalties and unifying tendencies: no absolute chaos, but diverse redintegrations of mutilated organisms, so to speak. *Esprit de corps*, or corporate spirit, is indispensable for any social body or system, whatever we may happen to think of its worth and chances of continuance. Nowhere do we actually find absolute social disintegration; and in spite of great cataclysms we commonly find some sort of continuity somewhere beneath the discontinuity. The disintegration and redintegration of the old Israel in the Exilic Age are as impressive as the different sorts of continuity in Palestine a few centuries later. Indeed, the comparative study of religions everywhere reveals so many resemblances *and* differences that it is useful to ask, not only why men differ or why systems disintegrate, but rather why the process has gone no farther. What are the checks, what gives a certain unity, solidarity and perdurance, however slight? There is a certain stability of types, forms, or configurations *as such*; though their qualitative differences make

---

[1] See his commentaries on Jer. xxxi. 33f, and Heb. viii. 6ff.

[2] Cf. 2 Cor. iii. 6: Rom. x. 4f. The practical problems of adjusting the religion of the individual and that of the social group arose both in the Exilic Age and at the rise of Christianity; for the former, see pp. 218ff., and for the latter, see commentaries on Rom. vii. and especially xiv. 1–xv. 13 (the "weak" and the "strong").

all the difference in the world. But there are varying patterns, and as we pass from one system (or system of systems) to another, one is led to ask what is the protective framework or environment which seems to maintain coherence throughout.   The chequered history of an individual, a people, a land, and even a body of thought, presents the same sort of problem.[1]

Long before men could look at things in a truly impersonal, curious, naturalistic or scientific manner, they had not failed to observe the regularity and permanence of some aspects of their world and the utter impermanence, changeableness and unreliability of other aspects.   It would be interesting to compare and contrast the impressions made upon early man by the coexistence of change and continuity, the continuous flux of all things, and the persistence of what seemed to them the more important.   Men came to feel that there were supernatural powers to be imitated, impersonal principles to which to adhere; and whereas *we* tend to start our enquiries from the world "outside" us, *they* relied essentially upon their knowledge of a world of which they felt they were part.

The Biblical view of the problem of change is of preeminent value because of its opposition to the belief in numerous gods, spirits and demons.   These have always afforded a much too facile explanation of life's haps and chances.   But the ideal of Ethical Monotheism—the One Universal God of a people united by ethical principles—like Occam's famous razor, avoided the multiplication of entities. It opened the way to—or rather, it compelled—unifying conceptions of process; and although it certainly aggravated the problems of life (see p. 112), a consistent Ethical Monotheism can alone co-ordinate our ideas of God, Man and the Universe.

The perplexing problem of Israel's changing fortunes sorely exercised the religious thinkers.   The old Israel was convinced that she had been "chosen" from the first; the disasters of the Exilic Age were due to her own faults, and were followed by a re-endorsement of the "choice"; then,

[1] See further, on this, pp. 265f., 311.

finally, Christianity arose on the ruins of the Jewish State.
Here was a tremendous tragedy which the student of Biblical
history finds far from of merely antiquarian interest.   Look
at the event through the eyes of contemporaries, while
noting the slightness of the information in Christian or
Jewish sources.   Earliest vicissitudes had been explained by
the recognition of an absolute Divine Righteousness, or
Rightness; but was God still righteous?   Even at the final
catastrophe the heart-broken author of 2 Esdras could feel
that God did not love Israel less than he himself did.[1]   A new
"Israel of God" was now claiming supremacy, and was
justifying itself by Israel's own sacred writings.   Yet, if the
old Israel had suffered grievously, might not the new?   The
old Israel had been warned that her relationship with
Yahweh was no "natural" or "immanent" one.   Yahweh
had chosen her and sustained her; but the very intimate
relationship—marital or filial[2]—did not remove the gulf
between Israel and the Divine Holiness.   Yahweh was
both immanent and transcendent: were he merely
the former there would be no gulf; were he merely
the latter, then indeed he could do neither good nor evil
(Zeph. i. 12).

St. Paul, one of the most loyal of the sons of Israel, with
much more insight than many of his followers, had as
sincere a grief for this old Israel as a Hosea before him
(Rom. ix. 3).   He must combine God's perfect freedom and
absolute righteousness with his conviction of the transition
from the old Israel to the "Israel of God."   If God were an
arbitrary being—like some Oriental potentate—what confidence could men have in Him?   But because He was and
always had been righteous, the new relationship was as
conditional as the old.   A righteous God who had chosen a
new Israel could, if necessary, repudiate it (Rom. xi. 17ff.).
So, nations are raised up or cast down, peoples are re-made or
unmade: there is an inexorable law or rightness.   God was
"true" to His nature (2 Tim. ii. 13); Man must be true to *his*,

---

[1] p. 113; cf. *O.T.R.*, pp. 177, 214.   Note the beautiful idea of
God as lover of souls, in Wisdom xi. 26, xii. 1 (see Goodrick's note).

[2] *O.T.R.*, pp. 120ff.

and the righteousness of God and that of Man are interrelated.   Where a non-religious treatment of the Biblical
history will find a confluence of causes and a multitude of
"natural" factors and explanations, on the theistic plane
God's righteousness no less means *His* naturalness.

We speak of the "choice" of Israel, of "election," or
better of "selection": God would use a prophet, a people, or a
people's foe; but the whole idea of "rightousness" implies
that, although God has absolute sovereignty and freedom
and makes His "selection," it is the quality of the "righteousness" of the man that makes the essential difference between
the good vessels and the bad (2 Tim. ii. 20ff.).   The potter
chooses good clay, but man is free and is responsible for his
intractability.   Thus, the theistic interpretation of history
is immensely far-reaching and combines the entire responsibility of the individual with his utter fraility.   For everything there is a rightness or reason, which a man can acknowledge—and by acknowledging it he puts himself in touch
with the universal Righteousness.[1]

We readily admit the debt that is owed to nations and
men of great endowment and opportunity; and rightly we
agree that for all great gifts an account of the trusteeship will
be required.   But democratic tendencies object to such
privileged recipients, and the individualism of the Exilic Age
and the insistence of Christianity upon the worth of every
individual bring the more vital question whether Divine
choice, election or selection is restricted solely (*a*) to the
outstanding, and (*b*) to the self-conscious.[2]   On the religious
plane the men whom God selects are trustees; even the men
of slight endowments—and who will confess he has none?—
must render account; every man is responsible to his

---

[1] The Jews suffered from Rome, but according to a Rabbinic
opinion Rome must have had merits which enabled it to be a world-
wide empire (Marmorstein, *The Doctrine of Merits in Old Rabb.
Literature* [1920], p. 19).

[2] The growth of the Pentateuch was roughly contemporary with
the vicissitudes of the Exilic Age (see pp. 1?, 236f.), and the highly
composite story of Korah's revolt (Num. xvi.) illustrates certain
phases of the opposition to men who—it was complained—took too
much upon themselves.

Creator (p. 118f.). So, while modern Humanism proclaims a man the master of his fate and the captain of his soul, Religion intensifies this, replacing an untutored self-sufficiency (αὐτάρκεια) by one that has the source of its strength in the Divine Relationship (Phil. iv. 13), replacing by a truer self that fatal weakness and dissatisfaction with self which most men feel in their solitariness.[1]

The course of Biblical religion, notably at the great epochs, does not point to an ever-developing God but to the development of convictions of the relationship between a Yahweh and his Israel, that is, between God and Man. The "spirit" of the pre-prophetic, pre-Exilic Israel, over-confident in its relationship, was in a very different "body" from the post-Exilic; and as we reach the new Israel and the "Body of Christ" we are impelled to the recognition that, although the relationship is "constant," the "spirit" and the "body" can develop together.

What can be said to develop or evolve is a relationship, a field, a nucleus with its environment; so that, although in Religion we may feel convinced that there is some relationship between God and the "body" as yet unconscious of it (p. 127, n. 1), we are led to infer that the character of the relationship between Man and the Divine Spirit depends on the degree to which the "righteousness" of a man is in harmony with the Divine Righteousness. A man, in so far as he is ethically or spiritually "right," is in harmony with a higher principle of "right." Because God is true to His nature Man must be true to his highest self; and when it was said of old that God "hardens" men's hearts modern psychology would speak of the "natural" consequences of a defective moral constitution. The "human" and the "divine" interpenetrate, and the account of the birth of Christianity should warn one that through some failure of "rightness," some defect, some inability to aim at a higher standard

---

[1] Few are the Stoics. The sturdy Stoicism and ethical integrity of the Victorian age have been followed by post-war disillusion and self-centredness—and the discovery of the emptiness of that self!

(Rom. x. 3), the thread of history, of individuals or of a people, may be broken.[1]

No one saw as clearly as did St. Paul that he was witnessing a tragedy: it was no time for vain-glorying.   Among his co-religionists there was religious zeal but no insight (Rom. x. 2), and in a sense they were the victims of their religion (xi. 9). That was the tragedy, and it is entirely intelligible when we observe the spread of religious fanaticism and the collapse of morale in the centre of a decaying Judaism.   The more, therefore, must one admire the sure faith and the un-quenchable courage of the Jews who refounded Judaism afresh, and who—whatever one thinks of St. Paul's vision of future possibilities—are confident that they have something to contribute.   It is not easy, perhaps, to look back at the first century A.D. in a detached historical manner, but no one who reflects upon all the changes that have brought us to-day will be so heedless as to judge harshly of the past.   The past, the present and the future are parts of one and the same process; and whether we regard it as "natural," in the narrower sense, or regard the Divine Process as "natural" in the more comprehensive sense, these old ideas of Right, True, Natural and the like are fundamental.

To bring these remarks to a close.   In the Amarna and Exilic Ages the consciousness of Right, Order and Law, found different expression among men and peoples of different types.   Israel's ethical monotheism had its implications for science and philosophy; but they were not   and could not be —pursued (p. 151).   In a world of widespread changes it was perhaps the impact of diverse modes of life and thought that made Israel play her unique part.   The Second Isaiah was possibly of Babylon, Jesus was of Nazareth of Galilee, and Paul was of Tarsus.   Amos knew of a wide world, and it may be added that Mohammed as a caravan-conductor had no

---

[1] As to the term "hypocrites" applied to the Pharisees, Dr. Lukyn Williams has suggested that it means *poseurs*, or better, play-actors, men satisfied with the mask rather than the reality; *Talmudic Judaism and Christianity* (1933), pp. 67–78, see esp. p. 74. Certainly, at every significant reforming movement the leaders go beneath the accepted beliefs of the age.

narrow outlook.[1] In no instance have we untutored Arabs of the desert, but men who by their very contact with the variety of life had a vision not granted to more cloistered or remote minds. None is of Jerusalem, yet—with the obvious exception of Mohammed—the universalising ideas are seen through rather local and national spectacles, and the old pre-Israelite or Canaanite "city of righteousness," where Yahweh once had his throne, holds the stage and inspires the imagery. By transferring the earthly Jerusalem to the skies the Christians gave a wholly spiritual significance to what was becoming a grossly degraded city; and we can well believe that those who cherished the old dreams of a glorious Zion, as in the post-Exilic visions, were sorely embittered as their own religious hopes were taken over by their rivals. As we pass from Judaism to Judaistic Christianity and thence to "Gentile" Christianity, we cannot fail to realise how little—fortunately—has been preserved of the impassioned propaganda that the successive steps must have called forth.[2]

In the envenomed passions and cruel strifes of contemporary Jewish life, as set forth by Josephus, there was little "corporate spirit"; and although Jews have very rightly drawn attention to much that was admirable in Pharisaism— more than it has been credited with during nineteen centuries—the old Judaism as an organism was fatally mutilated. For a new corporate spirit we must turn to the new "body of Christ." This was no "fashioning" but a "transforming" or metamorphosis (Rom. xii. 2). Christ is moreover, "not only the creator of all that is, but also the continuous immanent principle of order in the Universe."[3] With God as the Father, and all followers of Christ as "sons of God" (Rom. viii. 14; Gal. iii. 26), the new religion gave

---

[1] Cf. also what is said of Moses at Pharaoh's court (Acts vii. 22).

[2] As regards the question whether the new religion was to remain a sect or become a world religion, E. G. Browne, *Materials for the Study of the Babi Religion* (1918, p. xxi), remarks that the problem also confronted Bahā-ullah. He cites elsewhere, as from Renan, the advice that to understand the genesis and growth of a new religion one must go to the East where religions still grow (p. xxiii).

[3] Gore, *The Reconstruction of Belief* (ed. of 1926), p. 378, cf. p. 389.

new expression to the joint immanence and transcendence of God which the old Israel—at its best—had sought to maintain. God, Man and the Universe are united again in a new manner; and as we look back upon pre-Exilic Israel, the Second Isaiah and the post-Exilic Israel, we cannot ignore the utter difference between the new cosmic, spiritual and ethical ideas of incipient Christianity and the dying land in which it arose.

The Christian Body, the "Body of Christ," is a conception that could have risen only in Israel. With its "corporate spirit," and its ideas of group unity, and the extension of the group, it links itself on to all that went before. The group idea, as such, is not at all specifically Palestinian or even Oriental,[1] although some of the best illustrative material— as Robertson Smith so brilliantly showed—is to be drawn from the relatively simpler conditions of Arabia.[2] That the desert was an actual factor in the history of religion in Palestine is highly probable in the Exilic Age, when the culture of the land had been sternly condemned by the prophets (p. 146). Moreover, when the "iniquity of the Amorite" was full (Gen. xv. 16, cf. Deut. ix. 4 f.) the invading Israelites are said to come from the desert, prepared to destroy the natives and their abominations (Deut. vii. 1–6; note Ps. cvi. 34). Also in the time of Elijah, at the close of the condemned dynasty of Omri, the desert is an important factor.[3] On the other hand, the desert peoples are by no means necessarily a reforming or purifying influence. The desert, it has been said, stimulates the nerves but starves the mind; and when Sir George Adam Smith speaks of Arabia as "fertile mother but poor nurse of men,"[4] there is indeed a certain fertility, subtlety and alertness, but the "nurse" has notably been Persia or Greece (pp. 138 ff.) and the influence

---

[1] See *O.T.R.*, p. 115.

[2] Alt, *Der Gott der Väter* (1929), has interesting illustrations from Nabataean, Palmyrene and Greek inscriptions of the early Christian period of gods of a tribe, of a family, or of a leading individual. (Alt is dealing with the Old Testament allusions to the God of the patriarchs.)

[3] See *C.A.H.*, III, 367 ff.

[4] *Schweich Lectures*, on "The Early Poetry of Israel" (1912), p. 29.

of the Old Testament upon the Koran should not be over-looked.[1] In point of fact, the Arab of the desert is not particularly religious, and although the desert brings a man face to face with himself, not every man who goes thither is an Elijah (1 Kings xix) or a St. Paul (Gal. i. 17).

There are peoples who, on geographical and physical grounds, living as they are in the desert, or remote from the conventional and accustomed lines of life and thought, are thrown back upon themselves. And likewise there are times when, in lands of old-established culture, the old ways and modes collapse and, through the disintegration of the individual "atoms," there is a release of energy and the opportunity for new patterns and types. But those who are thus thrown "out of" themselves or "back" upon themselves do not by any means necessarily find a deeper, worthier and more fundamental self. The possession of an inherited tradition, a content, means more than "bare experience": it is the coherence that gives sanity to the individual and makes him a *socius*. The examples of "numinous" experience—all doubtless subjectively impressive—range from the sublime to the silly, from the fertilising to the futile and fatuous, so that the conceptions of the Holy and of the Righteous are most effective when they are complementary (pp. 109, 131). There can be no hasty appreciation of the "spiritual" *as such* (1 John, iv. 1), "by their fruits ye shall know them" (Matt. vii. 16).

There can be no gainsaying of the broad ascertained facts of history, and this age has everything to gain from a critical study of the epochal periods deeper than has here been out-lined. Why was the reformed Yahwism of the Exilic Age subsequently followed, not by a re-fashioning, but by the new Christian organism? From time to time there are great periods, individual or national continuity is jarred or broken, old patterns or configurations give way to new ones; but the ideas of reality are not solely of the physical universe,

---

[1] Islam did not arise in an area with a lengthy cultural history behind it as did Yahwism or Christianity. The last of the old Minaean–Sabaean culture—intimately related to that of the rest of the old Near East—had disappeared; the Age of Ignorance, the *Jāhiliyya*, intervened (*c.* 500–622 A.D.).

or of humanity, or of a supreme Personal Being, rather are the three found to have a new interconnection.

Hence one must not treat the Bible in any partial or one-sided manner. It is, we repeat, not precisely "Hebraic" or "Semitic," and we may not take our stand upon any one particular conception to the exclusion of the rest. Any tendency to emphasise the idea of Immanence alone or of Transcendence alone is equally misleading; for it is only through the relationship with God, which He grants, that men have gained their vivid consciousness of the reality of Divine Grace, and that He is "outside" the universe of our natural sciences. The awareness—the "knowledge by acquaintance"—of a God whose thoughts are wholly other than man's, leaves a gulf between the religious experience to which this conviction is due and the intellect with its description of the total world in which a man finds himself. But this does not open the door to obscurantism. God has His "Israels"; and if we believe, not merely that there is this relationship, but that He can choose, elect or select men in proportion as they are at a stage to respond, we may further believe that the nobler the embodiment the nobler the spirit: men are actually or potentially temples of the Living God (1 Cor. iii. 16f., vi. 19, 2 Cor. vi. 16). The Righteousness of God means an Eternal Right, Truth or Justice that would condemn Man were there not also an Eternal Grace[1]; and in so far as this is "natural," due to the Divine "Nature," so too the "choice" is not arbitrary but, as it were, "Natural Selection" on the theistic plane.

---

[1] "Though justice be thy plea, consider this—that in the course of justice none of us should see salvation."

CHAPTER IX

Ethical Monotheism in the Light of Comparative Religion[1]

To the immense amount of work that has been done in the Comparative Study of Religions from historical, psychological and other points of view it is unnecessary to refer. It is the study of what men have felt to be most real, most true; it is deep-reaching, and apt to cause impatience, pain or indignation. It cannot be too emphatically stated that the eminently readable and delightful collections of miscellaneous beliefs and practices sooner or later lead to the investigation of more intricate questions of a technical character (e.g. tabus, marriage-customs, social divisions), and that in due course we reach what might be called, not Comparative Religion, but "Comparative Theology,"[2] and the most delicate problems of Religion are involved.

It is impossible to approach the subject without some bias or preconception. This, however, can be tested and corrected as one proceeds; and it is a useful principle to set before oneself the "Golden Rule" of all criticism, namely, to treat the beliefs of others as we would that they should treat our own. No doubt it is diffcult to maintain such an attitude, more especially when one is dealing with beliefs and customs which are remote from current modes of thought. But the present conditions in the world of Religion justify a candid treatment, and it may surely be urged that Religion has been so potent for good and for evil in the past that a study of its salient features should be as thorough-going as one can make it, and that one should be ready to follow the road to which the evidence points.

[1] This chapter in its original form was a lecture to the West London Synagogue Association in February, 1932, and was subsequently expanded and published (by the Association). It is here further revised and expanded.

[2] A useful book under this title was published by J. A. Macculloch (1902).

It is often felt that Christianity is, or at least seems to be, embarrassed by Comparative Religion. There are what are often called "Pagan Christs," and it is now freely recognised that "Glimpses of a Saviour"[1] can be found in many parts of the world. Of this type of belief there are many varieties, and it appeals to many different types of mind, East and West. We are told that the Indian will say to the Christian: "your Christ whom we call Krishna," and *vice versa*; and in China a perfectly literal Buddhist adaptation of a very well-known Christian hymn has been heard[2]: The man Gautama, the human Buddha, was deified; and in eastern religions there are theological problems which, *mutatis mutandis*, are so closely parallel to those in Christianity that they raise the profoundest questions of the psychology of Religion, and the Spiritual Reality that lies behind.[3] But although this and other evidence that has been collected might appear to deprive Christianity of its originality and its uniqueness, the Christian will feel that beneath the formal parallels are essential differences; even as the Jew is conscious of a qualitative difference when Comparative Religion proceeds to compare and co-ordinate the beliefs of Judaism, Islam, Brahmanism, and other forms of theism.[4]

---

[1] The title of the ninth chapter of Macculloch's book; cf. also W. St. Clair Tisdall, *Christianity and other Faiths* (1912), Chapter XI.

[2]
> "Buddha loves me, this I know,
> For the Sutras tell me so,
> Little ones to him belong,
> They are weak, but he is strong."

Cited by Professor Soothill in *The Modern Churchman*, XII (1922), 390. He remarks that Neo-Buddhism has adopted Christian prayers, etc., and that the subject demands sympathetic study.

[3] Vishnuism in the thirteenth century had its synergists and its Augustinians or Calvinists. The issue was whether man was saved like the baby monkey which clings to its mother when she rescues it (the "monkey doctrine"), or has no more part in his own salvation than the kitten which is seized by its mother and carried out of danger (the "cat-hold theory"); see G. F. Moore, *History of Religions*, I (1914), 337.

[4] So also in early Palestine the syncretistic tendencies which would equate the God of Israel with Marduk of Babylonia, Khnum of Egypt, or the Greek Zeus would cause searching of heart. See *O.T.R.*, pp. 156 ff.

N

The chief points which are to be made may be conveniently grouped under twelve heads. They turn upon the importance of reconsidering the full significance of Ethical Monotheism, and it will be useful to start with some introductory observations upon the interconnection of the Old Testament and the New.

I

From time to time the religious value of the Old Testament comes up for adverse criticism; but hitherto, at least, there has been a characteristic English or British tendency, not merely to uphold an undivided Bible, but to lay special stress upon the Old Testament.[1] In times of wrong and injustice we turn to the Hebrew conception of righteousness. In times of war, disaster and revolution, the prophets and psalmists inspire us. In times of grave stress, and perplexity, we may feel with the writer of Isaiah lxiii. 19, that we have become as those over whom God's Name had not been called. We talk freely of the "Divine Discipline of Israel," but we may have to learn that the Western world must ask itself what this means for it: certainly, for the problem of sin and suffering the Old Testament is indispensable if we would understand the treatment of it in the New. And finally, if a Church is tempted to dwell too proudly upon the absolute superiority of its religion, a Hebrew prophet (Amos iii. 2) warns it of the danger of spiritual pride.

To-day we place the Old Testament upon the background of ancient history and religion. We follow its contents to Daniel and the Maccabaean Age, to the Wisdom Literature and Ben Sira. The apocryphal and apocalyptic literature —notably 2 Esdras—carries us insensibly into the Christian period, even as we may read Josephus and are suddenly aware that the Christian drama has begun; or we trace Palestinian archaeology and excavation back and down

---

[1] Even the entirely unhistorical Anglo-Israelite belief that the Anglo-Saxons are the remnants of the Lost Tribes ("Isaac's sons") may have its psychological basis in a genuine feeling that the Old Testament has a unique significance for this country. At all events, in Comparative Religion it is frequently necessary to go beneath the external forms of beliefs and customs and consider—if possible— their psychical foundation.

through Arab, Byzantine, Roman, Hellenistic, Jewish and
pre-Israelite periods, and are not conscious of gaps.

Again, in the New Testament there are the strongest
Jewish elements (e.g. Luke i., Epistle of James); and in the
Apocalypse or Revelation of St. John we seem to have the
last traces of archaic ideas of a distant past, yet in harmony
with the archaeological evidence for the persistence of many
varieties of belief in Palestine. In fact, it is not enough to
say that so-and-so must be *either* Jewish *or* Christian; it may
be just broadly "Palestinian." In the Fourth Gospel and
in Paulinism there is more that is Jewish—or rather,
"Palestinian"—than has often been thought; and it is now
more clearly recognised that the evidence for Hellenistic
influences in the New Testament must not obscure the
extent to which it is the ideological sequel of the Old Testament.[1]

The religious development behind the Old Testament and
the New is a complex one; but in the characteristic teaching
of the great prophets we recognise a profound religious
reformation. It is upon the significance of these prophets
that the "Higher Criticism" of the Old Testament may be
said to turn. The land of the Bible was never, or at least
rarely, isolated; and it is not easy to determine all the
factors in the development.[2] But just as a man's social
philosophy may be stimulated and shaped in reaction
against an "——ism" with which he has no sympathy, and
as Roman Catholicism betrays the presence of a Protestantism which it does not acknowledge, so, when we study the
Bible, we seem to see traces of reactions and protests, and
the prophets are of lasting historical interest for their fight
against beliefs and practices which they—and surely rightly
—felt to be contrary to spiritual religion. It was the fight
of good *versus* bad religion; it is on this account that the
Old Testament is of permanent value, and one must deprecate
any endeavour to maintain that throughout, from first to

---

[1] The character of Jewish religion in Alexandria and the variety
of belief in Palestine itself go far to explain the differences when
Rabbinical Judaism and Christianity became rivals.

[2] See Ch. VIII.

last, every constituent element is of equal spiritual, ethical or historical worth.

Now although we owe the fight for Ethical Monotheism to Israel, there are those who find the Old Testament a stumbling-block because of its "lower" elements. But this is to ignore both the ethical theism of the prophets and the simple piety of the psalmists. To contrast the Old Testament with the New is to contrast the religious vicissitudes of a virile and self-conscious people over centuries of stirring history with the religious idealism and programmatic aspects of incipient Christianity. It is to forget both the speedy rise of abuses in the Christian Church and the dark pages in the history of Christendom when the new religion came out into the world. The Old Testament faces the stern facts of human experience. After all—implicitly or explicitly—the history of Christendom manifests *Christian* conceptions of its God as truly as the Old Testament has set forth in black and white the lower as well as the higher levels of Religion.[1] And when it is said that Christianity unfortunately came under the evil influence of Psalms of Vengeance, the cruel extermination of witchcraft, and so forth, it is the more lamentable that the ethical and humane teaching of the Old Testament was ignored and that men dwelt more upon the sternness of the God of Israel than upon His compassion and righteousness.[2] Finally, when it is frankly realised that it was human nature that men should seize upon the cruder and less ethical aspects of the Old Testament, it is no less human nature which accounts many centuries earlier for those unlovely elements to which our attention is often directed.

In general, it is necessary to recognise both that there has always been bad as well as good religion, and that there has been development in the history of religion. How readily retrospect will arouse the conviction that there has been an

[1] Whence the Hindu will see little to choose between the European Christ as exemplified in the practice of European Christianity and what some Christians see in the "angry Jehovah" of Israel, see S. Cave, *Redemption Hindu and Christian* (1919), p. 143.

[2] See on this the remarks of W. B. Selbie, "The Influence of the Old Testament on Puritanism," in *The Legacy of Israel* (1927), pp. 407 ff., esp. p. 418.

advance needs no telling. The religion of Israel was
certainly felt to be an advance beyond the old pre-Israelite
religion, and Christianity an advance beyond the Old
Testament. Protestantism will feel that it has advanced
beyond Mediaeval Catholicism; and, if we were to go outside
the Bible, we should find that Islam believes that it has taken
up the figure of the Founder of Christianity and gone
beyond.[1] As a matter of fact, two different and contradictory types of feeling prevail: the one, that the most recent
stage of a religion marks an advance upon all its predecessors,
and the other, that the older the religion the purer, and that
at times there must be a return to that earlier stage before
it became contaminated and began to deteriorate. A
judicious treatment of the history of religion must take into
account the facts that point to some progressive development
as also those that suggest a "return," since it frequently
happens that instead of a "return" old elements reappear in
a new form (p. 85f.).

The contention I have here wished to put forward is a
three-fold one: the inseparability of the Old Testament and
the New, the admitted facts of "lower" and "higher"
elements in Religion, and the historical process in its
development. The Bible thus becomes a unique source for
the philosophical treatment of the vicissitudes of Religion.

II

The second point concerns the place of Christology within
Theism. Christianity looks back to certain great creative
movements both within the Bible and outside it (e.g. the
Reformation). The rise of Christianity can be viewed as a
great prophetic movement; and one can the better understand John the Baptist, Jesus and St. Paul when one comes
to them fresh from a study of their earlier predecessors, the
Hebrew prophets. Their uncompromising outspokenness
reminds one of, let us say, a Jeremiah on the one hand and
Protestant Reformers on the others. How deep-reaching

[1] It is claimed that the Koran in turn is superseded by the Beyan
of the Babis, and this in turn by the revelation to Baha Allah
(G. F. Moore, *op. cit.*, II, 513 ff.).

are all such movements! How Man is thrown back upon God! Man is clay in the potter's hands; God has perfect freedom; men have no rights before Him; all are unprofitable servants! There is a thorough-going theism which is more Hebraic or Semitic than Hellenistic or Greek.

St. Paul's sternness and his attitude to the Torah remind us of Jeremiah and the prophets. Yet, like even Jeremiah, he is at heart an Israelite. He believes that the restoration of the Jews will be the consummation of God's universal purpose, and he thus implies that there could be a synthesis (Rom. xi). A new shoot has been grafted on to the old stock; but there must be no undue exaltation, for it could easily be rejected. The line of evolution—as we might say—could again take another direction.[1] Paul has a very significant conception of the historical development of Religion, though it is not easy to say precisely how it is to be interpreted. Indeed, his philosophy of history, as it may be called, is a remarkable one: through the first man, Adam, sin entered the world; and through Christ, the Second Adam, there is redemption. Adam, in Luke's genealogical table, is a Son of God—it is a reminder that the human race is of Divine origin, and was probably added for the sake of Gentile readers.[2] Through Christ, our Brother, Man is brought into a new relationship of sonship with God (Rom. viii. 29, cf. Heb. ii. 11). Moreover, just as Jesus came to bring in the Kingdom of God, so Christ will ultimately hand the sovereignty over to God, who is the Father (1 Cor. xv. 24). If, then, the Law had been, as Paul calls it, a "pedagogue" (Gal. iii. 24 f.), it was the function of Christ, too, to conduct men up to God's rule. In other words, Paul's philosophy of the history of Religion culminates, not in a Christology, but in a Theism. And here the Old Testament and the New are at one, in that from Genesis to Revelation the entire history of Man—past, present and future—is placed within the

---

[1] Cf. Sanday and Headlam (*Commentary on Romans*, p. 327): "any virtue that (the heathen) may have comes by no merit of their own, but by virtue of the stock to which they belong . . . it will be a less violent process to cut off branches not in any way belonging to the tree than it was to cut off the original branches." See pp. 164 ff.

[2] Plummer, on Luke iii. 38.

creative work of a Transcendent God who is above both Israel and the Messiah, a God who, as the Jew and the Christian respectively hold, works out His purposes through them.

Judaism and Christianity, each in its own way—and very different ways—recognise the Immanence and Transcendence of a One and Only Ethical God; and we have next to ask, Is this a "religious" doctrine and nothing more?

III

The extraordinary realism of the old religion of Israel is my third point. It is often said that Semitic religion is "this-world-ly" in contrast both to certain "other-world-ly" aspects of Christianity and to the pantheism and quietism of Indian religion. The Semitic religions are characterised by remarkable and intense extremes.[1] We admire the vivid realism and the sublime idealism of Israel, her restrained and sober mysticism: God and this His world are alike tremendously real. Her ethical monotheism has given her a unique and permanent value, and those writers who find Ethical Monotheism a rather "bloodless" and uninspiring conception do not appear to realise that we, like old Israel, have our own problem of co-ordinating our own ideas of the realities of Man and Nature.

A Jewish anthropologist has recently argued, and rightly, that monotheistic or monotheising tendencies can arise anywhere and at any age.[2] This can be admitted. There is no special merit in monotheism as such. Religion in itself can be good or bad: it is the social, moral and intellectual setting and its continuity that make the difference between the admittedly impressive subjective significance of religious and mystical experience and its more objective worth. Inevitably

---

[1] See *C.A.H.*, I, 194 ff. Robertson Smith, *Lectures and Essays*, p. 425, wrote (in 1877): "*Corruptio optimi fit pessima;* the very tone of mind which makes Semitic heathenism the most hideous of false worships enabled the Hebrew nation to grasp with unparralleled tenacity and force the spiritual idea of Jehovah." (The term "Semitic" is, of course, open to criticism, see p. 138f.)

[2] Paul Radin, *Monotheism among Primitive Peoples* (the Arthur Davis Memorial Lecture for 1925); *Primitive Man as Philosopher* (1927), Ch. XVIII. Cf. p. 226.

and justly we contrast the ethical monotheism which arose in Israel with what we also find in the Old Oriental and other religions: superstition, cruelty and coarseness. We need a wide term to embrace our evidence, and we may speak of the "numinous."[1] When, therefore, we take a very wide view of the "numinous" we find religion that is spiritual and unspiritual, moral and unmoral; mysticism that is sublime or degrading; magic, spiritism, occultism, and so forth. All "numinous" experiences and convictions are subjectively very real and authoritative, yet they vary enormously in their ethical, social or intellectual fruits. The problem of good and bad religion is an exceedingly difficult and delicate one, and our attitude to it will be shaped by our personal religion. If, then, we are convinced of the supreme value of the effectiveness of that religious development which can be traced back to the Old Testament, Ethical Monotheism should be our criterion.

Yet, at the same time, should we not have to confess that the old monotheism, the old realism of the religion of Israel, is not so real to us to-day with our vastly greater store of positive knowledge? To put it more generally, we think we understand the immediate reality of the world of space and time; we may agree that there is ethical reality, in the sense that without morality, social order and brotherliness, we should sink back and fall below the level of *homo sapiens*; but "spiritual" reality is on another footing. We may have the firmest subjective belief in a Deity; but can we to-day co-ordinate Spiritual Reality with the rest of our knowledge, whether ordinary or scientific? In other words, is it possible to replace the old religious realism by a new one?

IV

Mathematicians make all sorts of postulates and then proceed to work out the consequences. Let us, in turn, be no less daring. Let us assume that the world's religions *do*

---

[1] The term, first coined by Rudolf Otto, *The Idea of the Holy* (Eng. tr. 1923), is now in frequent use. It is here employed of the religious, mystical and all related data which belong to the realm of the supersensuous and cannot be classified under definitely non-religious terms, see pp. 105 ff.

reveal, or involve, or imply, or suggest something that is "really" real and actual.   And my fourth point is this: we know of "theories" of Religion; can we, with the help of Comparative Religion, describe what we may call the "Theory of Religion"?   In other words, can we find out what Religion has to say for itself?   Such a task would be more ramifying than Frazer's *Golden Bough*, indeed, it might be difficult to see the Golden Wood for the Golden Trees!   Yet I venture to think we could condense our results into a sentence.   If we take a world-wide view of Religion, or rather of the numinous, we should, I think, find that the evidence would fall into three main groups, and that it would tell of an exceedingly close and vital relationship (*a*) between Man and the world or universe, in so far as it is understood by him; (*b*) between Man and gods, spirits and the unseen world; and (*c*) between the latter and the Universe.   This triangular relationship: God, Man and the Universe, is more or less clearly implied or expressed in very many different ways, and they combine to demonstrate the inherent weakness of any Naturalism which ignores Human Nature—even its alleged "illusions"—and of any Humanism which confines itself to Man and ignores the cosmos of science.[1]

I have space to make only a few miscellaneous remarks by way of justification.   That Man is organic to Nature needs no proof; and all deeper thinking has led him to Nature or to Nature's God.   Man's relationship to the world and the gods' relationship to it are often parallel or analogous; thus men and gods are *over*, or in some sense *in* Nature or part thereof: they are now, so to say, the electrician and now electricity.[2]   There are cosmic or nature gods, cosmic or nature human powers.   It is true there is a gulf between gods and men, but it is readily bridged; and mysticism and personal religion attest the profoundest experiences of communion and union, though not of identity.   Often the god is father, husband, uncle, or even brother; and there is

[1] On the Old Testament conceptions of the interrelation between God, Israel and their world, see *O.T.R.*, Ch. VII.

[2] See *Rel. Sem.*, p. 638.

abundant evidence for a divine or supernatural element in ordinary human birth. God, says the Koran, comes in between a man and his heart, he is nearer to a man than his neck-vein (Koran l. 15, viii. 24); and just as the body is called the city of Brahma, so to Paul it is the temple of God (1 Cor. iii. 16). In Indian thought, he who knows himself knows the Universe. The Chinese sage Mencius and Clement of Alexandria agree that he who understands his own nature will understand God. Deeper reflection upon God and Man, and the higher types of anthropomorphic religion lead to more intimate conceptions of both the nature of God and the nature of Man. In ways untold we meet with this triangular relationship: God, Man and the Universe, in theology, philosophy, and rudimentary belief and cere-monial.

All the religions make extraordinary claims, and one may, perhaps, sum them up suggestively in the old and famous Indian formula, *tat tvam asi*, "*that* art thou." It is the ultimate identity of the Self or Ego and the Universe or its God, of Man's soul and the Universal "Soul of all things."[1] This formula, it is true, is pantheistic; but if we take it as the "Theory of Religion" that Man is, *in some sense*, intimately related to God and His Universe, I venture to believe that we can co-ordinate and understand in large measure the data of Religion. *Tat tvam asi:* this ultimate, or actual, or potential, or conditional relationship—Man's cosmic exis-tence. This is my fourth point.

V

I turn now to the bearing of this upon our thought and our ways of thinking. We draw lines between Man and Nature, between God and the world. But our concept of "Nature" is far from primitive. In Indian thought we find one single order: one law runs through man and nature; and this law is sustained by the ethical god, Varuna, comparable

---

[1] Cf., e.g., R. W. Frazer, *Indian Thought Past and Present* (1915), pp. 53, 71, 94; J. Estlin Carpenter, *Theism in Medieval India* (1921), index p. 549 (under "That art Thou"); Sydney Cave, *Living Religions of the East* (1921), p. 29 ("the psychic and the cosmic principles are one").

only to Israel's conception of her own national deity.[1]   We have formed the concept of Nature by a process of abstraction and, having abstracted all that belongs to Man and God, we proceed to comment upon Nature's indifference; it is as though we placed apart in a large hall the blind, deaf and dumb, and then proceeded to comment upon the indifference of our audience!   Our Western concept of "Nature" is quite a secondary growth (see pp. 145, 201 f.).

But however strong may be a man's belief in a Supreme Being, it is surely difficult to conceive what were His attributes before Man appeared, or before there was life; as little could ancient Israel conceive her God to exist apart from His own people.   Yet the religious consciousness feels that God is First and Last; in Him we live and move and have our being.   Because of this faith the ultimate dissolution of this mysterious Universe, as we know it, means little or nothing, and so Emerson, that grand old idealist, could declare that he did not fear the end of the world.   This is due, not merely to religious faith, but to the ultimate validity of certain personal experiences and convictions; these are not kept apart in some watertight compartment, as it were, but are above and behind a man's knowledge of and reasoning about this world of space and time.   There is, in truth, a certain fundamental unity of consciousness, the same man having different sorts of experience at different times; but the difficulty has always been to relate to one another the two hemispheres of existence: *this* world and all that seems to take him away to some other and vaster existence.

In the religious growth of a man, when he comes to acquire religious convictions, he does not launch out and merely "add" to his knowledge.   When a man learns a new language and for the first time enjoys Shakespeare, Goethe or Dante, we may distinguish what is "additive" (e.g. the new language) from the "qualitative" effects of his new acquaintance with the great classic.   Much more marked are the "qualitative" effects of Religion, and we ask, How are we to formulate the process?   Religion asserts that God

---

[1] Cf. Cave, *op. cit.*, p. 19 f.; *Redemption Hindu and Christian*, pp. 26 ff.   See above, pp. 24, 140.

knows us before we know Him, He chose us first, and He made us for Himself, in His likeness. The data of religion and mysticism, the common belief that there is a supernatural factor in human birth,[1] and the *a priori* or transcendental nature of the processes of religious development combine to supplement the "Theory of Religion": Man is part of a vaster existence or shares in a vaster life before he consciously is religious, or has any explicit conception of God.[2]

Accordingly, instead of supposing that in religious development something "new" emerges from within—that there is "emergent" evolution—it might be better to say—and not in the case of Religion alone—that the individual gains a new and heightened or transformed consciousness of his environment, his world of activity and his place in the Universe.[3] In such experiences a man often seems to repair a sundered relationship, to resume unity with a Reality of which he had always formed part, to return to a heaven which is his home. Indeed, it is through the prevalence and persistence of experiences of this type that we may explain the rudimentary ideas of rebirth, reincarnation, and the like; and while to Tennyson pre-existence was a ground for belief in existence after death—death leading to a return to a pre-existent state, others have felt that the idea of immortality necessarily involves that of pre-existence.[4] That is to say, the experience of becoming an organic part of that which was already in existence is interpreted as though the actual individual himself had pre-existed.

VI

I venture to think that I can now more decisively make my sixth point, namely, that man's non-religious as well as

[1] See *Rel. Sem.*, p. 513; cf. *Kiddushin* 30b: "There are three partners in every human birth—God, father and mother" (cited by I. Abrahams, *Studies in Pharisaism*, II, 150).

[2] Cf. Tennant, *Philosophical Theology*, I, 326: there may well have been *rapport* between Man and God, before Man has religious experiences. See also p. 127, n. 1.

[3] Cf. p. 299.

[4] McTaggart, *Some Dogmas of Religion*, Ch. IV, cf. Tennant, *op. cit.*, II, 257.

religious modes of life and thought are influenced unconsciously by his place in the cosmos or his relationship with
God. If we agree that God knows Man before Man knows
God, we do not mean by "God" a solely spiritual reality,
over *there*; we mean, rather, that Man has some deeper
consciousness of his place in the Universe, of his relationship
to a God who is in His Universe and not apart from it.
This, at least, seems to follow from a study of the influence
of a man's religion upon the non-religious spheres of his life
and thought, and the reverse (see Ch. I), and from the inter-
connections between religious and non-religious though
closely related experiences (e.g. Religion and Art).   Accordingly, mental development will be due, not merely to
ordinary social intercourse, but to what may be called a
cosmic relationship.   "The objective mind that is at once
immanent in and dominant over its several members"[1] will
be that of which the whole human society itself is part.
In any case, whether the quotation be the best explanation
or not, the relation between the hemispheres of the "religious" and the "non-religious" is such that a place must be
found for Religion in one's conceptions of Reality and of that
Universe of which the universe of science must be so defined
as to be only a part or phase.[2]

William James, in his *Varieties of Religious Experience*
(p. 389), suggested that Hegel's idea of a perfected Being
was due to the prominence in the philosopher's consciousness
of mystical moods.[3]   Also Edward Tylor (*Primitive Culture*,
4th ed., I, 497f.) found a remarkable connection between the
doctrine of ideas of the Greek philosopher Democritus and
the current notions of spirits; he speaks of his "decanting
into his metaphysics a surviving doctrine of primitive savage

---

[1] James Ward, *Realm of Ends*, p. 129f.

[2] For the intellectual activity of the scientist, scholar or critic,
as such, does not represent the whole Self, but an isolated aspect
of it.

[3] J. W. N. Sullivan (*The Contemporary Mind* [1934], pp. 124, 134),
refers to Einstein's remark that modern scientific speculations
spring from a profound religious impulse; Sir James Jeans agreed,
provided that the word "religious" were sufficiently widely interpreted.

animism." Again, Cornford (*From Religion to Philosophy*) demonstrates at length the close connection between the religious and the philosophical thought of early Greece; and other evidence could be adduced to illustrate the relation between typical religious, philosophical and other reactions to the "outside" world.[1] The mediaeval ego-centric conceptions of Man and the Universe are so far justified that we are now told that the earth may be unique.[2] Be this as it may, such ideas are explicable if men are not isolated units here and now, but are in some sense one with God and His Universe, and through this relationship construct each his own ideas of a Universe with himself as centre. That is to say, man's relationship with God or with the Universe makes him think, not merely as an earth-born individual of a few decades, confined in space and time, but also as in some sense a cosmic or universal being.[3] We live in a world of space and time; but when we think "religiously," it is in a sphere wherein ideas of time and space have no relevancy. Indeed, are not our problems of Subject and Object, of the One and the Many, of ourselves here and now and the so-called "external" world, hopelessly complex simply because we exist in two worlds or spheres of which that of space and time is only one?

How does this affect our ideas of right conduct? Not only is there both good and bad religion, but one cannot ignore the fact that there are men of the finest ethical and moral character who seem to have no need for "religion," no sense

[1] For example, Pattison Muir, *Mind*, 1913, pp. 48–61; cf. the present writer, in *Essays* . . . *presented to Wm. Ridgeway*, p. 406f. (on "the evolution of primitive thought").

[2] Or rather, the earth, though not of course the centre of the Universe, is an extraordinarily rare sort of celestial body (Needham, *Journ. of Philosoph. Studies*, VI [1931], p. 31).

[3] On the "religious" origin of Newton's metaphysis, see Bishop Barnes, *Should Such a Faith Offend?* (1927), p. 304, cf. p. 257. See also A. N. Whitehead, *Science and the Modern World* (1925), pp. 16 ff., on the influence of mediaeval theology upon the scientific faith in the rationality of the Universe; also T. H. Sprott, *Modern Study of the Old Testament and Inspiration* (1909) pp. 90 ff., on the ideas of Nature's trustworthiness as generated by the Bible; cf. Leon Roth in *The Legacy of Israel* (1927), p. 441.

of it—at least in the conventional use of that word. A
Theory of Religion must certainly take into account not only
bad religion, but also righteous living that is—or appears to
be—without "religion."[1] Many will no doubt agree (a) that
the ethical integrity of a man who has no "religious sense"
is decisively better than bad religion; further, (b) that theism,
as such, has given a special, more intense, and more personal
shape to a man's life than non-theistic convictions; and
finally (c) that the ethical theism of the Old Testament
and its fervid realism, have, if we accept the verdict of
history, surely given a direction to the development of
human life and thought absolutely more effective than other
vaguer and ethically defective forms of Theism. Monotheism should show itself in both right living and right
thinking.

VII

Now the essential feature of the ethical monotheism of the
Old Testament is the absolute righteousness of God: He is not
arbitrary, capricious or untrustworthy; He is righteous, and
is at once Immanent and Transcendent. This brings me
to the seventh point: the God who is both in and behind all
history and the Universe. Let us recall, first, the superb
faith in God, even though He may seem helpless, indifferent,
or even hostile: one thinks, for example, of Dan. iii. 17f.
(even if our God does not save us we will not worship thy
gods), or Habakkuk iii. 18 (in spite of calamities and though
earth's blessings fail, "yet will I rejoice in the Lord"). Not
only some conspicuous words of Job (e.g. xvi. 18–22, xix.
25–27), the whole drama of the book leads on to the belief
in the God who is behind the God of man's experience, and
it calls up the saying in the Koran (ix. 119), "there is no
refuge from God but to Him."[2] He is behind the processes of
history (see pp. 112, 221f.). The disasters of the Exile which
might seem to show that God had forsaken Israel actually
brought the grander perceptions of His Reality: this makes

---

[1] See pp. 109, 195f.

[2] Cf. G. H. Box, *Judaism in the Greek Period* (*Clarendon Bible*,
V, 1932), p. 130: appealing from man's God to God's God; see
O.T.R., pp. 158ff., 241.

the Second Isaiah (Isa. xl. ff.) the climax of Old Testament religion. Though He might appear to be remote or negligible (as in Zeph. i. 12), He was near at hand, and separated only by the breadth of men's thoughts. And when the prophets condemned the religion of their day, and went behind history, the temple, and the culture to the God of the Universe, we perceive the vital fact of *all* development, religious and other: the thoughts, ideas and concepts which at one time are felt to lead to a goal, at another time are found to be a hindrance. The study of the world's religions, viewed broadly and dynamically, unmistakably points to the fact that there is some process, some greater and still transcendent Reality, behind or above the particular religion which at one time has made for progressive development, but at another is below the aspirations of the prophet or the reformer.

The implications of this are evident. Our most earnest thinking by no means always leads us direct to our goals: the important fact is that we constantly make this discovery for ourselves. True Theism never remains stationary. We human beings have not reached the limits of our own personal development, nor can we sound the depths of Divine Personality, or discover the last secrets of a Universe which is in the hands of One, who "will be what He will be" (Exod. iii. 14), but who will always be found to be "righteous"—that is, if we take our stand on Ethical Monotheism. God transcends our knowledge of Him; and our Ego, or Self, transcends us, imperfect beings that we are, with our religion or philosophy of the day. This ultimate Self is a greater thing than its most elaborate philosophy. By reason of our cosmic or theistic existence, that is, in or through God, and because we are also creatures of here and now, in space and in time, there will always be contradictions and paradoxes in our syntheses. Our thinking will give us the *road* to Ultimate Reality, but not that Reality itself in the fullness of the Truth and Beauty and Majesty of a Transcendent God. Can Man see God and live? If this seems to take us back to the simple faith of Israel at its best, it is to the *spirit* of Ethical Monotheism rather than to the *letter*; for our intellectual and other problems to-day are vastly more complex than those of ancient Israel.

VIII

What has been said on Divine Transcendence and the Ultimate Reality leads to the eighth point—the roads to reality, that is, in particular, Man's ideas of gods, spirits, angels, and intermediaries. A whole chapter or series of chapters of Comparative Religion must be condensed into a few words. Speaking generally, we may say that gods, spirits and the like arise from *personal* experience or feelings of relationship. But they also answer to spiritual, moral, intellectual and logical needs. Frequently the gods are *causes*—e.g., of rain or crops—and as such they do not necessarily stand in any relationship to man. Often they are grounds of existence, coherence, or persistence, principles of unity and of continuity.[1] At one end of our scale are the personal gods and other spiritual beings; at the other are necessities of thought—where and how shall we draw the line?[2]

No one would wish to belittle the profound value of the saints in Mohammedan and Roman Catholic communities; and while the Virgin Mary of Christendom is the successor of the Mother-Goddesses of old—though the ideas are heightened by Christian idealism—in the East the need for

[1] Cf. the Roman *genius*, the permanent principle of highly organised institutions (W. Warde Fowler, *Roman Ideas of Deity*, p. 21 f.); and for ideas of "corporate spirit," *esprit de corps*, etc. as provisional entities, see H. Sturt, *The Principles of Understanding* (1915), p. 174 f.

[2] The varying orthodox and unorthodox views of the Mēmrā and other Jewish terms find analogies elsewhere (see J. Abelson, *The Immanence of God in Rabbinical Literature*). To the supposition that God Himself may be a projection, a mental necessity, or focus, it may be replied that Man persistently finds a *personal* Reality beyond those inherited and current conceptions of God that are found to be inadequate, and that he demands this in place of any *impersonal* process or principle. Moreover, on intellectual grounds, the (empirical) Self seems equally elusive, and it is not surprising that Buddhism could argue away its immortality. But his own personal development is a guarantee that no individual can claim to have reached the limits of his growth, and his deeper experiences can convince him that in some sense he "transcends" all phenomena, and the most logical of his intellectual constructions.

a female deity is supplied by the figure of Kuan-Yin, who is derived from a male deity. The Babylonian Ishtar was also a Compassionate Mother, to whom is addressed one of the finest of Babylonian hymns; and while the monotheistic Israelite placed his Deity above sex—though finding in him all the tenderest attributes—among his neighbours the deities were sometimes bi-sexual in theory or were so represented in art.[1] Again, consider the "Christ-idea" and the parallels, e.g. the earlier Marduk, Osiris, Attis and Adonis, and the later Krishna, Buddha and Amitabha. Some may have no historical foundation, and the figure of Krishna has been admittedly cleansed.[2] The Jesus of history has become One in whom Christians will always find an accessible and realisable centre of the loftiest ideals; but while we do not forget that these have an Old Testament ancestry, He has also become an embodiment of social and other ideas which, like the "child Jesus," distinguish modern thought rather than the Founder of Christianity Himself.

When we read of the "God of the Old Testament" and the "God of the New," we understand that the writer has in mind different types of doctrine or belief concerning the Supreme Being, even though his wording sometimes implies that there are two distinct deities. We do not suppose that corresponding to the many local Madonnas venerated by the Roman Catholics or the local Elijahs of the Near East there are as many Spiritual Beings.[3] It is no less impossible to suppose that there exist *all* the spirits, saints and other spiritual or supernatural beings in whom men of all ages have genuinely believed and have been comforted and helped thereby. Sometimes a historical figure lies behind them, but not always; and all that can be said is that our

---

[1] See the writer's note in *Rel. Sem.*, p. 516; and cf. Vincent and Dhorme, *Revue Biblique*, 1926, p. 357.

[2] Cave, *Redemption*, pp. 3, 110. See also the discussion in the *Hibbert Journal*, V (1907), 74 ff., VI (1908), 422 ff.

[3] Cf. Tennant, *Philosophy of the Sciences* (1932), p. 170, also p. 178: religious experience itself cannot say whether there is a real or actual counterpart to its objects. How very genuine and effective are the beliefs, especially among rudimentary tribes, cannot be gainsaid; see R. R. Marett, *Faith, Hope and Charity in Primitive Religion* (1932), *Sacraments of Simple Folk* (1933).

nature is such, or the nature of the Universe is such, that Man can seek for and find these supersensuous beings within his private world, whatever be their authentic background in human history.[1]

Here let me refer to the Archbishop of York, when he says that "the One God of Heaven and Earth used the figure of Yahweh, the God of Sinai, as the means of revealing Himself to a particular nation."[2]   But if this be so, is it not more widely true?   Has not God elsewhere used "figures" of contemporary belief as the medium for His revelation of Himself?   Comparative Religion is forced to recognise the noble and fine attributes often attributed to "pagan" gods: the Babylonian Sin and Shamash, the Indian Varuna, and many another.   If any attempt is to be made to understand the problems brought by such facts, only from the standpoint of Ethical Monotheism does it seem possible that this can be done.   Is not Comparative Religion examining the ways in which the One and Only God has been apprehended?   If so, how far may one go along this line of thought?   There can be no doubt that in their deities, saints and intermediaries men have everywhere found consolation, companionship and inspiration: they have led men to a goal—as "pedagogues," we might say, using St. Paul's word.   Yet, just as the orthodox Jew will have no divine figure between him and his God, so the Protestant rejects the cult of intermediaries, saints or Madonnas.   A theist, too, might even say that, though the Christian believes that God has revealed Himself in Christ, there are certain types of Christianity that seem to keep men away from a fuller knowledge of God.

---

[1] Some of the descriptions of the development of Yahweh from a Kenite local god onwards read like biographies.   They encourage the fatal conception that man is improving the character of the Deity, cf. Geden, *The Evangel of the Hebrew Prophets* (1926), p. 248.   The late Professor Kennett told of a school examination paper where a little girl wrote: "God began by being rather fierce; but He improved as time went on until at last Jesus made Him almost as gentle as Himself."   Unfortunately that sort of thinking is by no means confined to children.

[2] William Temple, *Mens Creatix* (1917), p. 304.   Further on, he observes, "God used this figure of contemporary belief as the medium for His revelation of Himself."

And did not the prophets find it necessary to lead the people from the cult, the temple and the history to the God who was hidden behind the religion of their day?

If we believe that the Supreme Being of the Universe is the Ultimate Reality—as distinct from the intermediaries, "pedagogues," and approaches—Comparative Religion forces us to follow out the implications of our data. Thus the question will arise whether we suppose that the dead, especially the saintly, the precious and the powerful, can really exercise any influence over or on behalf of the living. We may agree that God could use them, or that He could use our ideas of them—and indeed of all supersensuous beings, whatever their actual origin—and we may agree that such ideas can be developed, purified and heightened. But on the Theory of Religion Man in his life-time is already in some relationship with God, and, if so, may he not already be used by Him? When a dear and valued life leaves us, "we doubt not that for one so true, there must be other nobler work to do"; but Ethical Monotheism cannot speculate whether the dead, *of their own right*, or *in and of themselves*, have any influence upon the world of the living. This is not to deny that it is so: it is to say that our conception of Ultimate Reality and of the road thereunto will shape our attitude to all our conceptions of transhuman reality.

In our search after Reality from the human side we are speedily at a loss. We cannot lay our finger upon transhuman reality; for although the Positivist or the Sociologist may find it in Society as a whole, or in Humanity, real or ideal, we cannot ignore the fundamental relationship between Man, Nature and the Universe; and, proceeding in this way, where shall we find Reality, and how shall we formulate it? Or again, consider the mystical and related experiences of Man's oneness with some vaster reality. Are we, as has been suggested, as the raindrops that are lost in the sea? If so, we are raindrops that can be conscious of oneness or relationship with the vaster reality—water. Or we may say that it is the oxygen constituent of the rain-drop, conscious of oneness with all else into which oxygen enters— both water and air. Mystical and other experiences might suggest that in some sense Man's soul is omnipresent, *Tat tvam asi*; but neither Pantheism, nor Pan-anthropism—if the word may be coined—proves satisfactory.

If we ask, is the Deity omnipresent, is He in some sense above, within, or behind the physical Universe, Comparative Religion will tell us of rites and prayers whereby men all the world over can come to feel the nearness or presence of a supersensuous Personal Reality. But as we pursue our enquiry we land ourselves in hopelessly pantheistic, obscurantist and materialistic positions until we recall Coleridge's words on "the presence of all things to God."[1] *This*, and not the idea of Divine Omnipresence, proves the more helpful line of thought, not only for the progress of Religion, but for the higher development of the human mind and all that turns thereon. So Man can, as it were, carry his God with him; and not for nothing did the religion of Israel have a nomadic ancestry.[2] Yet from time to time men need a Jeremiah (Ch. xxix.) to tell them that even in exile, away from the local centre of their religion, their temple, and their land—i.e. from all visible and material aids to Religion—they are not removed from the Divine Presence.[3]

IX

In our quest after Reality we follow old and well-tried usage when we make Personality Divine and Human our highest category. This is my ninth point.[4] Anthropism has

---

[1] This, he remarks, is alone safe and legitimate (*Aids to Reflection: conclusion*).

[2] Cf. pp. 155, 169. Two quotations may be made: (*a*) Epictetus, "Thou bearest about with thee a God, and knowest it not . . . in thyself thou dost bear Him and seest not that thou defilest him with thine impure thoughts and filthy deeds . . . In the presence of God Himself within thee, who seeth and heareth all things, thou art not ashamed of the things thou dost both desire and do." (*b*) Theodore Herzl (letter of 16 June, 1895), "the Promised Land . . . everyone carries a piece of it in himself and the Promised Land is there where we carry it" (from *The New Judaea*, 7 Jan. 1927, p. 148).

[3] On that remarkable chapter of Jeremiah, see especially John Skinner, *Prophecy and Religion* (1922), pp. 285–297.

[4] By a "personal" God is naturally meant, in the first instance, One whose relationship to man is experienced in a way that cannot be otherwise expressed; although the *quality* of a man's idea of such a God rests upon his moral and spiritual development; cf. Ps. xviii. 26, and see pp. 106, 171.

its obvious and recognised dangers; it is helpful to think of
the Deity as Father—once in Israel it was as husband[1]—
but to pursue our thoughts along the line of human relation-
ships, is, to say the least, to attempt to understand the
higher from the lower.   Yet this "personalism" has endless
possibilities, because of the transcendent Ego, the Self, and
the transcendent God and His Universe.   Indeed, we can
even trace from early times the tendency to think of God in
terms of mind and to utilise the knowledge of the mind and
of mental processes.[2]   Hence, it is sometimes suggested that
the Deity realises himself in His Universe, as does a man, a
Shakespeare, in his creative work.   Or, if we recall Coleridge's
words, we may say that, though we are not omnipresent
in all the contents of our mind, they can be in our presence;
and whereas we dismiss those thoughts that do not serve our
purpose, we, if we are as God's thoughts, may haply be of use
for His ultimate purpose.   Or again, when we think of
Transcendence and Immanence—terms that prove to be
absolutely necessary when we consider men's ideas of God—
are we not at one time outside and above our thoughts, and
at another time inevitably living and incarnate in them, and
sometimes even thwarted by them?

Herein lies the possibility of further developments of
knowledge, for if—on the Theory of Religion—we consider
the relationship between God and Man, we, when we think
of Him in terms of mind, are deepening our knowledge of the
human mind, and so, in turn, are acquiring better instruments of thought for thinking out the ultimate problems of
life.   But while I believe that along these lines there may be
great advances in the future, Biblical realism will forbid us
to think of the Universe as Mind, or to reduce everything to
Mind-stuff.   Though it has seemed helpful to think of the
Universe as a system of minds embraced in one supreme
Mind (so e.g. Plotinus),[3] a system of Persons or Selves, in one

---

[1] See *Rel. Sem.*, pp. 513 ff., 617.

[2] Not only in the "Logos" and the earlier Biblical "Word of the
Lord," but in Babylonia, Persia, and elsewhere.   Cf. above, p. 144 n.

[3] E. Caird, *The Evolution of Theology in the Greek Philosophers*
(1923), ii. 270.   But Personality is a higher conception than Mind.

Supreme Personality, may be a more fruitful conception. Yet, whenever we attempt to explain the interaction of Persons some theory of Monads appears to be required, we seem to need some connecting agency, substance, or other ground of our interrelations.   We may be firmly convinced that A can pray on behalf of B who is far distant, but here God is the medium, and to the religious soul this is all-sufficing; but once we attempt to understand our faith in this Ultimate Reality we seem to need what one might call a psychical or spiritual "ether" to explain all action at a distance.[1]

<h1 style="text-align:center">X</h1>

My next point is that though the Ultimate Reality transcends us, the prophets' conceptions of ethical righteousness open out most suggestive lines of enquiry.   The prophets laid greatest stress, not upon cult but upon conduct; cultus without conduct is empty, but righteous conduct—to do justice, to love mercy, and to walk humbly before God— brings a man into relationship with God.   This relationship with the Ultimate Reality does not necessarily come through the sacrificial system, or the ceremonial transition from some secular state of every-day life to a special holy or sacred psychic state, but through right living (p. 108f.).   Here there is no substratum, medium or "spiritual ether"; but the object of Man's quest is in some sense already and unconsciously attained by what is essentially parallelism or imitation—the adherence to certain ideal modes of behaviour.

Of the numerous utterances that might be mentioned here, one of the most striking is, perhaps, Meister Eckhart's "If I am pure God must of His own nature give Himself to me."[2]

---

[1] P. W. Bridgman, *The Logic of Modern Physics* (1928), suggests that there should be no *a priori* objection to the idea of action at a distance (p. 46); his notion of the immanence of the entire (physical) universe (p. 183f.) has much in its favour from the psychical point of view.   See below, on "fields" of force, p. 298f.

[2] The child-like and utterly naïve confidence that is found in certain types of religion finds abundant illustration; one may note among the early Christian martyrs the consciousness that as martyrs they had the right to demand revelations from God.   On this "naturalness," see also p. 164f.

With the right mode of life, with the right wave-length, so to say, God and Man are not remote from each other. This fundamental belief, expressed in many different ways, is of the first importance for all conceptions of Religion and Reality.[1] It is part of an immense topic. It is hardly necessary to refer to sympathy as a road to understanding and knowledge, to imitation as a means of acquiring certain attitudes, or to the conviction of the necessity of imitation of or adherence to a cosmic or divine norm or law. Although the psychical states of religion and mysticism—of the "numinous" in general—are overpoweringly impressive, right living—even if a man has no evident sense of "Religion" —is more significant than a religion that justifies or encourages unrighteousness: at least if we take our stand on Ethical Monotheism.[2]

The prophets' insistence upon social conduct is characteristic of the religious realism and practical mysticism of Israel. Her "this-world"-ness stands in contrast to Greek dualism of body and soul, on the one side, and, on the other, to an ultra-spirituality which runs grave risk of being empty words. But to-day there is a definite drift away from dualism to a unity of spirit and body, from the Greek idea of an incarnate soul to the Hebrew and primitive emphasis on the bodily organism as a physical and psychical unit. It is only one of other indications that we must go back, not only to the foundation of Christendom in the New Testament, but to the realistic spiritual idealism of the Old Testament before it came under the influence of Greek speculative thought (see pp. 216ff.).

XI

My eleventh point arises out of the religious realism of Israel. We contrast the realism and virility of Old Israelite life and thought at its best with Indian pantheism, quietism and mysticism: *Tat tvam asi*, the Soul of Man and the Soul of the Universe are ultimately one! All that comes in

---

[1] Special mention may be made of the fine essay on "the Imitation of God," by Israel Abrahams, *Studies in Pharisaism*, Vol. II, pp. 138–182. See also *Rel. Sem.*, Index s.v. Imitation.

[2] See pp. 268f., 288.

between is Maya, illusion, unreality. Whereas Maya depreciates this world of space and time, the Israelite accepted the world and lived in it an intense life, with his ideals of Righteousness; while the West, far less emotional, by immersing itself in the world of sense-data, has gained its knowledge of the mysteries of human nature and of the Universe. It is a knowledge not to be lightly valued or allowed to remain stationary, since, on the Theory of Religion, it is a knowledge of God's Universe, which is *our* Universe, through the relationship between God and Man, and increasing knowledge only gives us profounder insight into His ways and the heritage of the "Israel of God."

Now this world of appearance comes in between the soul of Man and the Ultimate Reality, and comprises the subject-matter of our sciences. It includes not merely the physical universe but Thought itself; for our thoughts are not so much the constituents of Reality, as guides to the apprehension and interpretation of it. Far from infallible, our thoughts, ideas and mental processes are our "human" tools—who can conceive the nature of man's activities in another existence after death without sense-organs? The world of thought as well as the world of the scientist are as a sea which both joins us to Reality and severs us from it; but it is a sea which is slowly and laboriously being charted.

Here we may recall the address of General Smuts at a recent meeting of the British Association. It was to the effect that in the evolution of the Universe we seem to pass from one level to another, each with its own concepts, its own laws and principles, but all bound together as members of an ascending series.[1] In the world of life, in the world of thought, in the evolution of the Universe, and in that not less vital "ideological" evolution of religious and other thought, which has now made us conscious of the past and not a little apprehensive of the future—here is a great field for further and fresher research. For the different processes, though on different levels, are—or seem to be—interrelated, and they have—or seem to have—as General Smuts said, "a fundamental unity of plan or organisation." As it

[1] *Nature*, Sept. 26th, 1931, p. 527, col. 2; cf. p. 523, col. 1.

has otherwise been expressed, "the structure of Mind . . . is cosmic structure at a particular level of activity."[1] Accordingly, on this view it would be futile to attempt to reduce everything to *either* Mind *or* Matter. The simpler method is to start from the known—the range or hierarchy of processes from the physical to the biological, the mental and the ideological, and from a comparative study of *all*—and not as is usual from a few only of them—more may be learnt of the evolution of Man in his Universe.[2]

One of the necessary tasks of the day is to reconsider our most important concepts, to unpack them, so to say, and pack them anew.[3] Thus, if we take a long view of the history of thought, it is not at all evident that the meaning of our terms "spirit" and "matter" has been finally fixed.[4] Certainly there is much that has been seemingly "religious" but had no "spiritual" worth; on the other hand, religious ideas that are enwrapped in ritual or ceremonial are not as such "materialistic." If by the term "God" we mean the Ultimate Spiritual Reality, we must admit that although a

---

[1] J. E. Boodin, *Hibbert Journal*, XXVIII (1930), p. 597.   Cf. also T. E. England, *The Validity of Religious Experience* (1937), p. 273, who remarks, "it seems to me that the one sole reality is neither creativity nor appetition, but the Universe; not the Universe in the physical sense nor in the pantheistic sense, but the Universe as a hierarchised whole, a dynamic structure in which physical, animate and mental activities are equally real, though of widely different values."   See W. M. Urban, *The Intelligible World* (1929), pp. 441 ff.

[2] See the suggestive "Herbert Spencer" Lecture by C. S. Myers, "Psychological conceptions in other Sciences" (1929); cf. e.g. p. 23, on the employment of the phenomena of Mind to throw light upon the phenomena of Matter. (Reprinted in *In the Realm of Mind*, 1937, p. 186.) On a "scale" of forms or processes, cf. R. G. Collingwood, *An Essay on Philosophical Method* (1933), p. 187f.

[3] When one considers how concepts are articulated from impressions, sense-data, ideas, and so on and so forth, and how these combine to form fairly compact units, the process that unifies them and makes them cohere is—so it may be suggested—not unrelated to the processes which make organic bodies of thought, a body of people, a species and many other sorts of "units."   See p. 267, n. 1.

[4] See, for some preliminary remarks, the writer's note in *Rel. Sem.*, pp. 676–686.   From the old point of view "spiritual" was that which the Divine Spirit informed (see especially, Isa. xxxi. 3); the common tendency to divorce the "spiritual" from practical work-a-day affairs often makes it verge upon the merely verbal.

given religion has been life-giving and inspiring, it has not rarely assumed forms that are static, ossified or dead. These have come between Man and newer and deeper conceptions of his Creator and, being as lifeless as dead matter, have shown that there can be a sort of "Materialism" in religion which has proved more subtle and destructive than Materialism of any other type.

Next, it is also necessary to reconsider the terms Nature and Natural. To the religious individual, and in supreme degree to such personalities as the prophets of old, what we should call the "Super-natural" was "Natural," in that God and His realm was a "natural" or integral part of the Universe. Whereas from one point of view we contrast the Natural and Super-natural, there is another and higher conception of the Natural which includes our Super-natural. But, if we widen our view and take into account bad religion, foolish myticism, occultism, and the rest, it is by no means the case that the "Super-natural" is necessarily of any lofty spiritual or other value. Moreover, approaching the terms from another and purely non-religious standpoint, we must be prepared to enlarge the realm of the Natural to include telepathy, second sight, and any other psychical phenomena from civilised and uncivilised lands that may be capable of verification. Certainly, proceeding in this way, we seem to open our doors too widely and to aggravate our difficulties, but a careful study of Comparative Religion demands that we should do justice to many embarrassing data. It may seem sufficient merely to tabulate the phenomena; but once we attempt to evaluate them, Ethical Monotheism must prove our criterion.[1]

The reason is clear. Ethical Monotheism must recognise as its only supersensuous and spiritual reality God, and all that "God" means for human experience and cosmic activity. It can find no place in its scheme of Reality for the merely supersensuous or the merely super-natural as such. It cannot treat that realm *apart from God* as "Real" in any

[1] Telepathy, for example, cannot be cited as a refutation of materialism, see C. C. J. Webb, *Group Theories of Religion and the Individual* (1916), p. 107 f. See also above, pp. 268 f., 288.

ultimate sense, though this is not to deny that the phenomena may be genuine. We may perhaps illustrate our
meaning thus: Music and Art of all kinds abound, but there
are ideals of Music and Art, and of Science, Literature, and
so forth. We may deplore or repudiate what is bad, we
may often be neutral, and frequently we may misjudge.
But if we are concerned with what seems to lead us to our
goal, we must follow our ideals and trust that any good
wheat among the tares which we are rejecting will not fail
in due course to produce food. In other words, so long as
Ethical Monotheism is our starting-point and our criterion,
this Ultimate Reality will be our guide when we are confronted with the problem of the existence of the Supernatural and the Supersensuous; and, in the words of Matthew
Arnold, God, the Ultimate Reality, is "the power not ourselves that makes for righteousness."[1]

XII

The Power in and behind the Universe is not arbitrary
(Num. xxiii. 19), and inasmuch as this conviction has
repeatedly prevailed in many different forms, we may ask
how far it is supposed that this dependableness, this
"righteousness," extends. Can it be merely an emotional
conviction of ours with no further meaning? In ordinary
life we trust our reasoning processes but we test them. If
our working-hypotheses or regulative principles break down,
chaos, chance or indeterminateness seem to prevail; although
it is a matter of common experience that in due course we
commonly find a more developed hypothesis or law or
principle which not infrequently covers a larger field of
action.[2] Of this there are outstanding illustrations. Whereas in Israel the belief in God appears to have broken down in
and about the Exile, the writings of the Second Isaiah show
convincingly that profoundly vaster conceptions arose—
precisely as often happens in research. But what ensued
was more than a solely "religious" development, since step

[1] *Literature and Dogma*, Ch. X, § 3 (beginning).

[2] See pp. 115, n. 3, 229ff.

by step we pass on to new stages in universal history wherein the newly reconstructed Israel laid the world under its debt.

To the Israelite, Divine Righteousness would manifest itself over an extensive sphere of activity because his thought was not so highly differentiated as ours. At his stage of mental development Divine Righteousness would often be manifested in processes which we call "natural" and have handed over to Science. But "the progressive rationalisation of the world by science is a continuous extension of our knowledge of God" (Pringle-Pattison). The concept of "Nature" has arisen by abstraction, and Man himself, only "a little lower than the angels" but organic with Nature, feels that he is in some relationship with the Divine Reality. If we believe that Divine Righteousness rules throughout, we have the highest type of Law, Order and Determinateness; and the repeated spontaneous recognition that the Ultimate Reality *is* Righteous is but further testimony to the link which Man feels between himself and that Power to which he gives the name "God."

One has only to consider the data of Religion to observe the extraordinary extent to which the belief has prevailed that the Universe—so far as it was known—is sustained by man as well as by gods. Man has felt it his duty to uphold the Right, to maintain Order and Justice, and even to help to sustain the gods themselves.[1] What the gods—what God—really requires of Man forms one of the most terrible, and yet one of the most wonderful chapters of Comparative Religion. Surely no sacrifice can be too precious, no offering too worthy; and yet (Micah vi. 8)—"what does God require . . . ?" Especially in the more rudimentary religions does there run the idea that if Man does his duty, Nature will do hers: Man and Nature—so far as understood—form a whole; one Law, one Order, rules throughout.[2] While it may be said that Nature, as such, is marked by a certain conformity

---

[1] On the last, as a fundamental principle of sacrifice, see W. O. E. Oesterley, *Sacrifices in Ancient Israel* (1937), pp. 20, 37 f., with reference to the theory of E. O. James, *Origins of Sacrifice* (1933).

[2] Although human laws are said to be "man-*made*" they depend upon some consciousness of the behaviour that is necessary if there is to be Social Order.

to type, Man is constantly realising the sort of type to which he must be true, the Rightness at which he must aim, the norm to which he must adhere. Man can use Nature so long as things are true to the laws of their being, and the Divine Process can use Man when he is true to his highest law.

Truth to Self is, then, the highest principle of life. In the lengthy history of Religion one sees that there have been decisive advances from lower forms, and that one cannot return to them with impunity. Everywhere and even in our own lives we see how much preparatory work has been done which, though inferior and of temporary value, has paved the way for what we hope may be of higher value and more lasting. Hence one cannot but believe that in one's weak and failing efforts to be true to oneself, to one's ideals of Righteousness—whether one be sceptic, agnostic or atheist, whether saint or mystic—one is always finding anew the Self to which to be true. And "the end of the matter" is that to be true to Self is to be true to the Ultimate Reality which is Man's quest. Adherence to one's highest ideals becomes the *Imitatio Dei*. When it is said that "all men are equal in the sight of God," what is meant is not, from the *human* side, the equal opportunity for all men to work out their highest aims, important though this is, but rather that they are equal, each man relatively to his highest Self and in his relationship to God and His Universe. May one not say, then, that a Divine will can work through men who are true to themselves, even though—despite Matt. vii. 1 ("Judge not that ye be not judged")—we may perchance judge their standards to be inferior to our own?[1]

In this chapter I have emphasised, first, the significance of the whole Bible for the study of the history of ideas of God (I), Christology itself lying within a theistic framework (II). In losing the realism of the old religions (III), we have lost the idea of man's cosmic existence (IV). Yet the fundamental relationship between God, Man and the Universe conditions our religious and non-religious thinking (V), and accounts for the complexity of our diverse modes of thought

[1] Cf. p. 228.

(VI).   God is both in and behind the Universe (VII), and is
approached by intermediaries (VIII).   Personality, Human
and Divine, is a more ultimate reality than the processes of
the human mind (IX), the relationship being, it would seem,
one of "parallelism" (imitation) rather than of "substance" (X).   Between the human soul and the Ultimate
Reality comes all that which both severs and unites Man and
God (XI), and in the Universe of a Righteous God the
"right" and "rational" are to be looked for everywhere (XII).

The Comparative Study of Religions is, I am persuaded,
contributing to some new stage in the history of Religion;
and just as Religion has led to Philosophy, in the development of the great historic religions, so Comparative Religion
may lead to some new stage in philosophical and other
thought.   It is one thing to collect and classify the data of
Religion, but to order them and follow out their implications
involves a theoretical treatment which cannot ignore the
religions which we consider the highest.   What I have called
the "Theory of Religion" perhaps satisfies the test of the
best theory, which is not so much the number of facts it
answers, but the way it answers rival theories.   It seems to
bring out more clearly the essential problems, not only of
Religion, but also of the relation between the religious and
non-religious spheres or aspects of Life and Thought.   The
"Theory of Religion" involves the unsuspected influence of
our cosmic or theistic relationship upon all our deeper
thinking.   Man as organic with Nature, Man as "son" of a
Divine "Father"—here are diverse modes of thinking; and
while men feel that they have contact with Divine Reality
in certain religious or mystical states or ceremonies, they
are not remote from the Divine Process in normal, daily,
"right" living and "right" thinking to the best of their
powers.[1]

[1] See further Chap. xi, to which Ch. x forms an independent
introduction.

CHAPTER X

The "Truth" of the Bible

I. THE PROCESSES

IN the light of the preceding discussions of special topics we may now gather up the threads and endeavour to give a synthetic view of the main argument—the "Truth" of the Bible.

The inverted commas are intended to draw the reader's attention to the ambiguous word and to invite him to ask himself what "Truth" he expects or desires to gain from the Bible, and also to consider what important "true" things are to be gained from the modern study of that Sacred Book. That we approach it in a way vastly different from that of earlier generations all will agree, but to-day our attitude either is or at least should be influenced by the actual conditions in which we live. The general world-situation to-day is one that arouses widespread feelings of uncertainty, if not of apprehension and pessimism. We can readily distinguish between such feelings, which we perhaps share, and the more or less confident assurances that such and such a road is the only one to be taken. But unfortunately there is no agreement whatsoever as to the precise road along which we should go; and only when one has had special opportunities of realising how over-whelming is the spate of literature on this changing world can one understand how deep and far-reaching are the convictions that vital developments are at hand.

The future of Religion is felt to be directly or indirectly at stake; and it would be wrong to suppose that it is Christianity alone that is involved. Broadly speaking, we find everywhere striking views of Religion that are styled "liberal," "modernist" or "revolutionary," confronted by a certain tightening or increasing narrowness, a closing up of ranks, as it were, in order to stand four-square against the attacks of those without—or possibly within the camp. There are not only the familiar anti-religious and decisively atheistic attacks upon Religion in any shape or form; but there are manifold varieties of thought claiming to be religious, even as there are admirable types of humanism which have at heart the betterment of man, which perceive that man has a "religious" nature that must be nourished, but which are decisively opposed to the typical beliefs and practices usually styled "religious." Hence not only the future of Religion, but the very conception of Religion itself, is at issue.

Besides the uncertainty and change in the world of life, there is a similar unrest and absence of harmony in the world of thought.   The masses of material in physics, chemistry, biology, psychology and sociology have become almost unmanageable; and the systematic treatment of the available data might sometimes seem to be more pressing than the search for new evidence.   A "philosophy" is needed that shall bring order into our scientific knowledge and our knowledge of Man and the Universe; and no sooner is this need recognised than we realise the impossibility of reaching finality: whatever be the ultimate "Truth" about Man and the Universe it is in outlook, method and guiding principles rather than in some final static elaborate body of ultimate facts that the way of life is to be sought.

Meanwhile there have gradually grown up profound changes in our knowledge of and attitude to the Bible. These are due partly to our newer knowledge of the environment of the Bible, of world-history, and of world-religion. The Bible comprises a fraction of the history and religion of a very small part of the Ancient East, during a few only of the many centuries of which we have some knowledge. It reached its present form in the midst of epoch-making crises: it is perhaps one of the most far-reaching of discoveries in all research that the Sacred Book can be viewed as a unique source for the enquiry into the developments that have ultimately made us what we are.   To say that the Bible has been of incalculable influence in human history

P

is in no wise to deny that other factors also have gone to make the western world. Our personal attitude to the Bible may range from an unintelligent and almost superstitious veneration to an antipathy that deserves the same adjectives. But whatever this or the other individual may think, the Bible has played a part that distinguishes it from all other books, and the veneration to which I have referred is more excusable than the antipathy, ignorance and indifference which are perhaps most noticeable among writers not otherwise lacking in intelligence. A man may, if he chooses, believe that the Bible has had its day, but the power of the Bible in the past should at least arouse an intelligent curiosity.

In so far as uncertainty pervades all departments of life and thought it is no exaggeration to say that there is a "cultural" crisis, and throughout this book the line has been taken that the Bible itself is a cultural force of the first magnitude. This is not to ignore that there are other religions besides Christianity, and that these have much to contribute to enrichment of religious thought—I think in particular of India. But the comparative study of religions has shown, not merely that the Bible contains numerous ideas, beliefs and practices that are very familiar elsewhere, but that they have taken a peculiarly pregnant form, and that it is this that has preserved them—at least up to the present. It is possible to conceive that the Western World and Christianity might slowly decay; but there are other religions, and the most cynical of opponents of Christianity would still be confronted with the lofty idealism and well thought-out doctrines outside the particular religion which attracts his criticism. And if he goes further and objects that he is not opposing Religion or a particular religion as such, but its general cultural effects, which he considers disastrous, we gain the very important admission at the outset that the real force of any religion does not lie in itself but in its effect upon its believers and their social life and thought.

The general "cultural" significance of the Bible can be illustrated in this way. For purposes of study we cannot

sever the Bible from Palestine and neighbouring lands: e.g.
for geology, geography and pre-history Palestine presents
many features of importance, and for sociological, psychological, and historical research both Palestine and the Bible are
invaluable.   That is to say, for purposes of *secular* research
the Bible cannot be ignored.   Furthermore, while the comparison of Biblical with Egyptian or Indian religion may
seem academic, there are writers who have associated the
Hebrew prophets with modern social reformers and revolu-
tionaries; and nowadays the points of resemblance and
difference between Communism and early Christianity also
come up for discussion.   Whatever the results of the
discussion, we learn more of the "sort of thing" that happens
when some new sweeping movement is initiated—successfully or otherwise—in life and thought, and in this way
light is thrown upon processes of development of all kinds
and on all levels.   Similarly, the historical vicissitudes of
great outstanding figures—Lenin, Sun-Yat-Sen, not to
mention others—enable us to consider more usefully and
with a better trained imagination the inner history of
epoch-making events in the past.   In this way, quite apart
from the interest aroused by the archaeological work in the
lands of the Bible which is serving to illustrate the past, the
study of the Bible becomes bound up with modern research
and living issues.   We may differ as to *how* the Bible shall
be taught; but the Bible is forcing itself to the front, and it
is for us to see that it is neither unused nor misused.

    In interpreting the Bible we invoke the ordinary principles
of textual, literary, historical and other criticism.   This is
secular research.   But it is not to be forgotten that we deal
with some of the most powerful events in past history.   It is
necessary to find the best tested principles and frame the
best theories and hypotheses.   In the attempt to understand
the nature of historical and religious development in the
past we are unable to ignore the present and the future; for
although the past has gone and will not recur, the view we
take of it affects the future, even as our "theory" of the
past, if we think it "true," is not confined to ancient history.
Our "true" conclusions in Biblical study and in secular

research should interpenetrate as certainly as do the principles employed; and by thus bringing the Bible into the field of methodical study, we so extend the "methodology" of the subject that the "metaphysical foundations" of Science tend to be extended to become those of the Bible.

In and behind the Bible are the great epoch-making changes to which frequent reference has been made in these pages. It will suffice merely to name Abraham, Moses and Joshua, Amos and the great prophets, the prophets of the Exilic period, Nehemiah and Ezra, Judas the Maccabee and his successors, Jesus of Nazareth and Paul. Of these it is the Exilic period to which special attention is directed, not because those that preceded or followed are unimportant, but because this can be more clearly understood and its significance traced. It is unnecessary to recall the outlines from the fall of the Kingdoms of Israel and of Judah to the inauguration of post-Exilic Judaism.[1] Modern criticism recognises the importance of this age, especially when it is viewed in the light of external history.[2] The Old Testament in its present form is not earlier than it, and the contrast between the old traditional and the modern critical view of the Pentateuch and of the general course of pre-Exilic history is scarcely less significant than the differences due to some of the sweeping discoveries in the realm of science. The Exilic Age was one of far-reaching internal changes in Israel and in Palestine, and it is very generally agreed that the Second Isaiah (Isa. xl.–lv.) is a supreme landmark in the religious development of Israel. A height was reached, to be surpassed only in the New Testament, and the re-statement of monotheism, the new covenant relations between Israel and her God, and the new mission for Israel make the difference between the "pre-Exilic" and the "post-Exilic" stages complete.

This prominence of the Second Isaiah, by the side of the other great prophets Jeremiah and Ezekiel, is one of the outstanding results of Biblical criticism, and to the modern

[1] See pp. 20, 44.
[2] See Ch. VIII.

student the Pentateuch in its present form stands at the head, not of Israel as a people (say about XIVth cent.), but of post-Exilic Israel as a Church (some 900 or more years later). But the historical writers in the books of Kings, Chronicles, Ezra and Nehemiah tell us little or nothing of the part played in the development of history by the great prophets, notably the Second Isaiah. That is to say, although we can gain much of historical importance (e.g. from the books of Jeremiah and Ezekiel), the actual thread of history which enabled post-Exilic Judaism to feel its continuity with the figures and events of the distant past gave only a very imperfect conception of the history of the most critical ages, by ignoring the conditions in (North) Israel or Samaria after the fall of the northern kingdom in 721 and in Judah and Palestine after the fall of Jerusalem in 586.

Consequently the "canonical" history has entirely obscured the circumstances of the post-Exilic reconstruction of Israel by its indifference to the work of the prophets; even as at the rise of Christianity "prophetism" was repudiated by a Judaism unaware of the debt it owed to its prophets for its preservation and persistence. This goes far to explain the historical differences between Christianity and Rabbinical Judaism. The "canonical" view of history which grew up after the Exile carried on Judaism and kept it alive; but what once helped, now hindered, and the religion which could command admiration for its lofty ethical idealism was challenged—and successfully—by the new Jewish offshoot which became Christianity. The "body" of history had preserved the old "spirit" of the religion of Israel; but the "Israel of God," Christianity, gave a new "spiritual" interpretation to the history it took over, and reinterpreted it from a specific Christian point of view, giving it a new "body"; see pp. 166, 169.

Thus the Old Testament of the Christian is not precisely that of the Jew, even as the pre-Reformation Catholicism of the Reformed Church is not precisely that of the Unreformed Church. However the facts may be expressed, the events of nineteen centuries ago exemplify the way in which both the "spirit" of a religion and its shell or "body" may undergo change; each needs the other. It is necessary to bear this in mind.

In pre-Exilic Israel, after Yahweh had gained the supremacy over other gods, reforming efforts were directed to the purifying of the cult. But political and social troubles weakened Yahwism, and in the exilic prophets and above all in the Second Isaiah we witness what we may call Israel's "re-discovery of God." Post-Exilic Judaism with its Law (Torah) had no doubt of the *reality* of God, and the Event a few centuries later is the *approach* to God, through Christ, who is the Way, the Truth and the Life. In the place of a confident nationalism, written and oral traditions and the possession of the Torah, the new religion offered a Person, and although the Yahweh of past national history had been and still was viewed more or less anthropically, in Jesus Christ men found combined a vivid and fresh human history tnd Divine Reality. There was discontinuity, and there was aontinuity. In the Exilic period, despite the internal changes, chere was continuity such that the post-Exilic Pentateuch could be regarded as genuinely Mosaic; and at the rise of Christianity, when Jews became Jewish Christians, and Gentile Christianity divorced itself from Judaism, an "Israel after the flesh" became an "Israel of God." In spite of the discontinuity, such is the continuity that to the ordinary reader the Old and New Testaments have always been felt to be organically interrelated. Yet even in the earlier period it is a "spiritual" rather than a "literal" Israel that has given the Old Testament its value (pp. 28f., 136); and enough is known of the heights and depths of the old religion of Palestine to justify us in saying that we are not to value "Israel" or "Yahwism" as such, but those ideas and ideals that have been effective forces through history.[1] For just as we may value a man not "as such" but for what he means for us, so although there is a history "after the flesh" which may be accurate, and, as such, "true," it is the history "after the spirit" by which we are inspired.

The Old and the New Testaments may be said to turn upon the sixth century B.C. (or the Exilic Age in general), and the

[1] Cf. *O.T.R.*, p. 221.

first century A.D.   Without the events of the former period
we cannot conceive how Christianity could have arisen, and
although we naturally regard the latter as a unique event
in world-history, the significance of the earlier is in no
circumstance to be obscured.   That those two periods have
many points in common, need not be detailed,[1] and in
instituting any comparison and contrast it is instructive to
add a third—the present.

At all three are found catastrophic forebodings; but the
hope of a New Covenant in Jeremiah (xxxi. 31 ff.), actualised
in the New Testament, is also the hope of those who have no
sympathy with apocalyptic and eschatological expectations
or extremist and destructive doctrines.[2]   The three "transitional" periods witness reforming, transforming and regenerative movements, and individualism extreme and disintegrating.   Political, social and economic difficulties combine, and the old Messianic dreams of leisure and the
abundance of good things have their modern counterparts.
Although at the second period the ethical monotheism of
Judaism might seem to satisfy men's spiritual needs, it was
not so; as in Jeremiah's time (vi. 14), the hurt cannot always
be lightly healed, even as a premature hypothesis may not
only fail to cope with difficult facts but may thwart or hinder
a better one.   Similarly to-day when men call for cures
more adequate or more radical than those that are offered —
whether within Religion, or without it—it is incumbent upon
us to observe that the best outlook upon life, like the best
"hypothesis" in thought, is the one that offers the best hope
and— what is as important—deals best with its rivals and
opponents.

At all three periods are prophets "false" and "true," and

---

[1] Besides the idea of the "Servant of the Lord," the contact
between the New Testament (St. Paul) and the Second Isaiah will
be recalled (cf. *A New Commentary*, Part III, p. 408 f.).   Cf. also
the following remark: "the originality of Jesus was rooted in a
revival of the true meaning of II Isaiah" (W. K. Lowther Clarke,
Divine Humanity [1936], p. 96).

[2] That even some clergy should believe that the Kingdom of God
can be brought in by violence helps us to understand how in the
first century A.D. Jewish priests could side with the Zealots.

the task of distinguishing between them, equally perplexing. In the New Testament we see how a religious revolutionising change is being introduced; in the Old we have more of the stages before and after a similar change. In both we perceive among the "weak" things of the world (1 Cor. i. 26–31) how one may seem despicable (Isa. liii.), and another be a complete disappointment from the point of view of *Realpolitik* (cf. Luke xxiv. 21). Especially is it instructive to take note of the fine ethical humanism that distinguishes both Deuteronomy and the "Wisdom" Literature. When all has been said in favour of Deuteronomy, its fanatical nationalism stands in contrast both with the theism of Jeremiah and the Second Isaiah and with the universal outlook of the priestly writer.[1] The Deuteronomic spirit failed, even as the later, distinctive humanism bore no fruit but was replaced by the Christian movement.[2]

History was made by the Second Isaiah and by Christianity, even as, to go back to an earlier period, the prophet Amos meets the troubles of his age with his insistence upon the Righteousness of Yahweh. So to-day, when the emphasis is laid upon the defects of institutions and upon economic, social and political difficulties, it is "true" history that the one indispensable factor in progressive development has been a religious rather than a secular humanism, and the doctrine of an all-embracing Divine Righteousness and "rightness" in men first, and only after that in the "man-made" institutions. Thus the three transitional periods are mutually illustrative.

Much more might be said: it must suffice to refer in passing to modern anti-Semitism and the ancient Israelite anti-Canaanitism; hymns of vengeance ancient and modern; the vital difference between words (Yahweh, God, Democracy, Liberty) and the "content" which indicates their meaning and gives them force; and the timely

---

[1] *O.T.R.*, pp. 185f., 197, 219; also *Mélanges Cumont* (1936), p. 547f.

[2] On this pre-Christian humanism, see especially Causse, *Mélanges Cumont*, pp. 525–537, and his earlier works, *Israël et la Vision de l'humanité* (1924), etc.

condemnation of an overweening religious assurance, spiritual pride and religious "imperialism."[1]

History is not cyclical; it does not repeat itself mechanically; the law of "righteousness" does not determine the form it will take. But though the events of history happen once and for all, there are processes which command our attention because we find in them what can repeatedly be verified in individual or national experience. The inspiration and stimulus which past generations have gained from the Bible have not been inseparably bound up with the history of the world between 4004 B.C., and A.D. 96, the dates in our A.V. margin, if so they would be of antiquarian interest; although it is the historical shell or embodiment of what has been felt to be true that makes the Bible a very great book in the way that can be claimed for no other book. To-day as in the days before the Reformation there is indeed a tendency to treat the Bible as a book from which to select those crumbs only that men think they need or that support their cause. But the trend of research is now to treat the Bible as a field, or indeed as part of a field, so that just as the earlier Reformers found it was living history, so we are now finding that modern knowledge is paving the way for an historical interpretation vastly more extensive and comprehensive than was possible when the Reformation began. Hence, whereas about four centuries ago men felt that in the Bible God descended into history and the Bible was living history, to-day we may reap the fruits of the Reformation in realising that the Bible may give new life to our own history.

We may understand our position more clearly if we consider in briefest outline some of the steps from the old Yahwism of Palestine to the "reformed" post-Exilic religion, the rise of Christianity, and the movement westwards from the land of its birth. The prophets gave a new ethical and spiritual value to the old religion. Such conceptions as the Fatherhood of God, the Church as the Bride of Christ, the Spiritual Rebirth of the Individual, and his Sonship—all these and many more go back ultimately to cruder, physical

---

[1] The old un-reformed Israel illustrates the conception of a God immanent in the State.

and gross ideas of the relations between gods and men, and what the gods needed of men.[1] Yahweh was a force, a destructive one at times (cf. Exod. iv. 24, v. 3, xii. 13–23), but not explicitly an ethical God; and although in all early religions ethical conceptions are by no means wanting— in so far as a religious cult unites men socially—they are embedded in a naturalistic shell, which prevents men from seizing them and reclothing them.[2] Religion was lived: men acted their thoughts. Man was an "animated body and not an incarnated soul," to borrow a concise statement of the facts,[3] and our differentiation into "body + soul (or spirit)" represents a definitely secondary stage in the development of thought.

At the earlier stage men imitate their gods externally, physically; the rite is the natural and indispensable expression of what we, at our stage of thought, can single out as an "idea."[4] As time passes, on the one hand, the religious rite is apt to become all important—the value lies in the act and not in the meaning it originally had: the "body" has lost the "spirit." On the other hand, the spiritual or ethical meaning may be recognised, it becomes explicit: examples are to be found in the history of religion, notably as we pass from pre-Exilic to post-Exilic Yahwism and to Christianity. But the idea itself may also tend to be isolated, devoid of substance, content or context; the ideas are words on the lips, no doubt subjectively valuable and authoritative, but without that social and objective significance they once possessed and which gave them a healthy "body." So, a rite, an object, a doctrine, or a religious, scientific, economic or philosophical dogma may come to lose that integrating

---

[1] In a famous passage Robertson Smith wrote: "Redemption, substitution, purification, atoning blood, the garment of righteousness, are all terms which in some sense go back to antique ritual" (*Rel. Sem.*, p. 439).

[2] *Op. cit.*, pp. 58, 263, 267f.

[3] H. Wheeler Robinson, "Hebrew Psychology," in *The People and the Book* (ed. Peake, 1925), p. 362.

[4] Cf. *idem*, "Prophetic Symbolism," in *Old Testament Essays* (ed. D. C. Simpson, 1927), pp. 1–17, and A. Lods, *ib.*, pp. 55–76.

complex or embodiment which once gave it more than merely subjective—or "autobiographical" importance.[1]

This is not to say that the working social and religious life of a group or the systematised corpus of beliefs or doctrines must, because it has worked hitherto, therefore be of lasting validity.[2] None the less, a social group, as such, entails a working harmony of beliefs and interests, and as society becomes more complicated and differentiated, the harmonious inter-relation of intellectual and aesthetic interests is no less necessary. The need that is felt to-day for a better adjustment of interests has arisen in the most natural and explicable manner as a result of human growth, an awakening of consciousness, and a dissatisfaction with the beliefs and customs that men of all colours and races find in their environment. In the past many invaluable ideas which men have found "true"—e.g. life after death, the personal relation between God and Man—have been embodied in forms which were rightly condemned—e.g. human sacrifice, religious prostitution— and sometimes men have "emptied the baby with the bath" and rejected the good and harmless along with the harmful and bad.[3] But whereas past reformers have found that which was spiritually, morally or aesthetically objectionable, to-day objections can also be brought from the intellectual side; and men who are attracted by some fundamental religious beliefs of the past, and feel their "truth," feel also the necessity of making them "real" in life and in thought by correlating the religious and the non-religious spheres of existence even as we find them correlated wherever the religion is a living and effective force.

As we pass from the Old Testament to the New we pass

[1] The adjective may be remembered as one that a famous Cambridge philosopher loved to employ.

[2] It would be instructive, e.g., to note step by step how the self-supporting body of beliefs around the old-time view of the Old Testament in spite of its long history gradually lost validity. It would be found that the "orthodox" view never had held the complete field, and that there was constant "interpenetration of opposites." Cf. p. 284.

[3] See *O.T.R.*, p. 137.

from older and more rudimentary physical and realistic types of life to those more familiar to modern thought. The Old Testament takes us back to primitive and ancient religious conditions; the New Testament leads us forward to our problems of to-day. In the attempt to understand the Old Testament we have also to evaluate all those religions wheresoever they may be, which we happen to consider "below" the level of our own religion. In our attempt to understand the whole Bible we have to correlate lower and higher types of religion, to ask ourselves in what way our conceptions of Inspiration, Revelation and Theocracy are effected. We have also to answer the question whether we suppose that the developments in Religion upon which we can look back have ceased.

The Bible raises questions of a philosophical character, so that one can justly speak both of the Religion and of the Philosophy of the Bible. We have seen that the age broadly of the sixth century B.C. makes a dividing-line between an old Oriental world and one that may be said to have lasted until to-day. There were sweeping developments over a wide area, and ethics, psychology, science and philosophy *in our sense of the terms*, can scarcely be traced earlier. There is a new dualism, an objectivity: the German philosopher, Dilthey, has described it as *eine wissenschaftliche Erklärung des Kosmos*.[1] It inaugurates the classical world of the Mediterranean.[2] The changes which the Biblical student associates with the Exile are part of the vaster changes which ultimately gave birth to our own culture. While in Israel we have the height of ethical monotheism—the Reality of God, in Greek lands we are in the centuries when intellectual activity produced the fruits which have made us grateful debtors to the spirit of Greek humanism. In the later post-Exilic age we pass to the Wisdom literature, the germ of a Jewish social philosophy; but although Greek thought stimulated the Jews, especially those of Alexandria, the ethical monotheism of Israel was not worked out philosophically.

---

[1] *Einleitung in die Geisteswissenschaften*, I (1922), p. 144.

[2] See pp. 81, n. 2, 135f.

When, in after centuries, Christians, Jews and Mohammedans did proceed to take up the implications of their
respective religions, they had to rely upon Greek thought:
the fact that this should be so is significant. The Greeks
gave us humanism, but not religion; the Israelites were not
philosophers, but they had behind them a lofty theism
which had, or was to have, philosophical implications. The
speculative thought of the Greeks was based upon the
relatively slight empirical knowledge of their age: they had
neither the national historical tradition nor the religious
feeling of Israel. It is true that Palestine itself had never
been isolated from the cultural influences of its neighbours;
and the alliances between Greek thought, on the one hand,
and Judaism, Christianity and Islam, on the other, have been
theologically and philosophically fruitful. But with the
progress of Science, Comparative Religion and Biblical
Criticism the alliances have become uneasy and new situations have arisen.[1]

We look back on the decline and decay of ancient Palestine
and Greece. We follow the disintegration of post-Exilic
Israel, the rise of a new religion, and the catastrophic fate of
the Jews.[2] The massacres and disasters in the Levant (e.g.
Cyrene[3]) will suggest that in the decline and approaching
downfall of their noble heritage maddened extremists and
fanatical Messianists by destroying the old Judaism paved
the way for the speedier conquests of Christianity. However that may be, the last traces of the ancient culture of
Palestine were washed out, as it were, and Islam in the
seventh century of this era had an easy victory and an
untilled field. Like the Communism of to-day, Islam had a
few simple ideas and offered much that seemed attractive.

[1] See pp. 97, n. 2, 157, n. 2.

[2] Cf. above, on the earlier period to 70 A.D., p. 156, n. 2.

[3] These began in 115 A.D., fifteen years before the founding of
the new Jerusalem, Aelia Capitolina, by Hadrian, and may be
regarded as the culmination of decades of revolutionary ideas of the
new age (see C.A.H., xi. 250f., cf 673). If Christian tradition has
been unkind to the Pharisees (see p. 187, n. 1), the unhappy fate
of the Jews at least obliterated the memory of the destructive and
ferocious outbreaks which were responsible for so much misery.

Meanwhile Christianity grew in passing westwards, and—as Renan hints—perhaps destroyed a dying Roman Empire. It reached an untutored West which in course of centuries began to feel and think for itself.[1] Helpful though it may be, in some respects, to speak of the "Dark Ages," we should not forget that the West had always been "dark" and that Greece failed to live up to its best and to keep the light burning.[2] It is the Western world that has gradually been realising that its inherited amalgam of Oriental religion and Greek intellect is alien to its genius; and, aiming after a new synthesis, feels the want of one that does justice to religious, social and intellectual needs. If the West has any genius or spirit that shall be as valuable to the world as that of Israel and of Greece have been in the past, it has not yet manifested it in its thought: but a "spirit" needs a "body," as truly as a "body," if it is to live, needs a "spirit." Civilisation is a *moral* organism.

Thus we have inherited the fruits of the alliance between Palestinian religion and Greek intellectual enquiry. We have in some measure come to understand how it is that we now think along the lines we do and not as those whose cultural heritage has had another ancestry. It is more important to understand the past as fully as possible before speculating on the future, and the rest of this chapter endeavours to go back to the Bible and observe what questions arise at once when we consider it historically.

It is generally recognised that there was a spiritual decline after the age of the great reforming prophets: the theism of these creative figures is contrasted with the ritualism of the priestly writers. Jeremiah and Ezekiel already represent the prophetical and the priestly types; and it has been easy to stress the gulf between religion of the heart and ecclesiastical

---

[1] Judaism and Christianity have flourished and have been fruitful in the West rather than in the East. Palestine belongs to the Mediterranean basin and not to Asia proper. See p. 158.

[2] In Babylonia and Assyria astrology paved the way for astronomy —thanks to the "scientific" spirit of the Greeks; but in Greece itself astronomy was followed by astrology (Jastrow, *Religious Belief in Babylonia and Assyria* [1911], pp. 256ff.).

organisation. Whatever Mosaism may have been—and
scholars differ widely—there was some subsequent relapse:
"Jeshurun waxed fat and kicked" (Deut. xxxii. 15).
Similarly, to come down later, the rise of Christianity is
irrefragable proof that some new spiritual impulse was again
felt necessary in the late post-Exilic age. But the contrast
between the prophets and post-Exilic religion has sometimes
been made too rigorously and harshly, and our estimate
to-day must be more judicious, and may even seem
temporising.[1]

The reforming prophets were, so to say, religious specialists,
men of intense feeling, and enthusiasts for their cause in a
way that could appear to border on fanaticism. Individualistic "prophets" may be, to use Burkitt's term, "social
nuisances,"[2] and may go further than even their disciples
can follow them. Keen, individualistic and enthusiastic
movements have constantly to be tempered by compromise,
adjustment, and the harmonious co-operation of men
differing in temperament and mentality. The history of the
earlier stages of the Reformation—even of Luther himself—
is as instructive an object lesson as the fortunes of some
pioneering research inaugurated by too independent and
individualist a thinker.[3]

To be more precise, we may notice two typical consequences, both due to the necessity of finding an adjustment

[1] One mistaken tendency was to treat the Priestly Writings as
representative of Judaism as a whole; against this the Jewish
scholars, Montefiore, Abrahams and others rightly protested. The
prominence of modern extremism also led to the feeling that the
spirits even of prophets must be tested (cf. 1 John iv. 1), while
with the spread of Biblical Criticism among the clergy there was
an at least unconscious revolt against the supposition that priests,
as such, were necessarily reactionary or obscurantist!

[2] *A New Commentary*, Part I, p. 430.

[3] As regards the influence of Hegelian ideas upon the criticism
of the Old Testament it may be said that the antithesis between
prophet and priest *does* represent a certain conflict between the
less and the more institutional and ecclesiastical interests. This
antithesis came to a head and made the great developments in the
religion of Israel at a certain period of its history, but to give it a
quasi-universal significance in Biblical history would be as great
a mistake as the Marxian absolute antithesis of Capital and Labour.

between a new movement and its environment. One is the weakening of the driving power and enthusiasm with which it is ushered in and greeted by its disciples; the other is the change in its content as it spreads among men who can grasp neither its original appeal nor the significance of the original ideas. We cannot live without ideals, but unfortunately in giving them an embodiment they are apt to become tarnished; and the very body in which they are incarnate may subsequently stifle them. Even in ordinary research the specialist must often simplify if he is to be understood; and the most sweeping tendencies in Science must be expressed in "parables" if the ordinary mind is to grasp something of their meaning.[1] One does not need to be either a Hegelian or a devotee of Dialectical Materialism to acknowledge that there are inevitable processes wherein the ideas of the single individual must be adjusted to the many, and that the many have conflicting intellectual and other needs to be satisfied which are not felt by any one individual.

Now, just as both prophet and priest were necessary—each at the proper time—to carry on the development of the religion of Israel, so also we should notice that the Deuteronomic spirit, Jeremiah, Ezekiel, the Second Isaiah, not to mention other factors, combined to make the change from the pre-Exilic stage to the post-Exilic. We could ill spare any one of these, even as our knowledge of Early Christianity would have been sorely impoverished had we not, let us say, the Marcan gospel or the Book of Revelation. How much richer we also are thanks to our possession of the apocryphal and pseudepigraphical literature! In a word, fortunate in what we do possess, we can see how easily our store might have been less, and how heedful we should be to make the fullest use of it.

We glance again at the men of the Exilic Age. What did Jeremiah, for example, think of Deuteronomy, and did

---

[1] B. Bavink, *Science and God* (1933), pp. 81, 82 f., cf. p. 91, speaks of the necessity of simplifying at the expense of strict accuracy, and warns his readers that a certain illuminating picture of a physical process is most probably not quite true.

Yahwism take the course that would have commended itself to him—or for the matter of that to Ezekiel, or the original author of the Second Isaiah?[1] In our own personal estimate of the religion of the Bible it is only too easy to ignore the diversity of minds that went to make it—it might even be better to say that no single estimate could do justice to "the Books" (τὰ βιβλία). More helpful is it when we recognise our debt to it—or them—to appreciate the wisdom of that movement—or school—which compiled our Pentateuch from the very disparate sources which literary criticism has discovered,[2] and to those Rabbis who, later on, included in the Canon the examples of Jewish erotic poetry, scepticism and religious megalomania which lie before us in the Song of Songs, Kohéleth (Ecclesiastes) and the Book of Esther. Wiser than most of us, they were under no illusion as to the earthen vessels in which religious truths could be stored. No synthesis of diverging or conflicting tendencies, no re-union or round-table conference bent on compromise and the smoothing-out of differences— we owe the Pentateuch, the Canon of the Old Testament, and the whole Bible from the Creation of the Universe to the vision of a New Creation, to occasions when the most legitimate of contrary and contradictory convictions must have been silenced in the timeless vision—such as is characteristic of the best of the old prophets—of a horizon reaching far outside the circumstances of the day.

How little we know of the inner history of the great turning-points! Memory concentrates upon a few occasions, and focuses upon a few names—e.g. a Joshua or an Ezra— what belongs to their age. Of the movement behind the Second Isaiah, and still more of the circumstances of so outstanding an event as the rise and early prominence of the Indian ethical god Varuna, we know nothing; the actors are among the countless "unknown soldiers" who have no memorial among the living. The more deeply

[1] Cf. Skinner, *Prophecy and Religion*, p. 117, on Jeremiah's dissatisfaction with the "official propaganda of optimism" (vi. 14), also *ibid.*, p. 150f.

[2] Contrast the elegant manner in which Josephus presents the Pentateuch to his Greek readers.

we delve into the history of our past, the more often do we
get glimpses, shadows or echoes of men who could have
graven upon their tombstones:

> After me cometh a builder,
> Tell him, I too have known.

Just in proportion as we admit any debt to the Bible
we must ask, at what point or points in the history that is
in and behind it do we recognise the hand of God? Is it
here, is it *there*, or is it in the whole process? Do we see it
in Jeremiah and not in Deuteronomy; in the Second Isaiah
and not in the Pentateuch? And if we proceed in this way,
shall we confine our questioning to the Bible, leaving out
the apocryphal and other writings that led up to Christianity?
Shall we indeed refuse to go outside Palestine . . . ? In
the history of research—Science or Biblical Criticism, for
example—the debt is to the third-rate as well as to the
leaders, to those who erred and forced others to clarify
their minds as also to the masters whose disciples have oft-
times been more devoted than wise. It is no disloyalty
to recognise where and in what respect the leader cannot
be followed; for the cause, the process, is greater than
any one of those who make it live or give it new life. One
generation sees evil in Biblical Criticism, another in
Darwinism, and yet another, it may be, in the comparative
and psychological study of religions. There is no doubt
that as we survey those processes in life or in thought
which have enriched the world we see errors, the correction
of old errors, and the perpetration of fresh ones. It is an
endless story of making right what is wrong, of reconciling
conflicts, and of bringing disharmony into at-one-ment; and
in the world of religion we speak of Righteousness, Sin,
Atonement and Forgiveness (Ch. VII). The processes of
history are on a vaster scale than our dim eyes can perceive,
and where so much good has come out of error and wrong
we must presume that the trans-human process demands that
each man, each age and each people should aim at being
true to its highest, for in being true to Self one is discovering
the Self to which to be true.[1]

[1] See p. 202.

In working out its national history Israel's best men were more than merely Hebrews or Israelites. They profited from the defeats inflicted upon them by their enemies outside; and the gross and cruel cults within opened their eyes to the secret of the relationship between their own God and themselves. The processes of history were not for one man or one people. Indeed, the very assurance and egotism of Israel led, on the one hand, to the truer conviction that even their own God cared for other peoples, like the Aramaeans, worshippers of Hadad, and the uncircumcised Philistines; while, on the other, this consciousness of national worth and destiny prepared the way for the recognition of the worth of every member of the "Israel of God." Much as the world owes to the people of old Palestine and to the Bible there must be no illusions. There is a vital difference between the undigested notion, the "Fundamentalist" belief, that the whole Bible is literally inspired— a belief that would have devastating consequences for our trust in God—and the knowledge that the Bible is a field, nay, part of a field wherein are treasures to be discovered by those who, like trained archaeologists, know where and how to dig. When we perceive that the essential truths of a religion are, as such, strictly independent of their particular embodiment, we have next to see that the "spirit" of the Bible is what it is because of the "body" which it informed; a less noble body would not have nurtured so life-giving a spirit.

Just as, in the national development of Israel, there were the more intense and outstanding occasions which alone gave new life and development, so it is in the history of the individual. Without the monotheism of the Second Isaiah, for example, one cannot conceive the progressive advance of Israel, although obviously the stages before and after form the occasion of the new inspiration and regeneration and sustain it. So also in the individual we understand how the rarer and intenser experiences re-invigorate and give new driving power; but they are part only of the whole life and are, as it were, the "nucleus" of the development. Religion itself, concerned properly with what is most real and true, may fill the whole man, but it is part only of the manifold phases of his daily existence. The significance of the religious impulse, indeed of all fresh, directive energies raises questions which unite the religious and non-religious spheres.

To start with the Mosaic Age, although there is no agreement as to the precise content of Mosaism there is no doubt whatever that the general period round about 1400 B.C. was an exceedingly important one for history and religion. Monotheistic or monistic tendencies can be traced in Egypt and South-West Asia.[1] Whatever was the religious culture of the Israelites on entering Palestine, in the land itself the general cultural conditions were of no low order; and the Yahwism against which the prophets had to contend, several centuries later, must have been a blend of the elements brought in by the invaders and those of native origin. Hence there are two ways of considering the course of events, (a) the development of the Israelites, from their sojourn in the wilderness outside Palestine after their exodus from Egypt, the settlement in Palestine and the inter-marriages, the monarchy, the Exile and the post-Exilic reconstruction; and (b) the development of Palestine, its ancient culture, its occupation by colonists and invaders (including the Israelites); and the persistence in Yahwism of elements whose native origin is beyond doubt.[2] Now while the former represents one evolutionary view of progressive development—in which, by the way, there is no room for the sweeping events of and about the sixth century B.C.—the latter is more true to life. We start with the relatively high conditions in Palestine in the Mosaic Age, the subsequent decline and deterioration justifying the work of the reforming prophets, the increasing disintegration followed by the new age inaugurated in the time of the Second Isaiah, and again the subsequent decline and deterioration until we reach the first century A.D. when, at the time of the rise of a new religion, Judaism itself evidently underwent some reinvigoration which nourished and preserved the scattered Jews after the final destruction of Jerusalem.

[1] Cf. e.g. Albright, *The Archaeology of Palestine and the Bible*, pp. 163ff. See above, p. 140f.

[2] See pp. 61, 63.

Alternations of religious impulse and decay to be followed by fresh impulse are everywhere familiar: we may speak of alternating de-spiritualising and re-spiritualising processes. The philosophy of history in Judges ii. 11ff., envisages, as it were, the swing of the pendulum from welfare to apostasy and defeat, and from repentance and deliverance to a new peace. But we never return precisely to the old position; a man does not return to the religion of his youth, though it may re-assert itself in his mature years. The process is irreversible; it only seems reversible when we treat it in the abstract, and compare it to the pendulum. The spiral would be a more suggestive figure, since the "return" is typically to a similar position on a higher plane or at a more advanced stage.[1]

At every fresh impulse there is no mechanical archaising return to the old, and the development in and behind the Bible illustrates a profounder conception of progress. We trace the ethicising and purifying of cruder and more physical ideas of the relations between God and man: some elements disappear, others take a new form, and others again are new. The Old Testament conception of "return" must be supplemented by the μετάνοια, or change of mind, of the New. It is the process upon which Dialectical Materialism lays such store, and its importance lies in the fact that it is, philosophically regarded, perfectly neutral.[2]

The process must not be severed from concrete history and universalised in Hegelian fashion. Nor can we ignore the difference between the development issuing in Christianity and that which resulted in Rabbinical Judaism and the Talmudism of Jewry. Nor again should we forget how often a new impulse, whether religious or not, leads to new growths that are "sectarian," narrower in their horizon, subjectively effective, but objectively less comprehensive than the parent. These are in some respects a devolution rather than an evolution. But the fact remains that one of the most familiar of processes is that where a new impulse gives a new

---

[1] Cf. *Textbook of Marxist Philosophy* (ed. J. Lewis, 1937), p. 385.

[2] See p. 284.

form to the old, and a new state of equilibrium follows after a preceding stage of disequilibrium.

The process to which we are referring may be supplemented by noticing the revived interest in the theory of a primitive monotheism. In the Bible there are the two outstanding epochs upon which turn the Old Testament and the New; also the Mosaic Age as a whole marks the difference between a pre-Israelite stage and one in which Yahwism was taking root. Other examples of powerful religious movements are to be found in Islam and in the introduction of the Indian Varuna. Much more could be said if we went further afield or included the occasions that are not so conspicuous. We should find that the religious impulse varied in intensity, content and continuance. It has to work upon the existing conditions in its environment; and just as widely different cultural conditions distinguish the monotheism of Islam from that of the Second Isaiah, so the latter (of the sixth century B.C.) cannot conceivably be identical with the Israelite or other monotheistic tendencies of the Mosaic or Amarna Age of some eight centuries previously.

Accordingly, when we turn to the impressive evidence for the belief in supreme gods even among savages, we may freely recognise that something of the nature of a mono-theistic belief must be regarded as a primitive phenomenon: that is to say, it does not come at the end of a progressive evolutionary series.[1] The profoundly interesting beliefs are to be found by the side of low, crude and savage beliefs and practices—an occurrence not unknown among more highly civilised peoples—but rarely are they historically effective. There is all the difference in the world between the most genuine of monotheistic beliefs among peoples high and low and the historical and continuous development of mono-theism in Israel.[2] The continuity is far more significant than

[1] See E. O. James, *A New Commentary*, pp. 672–6.

[2] As the eminent Roman Catholic, Father Wilhelm Schmidt, the most learned and energetic defender of the theory of primitive monotheism, especially mentions the tendencies to monotheism among the pre-Islamic Arabs (*Origin and Growth of Religion* [1931], pp. 192 ff.), it should be observed that it was not these, but Mohammed himself, that made Islam a force in history.

the world-wide prevalence of religious impulses of whatever quality, even as the subjective conviction that God exists is not so vital as the significance of that conviction for a man's co-ordinated life and thought.

Some generalisations may be safely made: (*a*) It seems quite impossible to understand intelligently the course of world-religion unless we postulate, *from the first*, religious impulses of greater or less intensity.   (*b*) But it is no less impossible to conceive at all intelligently the content of the religious beliefs and practices of human beings, living under the remotest prehistoric conditions.   (*c*) The same may be said of the dawn of religion in the individual; e.g. to "explain" the belief in a Deity from the infant's earliest experiences is to "explain" parental love from the child's love of dolls and toys.   If, on the one hand, the "Theory of Religion" has its explanation of the origin of religion, one which is accused of begging the question, all the alternative theories introduce, however unintentionally, the very factors which need explanation.   (*d*) The religious impulse is conditioned by the general cultural level of its environment. It would be generally agreed that there would be a real advance if only our religious, social, political and intellectual questions were so adjusted that we could face the future with greater confidence and unanimity than we do.   And further, were there any impressive and successful religious revival that might seem to point the way to a new stage of equilibrium, it would undoubtedly have cultural repercussions sooner or later, for the real strength of a religion lies in the meaning it has for the total environment.   That is to say, throughout we know only of what may be called despiritualising and respiritualising phases, never of actual beginnings or origins.

(*e*) Finally, at the respiritualising stage the old elements will constantly emerge or be reasserted in a new form or context.   Both the earlier "religious" and "secular" elements will contribute—even as, at a higher stage, Christianity gained from the pre-Christian "secular" philosophy of the Greeks.   But the despiritualising process is so familiar that it has been wrongly imagined that in the long

run there will be nothing left for Religion, all the religious
aspects having been sloughed off.   This, however, is as
illegitimate as to carry back the process and imagine that
there was once a wholly religious stage out of which law,
science, etc., have gradually developed.   The fact is that
we are always finding differentiated conditions—"religious"
and "secular" or "profane"—on however humble a scale—
but that the sort of differentiation varies.[1]

Both within the Bible and outside of it are illustrations of
religion good and bad and of higher and lower tendencies.
The history of Religion as a whole is one of repeated demands
for beliefs and practices higher than those in currency.   The
estimate we have of "pagan" religions involves our conceptions of the relations between God and Man, and to believe
that God has revealed Himself elsewhere than in the Bible
does not make it less *sui generis*.   On the contrary, the more
we seem to see of the Divine Process in human history the
greater becomes our own responsibility; for It is no respecter
of peoples or even of religions, and transcends all human aims
and ambitions.   When the great prophets utter their conviction that God is near to those who do His will and conform
to the attributes we ascribe to Him, we may find a clue to the
vicissitudes of Religion.   Many of the social and religious
practices in early and rudimentary religion are unlovely and
crude from modern standpoints, but they persist.   Is it not
that there is sufficient conformity with Divine Righteousness,
the ultimate Reality, on these lowly levels of man's childhood?
To be unconscious of one's childhood is one thing, but it is
quite another when men consciously choose what they know
to be the lower of the alternatives presented to them, for this
is not the ignorance of higher possibilities, but the failure to
aim at them.   It would be contrary to all reason if the lower
choice could be repeatedly made with impunity.   We may
believe that God moves in a mysterious way, and the
processes of history do indeed transcend the individual
actors; but everywhere men are found to be aware that for
them there is a right and a wrong.

[1] It is in much the same way that there is everywhere a recognition
of things that are "right" and of things that are "wrong"; but the
contents of the two groups vary.

In endeavouring to understand as carefully and completely as possible the nature of the epoch-making developments which have made human history, the despiritualising
and respiritualising processes require a fuller treatment than
can here be given them.   Along with the former we see not
only a weakening of the early impulse, but a certain isolating,
narrowing and specialising, while in the latter the processes
are synthesising, systematising and re-creating.   They recur
on the largest scale in and behind the Bible; they can even
be traced in our treatment of the Bible.   Consider, for
example, how we may isolate a problem in order to handle it
more effectively—we take J and E (the Yahwist and Elohist
sources) or D (Deuteronomy), we isolate them from the rest
of the Pentateuch, but ultimately we find that questions
arise which concern not only the Pentateuch but the Old
Testament as a whole.[1]   In like manner New Testament
problems are found to involve the religious and other conditions of the age.   We have seen how much the Bible gains
when we look at it in the light of ancient history and religion
instead of regarding it in isolation; similarly religious problems suffer if they are kept apart from the claims of the non-
religious disciplines, just as, on the other side, the intellectual
part of ourselves may be over-developed so that the wider
spiritual claims become obscured.   Everywhere there is the
possibility of excessive isolation or of premature systematising.   Yet the criticism of the Bible has progressed by
intellectual concentration upon problems, and its spiritual
and religious value has been so greatly enhanced that we are
justified in our faith that neither the Bible nor Religion has
anything to lose from the most penetrating criticism,
provided only it is remembered (a) that whatever we isolate,
in order to facilitate our scrutiny, belonged to an environment
which sooner or later claims our attention, and (b) that the
intellectual activity of a man is only a part of a larger

---

[1] Cf. Kennett, *The Church of Israel*, pp. xix.ff.   Again, literary
critics, following Wellhausen, narrowed their field and worked upon
a smaller canvas than did Ewald and Stanley; but when they began
to widen their horizon, they found a fuller and wider field than
was available to their predecessors.   This narrowing and isolating
was a necessary step; see pp. 79, 89.

existential whole whose claims are not confined to the intellect.

To Wordsworth's Peter Bell a primrose was not "the meanest flower that blows," giving "thoughts that do often lie too deep for tears," but a flower and "nothing more." But Tennyson's flower in the crannies, like the hyssop on which Solomon is reputed to have discoursed, can lead one on from question to question:—

> If I could understand you, root and all, and all in all,
> I should know what God and man is.

It is by successive processes of isolating and despiritualising that we pass from "the earth is the Lord's and the fulness thereof" to "the land belongs to the people." In the same way we pass from the mutual claims of the group and the full-blooded member to the one-sided notion that state-help calls for no reciprocal contribution; or we pass from the necessary combination of liberty *and* responsibility to the misleading half-truth that men are born free. Above all, in the sphere of Religion itself the most sterile and emasculated conceptions of a Supreme Being will come to prevail. And as "God" becomes a name, and scarcely more, men continue to use it seriously, though sometimes in the most naïve of ways, forgetful or ignorant of the wealth of content which once gave it force and fullness of meaning. Consequently, as the despiritualising process continues and earlier bodies and patterns of thought disintegrate, the religious and the non-religious spheres are more widely separated than is recognised by scientists and others who still appreciate the value of Religion, and by the religious who freely appreciate what the scientific and other fruits of the intellect have to contribute. Religious thought can scarcely yet be said to have assimilated the implications of those results of science which it has recognised.

With what sort of assurance could we say that "the Fear of the Lord is the beginning of Wisdom" (Ps. cxi. 10), or that we have first to seek the Kingdom of God and that a Heavenly Father knows His children's needs (Matt. vi. 33), or that not a sparrow falls to the ground without His knowledge (x. 29, cf. vi. 26)? We may grant that these are of profound *religious* importance; but it is well to remember that at earlier and less differentiated stages of thought convictions of this sort could be held with as intense a realism as our convictions of the reality of wireless waves, unable though we may be to visualise or explain them.

However incredible it might seem that any new religious revival, any fresh "respiritualising" process, should re-capture a religious realism at all comparable to that of the past, three facts should be borne in mind. There is first (*a*) the obvious fact that the vast majority of mankind do not share the particular cultural world of the more educated and the mentally more complex Westerner, so that their pro-gressive development is more likely to be upon their lines than upon ours. Next (*b*) there is no reason to suppose that individualistic pioneers, leaders or the like, will bend the environment to their own way of thinking; at the best they leaven the lump. Finally (*c*) at the greater epochs new positive developments make their appearance, called forth by the advances of thought. Thus the middle of the first millennium B.C. makes a distinct landmark when ethics, psychology, and philosophy begin to be prominent, along with the new consciousness—in Israel—of the Divine Reality. But the philosophy which once seemed to unite the religious and non-religious aspects of life and thought now fails; the comparison of religions, of philosophies, and even of the similarities and differences in the realms of the religious and the non-religious realms, brings as distinctive a problem as that when scientists began to apply the compara-tive method throughout all Nature, and were searching for the most effective way of handling the ever-increasing masses of material, and of correlating the points of similarity and of difference.

If we are impressed by the positive gains to our knowledge of Man and the Universe, the history of the factors in the growth of this knowledge is not less impressive; and the Bible, of unique influence in past history, throws unique light upon processes familiar elsewhere. In the respiritualising pro-cesses, not merely is the old re-stated or confirmed afresh, but there are new advances, even as in the evolutionary process there are mutations which are viable and endure. But not all changes are lasting; the new growth may not be able to adapt itself to its environment; or, what is more important, it may not be able to create the environment in which it could flourish as its "nucleus." Changes can come in "'from outside' as it were,"[1] that is, outside the field of attention, outside the run of things, outside the general environment of life and thought. The events which we can watch historically, step by step, or "quantitatively," give way to a "qualitative" change.[2] Thus was a new stage inaugurated in religion at the rise of Christianity; and in research a steady succession of steps will constantly be followed by the rise of a man or of men who strike out a new line which is thenceforth taken up, until once more some new development is inaugurated. It is on such occasions that old problems are not necessarily solved, but old questions are replaced by new ones; there are new and more hopeful outlooks, new ways are opened up, and there is a new life. It is this familiar process, replacing a series of interlocked steps by some fresh "start-off," that is felt to be the philosophical justification of a world-wide social revolution. Its fatal fallacy is to overlook the true nature of the historical process, and the epochal stages in the past.[3]

Our survey of the past, above all, our conception of the course of Biblical religion, may assure us that there has been a "progressive revelation." On a closer survey it is seen to be not one of spirit alone, but of spirit and body. In certain respects there might seem to have been no progress in Religion itself; but the recurring spiritual truths are as skeletons or vertebrae, reappearing in new bodies of life and thought. It is this combination of spirit (or soul) and its embodiment that we are learning to understand, going behind a false dualism which, however useful in directing intellectual enquiry, obscures the proper unity of life. There can be no effective "respiritualising" process without the body which it informs (cf. 1 Cor. iii. 19), and through the

[1] See p. 99f.
[2] See pp. 258, 262, and index, s.v.
[3] See pp. 66, 72, 208, 210, 213ff., 224.

growth of which comes the fullness of the "spirit" (cf.
Eph. iv. 13); hence any "recall to Religion" raises the
question more precisely of the "body" or content of the
religion to which men are to be recalled and of its cultural
implications and value.

But if we are impressed by the part played by the Bible
in the past we may recognise a certain directive line.
Through Israel we have gained the conception of the conditional worth of the individual in the relation between God
and himself; and, as we pursue the line, we reach the
conception of the ideal Man, the Christ, in whom Divinity
and Humanity coexist.   Thus does the Religion of the Bible
indeed lead on to a Christian Philosophy; it is that of the
normal interrelation within the individual of those experiences, intuitions and ideas which we divide and sever into
the "Religious" and the "Non-Religious"; and in this
inter-relation the old religious realism would take a new
form.

The "Truth" of the Bible lies not only in that which the
religious mind has found, tested and verified, it lies also
in what we can learn from it of principles and processes that
have made individual and national history.   It is this
aspect of it with which the present chapter has been mainly
concerned; in the one that follows the question of religious
realism will be considered under other aspects.

CHAPTER XI

The "Truth" of the Bible

(continued)

II. RIGHTEOUSNESS, ORDER AND TRUTH

WHEN the Bible is placed within the framework of world history and religion there must be a natural and intelligible connection between it and modern thought. This is not to force one into harmony with the other, for modern thought is at a definitely transitional stage, and, as regards Religion, we are living, as Renan said half-a-century ago, "on the perfume of an empty vase." But since any discussion of the necessary adjustment would involve what one might call "the Philosophy of the Bible," i.e. the philosophical questions arising out of the Bible, it must suffice to indicate some preliminary steps along the lines of the preceding chapters.

To start with some elementary remarks. It often happens that profound satisfaction is felt when Biblical details are corroborated by some external discovery, e.g. the name Abram, the fall of Jericho, traces of volcanoes, etc. The "truth" of the Bible, as a whole, is felt to be confirmed by the accuracy of the details, even as, conversely, the inaccuracy of details is felt to shake or destroy the whole. This very familiar fact, which is constantly being illustrated, testifies to the way in which our convictions can be so embodied or materialised that we cannot sever the "spirit" or "soul" of the Bible from the "letter" or "body." Everyone's ideas about the Bible rest upon a more or less unsystematised collection of beliefs based upon a *selection* of its contents. It is absolutely impossible to form a coherent system upon *all*; and it may be taken for granted that any body of belief with which the reader is familiar and satisfied is founded upon a *selection*, to the exclusion of data which for one reason or another find no place in it. Now, such undue stress is often laid upon the accuracy or inaccuracy of details in the Bible that there is a danger of losing the "spirit" of it, that which gave it its living value as Truth. Just as the soul (or spirit) and the body (or letter) need each other, so the "Truth" of the Bible is enhanced when there is a better "body" of ideas concerning it. This is the goal of Biblical criticism. A better conception of the Bible, a better approach to it, means that it has a higher "spiritual" value. The soul and the body need each other.[1]

But when we speak of the accuracy of details we must not take too narrow a view of Truth. In the case of parables, dramas and inspiring fiction we do not ask for "truth" in the narrow sense; it is their significance for ourselves as a whole with which we are concerned. Their "spiritual" value is by no means necessarily bound up with their conformity to actual fact, even though the personages and events that never actually lived or occurred prove on a sufficiently minute analysis to be compounded of innumerable details, each of which could doubtless be substantiated in actual life. If a thing is "beautiful" its photographic accuracy may be irrelevant, and though a piece of music may be in accordance with the best canons it may have no thrilling effect. So, as regards Religion itself, we must on analysis distinguish the "spiritual" aspects—all that makes a religion inspiring, genetic, and so forth—and the character of its content. This has already been seen in the case of the stages of religion in Palestine: (a) the pre-Israelite (before the introduction of Yahwism), (b) the pre-prophetic (before the prophetic reform), (c) the post-exilic (the reformed Israel), and (d) the Christian stage (the New Israel).[2]

In the course of Biblical criticism much has been "confirmed" that never was or need have been questioned, but fuller knowledge has undoubtedly imposed caution upon one's affirmations, no less than upon one's denials. We may not say that a certain datum (e.g. a person or event) is

---

[1] Cf. p. 232f. Coleridge (*Table Talk*, p. 144) says: "a true religion must consist of ideas and facts both; not of ideas alone without facts, for then it would be mere philosophy; nor of facts alone without ideas, of which those facts are the symbols, or out of which they are grounded, for then it would be mere history."

[2] See pp. 60ff.

fictitious, because it contains sundry incredible elements;
for if so, many excellent persons (e.g. Alexander the Great)
would be wiped out.   Nor may we say that the datum is
true because of sundry perfectly credible elements, since they
are also to be found encircling fictitious persons and events
and non-existent supernatural beings who for a space of time
have been intensely "real" to those who believed in their
actual existence and perhaps worshipped them.   Consequently in practice we often reach two typical conclusions:
(1) we are led to decide that X is essentially or substantially
true; there are untrustworthy elements, but we find some
essence or substance that answers our needs.   Or (2), we
are led to decide the opposite: X is not trustworthy, although
we know or must not deny that there are trustworthy
elements.   In this volume the second conclusion is definitely
taken as regards the Pentateuch and the first as regards the
reality of Religion.[1]

Even in the case of the Pentateuch the view that it can,
with all due caution, be correlated with the Exilic Age as a
whole has had some interesting results.   In it we may read
of the entry from Exile into a Promised Land—the land
of the fathers—of the futility of "short cuts" and of the
danger of ill-considered ascents to the heaven of one's dreams,
of the more "popular" and the more "ecclesiastical" phases,
and especially of the recognition that God is above and behind all things and must be treated as Holy.[2]   Thus, quite
apart from innumerable trustworthy elements of importance
for the earlier history, we find various fundamental ideas that
are immensely suggestive for us to-day.   Knowing, as we do,
that the ancient Hebrew writers were more concerned
with the meaning and the spiritual value of history than
with mere annalistic records—history in the narrower sense—
we may see in the Pentateuch, not so much ancient history
down to about the Amarna Age (p. 61), as history written

[1] Note that although scholars went too far in rejecting the historicity of the Homeric poems, which, as can now be seen, are in certain
respects historically valuable, no one in writing the early history of
Greece would use them *au pied de la lettre*; see Bury, *C.A.H.*, II,
510 ff.

[2] See pp. 47 ff., 102, 103 ff.

and re-shaped in accordance with the conditions leading up to the inauguration of post-Exilic Judaism.[1]

Again, the first eleven chapters of Genesis are of value, not for pre-Abrahamic history, but for what was thought concerning the beginnings of things, especially when we compare these chapters with other accounts of Creation, Paradise, the Dawn of Civilisation, the Deluge, etc.[2] The books of Chronicles are essentially and substantially untrustworthy for the history of the Israelite Monarchy. They do indeed contain various elements of historical significance for the pre-Exilic period, but their greatest value is for the light they throw upon post-Exilic conditions in the days of the Second Temple: the growth of tradition, ecclesiastical rivalries, the "Davidic" hope, etc. In fact, the whole trend of Biblical criticism has been to illuminate—at the expense of the pre-Exilic Age—the vital centuries from about the Exilic Age to the rise of Christianity. In this way the search in a scientific spirit after ascertained facts brings what we call "losses" as well as "gains"; but the gains add immeasurably to our knowledge of the history of Religion and meet *our* needs.

Similarly in the case of the New Testament, the "secular" enquiries into the historical background, literary forms, and the rest, ought not to be narrowly scrutinised, as each new book is published, with the object of determining whether Christianity is or is not being "confirmed." Biblical criticism is a work of faith; and, to quote the words of one of the keenest and most reverent of Biblical scholars, "the

---

[1] We have to avoid the danger of allegorising. To those who do not take the above view of the Pentateuch the "interesting results" will seem mere pulpit homiletics (see p. 247). The danger is, in fact, a very real one. It is very instructive, therefore, to contrast the sort of allegorical treatment that we find in Philo with that much more fertile treatment in his later contemporary St. Paul. We may also contrast the systematic allegorising by the Stoics and others of the popular religion with our modern use of the material for the study of the ebb and flow of religious ideas, a treatment far more fertile than the ancient one.

[2] We can then agree with the boy who said of the story of the Deluge, "all this sounds very terrible, but it would be still more terrible if it were true."

only time when Christians will have cause to be afraid is when the far-off figure of Jesus Christ no longer attracts the critic and the student."[1]   The New Testament belongs to an age of grave unrest, when religious fanatics and assassins were illustrating the old conviction—evidently born of experience—"whom the gods wish to destroy they first make mad."   Not only are the facts in and behind the rise of Christianity of much more than ordinary "religious" significance, but the modern interest in problems of "the last things" (Eschatology) illustrates the way in which current conditions can lead thinkers—however unconsciously —to certain problems of an earlier age that prove topical to-day.   And so, too, when we look back upon the first century A.D. we may ask how far the approaching cataclysm of Judaism (70 A.D.) is foreshadowed in the contemporary literature.   But just as a dying culture may contain—as it then did—the seeds of its successor, and as the end of one series may be the beginning of another, so it is not without interest to-day to observe the attention that is paid to the idea of the Divine Kingship, i.e. the worth of outstanding individuals as a prelude to the recognition of the potential worth of every man (p. 118 f.).   Also in this age of unrest and disintegration we may note the effort to go behind the inherited modes of life and thought in order to gain a truer reality—even a "sur-reality."   Finally, of special value for this chapter is the study of integrating and unifying "patterns," and all else that throws light upon disintegration and redintegration in Nature and Man.[2]

In this way we get in and arising from the Bible vastly

---

[1] F. C. Burkitt at the close of a paper at the Liverpool Church Congress, October 1904, on St. Mark's account of the Birth of the Church.   The words preceding are also worth noting: "the mistakes of critics are demolished more quickly than even the errors of ancient tradition."   On another occasion Burkitt stilled expostulation with these words: "if the Christian cause perishes at last, it will not be because historical critics have explained the Gospels away, but because the followers of Christ are too faint-hearted to walk in the steps of their Master and venture everything for the sake of the kingdom of God." (*Francis Crawford Burkitt*, 1864–1934, p. 12, reprinted from the *Proceedings of the British Academy*, XXII.)

[2] See Index, s.v., " Patterns."

more than could ever have been obtained before. The Sacred Book becomes of living interest to-day. Although criticism seems to be at times disintegrating and destructive, it is admittedly incomplete unless it is also constructive and redintegrative. Emphasis is being shifted. If we lose what was believed in the past to be "true," we gain what is "true" for ourselves and the future. What we find to be untrustworthy in one context becomes trustworthy in another, and modern psychology and mental science gain what may be lost to ancient history and religion. Much remains insoluble, and often we must leave the dead to bury the dead: what actually happened or was believed becomes less important than our own needs to-day. The things that have been tested and are true for to-morrow counterbalance what was true for a dead past. The things we know we should do are invariably more than we live up to; and so long as we fail to live up to the truths we accept we are not entitled to complain of the losses we think we have suffered.

The wise teacher will echo the words of Gautama that his disciples should be "men-who-have-the-Self-as-lamp," each "a lamp unto himself."[1] He will desire that they make their own what they gain from him, and will awaken them so that each may develop further *along his own lines*, and can correct and go beyond his teacher. The truths which we have really made our own become independent of their origin: we have our own responsibility for them. They may have to be authenticated afresh, and given fresh fertilising power; they have been tested by our own experience and not accepted at second-hand on authority.[2] What seems true to A is not identical with what seems true to B; but an interconnection between them can be established, partly because, on the claim of Religion, God is at least potentially in relationship with men (pp. 127, 184), and also because, on the human side, there are the ordinary biological, physiological

---

[1] See A. C. Bouquet, *Man and Deity* (1933), p. 229.

[2] The notion that we believe what we do believe simply because certain beliefs have been handed down to us on authority has proved a stronger weapon for those who attack Religion than for those who defend it.

and psychological contacts. Comparison of beliefs and customs establishes so many resemblances everywhere that the world of human life and thought and the world of Nature present alike the problems of classifying points of similarity and difference and of understanding their interrelations.

So, as regards the question of the "true," the answer to the enquiry, Is this true? depends on the mental stage and needs of the enquirer. If, instead of two different individuals we consider the same individual at different stages of his mental development, we should naturally find points of similarity and of difference. But if only we could grasp clearly the general principles of mental or ideological development, not only might the child have less to unlearn, but we might come to understand the process of unlearning and rethinking. All this requires a knowledge, which we scarcely possess, of the real relation between different minds and between minds at different stages of their development. There is, however, all the material for it; and what might seem to be a purely academic problem has immense practical value.

As we come to "look at" things differently there is a change in the perceiving subject, a change in the data—as they come to have a different meaning—and a change in the relationship which enables us to affirm or deny. One can develop to the stage at which a thing comes to be recognised as true: the ground can be so prepared that the subject is so placed and the object so presented that there is the appropriate relationship. The Bible is often unintelligible, not because of the ignorance of the unprepared subject, but also because the ideas in it, as presented, are too strange. There is no longer the general cultural *milieu* which enables the one to approach the other with understanding. For religious instruction, and indeed for the "reconstruction" of Religion, there is not only the question whether to use new words and phrases which the recipient at his present stage of development can at once understand, but also the question whether it is not equally necessary to prepare the recipient so that even the well-worn and familiar ideas have their full meaning. Much of Religion to-day seems devoid of "truth," not only because the phraseology and ideas appear strange (e.g. Divine Grace), but because the subject has not the right approach.[1]

It is a common tendency to rely more upon the evidence of the senses than upon purely intellectual argument. In Biblical Criticism archaeology has sometimes been considered a sounder guide than the internal criticism of the Bible, on the ground that the former is obviously objective and the latter purely subjective.[2] But the former, though dealing with perceptual objects, can be thoroughly subjective; and the latter, though dealing with numerous data that are "held in the mind," may base its conclusions upon so many lines of evidence that they are irresistible.[3] Yet the notion is instructive; it means that we accept X as true because of its relationship with Y, which we more readily and perhaps already accept as true. Now suppose we look at the "arm-chair" scholar and the "field" archaeologist and the objects presented to them: results of excavation, data in books, testimony of witnesses, and so forth. We have, let us say, two material objects, one of clay, the other of metal, suitable as missiles, book-weights, etc. They are recognised *by competent eyes* as a fragment of a particular type of pottery vessel and a weapon of peculiar shape. It may be necessary to verify this, to ensure that each was found as reported, that the ground had not been "salted," and that there had been no disturbance of strata. Only to the *equipped* observer with the trained "approach" do the texture of the clay of the vessel and the shape and pattern of the pottery

[1] What is done in Roman Catholicism is familiar. Also in Communism the effort is made to provide a natural relationship between the fundamental tenets it is desired to spread and the general cultural preparation of the recipients.

[2] On the "external" and "internal" evidence, cf. *O.T.R.*, p. 81, and *ib.* p. 79f.

[3] I may mention, in passing, that to the best of my knowledge no one of the critical views in this book is refuted by archaeology. On the contrary, archaeology has provided the best evidence for the strength of the pre-Israelite (Canaanite or Palestinian) elements in Yahwism, thus confirming the view taken of the development or evolution of the old religion of Palestine, and all that results therefrom (pp. 61ff., 141). See also p. 19, n. 2 and p. 29, n. 1.

tell their tale; both vase and weapon may then be of real historical value, telling of contact with, or the actual presence of, a certain people, and possibly even seriously dislocating current theories of the date and distribution of the pottery type or the use of iron.   Thus, what the perceptual object "really" is depends on the way in which the percipient approaches it; and it is useless to say that we should think "concretely," and go from things to concepts and not the reverse, seeing that the thing is nothing for us apart from its use and meaning.   Indeed, it has first been necessary to distinguish the "thing" from the rest of its context.   So, also, it is not particularly helpful to say that a book—e.g. a Sacred Book—is undeniably a combination of letters, or, if read, a combination of sounds; and when we ask what a thing "actually" or "really" is, or is "in itself," the answer seems to depend upon the particular approach. To ask, What is the Universe "really"? is not so important as to determine whether by a better approach we can gain a better knowledge of it; and, in like manner, when we are considering the "Truth" of the Bible, the really important task is so to equip ourselves that we gain from it all it has to offer.

Throughout there is risk of misinterpretation and error and the necessity of revising accepted views.   At one time new data fall into place within them or supplement them—these we may call *quantitative* changes; at another, some adjustment becomes necessary, and the changes are *qualitative*. We cannot make laboratory experiments; but the laboratory of the Universe is constantly putting our views, theories and regulative principles to the test.   We test our theories by the use we make of them; and when new evidence turns up we may even adopt the methods of Procrustes and force it to our liking.   Yet from time to time the new data become ever more clamant; and even our extensive theories, bodies of thought, and the like, will need adjustment.   There is no rule-of-thumb as to when we are dangerously "Procrustean," and when the data we have ignored or twisted are dangerously disturbing the equilibrium.   The fact remains that the transitions from one state of dynamic equilibrium or position or "truth" to another bring exceedingly perplexing problems. We see them in the actual development (a) of research, (b) of religion in Palestine, (c) of our "conservative" and "critical" views of the Bible, and (d) in particular, of this age itself.

Now "truth" from the old Biblical point of view *is* "righteousness," while the root idea of the Hebrew word translated "truth" (*ĕmeth*) connotes faithfulness, continuance and reliability. When reference is made to prophets "true" or "false" the difference between them is instructive.[1] For example, the false prophet does not speak in the name of Yahweh; he draws men away from the accepted truth; and his teaching is inimical to it or would have consequences that were so. What the true prophet says is confirmed by its results, and popular belief tells of men who know what will happen, who know the "truth" of things and can utilise it; they can even sweeten bitter waters (Exod. xv. 25) and make the sunken axe-head rise to the surface (2 Kings vi. 6). But the true prophet, whatever his more spectacular gifts and his unusual psychical states, has the knowledge of the principles or patterns of life; he is, so to say, in tune with the Eternal Truth of things; he knows the Divine Righteousness. Hence just as there are the psychical states which seem to take a man away from *this* world into a vaster experience, so "real prophecy has, we might say, a cosmic significence."[2]

All moral, social and political disorders, like the great cosmic disorders—drought, earthquake, etc.—were once thought to indicate that there was no "right-ness" in the world (cf. p. 117). Yet it is just this disorder—like the disintegration in the Exilic Age—that brought the conviction of the reality of a universal God and *His* Righteousness, not as an abstract truth, but as one to be embodied in life and thought. We pass—to generalise the transition—from one stage of accepted religion through the transitional and

---

[1] See *O.T.R.*, Ch. X; also Jackson and Lake, *Beginnings of Christianity*, V, 110f.

[2] Skinner, *Prophecy and Religion* (1922), p. 199; see the whole passage, pp. 194 ff. The test of prophecy, he points out, is not a psychological one.

indeterminate steps to another stage when equilibrium is restored. What was true and right in the earlier religion— e.g. the sacrifice of the first-born—is no longer so, and the new truth proves itself by its viability, its coherence and its reproductive power. Like some sweeping theory, every new truth has to win its way against the compromisers (cf. the Jewish Christians), and against those who—whether we choose to call them cautious or reactionary—hesitate to relinquish what has justified itself hitherto, even though it is only by Procrustean methods that they hold out against new facts and against a new position that subsequently approves itself in a natural and normal manner by its new environment.

We have seen how, in Palestine, ideas of Righteousness gained a new content; the dialectic of periods of stability and instability represents a process of universal validity. Right-ness *is* Truth. The old term has a large range of interconnected ideas: what is as it should be, what is true to its nature, and therefore genuine, effective, reliable. Hence there are also the questions, what should such and such a thing be in order to be as it should be, what should it be, and how is it to be made so? In Israelite religion "Rightness" is the attribute of the God of the Universe and all His works; and in course of differentiation we look for Truth and Order in Nature, Truth and Order in conduct and morality (cf. p. 144). Primarily it is Truth and Order in an undifferentiated Nature and Man; and consequently we should expect, not precisely the same "Order," but different grades of Order in the different departments into which the subsequent development of thought divides the Universe.

In Buddhism the famous Middle Path, the "Noble Eight-fold Path," demands right belief, resolution, speech, conduct, means of livelihood, effort, reflection and absorption (i.e. concentration, a mystical discipline).[1] Certainly, Right Thinking is not less important than the Right Living which

---

[1] See G. F. Moore, *History of Religions*, I, 285, 295. The conception of *dhamma* (Sanskrit *dharma*) corresponds to the older *arta* or *rita* (see p. 141), and is used of right, moral law, cosmic order; cf. Mrs. Rhys Davids, *Buddhism* (Index s.v.).

both tests it and is inspired by it.[1] When Marxists protest
that "the philosophers have only interpreted the world, our
business is to change it," they overlook what is due to the
thought of the past; and their efforts to frame a theory of
knowledge that shall produce and justify a revolutionary
social change are a proof that Right Thinking is more
necessary than ever.[2] Now, no far-reaching change in our
conceptions of Truth and Order can afford to leave out of
the reckoning either Nature or Religion; and just as a theory
of national or social reconstruction necessarily requires an
intelligent attitude to Religion, so also a religion that continues to be out of touch with the movement of thought
cannot play a worthy part in the progressive development of
mankind.   What has proved all-important in inaugurating
great movements has been the first step;[3] and there is a vital,
a fatal difference between (1) doing wrong that good may
come out of it (i.e. the end justifies the means), as in forceful
revolutionary plans and bloody practices (p. 156, n. 2), and
(2) the inaugurating stage of an *arkhē*.[4]

Among the factors of pre-eminent significance for the
course of thought to-day are (1) the massive *corpus* of
theological and philosophical teaching of the Roman Church,
universal in its outlook, and definitely a preserving and
conserving factor; (2) the more nationalistic systems with
their own totalitarian attitude to Religion (as in Fascism
and National Socialism); (3) the deliberately revolutionary
Communist aim of introducing a new social order with its
own principles of Truth and Order, anti-religious and

[1] On the influence of ideas on practice and hence of true or false
theologies on life, see especially Oman, *The Natural and the Supernatural* (1931), pp. 95–98.

[2] The anti-intellectualism of the day seems typical of an Age that
has stopped thinking, that seeks a ready outlet for its emotions, and
finds current thought sterile, with nothing into which to get the
teeth.   Hence it is ready to accept any seemingly satisfactory
emotional or intellectual system.

[3] Cf. A. Lods in *L'Ethnographie*, 1931, pp. 67–77: "l'Importance du
premier pas dans les croyances et les rites de l'ancien Israël."   For
an example, see on Wellhausen, p. 8, above.

[4] See above, p. 101; cf. on this especially C. F. Burney, "Christ as
the ἀρχή of creation," *J.T.S.*, XXVII (1926), 160–177.

universal in its scope; and (4) the many reforming and transforming endeavours in Philosophy, Religion, Biblical
Criticism, Science, and other fields, feeling their way to better
conceptions of Truth.   A distinction can and must be
drawn between all movements that are more or less assured
that they have found Truth and those more tentative ones
that work for a Truth that shall be more in accord with
current trends of thought.

Throughout we shall find a certain similarity of method.
Thus (a), in every case there is the appropriate selection and
presentation of the relevant evidence.[1]   (b) There is an
arrangement by means of regulative principles so that the
material is—to quote Lord Acton's words àpropos of Universal
History—"not a burden on the memory but an illumination
of the soul."[2]   Thus, just as one is wont to treat the Old
Testament as a *Praeparatio Evangelica*, it is here proposed
to associate both Testaments by means of the epochal
changes to which they testify.[3]   Again (c) it is not the
"letter" that counts, but the "spirit."   A "true" biography
of a man will not inspire us, but will remain dry bones unless
it is so written that his life calls out some response in ours.
The Bible, which must mean *something* to every intelligent
reader, gains in meaning according to our cultural approach
and the "spiritual" interpretation of its contents: this is
the difference between the purely intellectual approach and
that which is expressed in the words, "God is His own
interpreter" (cf. 1 Cor. ii. 10f., 2 Pet. i. 20).   In this way
there is the appropriate relationship between the cultural
and spiritual approach of the individual and both the
"letter" and the "spirit" of the Bible (p. 232).   In general
(d) the appeal is made ultimately to the "spiritual" or
emotional side of the individual.   Hence there is the appeal
to self-sacrifice, an "Israel," a World-wide Brotherhood, the

___

[1] In the Bible itself allowance must be made for a certain antipathy
to Canaanites and Philistines in the Old Testament, and for an anti-
Jewish and pro-Roman feeling in the New.

[2] Consider, also e.g. how easily Marxism is presented by means
of such counters as (a) capitalism, (b) the class-warfare, and (c) the
socialist state.

[3] See p. 232, n. 3.

Church, the Remnant, the Self-conscious Minority, the General Strike, the Historic Task of the Proletariat, Labour's Historic Mission. The point is that by some such appeal, and not through the intellect alone, are men stirred in the world of religion and of active life.[1] There is need of Plato's "noble lie."[2]

But to idealise is not to put in what is not there, and when we contend that "true history teaches true religion" we have constantly to enquire whether the "letter" justifies the "spirit."[3] What is "spiritual" requires some more concrete justification; and the question constantly arises whether we are extracting too much out of our material, or rather "reading in" too much. When, for example, the Koran (xvi. 9) states that Allah created horses, mules, etc., and "shall create other things which you do not know," it has actually been maintained that the Koran *foresaw* the age of locomotive engines and motor-cars, though with more plausibility the passage has been used to *justify* them, and so to quiet the fanatics of Mecca when the holy places were being "defiled by these inventions of devils."[4] Difficult principles of interpretation are involved; and it must suffice here to note the observation that since a man's utterances are the products of a mental content immensely larger than

---

[1] Of Elijah, Wellhausen wrote: "legend and not history could alone preserve the memory of his figure" (*Prolegomena*, p. 462); and Milburn (*The Logic of Religious Thought*, 1929, p. 54) remarks that the same could be said of Jesus. The demands of the imagination—everywhere illustrated in myths and legends—find modern examples when Walter Scott (in *Old Mortality*) in spite of protest would still hear the drums of the cavalry beaten at night(!); and when, despite criticism, Sir James Frazer loved to hear the bells of Rome at Nemi "if it be only in imagination" (*The Magic Art*, p. xxvi. f., *Balder The Beautiful*, II, p. 308f.).

[2] *Rep.* 414 B. Cf. A. J. Toynbee, *A Sudy of History* (1934), i. 248.

[3] A case has arisen already above, p. 237, n. 1. Note also the contention that the human personality of Jesus of Nazareth must have been such as to justify the rise of Christianity, and this the Jesus of "Liberal Theology" and the "Captured Christ" of party-propaganda fail to do.

[4] So an Arab writer, cited by C. S. Braden, *Modern Tendencies in World Religions* (1933), p. 206. Cf. the use made of the Old Testament by early Jewish and Christian interpreters to substantiate their views.

that which is explicitly within his consciousness at the time, the profounder the persons interpreted—Plato and Shakespeare are given as examples—the more may the true interpreter seek to get behind their words to the "real content" of their minds.[1] They are then no longer merely different minds of different ages and lands; in going down we reach a common "substance," as it were, and one soul answereth to another.

The difficulty of writing a "theology" of the Bible on the basis of contradictory ideas and beliefs ranging over several centuries has long been felt: but the deeper study of the "spirit" and "letter" of the world's great religions has brought a new situation. We have not merely to reinterpret and justify afresh the religious values, but rather to recognise that in the world's religions Humanity is thinking out somewhat similar problems with very similar patterns and along not wholly dissimilar lines. The present crisis in Religion is too widespread and fundamental to be approached in any particularistic manner. A crisis is a time of testing. Repeatedly has primitive man been able to find, not in some beautiful image, but in some crude idol or fetich, the spiritual encouragement and stimulus that Religion alone can give; but there has come the time when the idol is only a block, no longer a god or the embodiment of one. So too, rites and ceremonies, doctrines and dogmas, myths, legends and histories are from time to time closely cross-examined and their defects revealed. The whole story of Religion is one of trying and testing; and only too frequently the attacks that are made upon the outward forms of a religion are deserved, and have forced men to recover the underlying Spiritual Reality which had once informed them.

The history of Religion is that of continued efforts to translate, justify and rationalise the awareness of a Reality transcending this world: the reasons offered in support may be bad ones, but the initial instinct cannot be explained

---

[1] See O. C. Quick, *The Christian Sacraments* (1927), pp. 189 ff., on the possibility of going beyond and seeing what was latent in the words and deeds of Jesus.

away.   It is a primitive consciousness, and the evidence
brings the twofold question: How does it manifest itself,
and how are we to understand ourselves accordingly?   The
common tendency has been to conceive a personal relationship between a man and this unseen reality; but the efforts
vary, and when men have spoken of their god as a father we
notice (a) that the conception of this Reality is thereby
enhanced, it responds to the conception; but (b) that
constantly the human term has proved inadequate, the
ordinary experience of fatherhood being pressed—as a
parable or symbol may be pressed—beyond its true limits.
An excellent example is afforded by the relation between
Yahweh and Israel, where Yahweh is both husband and
father (Ezek. xvi. 20f.).   On the one hand, the idea of a
marital relationship encouraged rites of ceremonial prostitution; on the other, the Covenant between Yahweh and
Israel demanded a higher type of relationship between the
Israelite and his wife (see Mal. ii. 10–16).   One is not
dealing with illusions: *because* the One God made both master
and slave Job is compassionate to his servant.[1]   It is a
gross error to suppose that this Reality is an inference from
ordinary experience: on the contrary, ordinary experiences
serve to express and develop the consciousness, and we must
distinguish between the primary awareness and the expression of it.[2]

Comparative Religion testifies to the persistent efforts to
restate the primary experiences.   There are de-spiritualising
and re-spiritualising processes which prove that some
ultimate reality must be postulated.   On the one hand are
the innumerable beliefs; on the other, the "no, no" of the
philosophic mind that goes behind them to an Absolute,
known only through its several manifestations, but in itself
devoid of qualities.[3]   It is possible, especially when we
consider the lengthy history of Religion in India, to conceive

---

[1] See the beautiful chapter, Job xxxi (esp. verses 13 ff.).

[2] Thus, it was possible to regard the blood as life itself and not as
the vehicle of life, even as an idol could be an actual god and not its
embodiment.

[3] Cf. J. Estlin Carpenter, *Theism in Mediaeval India* (1921), p. 194 f.

a scale of "God"–concepts ranging from the crudest
anthropism of the simple native to the most abstract
conception of the philosopher. The intellectual notion of
impersonal powers or agencies has constantly given way to
the belief in powers in a *personal* relationship: "Thou," not
"It." The data adduced for "primitive monotheism" prove
how invariably men need gods or spirits that are accessible
and effective (pp. 189ff.). Even in the Old Testament
the monotheism is no simple one: the Name, Presence (or
Face), Angel (or Messenger) unite the Supreme Being of the
Universe and the worshipper. At successive stages, as is
especially illustrated in India, a new development in a
religion is conditioned by the current cultural situation and
religious phraseology, and a reforming movement will
introduce a new god or else a new conception of an old one.
An intermediary between man and a transcendent Being
may also become transcendent, and then a fresh intermediary is demanded. In general, unless we are genuine
polytheists it is natural to recognise Man's varying efforts to
express his religious convictions of some One Ultimate
Reality in the terms of his environment; and everywhere
this environment is undergoing change.

Comparative Religion leads us to the point where we should
ask ourselves, of the various historical conceptions of an
Ultimate Reality, which gives the best approach to life
and thought? The word "God" must have *some* content,
if it is to be used at all seriously, and with meaning; and
when men protest that there cannot be a God, on the
ground that if there were, certain things would not happen,
it is reasonable to ask what place in the world of life and
thought their convictions already assign to Him.

The data of Religion and the experience of missionary
work testify to the universality of the religious consciousness.[1] There is a "spiritual" potentiality, and through this
Spirit in men the most rudimentary of individuals can accept

[1] See p. 127, n. 1. Cf Christopher Dawson, *Enquiries into Religion
and Culture* (1933), p. 197, developing Ruysbroeck's conviction that
every man possesses deep down in his soul an immediate contact
with God, but is usually without the realisation and enjoyment
of it.

for themselves and prove by intimate personal experience the content of the Reality which has been offered them. If this be so, we must accept the implications. Christianity has expressed the facts of experience when it says (a) that no man can regard Jesus as Divine save through the Holy Spirit (1 Cor. xii. 3, cf. John vi. 44), and (b) that in accepting the Divine Christ men see through Him the God of the Universe (John xiv. 6, cf. Eph. ii. 18). But the missionaries may be Christian, Buddhist, or Mohammedan, and when they are compared, though there are noteworthy resemblances, there are also significant differences of content or "body," so that the "spirit" of the religion varies accordingly.[1]

At the rise of Christianity there was nothing strange in the conception of a son of a god, and the idea of an approach to God mediated through Jesus would, in itself, be quite intelligible.[2] Extending our survey we should include such figures as Mithras, Krishna, Amida, and the earlier cosmic Pharaohs and divine kings who aroused profound feelings which ordinary individuals could not.[3] Under external religious influence the accepted figure of Krishna has been elevated, and it is possible that Christianity has elsewhere impelled men to enhance their own native religion.[4] But Christianity must observe how often a religion is only a veneer, and it must not be misled by the mere use of Christian

---

[1] Some informal words of Burkitt may be quoted without comment: "What I especially like in Orthodoxy is the Doctrine of the Trinity; the *Son* is God in history, a real individual who had a Career and is an historical inspiration for us. We are attracted to Him and can (in some measure) answer His call, because we have, or may have, within us something really akin to God. . . . This something is the Holy Spirit. . . . Through the Spirit in us we are in a sort of real, though not immediate, contact with this great Reality. . . . The advantage of the Doctrine of the Trinity is that with it in our minds we need not try to connect up all Deity into either Jesus, the Prophet of Galilee, or ourselves." (Page 19 of the reprint noted above, p. 238, n. 1.)

[2] A. D. Nock, *Conversion* (1933), pp. 232 ff.

[3] Cf. *O.T.R.*, p. 90.

[4] For Krishna, see p. 173. See also A. P. Elkin, *Hibbert Journal*, XXXV (1937), 544, on native religion; and for North American religion, Paul Radin, *Crashing Thunder: the Autobiography of an American Indian* (1926), *Primitive Man as Philosopher* (1927).

phraseology or rites: the spirit and the content or body of a religion are interconnected. Psychic phenomena—mysticism, revivalism, occultism, etc.—are not necessarily themselves of genuine spiritual value; and Comparative Religion enables us to realise what is involved when the sacred "embodiment" is an animal (strong like a bear, or keen-eyed like the eagle), a well-shaped statue of Zeus, the all-seeing and universal sun, and so forth, and also to understand how what at one time may be a spiritual help and inspiration can later become a hindrance to further growth.

Men cannot "return" to the past and all its attendant circumstances. The national history of the Old Israel was attacked when St. Paul placed it within a larger framework and included the Gentiles. Modern thought, too, by placing the Bible history upon a larger historical background and by its more human—if not more religious—attitude to the world's religions may no less wound the susceptibilities of Christians who have forgotten the spirit of Christianity. The great epochs of Biblical history are in themselves a token that, if the Old Testament led up to the New, the Bible as a whole is to lead up to some new fulfilment. The idea of the Messiah, the Christ, as the approach to a Spiritual Being, the God of a Universe inconceivably vast in space and time, has an intrinsic finality. Like the ideas of Holiness, Truth and Righteousness, the conception of One who is the Way, the Truth and the Life is capable of continued development so long as men are seeking after the Ultimate Reality they call God.[1] And to be a *human* being and to seek after God are one and the same.[2]

---

[1] On the richness of the conception of "the Christ," reference may be made especially to M. Milburn's analysis, *The Logic of Religious Thought* (1929), pp. 69 ff.; and Christopher Dawson, *Enquiries into Religion and Culture* (1933), p. 327. What Asiatic religion has made of "(the) Buddha" should not be ignored; cf. p. 318f.

[2] At the rise of Christianity a Messiah who should introduce the Kingdom of God would be understood in the light of current Messianic hopes and the Jewish ideas of God. But amid the current political strifes when the zealots and *sicarii* were as "theistic" in their phraseology as any one, it was necessary for Christianity to purify its conceptions of God, even as Israel had formerly severed its conception of Yahweh from the current ideas of the land (cf. e.g. Hosea).

Unless the God of the Universe, the "God in Christ," is thought of as transcendent, ordinary human ethical ideas of Jesus of Nazareth limit the spiritual growth. "Transcendence" involves the idea of continued attraction, and has many analogies. The preacher and teacher must not be too much above the heads of their hearers nor "play down" to their level. The personal or intellectual subject that attracts us must be neither outside our grasp nor, of course, one which we have exhausted. That to which we give whole-hearted devotion is absorbed consciously and subconsciously; we grow into it, and it infuses us: we in it and it in us. And when the subject is a person, although the psychological processes are everywhere similar, there are significant differences depending upon the nature of that person. How much more so when it is the transcendent God of the Universe, and the word "God" has a full and inexhaustible content! The true transcendent is "a beyond which is akin."[1] There is a striving after a certain satisfaction, completeness and expression of Self or Type. And as such it runs through Nature and Man: from the most elementary of tropisms to the effort of the organ to maintain and repair itself, and to grow, and finally to the search of the Spiritual Self after completeness (Col. ii. 10). We can describe it, according to the several examples of the process,

---

"God" remained the Supreme Being of the Universe, and "the Christ" is essentially man's Saviour and Redeemer. Had the conception of a *cosmic* Christ (Col. i. 15 ff.) been pursued and developed, as it was to some extent in the Logos Christology, Christianity would have had a different history. Note, e.g., the sort of "Christianity" that appears in Manichaeism and Gnosticism. (Cf. p. 323, n. 4.)

[1] W. R. Matthews, in *The New Learning* (ed. Raby, 1933), p. 307. C. C. J. Webb, *Religion and Theism* (1934), pp. 15 ff., suggests that there are two features in all instances of religion—*ultimacy* and *intimacy*. D. M. Edwards, *Christianity and Philosophy* (1932), p. 169, developes the phrase used by Émile Boutroux, "the Beyond that is within": "it is supernatural and transcendent in relation to the whole finite-temporal order, but is increasingly naturalised—shall we say 'immanentalised'?—in the ascending series, most of all in man and social organism." R. F. Rattray, *Fundamentals of Modern Religion* (1932), p. 33, speaks of the Law of Familiarity and Unfamiliarity: "to be assimilated heartily a thing must be neither too familiar nor too unfamiliar to the assimilator."

as the inherent seeking after a larger field, environment, or unit of existence.

In the world's religions the realm of the sacred and holy ranges from objects of perception to names, words, or myths: they may not be lightly heeded (p. 104). The mystical state has its ineffable experiences, the unspeakable words no man may utter. In his Essay on "Intellect," Emerson tells how he could not put himself in the attitude to look an abstract truth in the eye: "I seem to know what he meant who said, No man can see God face to face and live." Any "truth" of ours is an embodiment and expression of Truth: as such it is not "revealed." The trend of modern thought is against the notion of "revealed" knowledge. Rather are the truths of revelation propositions which express the result of correct thinking.[1] Theological doctrines are not revelation, but more or less adequate interpretations of it. The Christian "would not be able to extract that dogmatic content out of his present experiences had it not been first interpretatively read into them."[2] "All revelation, and everything which is truly 'given,' must be given in proportion to the capacity of the recipient."[3] "What is offered to man's apprehension in any specific revelation is not truth concerning God, but the living God Himself."[4] Thus we regain "the Biblical conception of revelation as the self-disclosure of God in human experience, in the lives of persons."[5]

The data of Religion and, in particular, the despiritualising and re-spiritualising processes in its history, testify to the interpenetration of Man and God, Who is the Spiritual Reality. God is both immanent and transcendent, and there is a relationship between Man and God before Man

[1] Temple, *Nature, Man and God* (1934), p. 317.

[2] Tennant, *The Philosophy of the Sciences, or the Relations between the Departments of Knowledge* (1932), p. 174, cf. p. 179f.

[3] Matthews, *op. cit.*, p. 310.

[4] Temple, *op. cit.*, p. 322.

[5] Matthews, in *An Outline of Modern Knowledge* (ed. W. Rose, 1931), p. 81. Cf. also G. Galloway, *The Philosophy of Religion* (1914), p. 319, on "the heightened spiritual consciousness which gives birth to insight." See below, p. 300f.

becomes conscious of it and seeks to express it. Yet the manifold forms of Religion—and especially its aberrations—are embarrassing; and because of its diverse fruits, not only are we forced to recognise qualities of Religion, but to allow for a difference between what is truly ethical, "spiritual" and life-giving and what is merely "psychical."[1] Now, if we already stand in a relationship with what is spiritual or psychical, by what sort of mental process can a man start from his current body of opinions and build up his religious, philosophical or other system? Is not his mind working towards the expression of a Reality with which he is already in some sort of contact? A comparative study of the main types of philosophy, with special reference to Oriental peoples who have not come under the influence of Greek thought and Christianity, should be suggestive. Here, however, one can only refer briefly to the intellectual efforts which are directed against the conception of a transcendent Spiritual Reality.

The fine idealism of Humanism and the ethical sincerity of its exponents are always attractive. Its aim is naturally for a "whole" and not a mutilated personality; and it welcomes art, music, poetry, and all that inspires a love of the Good, the Beautiful, and the True. The longing for a fuller Self takes innumerable forms; and once we go outside the practical, working life we find as wide a range in the non-religious fields as we do in the religious, depending likewise, in each case, upon the individual who goes "outside."[2] Psychical experiences (as under an anaesthetic) are, as such, thought to be spiritual, and the endeavour is not always to adjust the Self to the brute facts of life or to find a fuller life, but to escape from the Self. There are strange pseudo-selves, the self whose transcendent attraction is the film-star, or the like, the self that finds in astrology, neo-Gnosticism and all sorts of superstition a satisfaction of its craving. In all these

[1] When Matthews says, "we cannot rule out the possibility of 'satanism'" (*The New Learning, l.c.*), we have the endeavour to explain what seems trans or super-human but is absolutely opposed to all our conceptions of God.

[2] Cf. pp. 99ff.

quests or escapes men are not living in separate water-tight
compartments, and consequently we can understand (1) the
argument that a man's private beliefs and fancies are his
own and are to be respected as long as they do not threaten
the accepted social-political structure, and (2) the endeavour
to satisfy his deeper needs for a fuller life in a way that does
not conflict with this structure but, rather, facilitates it.
The position of Religion to-day illustrates typical problems
when the necessity of enhancing men's lives otherwise than
by *panem et circenses* comes up for discussion.

Humanism will voice a wholesome protest against a false
supernaturalism: an imperfect or inadequate religion sooner
or later brings its Nemesis.   Humanism corrects religiosity
and self-centredness; and in forcing attention to those outside
our particular group enforces the religious conviction that
the God a man strives after is also the God of others.   But
Humanism has not the strength of Religion, and in spite of its
lofty ideas of brotherhood and toleration, men would not
perhaps love others half so well loved they not Someone
more (1 John iv. 21, iii. 11).   Humanist ideals have not the
philosophical background of the real unity of Mankind,
whereas, for Ethical Monotheism, the real relation between
God and Man does depend upon that between man and man.
With all its concern for men Humanism does *imply* a
religion; but, although not a religion in itself, it has that
which Religion should re-spiritualise—and rationalise.[1]

For Humanism is philosophically imperfect.   Man is a very
recent arrival in the evolutionary process, and on all counts
there should be some interrelation between the processes of
Nature and those that produced Man and are still working
in him.   All are united through the Ultimate Reality, the
Righteous God of the Universe.   Hence when we think

[1] There can be no religion worthy of the name if it be without a
belief in a transcendent God in personal relation with Man.   The
Hīnayāna Buddhism is not a social-religious system, but the religion
of a special class or type; see John Baillie, *The Interpretation of
Religion* (1929), p. 386f.   On the defects of Humanism, see H. G.
Wood in *Christianity and the Crisis* (ed. Dearmer, 1933), pp. 513–42;
C. C. J. Webb, *Religion and Theism* (1934), and Cairns, above, p. 115,
n. 1.

about the world, however necessary it may be to differentiate, specialise and isolate our experiences for the sake of simplicity, it must not be forgotten that there has been "isolation."[1]   What then is the real "whole"?   Our synthesis will be lamentably inadequate if we forget (a) that Man is a relatively late comer in the history of the Universe, and (b) that as a thinker, he is drawing upon part only of his total consciousness.[2]   When from the religious point of view it is said that God "created" the Universe, the intention is to express the consciousness of a Spiritual Reality immanent in but transcending it (cf. p. 127 n.); and principles of Rightness, Order and Law are found to run throughout the Universe, a Whole of which Nature and Man are integral parts.

If we think that *we* have at last reached the true view of the Universe, do we imply—whether we include or exclude Religion—that what we have discovered was true, even before we discovered it?   No one can deny the efficiency of Nature—the "instincts" of animals that enable them to live, and the "intelligent"[3] processes that enabled Man to conquer the world, and lay the foundations of civilisation countless years before continuous history begins.   As the ages pass, what is implicit in rudimentary beliefs and practices becomes explicit; if there are de-spiritualising processes, others are re-spiritualising; there is selection, re-assertion and social acceptance; and a certain continuity underlies discontinuity.   The dawn of the true scientific spirit can be discerned (p. 144f.).   Thus the whole course of history warns us that, while practical social idealism is vital for the progress of Humanity, no deep-reaching theory of social reorganisation can endure if it ignores or treats in "Procrustean" manner the deeper facts of

---

[1] On the danger of "isolation," see H. Levy, *The Universe of Science* (1932), pp. 20, 43 ff., 102; and in *Aspects of Dialectical Materialism* (1934), pp. 1–30.

[2] The "intellect" literally discriminates, picks out (*inter-legere*); see E. I. Watkin, *Philosophy of Form* (1935), p. 253, citing P. Wust, *Naivetät und Pietät*.

[3] See C. S. Myers: "Instinct and Intelligence," *Journal of Psychology*, III (1910), 209–218, 267–270, who concludes: "throughout the psychical world there is but one physiological mechanism; there is but one psychological function—instinct-intelligence."

life. Only a religious view of the Universe can give a
rational view; and it can, and always should, take a more
human view of the development of Man than those exclusivist systems—religious or anti-religious—which can only
justify their position, propaganda or polemics by aspersing
others. Our most measured conception of Reality involves
our conceptions of God, Man and the Universe.

A "religious" view of the processes of history—in its
widest extent, and therefore covering the whole Universe—
is indispensable. Hence the anti-religious view taken by
the "Dialectical Materialism" of Communism is instructive,
especially as its appeal is to the intellect. It recognises an
inevitable process in social and economic development, an
inherent cosmic necessity, whence the genuine Communist
who feels himself in accord with it has all the subjective confidence of the man who is "on the Lord's side." In the
dialectical process, in general, there are relatively gradual,
successive and "quantitative" changes leading to leaps,
discontinuities and "qualitative" differences, when, besides
what is positively new, there will be the old, but in a new
form.[1] This sort of process is illustrated from the scientific
field, and can be further applied to it; so that dialectical
materialism as an interpretative method calls for a less
partial understanding of processes which have been isolated
for special scrutiny, but must be seen more in their natural
wholeness and comprehensiveness. But the processes of
change, of forming mutations that persist, and of producing
the old in new forms and new wholes, run through the history
of Nature and Man. In fact, in and behind the Bible, as
we have seen, are the most sweeping changes and mutations
in human history of which we have knowledge. We can
ignore neither the data of Religion nor the epochal events
that have made our history: and a synthetic view of world-
process is doomed to failure if after "isolating" its field of
social and economic material it fails to place it again in its
proper environment.[2]

[1] Lenin, for example, spoke of a spiral-like movement. Cf. above
p. 225.

[2] See further below, p. 293.

The popular idea of "evolution" as a sort of linear process was objected to since, on a strict interpretation of continuity, significant changes remained inexplicable or were explained away. But questions of continuity and discontinuity are always recurring. On close analysis the more gradual and quantitative changes will reveal breaks and discontinuities, and what seem to be impassable gulfs—e.g. between the inorganic and the organic—also seem to recur in the world of thought.[1] It may be recalled that T. H. Huxley originally expressed his belief in "the absence of any real transitions between natural groups," emphasised the spontaneous appearance of marked differences giving rise to new varieties, and thought that Darwin had loaded himself "with an unnecessary difficulty in adopting *Natura non facit saltum* so unreservedly."[2]

If there is actual or potential relationship between God and Man, why is He not more generally recognised? In the first place, lovers of freedom and liberty may repudiate the notion that they should be controlled by a "God" who is nothing to them, or only a name. But no one who is devoted to a cause is conscious of or rejects control and discipline; and Religion affirms that the Truth makes men free and that His service is perfect freedom. Freedom is a knowledge of necessary conditions and, as Nature is conquered by our obedience to her laws, so we have greater freedom and potentiality by adherence to the ultimate law of our being: *cui servire regnare est.* The cry is for Freedom and Liberty; but without the proper cultural background the concepts mean what we choose. Moreover, religious experience testifies that God does not compel or restrict; He enlarges

---

[1] Inge, *God and the Astronomers*, p. 63, quotes Whitehead (*Process and Reality*, 1929, p. 132): " the modern quantum theory with its surprises in dealing with the atom is only the latest instance of a well marked character of nature." Cf. the *Textbook of Marxist Philosophy* (ed. by John Lewis, 1937), p. 300: "the evolutionary process is not strictly continuous, but consists of partial reverses, breaks or leaps. See pp. 87, n. 1, 296, n. 1.

[2] See W. R. Sorley, "The Interpretation of Evolution," in *Proceedings* of the British Academy, IV (24 Nov. 1909), citing Huxley, *Life & Letters* (2nd ed.), I, 250, 254 (letters to Lyell, 25 June, and Darwin, 23 Nov., 1859), and *Collected Essays* (1893), II, 34 ff.

man's freedom; and when, as to-day, so much of the expression or embodiment of Religion is out of harmony with the highest aspirations of right living and thinking, it is not the *existence*, but the *meaning* of God that men ask for.   To *what* "God" shall they give themselves?   For many are the altars to Unknown Gods.

In the varying temperamental, emotional and intellectual urges that predispose one's choice and selection throughout all life and thought there are the "patterns," modes of thought, regulative principles and the like that encourage some ideas, and reject, squeeze out or exclude others.   They canalise our thinking, prevent us from changing more than we do, and distinguish us from our neighbours.   These prepare us to accept or reject the claims of Religion.   If they already give us a feeling of completeness, an assurance of Truth—or at least of the right way to it—why disturb our ways of thinking, our modes of thought?   Thus they play so indispensable a part that we must now briefly consider them.

It is the peculiar significance of this age that, besides our more or less systematic religious, political and other bodies of practical life, the effort is being made in the world of special studies to systematise the different fields and their interrelations.   The aim is to seek guiding principles, regulative ideas, the best concepts, modes or patterns.   In this "re-thinking" we are performing with the utmost deliberation and at a high stage of consciousness what was done among rudimentary peoples at lower stages of consciousness. For they organised their experience and their various social religious activities, and paved the way that led to our stage of development.   We, in turn, are endeavouring to organise our life and thought; and, with our vastly superior accumulation of data, we can attempt both to correlate the higher and the lower processes in human development and, going outside Man, to correlate them with the processes in Nature.

Reference has elsewhere been made to the processes of disintegration and redintegration, of breaking up into "parts" what are given as "wholes," and of making fresh "wholes."[1]   Individuals become groups and groups become

1 See pp. 162, 170.

individuals, and throughout we seem to find wholes, systems, organisms or units arising from some disintegration or tending towards a new redintegration. All the processes come between the extreme limits of disintegration and of redintegration. In Man we see a supreme Self harmonising and integrating all his sub-activities; but an absolutely perfect Self would allow of no modification. There must be room for growth. In our intellectual efforts to systematise our material we take heed lest we restrict further development and thus become the victims of our system. As in the processes of Nature, our data may at first be plastic; but as we proceed to build we restrict their potencies.[1]

We do not anywhere precisely "discover" order or system in our material, for we also find the absence of it; and even when we feel we are successful others may not agree with us. We neither "discover" order nor "put" it there, but only when we approach, view or think along certain lines do we feel that we think truly. This starts low down in Nature: even the percept is the result of an integration, a pattern; and as we ascend there are configurations of configurations, units in a higher integration,[2] smaller patterns falling within larger ones and dominated by them.[3] Postulates must be provisionally assumed before they can be proved; there must be preconceived ideas, which may prove premature; and it is through error and opposition that our approaches, views and modes of perception and conception are corrected and improved. So, when we say that a thing is or is not true

[1] Hence, although the systematising organising process is necessary, it may be continued too far, and then one becomes the victim of one's own closed and "immanent" system. For the similar biological process of growth towards increasing stability, cf. J. Needham, *Order and Life* (1936), pp. 57 ff. See below, on "inertia," p. 273, n. 4.

[2] Sir J. H. Parsons, *Introduction to the Theory of Perception* (1927), e.g. pp. 43, 46, 49; J. T. MacCurdy, *Common Principles in Physiology and Psychology* (1928), especially Ch. XXVII.

[3] Cf. A. N. Whitehead, *Science and the Modern World* (ed. of 1927), p. 134; MacCurdy, *op. cit.*, pp. 254, 274 f. So, too, the *Textbook of Marxist Philosophy* (ed. by J. Lewis, 1937), p. 244, speaks of "a determined species of movement which embraces all the others, subordinates them to itself, and is characteristic of the thing as a whole, constitutes its uniqueness, its distinction from other things, forms the basis of its stability."

to its nature, when a Henry Drummond finds "Natural Law in the Spiritual World," and Religion sees God in history, there is a sort of parallelism between the Subject, the Self, and its patterns, on the one side, and, on the other, the "meaning" that the Object has for him.   It is this harmony that gives confidence and strength; although the fact that men do not agree, and that a man will pass from a "lower" to a "higher" truth proves that the process is essentially incomplete.

In systematising or organising our material our concepts must be defined with due regard to our needs.   If we take a cross-section of our systems we note the vicious circle, maintained by the meanings we give our terms.   So a is conditioned by b, b by c, and c by a[1]: it is a "circular definition."[2]   Thus the system becomes self-supporting, and "the outstanding achievement of twentieth century physics is the recognition that we are not yet in contact with ultimate reality."[3]   If, instead, we consider the dialectic of Nature and Man, we can follow the historical "cycles" over large fields of experience: the impetus caused by opposition within the field or without, and the alternations of stability and instability.[4]   But in our regress neither the Hegelian absolute nor the Marxian political philosophy finds confirmation. We never get back to actual origins; and when we look forward, our view of the cycle is influenced by our present predispositions.   In the past we find repeated continuous or "quantitative" series arising from and leading to "qualitative" changes.[5]   And the further back we go, the more removed are the conditions from those that we can understand; our concepts fail us.   Our examination of the theory

---

[1] Cf. Sir A. S. Eddington in *Science, Religion and Reality* (ed. Needham, p. 204).

[2] L. M. Parsons, *The Universe of our Experience* (1933), p. 59 f.

[3] H. Levy, *The Universe of Science*, p. 28, citing Sir J. H. Jeans.

[4] Lord Acton, in his inaugural lecture on *The Study of History*, speaks of the "logic of discovery" and the part played by opposition, error and contradicting facts (ed. of 1905, pp. 55, 118–123).

[5] James Ward, *The Realm of Ends* (1911), p. 73, remarks that the tendency to attribute the earliest arts to gods and heroes shows "how little this generation of new natures is to be regarded as the inevitable consequence of the antecedent routine."

of Primitive Monotheism has shown that we must postulate repeated occasions of spiritual impulse; but the nature of the conditions in actual prehistoric ages entirely elude our comprehension (p. 227). The world in which God is "immanent" must have been "created" by the God we find to be "transcendent," although it does not at all follow that it was created *ex nihilo*, whatever that may be supposed to mean.

The Self, in finding that there is *Something* outside the sphere of positive knowledge, is transcending its cycles and its circular definitions or cross-sections—what we might call Time and Space respectively.[1]   What is this Self?   Analysis takes us to energy at different levels, of which the mental activities are the highest; it tells us of patterns, configurations or modes; they are the ways in which material is organised and in which the organism organises itself by maintaining itself and reacting to what is presented to it.[2] Like the Platonic "ideas" (i.e. types or forms of things) the different irreducible patterns or types are "given," and early thinkers were soon led to the conviction, even in their day, that coeval with the "creation" of the world by God there was a Mind, Wisdom, Reason or Logos.[3]   Through this Reason, slowly, painfully and with many errors, we come to know our environment.

[1] Mystical or other experience which takes—or is felt to take—the individual to the Ultimate Reality does not justify the view that we can bridge the gulf intellectually between the Eternal God and the actual original state of the world as known to us. See further, p. 305.

[2] We may speak of "schemes" of perceiving (F. C. Bartlett, *Remembering* [1932], p. 20, etc.) or of a totality of *Gestalten* one above the other (Bavink, *Science and God* [1933], p. 112f.).   For the general argument, cf. both Marxist philosophy and also the neo-scholastic point of view in E. I. Watkin, *Theism, Agnosticism and Atheism* (1936), p. 80f.

[3] W. L. Knox has argued that the Jewish "Wisdom" and the goddess Isis were equated (*J.T.S.*, XXVIII [1937], 230ff.), and we may recall that the "Name" or "Face" (i.e. Presence) of a deity could be represented independently as a goddess (S. A. Cook, *Rel. of Anc. Pal.*, p. 179, n. 2).   When Wisdom is especially located at Jerusalem (Ecclus., XXIV, 8ff.), this corresponds to the older conception of the "city of righteousness" (p. 141 above); cf. also Isa. ii. 3.

Yet, while the world may last for as many millions of years as the physicists and mathematicians may decide, men become conscious that it is transitory compared with a God who is the First and the Last, the Alpha and the Omega. This is not a transference to God of Man's feeling of his own transcendence, but the consciousness of a supreme Reality above Space and Time. Mysticism, it is true, will speak of an immediate or direct relationship between the Self and God *in and for Himself*: "alone with the Alone."[1] But one must ask with Dr. Inge, "can any finite spirit so transcend the conditions of its existence"?[2] Christianity bids us strive for increasing "fullness," a spiritual growth (Eph. iv. 13–15). Undoubtedly all the experiences—even those under anaesthetics—which take one away from our world must find a place in the completest account of life; and there is a quiet beauty in Nature, notably in the "patterns" in flowers,[3] which speak of joy and peace and "rest in the Lord," that prepares one for fresh activity, rather than for eternal passive contemplation. For if to "know" God is "life eternal," like man's "love" for God it is not merely the climax, the finale, but the starting point of new endeavour (p. 124). And though it is *we* who know and love, it is through *Him* we have this consciousness.[4]

The Self, however, when immersed in its ordinary activities, is not precisely the same as when it subsequently passes judgment upon its own thoughts and actions; and still less

---

[1] That the ultimate knowledge of Self is also knowledge of God is a conviction that has taken many forms; cf. p. 182 above, also R. Otto, *Mysticism, East and West: A Comparative Study of the Nature of Mysticism* (1932), p. 81, etc.; S. Cave, *Redemption, Hindu and Christian* (1919), pp. 66–68.

[2] See his helpful remarks in *Science, Religion and Reality* (ed. Needham), p. 386f.

[3] See especially the exquisite designs in K. Blossfeldt's *Art Forms in Nature* (with introduction by K. Nierendorff, 1929).

[4] Gal. iv. 9 (cf. 1 Cor. xiii. 12), and 1 John iv. 19. In Jer. xxii. 15 ff. to "know" Yahweh is to use the knowledge creatively—the Hebrew use of the verb will be recalled; and conversely, right conduct is in itself an (unconscious) knowledge of ultimate truth (p. 195). On "love," cf. Jesus and Simon Peter (John xxi. 15–17). Our modern tendencies are practical, activistic, and historical; and concepts should be effective, "operational"; cf. P. W. Bridgman, *The Logic of Modern Physics* (1928), pp. 5f., 31, 56.

is either of them the Self when conscious of its transcendence
above a transitory world.   In this sense there are different
phases of a single unitary Self.   Now just as our own
thoughts and actions can be our data or material, so also the
data of history, religion, economics and the rest, are
"material," or rather "matter," which can be selected and
"formed" so as to produce useful results.   But the "matter"
is due primarily to individuals, who were themselves working
upon "matter"; and, as we pursue our analysis throughout,
we find "matter" which is passive, plastic, potential, and
determinable being actively operated upon.   To adopt the
Neo-platonic view: "matter is matter only as the passive
recipient of 'form' from above it; the same thing may be
form in relation to what is below it, and matter in relation
to what is above it."[1]   "Matter" in the old popular sense
disappears; but it comes back in a more comprehensive and
dynamic sense.   "Matter" is relevant to that which forms it;
the notion of an absolute dualism "Mind *versus* Matter" recalls
the dualism of "Good *versus* Evil" or of "God *versus* Satan."

Moreover the concepts of "Mind" and "Substance"
undergo reconsideration; for on analysis we find processes
and activities on qualitatively different levels, the mental
being the highest, so that a thing, a creature or unit is what
it does and—on the highest level—thinks.   Physical and
intellectual acts are lower and higher forms of energy.   And
when, in accordance with the modern tendency, we look at
things dynamically and "historically," we find more or less
stable types, preserving—amid change—unity and a certain
constancy of form.   They are unit "events."[2]   Thus we

---

[1] The citation is from Inge, *God and the Astronomers* (1933), p. 264.
From the "matter" furnished by rudimentary peoples, anthropo-
logists with their "forms" furnish views and effective theories, and
so forth, and these become "matter" to those who review and criti-
cise their works!   This statement is no crude anthropism, but an
illustration upon an intelligible plane of the processes that recur on
different and qualitatively lower planes.   (For similar sorts of
process compare the fin of a fish, the wing of a bird, the forelegs of a
horse and the arms of a man.   See below, p. 310 n.)

[2] See e.g. Bavink, *op. cit.*, pp. 62, 66, 68 f ; H. Lowy, *Universe
of Science*, p. 39; *Textbook of Marxist Philosophy*, p. 242 ("a
stability of types of movement").   The term "events" is of course
Whitehead's.

may compare the relative perdurance of a flame, candle, candlestick, house, its owner, the World War, a nation, a continent, this planet, and finally the whole world. Throughout it is a question of the relative stability of every unit creature or event in life, in thought (e.g. a theory, a doctrine, a body of thought), and in the world itself; and this dynamic stability depends upon the adjustment of its relations with the relevant ever-changing environment or field. Each is a Whole within a larger Whole: there is no absolute permanence, and the human "event"—an integral part of a vaster history—when it becomes conscious of this must at last find permanence only in his relation with the Eternal Spirit.

In this world of units, events, patterns, etc., we have not so much operators as modes of operation, centres of function and process. While early advanced thinkers conceived a primaeval Mind or Logos, an earlier and more fundamental tendency has been to explain processes animistically. After all, what makes a unit or event endure and live; what makes the constituent elements of each associate and cohere? Spirits, demons, angels, gods, patron deities, the *genius* (p. 189, n. 1), all have played their part; and we still instinctively speak of *esprit de corps*, the "spirit" of a thing, the "soul of a movement." While philosophical argument will take us away from animism, polytheism or pluralism to God, the Eternal Spirit, as the ultimate ground of coherence, the religious argument will suggest that "spirit" informs a man according to his body or "form," and that his own soul or spirit depends on God.[1] Unless the line be arbitrarily drawn, "Spirit" pervades all creation, although the religious consciousness—however monotheistic—repudiates the notion that God can be responsible for all spiritual, psychical and other manifestations of action whatsoever. But although we cannot speak of an "evolving" God, the attributes of God can be sought in the order and rightness that we find in Nature and Man. Hence we may speak of degrees of

---

[1] Cf. above, pp. 166, 171. In Col. i. 17, Christ is the basis of all that exists (cf. p. 168, n. 3). A distinction can be drawn between "theopanism" (no reality except God) and "pantheism" (the universe as known to us *is* God); see on this, E. I. Watkin, *Philosophy of Form* (1935), p. 376; *Theism, Agnosticism and Atheism* (1936), Index s.v.

"Spirit" or energy which we estimate according to their forms and fruits, and classify as physical, organic, psychical or spiritual (in a definitely religious sense), and evaluate according to our criteria for differentiation.[1]

When we look "historically" at any continuous flow of activity—mental or other—controlled by patterns and cycles, it is evident that they are not closed systems, else there could be no modification. There must be "open minds," minds with "windows." Every unit is within a larger field or environment which protects and ultimately controls it. There is a striving after completeness, even as a man at any time has urgent needs in some directions but satiety in others. But disequilibrium or instability does not supervene at once at every deprivation or over-indulgence; and the religious conviction of a *transcendent* God implies a continuous striving after a completeness the nature of which the human mind cannot conceive (p. 253). Yet Religion recognises the possibility of a *spiritual* death which is worse than physical dissolution; and, corresponding to the devastating results of self-sufficiency—if logically pursued to the end (p. 49)—is the conviction that a purely immanent God, that is, one completely represented by and confined by His manifestation, in a people (cf. ancient Israel, p. 213 n.), an object (image), or a stagnant doctrine, is "idolatrous" and brings death.

Change, as such, is by no means necessarily a progressive development; and, since every growth depends for its structure upon its relevant environment, every new stage as it emerges depends for its survival—whether it be deemed a re-fashioning, transformation or a higher type—upon the total environment.[2] The *fact* of change is not so significant as the processes that evidently sooner or later control or

---

[1] Robertson Smith's fundamental theory of a group of worshippers united by their god (see *Rel. Sem.*, pp. 503 ff, and Index s.v. Groups) raises the question, What makes any group cohere, what makes the doctrines and principles which unite them cohere? What is worked out on the religious plane in terms of gods, men, social customs, covenants, etc., is significant for our ideas of coherence and completeness on other planes. See p. 311f.

[2] On new movements in religion and thought, cf. p. 272, n. 3.

restrict change; and if this would seem to imply an absolute Determinism, it is rather that there is freedom within the relevant patterns, units, and so forth, and "evolution" rather than "revolution" has the last word. This is important for the question of the possibility of radical changes. Our growth is an integral part of the growth of the Universe, and the situation to-day is such that we ask, Amid all possible changes what shall determine our outlook?

What is the real Universe, what is Reality? The answer would seem to depend upon the level of consciousness from which we view it. Analysis reveals different levels of activity, and it is clear that although only the highest, the intellectual, can tell us of the lowest, for us the world we live in is not "mind," but rather a hierarchy of processes. Our question should be, Can we view the Universe better than at present; are we perceiving and conceiving our environment progressively? Alike the prophet and the scientist will tell us of principles and patterns rather than of their embodiment;[1] and the religious conviction of Spiritual Reality and spiritual growth (Eph. ii. 21, iv. 15) implies a progressive knowledge of our ultimate environment. Meanwhile we are actually aware of the limitation of our senses; and the data of telepathy, clairvoyance, second-sight, and so forth, tell us, even after the most necessary scepticism, that our actual world is more than we know, and that—to judge from the often scarcely "spiritual" character of the circumstances—a distinction between the Psychical and Spiritual must be steadily maintained.

As for the dead, and pre-eminently those who have so greatly enriched our world, we can ignore them as little as Roman Catholicism ignores the question of angels and hierarchies of angelic intelligence. On the one hand is the necessity of a systematic treatment of all the higher and supernatural experiences and beliefs;[2] and, on the other, the equal necessity of a critical consideration of the implications of tested facts. On the one hand, is the conviction that we can pray to God on behalf of those distant (cf. p. 299), and

[1] Cf. *O.T.R.*, p. 109 n.
[2] Milburn, *Logic of Rel. Thought*, p. 151, cf. pp. 120 ff.

even that thought has a real efficacy;[1] and on the other, is
the increasing diminution of individual differences as
unanimity is reached (termites, flocks of birds, etc.), suggesting that at zero point there would be real telepathy.[2]   On the
one hand is the suggestion that when we think "religiously"
we may be thinking "cosmically," and on the other the
inference that the data of telepathy point to some common
pervasive medium.[3]   "It is surely significant," remarks
Inge, "that panpsychism is once more being taken
seriously."[4]   *Tat tvam asi* is certainly a formula that covers
a large field of evidence (p. 182); and the belief that Nature
and Man are one, and that the regeneration of the latter
meant that of the former recurs in the Jewish Messianic
ideas and in St. Paul's view of the future (Rom. viii. 18ff.).
The Universe, like man himself, consists of the physical,
the psychical and the spiritual.

But a convinced belief in another existence after death is
not in itself spiritual or religious: all depends upon the
relation between the individual and the Eternal Spirit
(pp. 123, n. 1, 288). It may even be that through this relation,
"the beatified spirit . . . by virtue of its assimilation to the
Father of spirits," may "share in His activity in the world of
space and time."[5]   But even if there are angelic intelligences
it is imperative both to avoid the supposition that the
"psychical" is, as such, "spiritual" and to adopt caution
in the use that can be made of both for our positive
knowledge.[6]

[1] See p. 195; and cf. Mahāyāna and Shingon Buddhism (G. F.
Moore, *Hist. Rel.* I, 30, 127f., 130).
[2] MacCurdy, *op. cit.*, p. 297.
[3] Cf. C. D. Broad, in the *Proceedings of the Society for Psychical
Research*, XLIII (1935), pp. 397–438 (concluding paragraph).
[4] In *Science, Religion and Reality*, p. 372.
[5] Inge, *God and the Astronomers*, p. 292.
[6] Gilson, *The Philosophy of St. Thomas Aquinas*, Ch. VIII (tr.
Bullough, 1924) deals with angels; but the notion of continuity and
of gradual quantitatively descending (or ascending) degrees of
knowledge is hardly borne out by all we know of qualitative changes.
And such changes sever men from the realm of God and—unless one
accepts spiritualism—the dead.   "Principalities and powers" above
there may be (Eph. iii. 10); but they do not come between God and
Man (Rom. viii. 38f.).

Religious and non-religious thought converge to make us regard individuals as "cosmic" beings, thinking partly as creatures here and now, and partly in a way that relates them to God and His Universe (p. 186). Hence we think, now along purely individualistic lines culminating in solipsism, and now as citizens of the realm of God. But the aim of scientific enquiry is to reach knowledge that is true for all, allowing for intelligible differences. This, also, is the direction taken by the comparative study of religions, i.e. of all that men evidently hold most true. Our frames of reference are our own; but as they converge and become parallel, as it were, an essential agreement outweighs the less essential differences. On a very low level of difference all are virtually one; on the highest level of organisation again all are virtually one, but how rich a unity!

If we consider the next step in any process we note how Man, for his part, has been impressed by the truth that what he sows he must reap. In the Indian doctrine of *karma* the deeds of a man in his lifetime cling to him after his death when he undergoes rebirth, transmigration. Salvation comes as an escape, in the knowledge that the ultimate Self is the sole reality. No longer locked up in a self-determined cycle by its deeds the Self can now pass outside. But instead of the *karma* of an individual, the Hebrew prophets of the Exilic Age were confronted by the protest against social *karma*: the fathers eat sour grapes and it is *we*—and not the fathers reborn—whose teeth are set on edge (Jer. xxxi. 29). But in the Exilic Age Ezekiel (Ch. xviii.) teaches the possibility of a definite change in the individual or his line; the thread is broken, for better or for worse.[1] No less definite is the change in the historical development of Israel, although the continuity is not less striking than the break (pp. 72f., 210, 319). Again, Christianity makes a decisive break: an old age (Aeon) is replaced by a new, but there is continuity. As in the great breaks in individual development, the earlier and later stages are by no means radically severed; and although *karma* may

[1] See *O.T.R.*, p. 118.

remain—the inevitable consequences of former actions—a new spirit, a new will, reorganises life and thought.   The old continuity is broken, but the absence of discontinuity points to a new and qualitatively different continuity.   As to the question of continuity and discontinuity after death speculation is useless, and thought dwells upon the instinctive feeling that in a just Universe right and wrong have their natural consequences and upon the justice, the mercy and, above all, on the love of God (cf. p. 132).

From the old religious point of view, God, in spite of the great changes or discontinuities, is wholly righteous and not arbitrary.   And if we consider the growth of the individual and those experiences which are regarded as a "revelation," there is, on the one side, the conviction that "there neither can nor should be any criterion of divine revelation assignable before";[1] and on the other, the revelation accords with the stage of mental or cultural development.[2]   In other words, there is the consciousness that God is absolutely free; but with it the practical assurance that what comes from Him will make no absolute discontinuity with the past.   For if it did, if the "revelation" violated reason or conscience, should we not say that it was of human origin, and not the Spirit operating on man?   In life and thought retrospect seems to show determinateness, purpose or teleology, whereas prospect offers only possibilities and probabilities. Yet there are strivings for completeness, patterns to be followed, and, on the religious plane, a transcendent teleology, God and Man seeking relationship.   If, therefore, at any

---

[1] I quote Brunner, *Philosophy of Religion* (1937), p. 178; cf. Butler's *Analogy* (1736) II, Ch. 3: *a priori* speculation is futile. Sprott, citing a lengthy passage from Butler, concludes: "we are not qualified to form *a priori* theories of Revelation any more than of Nature" (*Inspiration and the Old Testament*, 1909, p. 48).

[2] Cf. A. B. Davidson, *Theology of the Old Testament*, p. 405: "in the present day we are more inclined to conclude that the methods pursued by revelation were simple, and, if we can say so, natural; that is, that its great object was to enable men in each age practically to live unto God, and that at all times it gave them light sufficient for this . . . it took men as it found them . . . penetrating and transforming other modes of thinking on many non-essential matters which they cherished.

given time there is lack of determinacy in life or thought,
rather is it a transitional state due to lack of balance, incompleteness of method, and the perhaps unavoidable failing
of trusting in a premature synthesis, the over-hasty solution
of a difficulty.[1]

Change will involve choice.   Although there seems to be
little or no evidence of choice low down in the scale of life,
our own life-history, as embryo and infant, illustrates the
fact that an organism at an early stage of evolution can be
an integral part of a larger unit before it becomes one in its
own right. *This* unit makes the choice: and what determines
its choice?   A larger environment protects the smaller; and
he who identifies himself with a cause, a group, a Church,
etc., can feel himself part of a more permanent reality.[2]
This relationship protects change.[3]   We need not ask where
sentiency and consciousness begin; all who build better
then they know—animals or men—are processes within a
larger environment than that of which they are conscious
(p. 222).   In Nature the growth is of patterns, types; in
Man there may be consciousness of patterns of life and
thought, and of the general type to which to be true—
though these are by no means necessarily "spiritual."   In
point of fact, every change, even the slightest, needs some
explanation; and if the dominating pattern, unit, or environment enfolds the subordinate, what ultimately enfolds
the whole if it be not the God of the Universe?   Changes
occur in the evolution of Nature and Man—"natural"
changes: the new emerges when there are the appropriate
conditions; and even in the realm of Religion the Eternal

[1] Cf. Jer. vi. 14.

[2] In primitive religions men often found confidence by placing a
part of themselves (e.g. a garment, rag, or their inscribed name)
in some sacred place or locality felt to be more enduring and
permanent.

[3] We may note, in the evolution of religion, how the first steps in
the rise of Christianity were protected by its organic connection with
current Judaism, until at last it became an independent organism—
as it were—existing in its own right. The same could be said
of powerful theories and bodies of thought, whose possible
significance is not at first recognised.

Spirit takes men as it finds them, heightening the types and patterns of their life and thought.[1]

Any desired change may be thwarted by our will, by contrary patterns and types of thought that hinder or exclude it. There are beliefs that allow movement only within certain limits. Animism, demonism, and the like have inhibited free enquiry into causes and processes. The Sacred Book (e.g. Bible or Koran), doctrines—and especially specific doctrines concerning God—these have shown how development of thought is in many varying ways dominated, repressed or stimulated. The use that any unit can make of the environment—accidents apart—is regulated by its patterns. Man and Nature exemplify misuse, atrophy, parasitism, failure to fulfil promise, and all the consequences of lack of balance.[2] The tendency of things "to work themselves out" is also that of the organism striving to conform to its type and to repair a mutilation; and how the individual repairs his mutilated "spiritual" organism is illustrated by the substitutes for a reasonable religion.[3] When a distinction is drawn between being born of flesh and born of the spirit (John iii. 6, cf. Rom. viii. 6), the intention is to emphasise the difference between ordinary development and the effects when a new spiritual impulse informs the normal man (cf. Isa. xxxi. 3).[4] To be as a child,

[1] Granted that something keeps every change from leading to an absolute disintegration, the belief in a *creatio continua* becomes intelligible (p. 3, n. 1); but not every cosmic change can be due to a God who gives His Universe freedom, even as not every "psychical" phenomenon can be called "spiritual."

[2] Drummond, *Natural Law in the Spiritual World*, pp. 330 ff., illustrates the defects of cheap and easy religion which encourages low standards; contrast Phil. ii. 12.

[3] Watkin (*Theism*, p. 30 f.) cites Baron von Hügel (*The Mystical Element of Religion*, II. 57 ff.) on morbid psychological phenomena and the price paid by man's body for the tension of a spiritual life for which it was not evolved. The effect of "heady" ideas upon ill-organised minds is also familiar.

[4] Cf. Watkin, *Philosophy of Form*, pp. 41, 45, on the vital difference between (a) inertia and static development within relatively confined limits along the same lines, and (b) the tension between the static and the dynamic, between the tendency to static development and the impact of the environment. This tension "maintains evolution organic and inorganic and constitutes the warp and woof of human history." Cf. below, p. 295 f.

to be reborn, is to go behind the customary patterns and modes of thought in which one is entangled and start afresh, and how realistically the feeling of a new birth is felt by primitive peoples is well known.[1]

At great crises God "breaks through," as it were; but Aquinas has summed up the common experience in the words *Gratia non tollit naturam sed perfecit*.[2] The revelation, the visitation or the new insight does not destroy the natural structure but perfects it, so that events which can only be ascribed to Divine Grace are "natural," even as new insight in ordinary affairs constantly develops and does not annihilate the past course of one's life and thought.[3] There is a co-operation between the Spirit and the Self; and even when this "breaking through" comes at a crisis it is not imposed violently; it is still a choice—and a "covenant." *He* knocks; but *we* open the door (Rev. iii. 20). The Biblical writers have turned religious experience into national history when they affirm that Yahweh and Israel once chose each other, though the choice was not due to any merit on the part of the people (Deut. xxvi. 17–19).[4] Such a "breaking-through" occurred notably at the Exilic Age and at the rise of Christianity. But the varying after-effects of *every* significant religious movement are not to be ignored (p. 144); and, as in the history of thought, the more sweeping the changes the more necessary the adjustment in the whole environment concerned.

The foregoing bears obviously upon the question of such drastic interventions as miracles. It is easier to understand the prevalence of the belief in them than the phenomena

---

[1] See *Rel. Sem.* s.v. "Rebirth."

[2] I owe the citation to Brunner, *Philosophy of Religion*, p. 176. But although he dissents, Biblical religion itself shows that even if there is no continuity to bridge the gulf between Creator and creature there is continuity behind discontinuity in the effects of the Spirit upon man.

[3] Cf. pp. 115, n. 3, 254 n.

[4] The conception of an actual covenant between God and Man is distinctive of Israel, and is one of the most striking that we owe to a people among whom the idea of Divine Holiness, Power and Righteousness attained its highest expression. The conception is, in a sense, the pre-Christian *kenōsis*.

described; and Jesus Himself denounced reliance upon "signs" as apostacy (adultery).[1] The wonderful events which stand at the beginning of national Israelite history are very freely rationalised or explained away to-day; but had there been no genuine and powerful conviction of Yahweh's might and His choice of Israel, the traditions of the Exodus and Law-giving on Mt. Sinai would not have taken the form they did. As it is, they give what would be an intelligible account according to the beliefs of their age; though we value them more for the "spirit" of the old religion than for the "letter." In fact, the whole treatment of the national career is based (a) upon the recognition of Yahweh's place in history, and (b) upon the desire to embody this in the records of past history, and so to "rationalise" it.[2] At the great critical periods the prophets, on the other hand, aimed at placing spiritual truth above the more concrete embodiments in rite and history. They would turn the people from the God of their past to the God of the present and of the imminent future. But once more there was, in the post-Exilic Age, an historical framework, though with a fresher meaning, and past, present and future form one unit.[3]

Instead of an ever-present God over and in the Universe, a common tendency has been to find Him only in the breaks and leaps of history and in the gaps of the knowledge of the day. Alleged marvels—whatever their credentials— if isolated, have not had the same effect as those that harmonised with the current life and thought. The latter were "true," or could be shown to be so. They evoked or strengthened men's faith. Whatever a past age might have thought of the wireless, the fact that the whole technique fits integrally into a large field of already accepted knowledge distinguishes it from any marvel that continues to be unique and isolated. There is no reason to suppose that God requires our blind faith; and the Will to Believe has

---

[1] Luke xi. 29. Cf. the Old Testament usage where the Baal cults are stigmatised as adultery.

[2] See especially A. Weiser, *Glaube und Geschichte im Alten Testament* (1931).

[3] See pp. 82, 85, 209f.

been caricatured.[1]   On the one hand, in the words of Lessing, "Accidental truths of history can never become the proof of necessary truths of reason."[2]   But, on the other hand, a quite exceptional occurrence may be but an outstanding example of what is otherwise familiar.[3]   The tremendous "breaking in" in the first century A.D. is a fact of actual world-history—like that in the Exilic Age—but the manner in which the spiritual facts were selected and embodied in the letter of the narrative in ways that were in accord with the thought of the age is not less in need of reverent critical enquiry than the Mosaic Covenant which theologians and others already freely rationalise.   But to "rationalise" is to satisfy not merely the claims of the intellect, but the deeper needs of Man; and it is also necessary to "re-spiritualise," if not to "real-ise," that is, to manifest anew the reality of the spiritual facts.

Some fundamental process is continuously striving to keep Nature and Man true to type and to improve the type, turning disorder into order, wrong into right, and working for "righteousness": reconciling, making at-one-ment, and forgiving "sin" in the widest extent of the word (p. 294). Re-establishing the right relation between Man and God, seeking for Man's willing loyalty, and, at his moment of extreme self-consciousness, his willing self-sacrifice, this process becomes intelligible only on the religious plane.

Sacrificial ideas and rites run through the world's religions, and Israelite tradition very naturally ascribed its elaborate post-Exilic sacrificial system to the founder of the national religion in the days of the Mosaic Law-giving.   It also

---

[1] See R. H. Thouless, *Introduction to the Psychology of Religion* (1923), pp. 275 ff.; the belief is really in what rationalises the different modes of relevant experience.

[2] See, for the whole passage, Creed and Boys Smith, *Religious Thought in the XVIIIth Century* (1934), p. 173.

[3] Note the use made by Robertson Smith of the evidence of Nilus for his theory of sacrifice.   Whereas some scholars thought it unsound to rely and build upon so isolated an occurrence, the evidence was really the crowning embodiment of the main ideas found elsewhere; see *Rel. Sem.*, p. lvi. f., and Oesterley, *Sacrifices in Ancient Israel* (1937), p. 53.

assigned a pre-eminent share in the priestly organisation
to the first Israelite king of Jerusalem, the founder of the
Monarchy.   And while the atoning-value of the "servant"
(Isa. liii.) points to a supreme landmark in the Exilic Age,
the Christian sect in their Messiah carried on and developed
further the fundamental sacrificial ideas.

The best explanation of sacrifice is disputable.   The
sacrifice was felt to institute, or, rather, to restore, some
relationship between men and their gods.   Subjectively, it
gave the individual—or more typically the group involved—
relief, strength, completeness and peace.   Objectively, it
was believed to please the gods, to maintain them, and to
enable them to function on behalf of their adherents.   The
sacrifice was to be of the best—worthy of the god's acceptance, and of real worth; the unblemished condition of the
sacrificer and of the sacrifice being necessary for the relationship with the unseen power.   Fundamentally the sacrifice
consists of what a man most values—even his son, the first-
born, his own self.   Prepare the sacrifice and the god will
accept it; present oneself as a living sacrifice and be renewed
and transformed (Rom. xii. 1f.).

The first century of our era was a new stage in world
history.   "God is spirit" (John iv. 24), and the ideas of an
unseen Spiritual Reality take many forms.   Through Jesus,
the Messiah, men raised to a new level the convictions of
God they had inherited.   Social and personal religion
entered upon a new phase; and in working out its convictions
of the nature of Jesus Christ the Church powerfully developed
the idea of human unity already implied in Ethical Monotheism and the harmonious interrelation between the
religious and non-religious phases of life and thought.   So
to-day we have, on the one hand, the ideal of personal and
communal devotion to God in Christ, and, on the other,
greater freedom for our searching out of the mysteries of
that Universe over and in which is the Eternal Spirit of God.
Through this Spirit, Man is ever led on to pursue his quest
for a whole life; starting from the impulse of the Spirit, he
is led on to find that God in Christ is the leader and finisher
of his faith.

Nineteen centuries ago great changes were impending in Palestine amid turbulence and unrest. Choices had to be made, and two of them changed the face of the world: that of Jesus which led through Gethsemane to the Cross and Christendom, and that of the people for Barabbas which led to the downfall of the State. "But on account of Him there have come to be many Christs in the world."[1]

[1] Origen, *contra Celsum*, VI, 79, cited by H. D. A. Major, *The Modern Churchman*, XI (1921), p. 276.

CHAPTER XII

The "Truth" of the Bible

(*concluded*)

III. Towards a New Culture[1]

THE last hundred years, indeed the last few decades, have witnessed a rapid and enormous increase in man's knowledge of himself, his past, and the world in which he lives. Not only in science have the great advances been made: psychology, anthropology, the study of early belief and custom, and the recovery of long-forgotten history have brought masses of material which are examined along characteristically "comparative" and "historical" lines. Novel sorts of enquiries and of problems have arisen; and the efforts to understand primitive modes of life and thought have combined with current conditions to impress upon us the necessity of reconsidering our own. In the attempt to articulate our material we are attempting also to bring order into our own minds: the two attempts are one. Our retrospect upon cultures less "advanced" than our own impels us to find fertile notions of development which shall help us to face the immediate future. In this way current tendencies in research may be said to be preparing the way for some new culture.

In many respects the most significant achievement of the last 50 years or so has been Biblical Criticism. Whatever the Bible may mean for the future, no one can be indifferent to the part it has hitherto played in the history of the West. Biblical criticism is a specific, practicable and important undertaking. It involves the effort to describe what has actually happened, to understand some profoundly vital religious developments, to estimate their place in world

[1] Pp. 279–82 are reprinted, with revision, from *The Cambridge Review*, 24th January, 1936.

history and religion, and to further that progressive interpretation of the Bible which began with the Renaissance and
Reformation in the sixteenth century.

Now, while the Bible is, to say the least, an extremely
valuable source for anthropological, historical, and other
"secular" pursuits, Biblical Criticism itself is in accord with
the principles that prevail in the various relevant ancillary
studies. The consequences are significant. The Bible
becomes an integral part of the ordinary world of learning,
vital conclusions drawn therefrom must be tested in the
light of ordinary knowledge, and our estimate of its religious
worth must not conflict with our estimate of what we consider to be the "real" world. To put it otherwise: not as the
determinant of all knowledge, but as an essential part of our
total knowledge of world history and religion, the Bible is
coming to hold a new position within the framework of all
branches of thought. And, this, above all, points to some
new culture.

From the very beginnings of this Universe to the present
day is one stupendous history. We learn something of the
cooling of the earth, the dawn of life, the appearance of man,
his rude efforts to satisfy his needs and answer his questions,
and, at length, the great forward steps for which the Bible
is our first authority. A stage of maturity was reached in the
Near East only some 5,000 years ago; and about half that
relatively minute figure separates us from those centuries
in Palestine, Egypt, Asia Minor, and other lands which may
be said to have inaugurated those developments that have
culminated in our efforts to-day to understand our position
and the direction we are taking. In this one single immense
history, with all its changes and continuities, we pass from
Nature to Man, from cosmic activity to man's creative
energy, and, amid unities and differences, we can now discern
whole series of hierarchies of processes from the cosmic to the
ideological, from the actual story of the Universe and ourselves to our feeble attempts to tell it intelligibly and
helpfully. A vaster survey than ever lay before the great
philosophers of the past confronts the organising and
constructive minds of the future.

Meanwhile, the world's religions testify to genuine personal religious experience and to all that men have felt to be most true and essential for life as a whole. In the effort to arrange and understand this great body of material we become conscious of the necessity of making our own conceptions of Religion in general—and therefore also of Theology and Philosophy—less exclusive and far more objective and comprehensive than they are. Research in this field classifies the many different varieties of religious, mystical and "numinous" experiences, and can point to the extraordinary if not tragic differences in their moral, intellectual and aesthetic effects upon men.

The complex history of Religion is that of man's constant dissatisfaction—due to his natural growth—with inherited usage and belief: a "super-social" striving to satisfy new and deeper needs. Dr. Inge has said, "Alike in religion and philosophy, the important question is not whether God exists, but what we mean when we speak of God." Certainly it becomes clear on several grounds, not only that the existence of the Supreme Reality men call "God" is vividly felt in new and impelling ways at great history-making crises in individuals and peoples, but also that there is a psychological tendency, an "emotional monotheism," as significant for the individual who experiences it as for our "Theory of Religion" (p. 181). And apart from the specific feelings and states which we label "religious"—and independently of their social and other value—we must recognise "God" also as the "Power not ourselves that makes for righteousness" (p. 200), even though there is no consciousness of this among men who "unwittingly do His will." In a word, the theoretical study of the world's religions, the "Theory of Religion," opens up far-reaching questions as to the relation between the various "religious" and "non-religious" aspects of life and thought and how our evidence is to be interpreted.

The reaction against religious conceptions considered to be outworn is not surprising when, for example, we consider the transition of terms from Hebrew to Greek, thence to the Latin world, and finally to the youthful West. Especially instructive is the opposition to the familiar "dualistic" views (e.g. this world and the "over yonder,") since it is opening the way to a re-statement of the earlier typical and fundamental realism, whereby God's sphere—whether we call it the "supernatural" or not—is not outside, but within the "natural": the profoundest realities of Religion are part of the world of accepted fact; God is a real part of a real world. Hence the opposition to "other-worldness" and the secularism and materialism of this age, in emphasising the "here and now," is preparing, not for a merely Immanent God or a pleasing and innocuous numinousness, but for the only conception which the Theory of Religion can entertain, namely, a God at once Transcendent and Immanent. This is due to a Christianity which has established the primary fact of the ideal paradoxical two-fold nature of the sons of men: the normal co-existence in the average individual of the two spheres of the human and the divine, the unitary individual, the *socius*, who can regard the Universe as a reasonable whole containing both the "here-and-now" and the Supreme Reality—the infinite within the finite.

But men always confuse the world of which they are gaining increasing knowledge with their conceptions of it. The survey of past notions of the Universe—so far as it was apprehended by primitive and ancient peoples—is thus a timely corrective, a warning against confusing the thing thought of with the processes of thinking. Only in the improvement of our ways of thinking shall we enhance our powers of experiencing, interpreting and describing the whole Universe. As it is, men have both read into and read out of the Universe, and have blended external history and their private world. They have looked back to some Golden Age or state of peace, a property-less and communistic society, a Fall, or the like; or they have looked forward, apocalyptically, to some almost cosmic catastrophe, or, more evangelically, to a New Covenant, or to some perfectionism or absolutely changeless harmony. Most characteristic perhaps is the feeling of the dawn of some entirely new era in the world's history.

Here the Dialectical Materialism of the day is of

outstanding importance because of its use to under-pin
Communism as an instrument for reinterpreting the past and
transforming the future.   Its standpoint is not static, but
dynamic; and, though academic and theoretical in its origin
—when Karl Marx gave a new turn to the Hegelian logic—
it became the backbone of a practical policy for changing
the entire cultural outlook of mankind.   Hence, quite apart
from its significance as an organ for revolutionising social
and economic conditions, it is of special interest in any
enquiry into the nature of the reformation, reconstruction or
re-creation of life and thought.   In a word, it involves the
philosophy of beneficial and effective change.

Dialectical Materialism involves three main points:(1)
Man is part of what we call "Nature," and the activity of the
human mind may be regarded as one of the "natural"
processes in the Universe.[1]   Certainly, the processes
culminating in Mind have made us increasingly conscious
of the past; but directly we view Mind as part of cosmic
structure some definite constructive attitude to the story of
man's religious convictions is indispensable.   But here,
Marxism, Dialectical Materialism and Communism are,
despite Marx's noteworthy aphorism (p. 96), as inexcusably
inadequate as is so much of contemporary philosophy.
Next (2), instead of the popular view of evolution, as a more
or less orderly series of gradual changes, we should recognise
that there are both (a) gradual "quantitative" movements,
and (b) new "qualitative" results, initiating fresh "quantitative" movements wherein the old will repeatedly re-appear
in a new form and "disorder" becomes "order."   This we
have already noticed, in the development of religious and
other thought.[2]   But although our retrospect will reveal
whole series of quantitative changes followed by some
qualitative change, series upon series, we never succeed in
reaching actual beginnings, but only some fresh starting-
point.   In fact, what we treat in terms of development or
evolution has been abstracted and isolated from an environment of which it had once been an integral part; and because

[1] See pp. 198 n., 265.
[2] See pp. 86, 258.

this unit or cycle belonged properly to some larger unit or cycle, we cannot regard the dialectical process as final or conclusive. Finally (3), what is known as the "interpenetration of opposites" will naturally occur when we have isolated a process from an environment from which it proves to be inseparable. This is especially noticeable when—for whatever reason—the realm of Religion has been ignored as irrelevant, and the effort has been made to form a complete synthesis without it. In this way, Dialectical Materialism is philosophically as one-sided and inadequate as would be any religious synthesis that should ignore vital social, scientific or other data.

Now the Dialectical Materialism of the day is felt by its adherents to be a complete and final statement of an irresistible process applicable to the world of social and economic conditions. But the Dialectic, as a process, is no respecter of persons. It can be argued, for example, that Communism leads dialectically to Fascism.[1] Moreover, a recent Roman Catholic writer has indicated how we can pass from the Dialectical Idealism of Hegel to its antithesis, the anti-religious Dialectical Materialism of Communism, and reach, as the synthesis, a Dialectical Ideal Realism which is, in a sense, a restatement and revision of the scholasticism of St. Thomas Aquinas. Indeed, he does not hesitate to regard Communism as "an evolution towards the truth," and as a preparation for the Kingdom of God which it is meanwhile seeking to destroy.[2] The Hegelian Dialectic thus takes a religious and philosophical form which, whatever may be thought of it, at least exemplifies the radical inconclusiveness of Dialectical Materialism.

Of course Dialectical Materialism took its rise from empirical facts. It is based upon actual social data, isolated

[1] Cf. John Macmurray, The Philosophy of Communism (1933), p. 85f., and in Aspects of Dialectical Materialism (1934), pp. 47–53 (in view of Bernal's remarks, p. 151f., it is difficult here, as often elsewhere, to distinguish orthodoxy from unorthodoxy).

[2] E. I. Watkin, Men and Tendencies (1937), p. 281; cf. The Philosophy of Form (1935), p. 194. He comments (ib. p. 159) on the futility of attempting to "prescribe the future course of history by the application of the dialectic."

from their natural context, and it ignores as irrelevant for
the purpose the larger field of life and thought.   Claiming
a universal validity and contemplating a change in Man
greater than any hitherto known, it remains indifferent to
those great epochal changes in human history which have
brought us to our present stage of thought—changes to
which reference has often been made in these pages.   A more
unscientific and uncritical procedure can hardly be conceived.
Now Hegel's Idealism handles the Dialectic in the most
absolute manner, and, not to mention the criticism to which
it has been subjected, it is exceedingly difficult for the
ordinary individual to understand.   As for Dialectical
Materialism, it is sufficiently in touch with human life
to make it a world-wide influence.   But not in this way
can any new era be introduced: the influence of Religion is
too great a force in human history to be ignored.   On the
other hand, Religion—relatively speaking—precedes Philosophy, and we may suggest that a no less absolute and far
more intelligible conception of the Dialectic can be found in
the familiar religious conviction that God was in the world
and reconciled it to Himself in Christ (2 Cor. v. 19, Rom. v.
10 f).

We have here no abtruse philosophic idea of the Universe
going out and returning to itself, no political philosophy
relying upon hatred and bloodshed for the inauguration of
its kingdom, but the thoroughly simple, if not homely
belief, that so many untutored souls have felt to be an
absolute Truth.   It is a final conviction of Ultimate
Reality which has had the profoundest influence upon men
and women irrespective of temperament, training and
learning.   It appeals to the whole personality and not to
some specifically intellectual aspect of the individual.   Yet
if "religious" and "non-religious" thought form interrelated
parts of one whole, what is felt to be "true" in the sphere of
Religion should not stand by itself isolated from the world of
life and thought.   If we affirm that God is reconciling His
creation to Himself in Christ, is this solely a "religious"
truth, or is it the supreme expression of the ultimate mystery
of God, Man and the Universe; and was the explicit

statement of this the greatest landmark in the evolution of human life? The remarks on this in the following pages are made in the completest consciousness of their tentativeness and inadequacy.

The division into the realms of the "religious" and the "non-religious" is a false dualism; they interpenetrate, and can no more be severed than these words from the page upon which they are printed. From the study of the data of Religion we must infer that the Power men call "God"— and everything depends upon what that word conveys to us—must be in some actual or potential relationship with men, even with those who deny Him, or whose ways of life and thought would seem to obstruct or exclude their recognition of His existence (cf. p. 260). God can, as it were, "break through" the shell men construct around themselves: He comes unsought as well as besought. He Himself stands in a "personal" relationship to men; and although we often do not seem to need the concept "God," it rationalises our knowledge. But it is important to observe at once that even a profound religious experience and our ordinary knowledge of the world in which we live very commonly fail to be adjusted one to the other.[1]

Again, the "Theory of Religion" leads to the conclusion that God evidently proceeds along "natural" lines, according to our measure of experience. None the less, religious experience finds a gulf between God and Man which only God can bridge. It is not that God is solely transcendent, for then He would have no real meaning for us; it is the transcendence of an *immanent* God that we so readily forget. The absolute consciousness of the inexhaustible riches and unsearchable wisdom of an eternal Divine Power is the

[1] A belief in God can rationalise our experience of our world, see R. H. Thouless, *Introduction to the Psychology of Religion* (1932), p. 281f.; cf. F. R. Tennant, *Philosophy of the Sciences* (1932), p. 184: the world as known to science has a reasonable explanation only in terms of theism. Inge (*Science, Religion and Reality*, ed. Needham, p. 389), citing Bacon's remark (above p. 53 n.), observes "we ought to add that the religion to which deeper knowledge brings us is not the same as that from which superficial knowledge estranges us."

inescapable paradox of the close and intimate relationship between human beings and the unseen God (p. 249).   But an immanent God is not merely the Creator of the Universe at some immensely remote beginning of things.   He is One that has always had some meaning for Man; though it is the question *what* that meaning is, and *what* God has meant even before Man appeared, that provokes enquiry.   Nor do we confine God's activity to any one aspect or phase of our existence—e.g. the specifically "religious" moment; and when it is said that "God is Love" this is born primarily of personal experience and of the conviction that His is higher than even the highest of human attributes.

If there is, in some sense, a relationship between God and Man, what is its bearing upon a man's actions and thoughts? The data of Religion may be said to point to a "Theory of Reality": there are beliefs and practices which make Man, as it were, a veritable cosmic being.[1]   There are mystical and other experiences of a oneness with things, as though we were in some way one with the actual world.   As we go deeper down individual differences disappear;[2] and from time to time men have believed that the Universe is essentially animate.   But if we are organic with Nature and an integral part of the actual Universe of our sciences, this in itself is not necessarily "religious."   It does not at all mean that there is a natural and unconditional relation between God and his creation—the Universe and Man.   Rather should one consider whether our convictions of the nature of the Universe and our convictions of God converge to direct us towards a higher truth.

Life is made fuller by romance, poetry, art and music; but mysticism, spiritism, occultism and the "numinous" also

---

[1] Pp. 117, 182.

[2] I quote from J. M. Wilson, *Cambridge Theological Essays* (ed. Swete, 1906, p. 222f.): "I believe that anyone who can faithfully express what is true to himself *may be drawing from a region of universal consciousness*; and may help others to interpret, even if not exactly in the same way, their own experience, and thus advance true knowledge" (the italics are my own).   Elsewhere (p. 245) he speaks of "the solid and permanent substratum of one common—may we not say Divine?—humanity."   Cf. also above, p. 248.

combine to convince us that existence in this world of space-time is not all.   Nevertheless, throughout we tend to value only what is true and good and beautiful and holy; and just as the psychic or "numinous" is not necessarily of spiritual value—and Religion itself has at times tolerated or encouraged what is bad—so we tend to value only what has personal worth and conduces to a higher and fuller life. Nowhere as here is the necessity of maintaining that there can be a vital difference between the subjective feeling of worth and its objective value more keenly felt.   Moreover, whatever may be the ineluctable implications of the more remarkable of the alleged psychic phenomena—e.g. telekinesis, levitation— we do not think of associating them with an omnipotent Deity; on the contrary, the usual tendency has been for Religion to view with suspicion whatever might seem "religious', but is felt to be its worst enemy.   Even among primitive peoples, where there is much that we should call "magical," a line will be drawn between their social-religious beliefs and practices and those that are denounced by them, although to the outsider all might seem to be equally "magical."   In general, Religion typically cherishes high ideals of Divine Reality, and it is encouraged to believe that a righteous and omnipotent God does not do all that His mere power might allow.[1]

Our thinking proceeds along two lines: one is the steady building up of positive knowledge; the other is based upon our convictions of a holy and righteous God.   The belief in the possibility or probability of *some sort* of existence after death is too widespread to be ignored; but rebirth (with the doctrine of *karma*) might be by no means a boon (p. 270), and to many the possibility of *some sort* of eternal existence is not less overwhelming than that of annihilation is to others. It is the *quality* of the existence and the relationship with the God of the Universe that alone are vital (p. 123); so that, whatever be the actual facts of human powers and of human destiny, the religious aspect is fundamental.   Ideas of the supersensuous, the beyond, and the invisible may or may not be well-founded—we may contrast wireless waves and

[1] Cf. in this connection the account of the Temptation of Jesus.

communication between the dead and the living—and no doubt we are only at the beginning of our exploration of our Universe; but there is a certain orderliness in the growth of our positive knowledge.

We may imagine a triangle at one corner of which we have all that a transcendent God may prove to mean for a Universe in which He is immanent; at the second we have ourselves, relying upon the world around us and reaching out towards the Divine and all that is unknown; and at the third we place the numinous, the unknown and all that may or may not prove to be *either* of spiritual worth and of value for our conceptions of God *or* of significance for the progressive developmment of our knowledge. There are contradictions in our existence, partly because we are bound up with existence in this world, and partly because we are in relationship with a God that transcends it.   There is indubitably much of value for our positive knowledge of which we are ignorant, but it would be as rash to deny that the countless dead have any significance for our fuller knowledge of Reality as to enlarge upon the possibility. Man is gradually building up his store of ordered knowledge and gradually testing and retesting his "religious" beliefs; his convictions about the God of the Universe test and direct what "non-religious" research has brought to light and are in turn directed and tested by it.

When it is asserted that God "created" the universe, the reference is not to an event in space, like a potter who moulds his vessel, it arises from the endeavour mentally to bridge the gulf between what Man knows and thinks of the world around him and the Supreme Being, for the origin and maintenance of the Universe is a problem that exceeds the limits of human thought.   If God is immanent, if He is a God of Love, there are far-reaching implications.   Evidently He gave His creatures a measure of spontaneity and freedom, as befits a loving Creator and Father (p. 114f.); and such a God, and not one who is essentially powerless, accounts for the mixture of good and evil that so often perplexes us.   To put it in very human terms, God is not the Father who cannot control His Frankensteins, but One who gives his creatures all liberty within limits, in order to draw and lead them to Himself.[1]

Our Mother Nature herself is beautiful, bizarre and brutish; and in all but the first she is easily outstripped by the human animal.   Her infinite variety, her efficiency, and the terrible, impartial ruthlessness which enables creatures to preserve themselves at the expense of others account for the conflicting verdicts Man has passed upon her; but his own inhumanity and self-sacrifice, his tenderness and fiendish egotism, blend the divine and the diabolical in a way that merits the same verdicts.

In many respects the Universe is terrifying in its immensity, its balance and its power, and its seeming disregard of ourselves with our three-score years and ten.   But Man has had a sufficiency of knowledge to enable him to feel at home in it, to progress, and to seek to wrest its secrets.   Nature and Man are so interrelated that it would be folly to ignore the objectivity of the processes at work in both; and our ability to describe and utilise them with a certain measure of success should not be allowed to cloak our real ignorance of them.   To-day, when we tend too much to take Nature and natural processes for granted, it would be a dangerous error to assume complacently that the evolutionary process running through Nature and Man must justify our laudable programmes.

The ethical demands of Man are the demands of human nature, of Man as part of a Universal Order; and from the religious point of view a God of Righteousness means a certain order and right throughout His Universe.[2]   Whatever exists will have had a certain justification; and we must not be surprised if there is enough "good" in what we consider "evil" to maintain it in a way that perplexes us, or

[1] We recall what Charles Kingsley put into Dame Nature's mouth: "You see, I make things make themselves," and the words of Paul Janet: "that which is precisely most worthy of a God is to have a Nature which creates itself" (cited by Sir J. Arthur Thomson, *Purpose in Evolution* [1932], pp, 23 and 12).

[1] Cf. pp. 110, 201; and to the references add especially J. Estlin Carpenter, "Conceptions of Law in Nature," *Hibbert Journal*, XXI (1923), 711–24.

if the "evil" in what we consider "good" persists in thwart-
ing it. A distinction is drawn between the *bonum sibi* and
the *bonum alteri* (p. 114); and when God is thought of as the
Power not ourselves that makes for righteousness, we are
distinguishing the processes of growth and change, as such,
and their value. Even on the plane of Religion, God's
processes are not arbitrary, but befit His righteousness;
although to think of them as unconditioned or guided by
human interests would be harmful, as Israel's prophets
clearly taught.[1]

Wrong and disorder, unrighteousness and disintegration,
the abnormal and the insane—these force our attention to
what should be otherwise. Thus we gain more definite
notions of systems, organisations and patterns, of regulative
ideas and principles, of approaches to our subject, and
of ways of selecting and setting our material in order so as
to give it "form."[2] In the case of our Biblical material we
have seen that through our own mental activity we reach a
position where we do not view it as a mass of data, but,
thanks to our selection and arrangement, reach meanings
which we feel to be true.[3] We may all see and use our
material differently; but it is not the bare observer and the
bare material, but to the forms, patterns, categories and so
forth in the observer there correspond the ways in which the
material has been organised, formed or patterned.

Patterning begins low down in organic evolution, so that
the organisms recognise each its own food, and the effect of
the sight of a pond on the chick is not what it is on the
duckling. The recognition of "forms" or "patterns" in
Scholasticism, in Science, and also in Dialectical Materialism
is the mediaeval and modern counterpart of ancient

---

[1] When Yahweh says, "I will be what I will be'. (Ex. iii. 14), Sir J.
Arthur Thomson observes that this is the God of Evolution (*op. cit.*
p. 55). We may contrast J. Needham (*Order and Life* [1936], p. 16),
who retains the conventional rendering, "I am that I am," and
remarks of it: a sublime expression, but for our research "the frank
confession of intellectual bankruptcy." (On the renderings of
Ex. iii. 14, see *O.T.R.*, p. 113.)

[2] See Index *s.v.* Patterns.

[3] See p. 234.

conceptions of Reason, Wisdom, Logos and the Platonic
"idea."[1] We can speak of forms of forms, or patterns of
patterns, or units of units, and dominating forms, all
enabling creatures to live each in its proper environment.
Although they are "natural," there has been a tendency to
feel that they are of transcendent origin—we have only to
think of the old ideas of the Divine Wisdom and Logos.
Kepler after his discovery of a scientific law is reported to
have exclaimed, "O God, we think Thy Thoughts after
Thee"; and often men have felt that their knowledge is
not of themselves, but that they are the agents of a higher
process. Some musicians, we are told, "have declared
that there must be a kind of heaven in which musical phrases
already exist," and a mathematician (Heinrich Hertz) felt
that mathematical formulae have an independent existence
of their own, they arise without prevision.[2] Between
instinct and intelligence there is no absolute gulf, and were
there no forms or patterns life would be impossible. Both
tragic cases of mental collapse and the present day breakdown of many of the patterns of life and thought enable
us to realise more clearly the reality of processes that
normally make existence so orderly that they are not
recognised.

Amid all our change and variety in the course of growth
something normally gives us stability and coherence. The
study of abnormal psychology illustrates the effects of its
absence. There are limits to our possibilities; and, while
in Nature we find remarkable developments and mutations,
roses simply do not become thistles; it takes a nightmare to
suggest changes of an incredibly absurd character. There
can be great permanent changes in our mental development;
but evidently there are conditions, since there are limits

[1] Watkin, *The Philosophy of Form*, pp. 84, 252; *Textbook of
Marxist Philosophy* (ed. John Lewis), p. 12. See also above p. 263.

[2] J. W. N. Sullivan (*The Contemporary Mind* [1934], p. 104, cf.
112f.), to whom I owe these examples, points out (p. 115) that
mathematics and music are the least dependent on experience; there
are creative prodigies at a very early age since they "can proceed to
create before they have learnt anything about the world, because as a
matter of fact there is nothing for them to learn."

to what we can assimilate and digest.   There are cases
where the whole-hearted acceptance of certain things as
true—e.g. in occultism—has had deleterious effects on the
mind.[1]   There are limits both to what we can grow into
and treat as regulative and to what we can impose upon
others, and the fact that this should be so is exceedingly
important when we are considering the development of our
patterns or forms of thought.

In attending to any object we isolate it; but constantly
we find ourselves forced to extend our horizon and ascertain
more of its context, environment or field—what we might
call its "ecology."   In so doing our approach likewise
becomes less narrow; much more is relevant than at first
we imagined.[2]   But when we enlarge our field there is a
great difference between the orderly growth of our knowledge of the object in its immediately relevant field, and the
common tendency to leap to some ultimate position which
satisfies our personal demands, and is personally rather than
merely intellectually satisfying.   From primitive peoples
upwards there is often an "immediacy" which the course of
research breaks down—we may contrast the Hebrew
attitude to Nature with our own.   To say "In Him we live
and move and have our Being" expresses the consciousness
of our ultimate limits and of ultimate truths; but the
orderly growth of knowledge does not take us there, but to
the point where we need a bridge.   We may indeed keep
apart our profound personal convictions and our positive
knowledge, and both Science and Biblical Criticism have
progressed by maintaining this severance (p. 229f.); but the
necessity of finding some adjustment is obvious when we
consider that a religion is most real when there is some
intelligible relationship between it and what we class under
the heading of the "non-religious."   On the one hand, it is
unwise to abandon a problem to the theologian or the
metaphysician because it is outside the limits of positive
knowledge; but, on the other, the implications of religious

[1] There have also been theories which resemble pins of which the
boy said that they had saved people's lives—by not being swallowed
by them.   [2] Cf. 229.

experience and conviction have a significance which "secular" research cannot ignore.

In all growth and change there is no absolute freedom but rather a choice of patterns or forms, and of lines to be followed. There are limits even to our private creations.[1] There is always the possibility of taking the wrong turning, of making the unwise choice and of selecting the inferior alternative. On looking back we can see how often there has been a process modifying, rectifying and repairing our mistakes; and in the realm of Religion we gain our convictions of undeserved forgiveness, redemption and atonement. Now it is some specific occasion where the wrong has been turned into right, and now the whole Self is transformed, redirected, and exercises its freedom differently. But in any case this repairing process involves a larger field of action, and if we may truly speak of the Power not ourselves that makes for righteousness, we may surely see the operation of an Immanent God throughout His Universe. The "religious" conviction raises to a higher plane and generalises a fundamental process.[2]

Change in itself is not necessarily a progressive advance, it may be for the worse, and, as in the case of an accident, there may be limits to the repairing process. Nature's marvellous power of repairing an imperfect, injured or mutilated organism has its limits; but in Man the Self can be superior to its bodily organism, and even the impaired Self can be re-organised on a higher plane. By sublimation a lower trend can be replaced by a higher one; but when some normal need is not satisfied the substitutes for Religion will show how the human creature's need is met by some less

---

[1] Miss H. Wodehouse (*The Presentation of Reality* [1910], pp. 138 ff.) remarks that once the novelist has created a fictitious character the rest is governed by the ordinary law of actuality; hence we can argue about a good novel rather than about a bad one. The hopeless inconsequentiality of dreams affords an instructive example of what can happen when there is no directive will.

[2] "If God the Creator is also God the Redeemer we should expect to find the creative redemptive process at every stage similar in character and method" (C. E. Raven, *Evolution and the Christian Conception of God* [1936], p. 20); cf. below p. 323, n. 6.

integrating impulse.[1]   Throughout there is an urge towards a fuller expression; there are, as it were, events to be accomplished, melodies to be completed, a striving after a state of equilibrium—but the results are subjectively satisfying, and there may be regression and devolution, and the road may lead into a *cul-de-sac*.

In the processes of development we may distinguish between the one more "intensive"—we may call it inertia[2]— and the one that departs from the line hitherto followed and goes "outside," as it were, and is "extensive" rather than "intensive."   For self-preservation and maintenance there must be a dynamic equilibrium or stability, and whatever is felt to be alien, disturbing and inimical will be rejected. A whole series of active movements may lead to a new stage where there is thenceforth a stabilising within what is now a relatively closed system, a self-contained field.   Thus after the conflicts—the "interpenetration of opposites" (p. 284)—leading to Bolshevism in Russia, once the revolutionary stage had been established all further growth and change must be *within* the new framework.   Again, at the rise of Christianity we may contrast the inertia of Rabbinical Judaism (p. 72, n. 2)—all subsequent development being within definite limits—with the active development of Christianity, until here, too, the carefully formulated theological and philosophical systems led to a state of inertia.[3]

Throughout we are dealing with a familiar process: the endeavour to maintain an existing pattern (or pattern of patterns) and the difference between the steps leading up to it and those that follow.   The changes within any given pattern are different from those outside it that might endanger it, and there is always the question how much any system or organism can stand without changing the

[1] Cf. p. 273, n. 3; also E. I. Watkin, *Theism, Agnosticism and Atheism* (1936), pp. 136 ff.

[2] So, Watkin, *The Philosophy of Form*, pp. 41 ff., 116, 267.

[3] Cf. also the introduction of the "Wellhausen" stage of Old Testament criticism (pp. 66f., 89), and the subsequent movement within specific literary-critical limits.

pattern or—so to speak—spoiling the tune.[1] The new
organism, like the old, is subject to its own laws; and there is
always the tendency for us to maintain a system in Procrustean manner (p. 242): we may have an "official theory,"
an interlocking body each part supporting and supported
by the other parts. There may be what M. Maritain has
styled "un jeu d'erreurs compensatrices," and so it may
come to pass that we don't *have* a system, it may have *us*.

Thus a system may be adequate within a certain range;
it has made its field and is so far untouched by the larger
field outside it; there is resistance to change, and this may
lead to atrophy. But do we know of any absolutely closed
system of life and thought? Inertia is not a final stage:
every unit system, pattern or "event" (p. 265 n.)—however
we name it—is essentially part of a larger whole, like the
flower in the crannied wall (p. 230), although now confined
in a smaller one. And even as we ourselves become conscious of incompleteness, so we may regard the constituents
of every unit as striving to be less "intensive" and more
"extensive," striving—let us say—like animated musical
notes who refuse to believe that the melody is finished.
This twofold movement is familiar. Constantly we find
ourselves going outside and taking in new raw material,
digesting it, fashioning and shaping it, and rejecting what
cannot be utilised. On a large scale we find this process in
the contrast between nationalism and universalism or internationalism.[2] We may regard it as the most fundamental
of all processes: the striving of any given unit (or unit of
units), which is essentially an integral part of a larger one,
within itself or to break down its barriers.

[1] The *Textbook of Marxist Philosophy*, p. 280, observes that
quality and quantity are radically different: "if a thing changes its
basic quality it ceases to be that which it was, it is turned into something else, whereas with a change of quantity a thing does not cease
to be itself." Of course, throughout, the whole question is how one
is to determine the difference in difficult cases.

[2] Cf. the remarks of A. J. Toynbee, *A Study of History* (1934), III,
248 ff., 254, etc., on withdrawal from the world and the return to it. In
primitive society we may contrast endogamy (marriage within specified
groups) with exogamy (marriage outside such groups), each naturally
having a different repercussion upon the social beliefs and customs.

There are processes in Nature which look purposive and teleological, like those in man.   There seems to be a striving after some specific end, an aiming at some more complex pattern or whole.   Writers speak of an urge or *nisus*, an *élan vital* (Bergson), or they resort to the old notion of an entelechy.   There is a proper disinclination among scientists to speak of Nature anthropically, in human terms; but it is certainly necessary to bear in mind that Man himself is not always so purposive as he thinks and that greater purposes and plans will take the place of the smaller ones that were more immediate and temporary and confined in their scope. In biology one reads of the "prospective significance" of the cells,[1] as they proceed to form specific predetermined patterns; but also in our own world we may—no doubt more freely and creatively—build up a system; yet there is a constant tendency for the constituent elements to become stabilised, to organise their implications, and to determine the further growth of the thought-structure.[2]   And while in Nature the process certainly *seems* purposive in its adherence to certain types or patterns, Man, too, although in many respects a Creator, has not—if he cherishes his sanity—a freedom that is unlimited.

In natural growth it can be seen how an individual unit, such as the new-born babe, can be entirely dependent upon a larger unit—with which it co-operates, however unconsciously.   But the "individual" units are everywhere variable, like the patterns and purposes which everywhere vary in range and complexity; and instead of reaching a specific end the units (being essentially integral parts of a larger whole) will merge into greater ones, each with its own pattern or purpose.   Religion recognises an *immanent* God, a Divine Reason, Wisdom or Logos, and we may distinguish between His—or Its—greater and lesser purposes. Men strive after a transcendent God and Reality; but what they reach are new stages in their growth, and sufficient insight and knowledge to carry them along to a higher stage.

[1] The term is Driesch's, see J. Needham, *Order and Life*, p. 53.
[2] Cf. even the limitations of the novelist (p. 294, n. 1, also p. 261, n. 1.)

We do not arrive at the ultimate purpose, but the "whole" has greater wisdom than the "parts," and our quest makes us fellow-workers with something that transcends all we know.

Every growing unit is part of some larger one, and to this we may look for an explanation of the appearance of what we regard as "new," that is, some peculiarity which cannot be directly derived from the immediately preceding stages. Changes can be regarded as quantitative or qualitative, according to our criteria[1]; and what is entirely unpredictable in advance may, on retrospect, seem natural and rational.[2] The changes normally come under the appropriate conditions. Thus, L. J. Henderson has shown how the unique properties of the three elements hydrogen, carbon and oxygen enabled the inorganic world to prepare for the organic.[3] In the case of the higher integration of functions, the many phenomena that arrest attention and provoke speculation are scarcely more impressive than the familiar changes in normal embryonic development which culminate in the ability of the young mother to suckle her first-born.[4] We should correlate the *natural* processes of the created order with those of the more spontaneous creative processes of man.[5]

It is through the larger field that we explain the phenomena of emergent or creative evolution, or creative synthesis, as it is also called. We do not know of any complete

---

[1] See p. 296, n. 1.

[2] See pp. 115, 270f.

[3] *The Order of Nature* (1917), Chaps. IX and X. We may also compare the *Praeparatio Evangelica* (cf. pp. 68, 174f. 319.)

[4] Cf. Needham, *op. cit.* p. 42, on embryonic development in general: the final product comes into being by a precise co-operation of reactions and events which, however, can be dissociated and thrown out of gear.

[5] It is interesting to see how Dialectical Materialism seeks to explain unexpected and outstanding figures or events. To speak of God "is intellectual suicide," and all "mysticism," and the like, is repudiated. "Historical necessity" is no explanation, and it becomes necessary to look to a larger environment for operations which previously had been considered irrelevant (Sidney Hook, *Towards the understanding of Karl Marx: a revolutionary interpretation* [1933], pp. 166–177).

self-contained system wound up in readiness; and no new
factor comes in for the nonce as a separate independent
agency—though the idea of a *deus ex machina* is one that
often forces itself upon us when a crisis has been surmounted;
rather is it that a larger field proves to be relevant for what
has hitherto been treated in isolation.[1] Hence we often
get the old in a new form; and when the changes lead to
some new system, some fresh co-ordination, we pass from
the earlier to the later, ignoring all that intervenes in a
way that recalls the conception of a quantum (p. 313 n.).
Moreover, this conception of a larger or even an ultimate
integral field of force can be invoked in cases of what seems
to be action at a distance (p. 195).   In our prayers to God
on behalf of those afar off we seem to imply that all are
parts of a single ultimate field; and outside the realm of
Religion telepathy and "providential warnings" might also
seem to imply an actual common substratum or substance
of which individuals are outcrops.[2]

God, the Creator, would seem to be already in our "field"
before we come to recognise His existence.[3]   From Primitive
Religion upward there is a belief in supernatural power
which Man can enlist conditionally: the sacred Power
(Mana) and the necessary preparations and precautions
(Tabu) are correlative.[4]   God offers Himself to those who
approach Him in faith (Luke xi, 9–13), and He can use
those who prepare themselves for His service (Jer. xv. 19).
But if there would seem to be a certain natural appropriate
growth in the relation between the "body" and the "spirit,"[5]
there is also a "breaking through," and the "emergence," if
it can be so called, is not so much a stage in a series as a

[1] See pp. 229 f., 293.

[2] Is it wise to ascribe to God all the occasions when a few receive
these "warnings" and escape while those not so favoured suffer and
perhaps perish?   The cause of Religion is not prejudiced if we speak
of God's Universe, with all its freedom and spontaneity—within
limits—rather than of God Himself.

[3] See p. 184.

[4] Cf. p. 107 n., and *Rel. Sem.*, pp. 552 ff.; and, above all, the works
of R. R. Marett.

[5] See pp. 166, 232 f.

disturbing factor, a qualitative rather than a quantitative change. The great spiritual intrusions are inaugural (cf. p. 124); they make discontinuities in what may later become only a more impressive continuity. This can clearly be perceived in the cataclysmic changes upon which the Bible turns, viz. in the Exilic Age and at the rise of Christianity; and it is surely significant that, just where we see epoch-making Divine interventions without a parallel in human history, as known to us, there is a final continuity which—when we take a long view—seems intelligible and natural. On the other hand, it must be recognised that spiritual impulses can be "sectarian" in their results, even as disintegration may lead, not to a vaster synthesis, but to minor syntheses or narrower bases than before. Similar sorts of process run through the Universe of Nature and of Man.

God grants His creatures joy, peace, help and love; and men are strengthened for the better exercise of their powers. He gives them illumination and insight; but can it be affirmed that He gives them truths unattainable by reason? As has been truly said, "the world is still at the beginning of the study of the nature of revelation."[1] The various religious doctrines, all the world over, present the result of human thought working upon religious experience and influenced by the social and intellectual environment.[2] We constantly need some "imaginary hypothesis" to set our material in order and reach the truth of things; but, like the happy ideas, and like the feeling that we sometimes have at night that our problems have been solved, all may prove illusory. There is no break in the series between the happy ideas that prove effective and an overwhelming realisation of the Truth—or of the way thereunto; the cardinal fact is the intuitive conviction that even the "revelations" claimed to be of divine origin are to be examined along "natural"

---

[1] J. M. Wilson, *Cambridge Theological Essays*, p. 221. He observes that inspiration belongs to minds not to truths apprehended by minds (p. 227).

[2] G. Galloway, *The Philosophy of Religion* (1914), p. 584. See above p. 254 n.

(ethical and rational) lines; the "spirits" are to be tested (1 John iv. 1).[1]

Through the changes in the general background of thought religious and other truths which were felt to be entirely credible and reasonable in their day may lose their effectiveness.   When those that were "supra-rational" are now felt to be irrational, it would be infra-rational to rehabilitate them in their old form.   An imperfect "body" impairs the "spirit."[2]   Rather must one seek to restate them in that supra-rational form that transcends and stimulates life and thought; for a "religious" truth is an active generative force and not an isolated sentiment, and a religion is strongest when it forms a triad with theology and philosophy. Illumination or inspiration is the "light which lighteth every man" (John i. 9, cf. Ps. xxxvi. 9).   And it must be a "true" light; for there can be an irrational and misguided impulse, subjectively felt to be spiritual, which at its worst recalls the forcible words on the light in a man that is darkness (Matt. vi. 23).

When the "new" emerges in evolution we have in mind the new relations or phenomena arising from some fresh impulse.   Now in Man we can postulate from a very rudimentary stage religious impulses, that is, some consciousness in the child and in the childhood of the world that found religious expression.   There is no reason—apart from doctrinal interests—to suppose that there was an actual primitive prehistoric monotheism followed by subsequent relapse and deterioration.   On the contrary, the unifying religious impulses, such as we come across in history, gave new strength and direction to the current conditions *whatever they were*.[3]   But we know as little of the inside world of primitive pre-historic man as of the infant; hence, in spite of each and every religious or even

---

[1] Raven, *op. cit.*, p. 35, remarks that "creeds and doctrines like formulations of natural laws are hypotheses."   Of course, if like "natural laws" they need restatement, it is in order to adjust them to the growth of human experience and knowledge, it is to "fulfil" and not necessarily to "destroy" them.

[2] Cf. pp. 166, 214, 266.

[3] Cf. p. 226f.; and see *J.T.S.* XXXIII (1931), 1–17.

monotheistic impulse, we can still attempt to trace some intelligible evolution. It is an evolution of the "body," so to speak, which undergoes quantitative and qualitative changes through the indwelling—or as we are often inclined to say—the "inrushing" spirit.[1]

We may think of an immanent God as "an indwelling differing widely in the measure of its fullness according to the capacities of the several levels."[2]   We would meditate on the care of a Heavenly Father for His creation (Luke xii. 22–31); but to be thoroughly realistic we have only to consider the economy and balance of Nature and the marvellous phenomena of instinct, self-preservation, protective colouring, mimicry, camouflage, all of which assures us that in His Universe the "whole" is more efficient and purposive than the "parts," and which impels us once again to seek to co-ordinate rather than to sever the realms of Nature and of Man.[3]   Yet there is so much in both that seems contrary to the attributes of a Divine Power that it would be difficult for us to speak of an "immanent" God, were it not that by so doing we gain truer conceptions of both.[4]   It was a great step—which, again, could not arise of its own accord in Man—to realise that if Man loves God, it is because God first loved him (p. 126 f.); and the readier we are to believe that the same Power is in and behind both Man and Nature—always according to their several levels— the more inevitable is the conclusion that if, on the one hand, there is a process that keeps Nature true to type, on the other, it is for Man, the free creator, to find the sort of type to which he himself must be true.

Evolution has brought greater possibilities of forethought, free ideas and constructive imagination. It has also

---

[1] For the bearing of this on Robertson Smith's theory of the "origin" of sacrifice, see *Rel. Sem.*, pp. xxxv., xlviii.

[2] Raven, *op. cit.*, p. 29.

[3] This is by no means to revive the old notion of "Design in Nature," rather might one enlarge on the lack of design and intelligent forethought in Man!

[4] It is one of those difficult convictions—like Divine Love (p. 113, n. 2)—that subsequently makes it easier to understand the processes in the Universe.

brought a duality of Thought and Action against which there is apt to be an anti-intellectualist reaction. But Thought both leads to action and tests it; and although we feel that we should *live* our religious and other truths, the history of Religion itself proves that the ideas and beliefs embodied in practice at any one time are not necessarily of the highest. Thought now hinders and now facilitates Action. Moreover, in dealing with primitive peoples we are constantly obliged to describe as explicit what is implicit. There is often an immediacy in their actions such that even their religious practices might seem to be as instinctive as the behaviour of the lower organisms.[1] They are manifesting their feelings, and we have to interpret them even as we do the actions of the infant. Here Feeling, Thought, Belief and Action are one.

Of course the fact that we do things with a certain measure of effectiveness is taken to be an indication that we are doing them as they should be done and that we are adhering to the Order, Truth or Nature of things. But constantly it is discovered that there are better ways and a less incomplete truth. At more advanced stages there are more explicit ideas of a Truth, Right or Order to be aimed at and followed;[2] and the highest state of knowledge is the knowledge of God's processes and demands. The unanalysed identity of feeling and action at one stage becomes, at another stage, the more explicit consciousness of adherence to or deviation from what is Right and True. At the same time, Man's increasing consciousness of the Universe has led to an immensely greater complexity of life and thought corresponding to the recognition of the complexity of the Universe. If it were at all possible to analyse minds we might expect mental categories, patterns, and the like, corresponding to the Universe as apprehended by those minds; and at the highest conceivable stage of intellectual and spiritual development a human being would the more completely embody in himself the principles of the Universe. There is a correspondence between the pattern

[1] E.g. ideas of rebirth, etc., see pp. 214, 274, n. 1.
[2] See p. 214, cf. p. 111 f.

of the man who speaks or writes and that of the man who receives and accepts; and unless there were some inter-relation between our minds and the Universe we could not apprehend it. The mental processes are thus cosmic processes at the human level, but at a stage immensely higher than we find them among primitive and ancient peoples.

The ultimate processes in the Universe cannot be external to us; we are part of the history of a Universe, the funda-mental principles of which are manifested in Nature and Man. Among early peoples we often find what implies a sort of co-operation between Man and Nature; there are magical or magico-religious practices[1] wherein men imitate, or rather they act or perform the processes of sunshine, rain, natural increase, etc. They are, as it were, carrying on the cosmos with or without the co-operation of gods, spirits or other functionaries.[2] In so doing they come to learn much of Nature and of what is or is not indis-pensable for their purpose. Later, in endeavouring to develop social and national life, the necessity of learning the same lesson is still felt. There is an Ultimate Reality against which neither Nature nor Man can contend; and, to adjust a noteworthy sentiment, this Reality is "a cyclone which sweeps away everything in its path." The feeling that one is co-operating with some objective cosmic or historic process can be immensely powerful: thought and action are one, the thing is true because *we* are doing it, living it. The activity *feels* sacred, because of the human depths that are sounded and the goal that lies ahead. Yet the feeling is subjective, the urge may be fanatical and irrational, and the light may be the light that is darkness. There can be no more impressive crisis than that nineteen centuries ago when, amid conflicting religious impulses, widespread disaster and ruin came through the passion of self-confident fanatics and a new direction was given to the history of thought by a Christianity which did not grow out of but in opposition to them. Right and wrong ideas of

[1] On the difference see pp. 150, 288.
[2] See p. 117.

God and Reality were in conflict, and the rise of Christianity is really a unique cosmic event.

Although we do not reach Ultimate Reality we do come to know more about ourselves; we live in a very real world with the knowledge that there is something more real. Science, writes Max Planck, "brings us to the threshold of the Ego and leaves us there."[1] We reach ourselves, and we discover that there must be something more real than the Ego and the best fruits of the intellect.[2] Impressive religious, mystical and numinous experiences support the Indian conception of Maya, the relative unreality and impermanence of this world (p. 197); and on the purely religious side we have the conviction that "all our existence is part of a mystery which surrounds even scientific thinking, so that nothing is left to us but grace or despair."[3] The bridge we try to throw from the Here-and-Now to the Ultimate Reality breaks down, and we can only acknowledge, at the end of our thinking, that the cosmos is no logico-geometrical scheme but an adventure of divine love.[4]

The fact of the existence of God is within our personal horizon, but the conceptions we frame will be conditioned by our knowledge of ourselves and this world. To quote the late Canon Streeter, "without some *objective* presentation of the conception of the Divine, the word God is a blank cheque, which the individual worshipper must fill in from the context of his own small personal experience and his own exiguous ideals."[5] The great historical religions have sought to fathom the mystery of all mysteries, and through Biblical religion we have come to inherit convictions of the nature and accessibility of God through a personal intermediary, and these have guided life and thought along a way that has been felt to be true.

---

[1] *Where is Science going?* (1933), p. 167.

[2] Cf. pp. 257, 263.

[3] A. Keller, *Religion and the European Mind* (1934), p. 79. This is the keynote of the Continental theologians Barth and Brunner.

[4] F. R. Tennant: the concluding words of his *Philosophical Theology* (1930), ii. 259.

[5] *The Buddha and the Christ* (1932), p. 127. See below, p. 323, n. 1.

Between ourselves and the Ultimate Reality we can conceive a hierarchy of processes, e.g. the subject-matter of physics, chemistry, biology, physiology, psychology, and sociology.[1] We may think of these as qualitatively different levels or strata—not without overlapping—with their own processes, patterns and appropriate conceptions. Such a differentiation does not, of course, lie on the surface of things; it is not to be found in the mind of the child or the childhood of the world. It is the result of a mental differentiation, the highest stage yet reached; it is the outcome of a lengthy mental development which has not necessarily ceased.

The various strata can be mutually suggestive and supply each other with helpful analogies. As A. N. Whitehead says: "there can be no doubt that the normal method of cross-fertilising thought is by considering the same, or allied problems to our own, in the form which they assume in other sciences.[2] J. T. MacCurdy finds an essential identity beneath physiology and psychology.[3] James Ward speaks of a sort of "mental chemistry," and finds more than analogy between organic and mental development.[4] Sir Edward Tylor compared cultural details with species, and found it at least a good working analogy.[5] G. F. Moore likened the multiplication of religious sects to the origin of species and the multiplication of low types of organism by fission.[6] Comte argued that political and moral crises are the result of intellectual anarchy, and that social and national disorganisation is due to profound divergence touching the general ideas that form a common social

[1] Some may prefer to conceive a triangle having at its angles (a) physics, (b) biology, and (c) psychology; this more readily illustrates both the contacts between them and the intervening departments.

[2] The Aims of Education (1929), p. 233.

[3] See p. 261, n. 2.   As long as the properties we are concerned with are present we can always ignore the irrelevant details (ib. p. xii,f.)

[4] Psychological Principles (1918), pp. 76, 103, 184, 410.   On ideas as forces, see T. Merz, History of European Thought in the XIXth Century, IV (1914), 237 f, 523 f, 723 ff.

[5] Primitive Culture (ed. of 1903), i. 8.

[6] The History of Religions, II, x., 368.

doctrine. (This means for us that the problem of world-peace is essentially one of ideological harmony.) Passing over the favourite comparison of social and biological vicissitudes, we may mention the view of Sir George Darwin that "the laws which govern stability hold good in regions of the greatest diversity," and that "homologous considerations as to stability and instability are really applicable to evolution of all sorts." This he illustrates from the fortunes of governments.[1]

Much more could be said, but it must suffice to refer to the long antiquated typology which traced more than a likeness between the processes in Nature and those in Religion, between the growth of structure in organisms and that in doctrine. Here we return to the real interconnection between ideas or "forms" in God's Universe of Nature and Man, in the field of Science and in the world of Thought.[2] The processes may be regarded as analogous or rather homologous, and the lower is contained in the higher even as—to take an elementary illustration—$x^2+2xy+y^2$ is contained in $x^3+3x^2y+3xy^2+y^3$. For although there might seem to the uninitiated to be no connection whatever between these we have only to write them as $(x+y)^2$ and $(x+y)^3$ for this to become obvious. So, in general, the aim is to find a way of co-ordinating our material in order to distinguish between unhelpful comparisons—suppose, e.g. the first of the two terms above had been x^2+xy+y^2— and those that enable us to cover as wide a field as possible with the utmost economy of effort.

Of all the processes physics might seem to handle the most fundamental, in that it enables scientists to speculate on the entire history of the Universe from beginning to end. But we know of no actual complete historical cycle—apart from abstraction—for each cycle is, in the last analysis, an integral part of a larger one. Besides, we should still wonder out of what and into what does the Universe develop. Indeed we cannot start from sense-data and discriminated

[1] In *Darwin and Modern Science* (ed. Seward, 1909), pp. 543, 547.
[2] A. B. Davidson, *Old Testament Prophecy*, pp. 210 ff., 326 ff. Some reinterpretation of the old phraseology is admittedly necessary.

perceptions, for these are constructs, interpretations.[1] Physics is not entitled to call the tune; the development of the human mind that can handle the data of physics is more fundamental than the data themselves.   Moreover, we need not ask how we can pass from the world of percepts to the conceptual or purely mental world; already the world of primitive man is much more what is "in his mind" than what is, as we should say, "external."   Man has increasingly "externalised" his world and thereby learnt more of the environment in which he is placed—a notable advance was made by the Ionian Greeks (pp. 144ff).   But we can view the more perceptual processes and the more conceptual processes as lower and higher forms of activity, even as in the history of Religion we can distinguish two stages in the expression of religious feeling; but the later does not grow out of the earlier.[2]

Of modern developments in physics it has been said that they have changed, not the material, but the interpretation of it; they have led to wider notions of Science and Mind.[3] Similarly Biblical Criticism does not change its material, but it covers a much wider field which it interprets afresh. In either case there are real data; but their real value lies not in the bare material as such, but in its meaning for us, and in the way in which our knowledge enables us to use it.[4] Instead of the dichotomy into mind and matter—the "matter" of the physical world and the mind of the human observer—we may think of processes at different stages of their development.   If Man has learnt in some measure to control the matter or material of the "external" world, he has often to deal with no slight intractable material in the,

---

[1] Cf. Sir J. H. Parsons, above, p. 261 n.; Tennant, *op. cit.*, i. 35, 37 f., 64; Watkin, *Philosophy of Form*, pp. 252, 84.

[2] See p. 214.   So as regards Robertson Smith's theory of totemism, the higher religions did not evolve out of it, they are higher forms of ideas or usages which find their expression in lower forms, in totemism, see *Rel. Sem.*, p. 541, cf. *J.T.S.*, XXXII (1931), 247.   On the *x* which takes these different forms *a* and *b*, see p. 310 n.

[3] Bavink, *Science and God* (1933), p. 57.

[4] Cf. the material of the archaeologist, p. 241 f.

fruits of the human mind.[1]   Not only is it unnecessary to confine the term "matter" to part only of the material with which we have to come to terms,[2] we cannot sever the external world and the world of human activity and thought; all are "events"—to use Whitehead's term—in one immensely long history.   Throughout this history there is a continuous flux from atoms to human happenings, but there is stability varying in degree from the inorganic to the organic and to the bodies of thought and doctrine which make history and are often—rightly or wrongly—as resistant to change as the "rock" upon which they are believed to be founded.

After all, it is through the highest activities of the developing human mind that we have learnt so much of the Universe and can include Man and his mental processes themselves among its constituents.   By thinking along certain lines we feel that we think, act and live effectively.   But it does not follow that the Universe is ultimately mind-stuff. Indeed, instead of conceiving of some undifferentiated stuff as the basis of the Universe, the more immediate task is not to demonstrate the unity of the Universe, but to unify our own way of regarding it.[3]   In any large field of material— e.g. in dealing with the Bible itself—the fundamental unity lies in the structure of our own life and thought.   Even if we were in a state of equilibrium, a dynamic stability, we should still have to ensure that the working system which we find to be a complete answer to our questions to-day was not one to hinder our successors in ten or a hundred years' time.   And this demands the explicit recognition of a transcendent Reality.[4]   Thus we aim first, not at a philosophy, but at a higher anthropism.   Men are *persons* before they are specialists in science, theology or philosophy, and the aim should be to help the average individual to understand the relation between his ever-growing Universe and

[1] See pp. 14, 113, n. 3, 242.   [2] See p. 265.

[3] Do we actually know of any undifferentiated matrix, apart from what we have abstracted and isolated?

[4] On the dynamic character of the conception of a God of Righteousness, see p. 112.

his ever-growing Self, to educate him so that he can realise how Man is the measure of all things, in a higher sense than is commonly meant.

The Self may be greater than all its functions, but we live in what may still be a very young world; confined in body and mind, we must be realists in a very real world; but our description of it is conceptual, and we shall continue to speak of our "external" world, although in the last analysis we may be "cosmic" beings and our Religion unites us to an Ultimate Reality. The interpretations and constructions by which we live give us, no picture of reality in itself, but what is effective reality for us: in the words of St. Thomas Aquinas, "the intellect does not apprehend things according to their mode of being, but according to its mode."[1] The "things" may be apprehended differently by different minds; and it is difficult to see why we should conceive of some hidden reality, when what we really need are less imperfect ways of utilising our accessible material.[2]

Such is the growth of knowledge that much more may prove to be importantly real than can be utilised by us at present. The world of Religion and of the numinous may induce us to speculate, e.g. on the implications for our positive knowledge if human beings are veritably cosmic, parts of one earth-soul, or if there are angelic super-intelligences. But it would seem as though we can assimilate only (a) what is analogous (or homologous) to what we know and (b) the inferences based thereupon. There is a sense in which progressive development is rational, orderly and step-wise; and one-sided specialistic development, especially in speculative thought, may easily outstrip the field or environment by which it should be supported and which it should, in turn, support.

---

[1] F. J. Sheen, *God and Intelligence in Modern Philosophy* (1925), p. 126, cf. *ib.* p. 135.

[2] The Platonic world of reals, patterns, eternal objects or archetypes would be one of "smiles" waiting to be materialised by "Cheshire cats." It is the world of logical entities. In the case of homologies and all other comparable things an x may take the various forms a, b, c, etc. (fin, paddle arm, etc.); but we know of no x in and by itself, although it is a necessary logical entity.

The not uncommon notion of a world-soul and the religious conviction of the relationship between Man and the God of the Universe represent a tendency the very opposite of which is to multiply souls and selves without limit. As is well known, animistic, polytheistic and pluralistic belief finds souls and spirits innumerable. They are agencies, organisers, causes and maintainers. They are unifying principles and forces; and one can reckon as many souls or spirits as there are units or individuals.[1] We have only to think of the "individuals" in organic life—e.g. a hive or a beaver-colony—and of the ranges of "corporate personality"—e.g. a clan, church, regiment or college—to understand the naturalness and utility of the conception. It would be difficult to say which was the more "real," the individual or the group, the social class[2] or the nation—we are led on to ever more comprehensive units until we reach the ultimate Soul or Self of which each is an integral part.

Meanwhile, if we substract the activities, functions and processes of any unit, what is left? The tendency is now to think, not of matter or substance, but of streams of energy, streaming centres of action, processes, constellations of activity.[3] As in human history itself, amid increasing change there are tolerably stabilised "events," the lesser merged in the greater, though without losing their individuality. But we cannot draw a rigid line between the human, the organic and the inorganic; and while human beings are held together by their "corporate spirit," there is a cohering principle even in the world of thought, the significance and effectiveness of which are readily seen when ideas, beliefs and doctrines break down.[4] In fact we have to describe the Universe by means of more or less stable

[1] See p. 266.

[2] Insistence on the social group and social righteousness may be narrow and intolerant and subjective; it may overlook the fact that a true objective righteousness should unite that wide variety of individual types which every social group should embrace, if it would live and expand.

[3] Cf. Bavink, *op. cit.*,, pp. 62, 66 ff.

[4] Cf. p. 162.

concepts and bodies of thought.[1] We pass from our souls
and selves—of which the transcendent and immanent God
of the Universe is the maintainer—to the cohering power
in the world of Nature and Man, the patterns, forms, configurations, and the like, through which we live, and understand and describe our environment. After all, the means
whereby they cohere is really remarkable and absolutely
indispensable! From the purely religious point of view
there is no difficulty in believing that in God's Universe
there is no rigid line to be drawn between the jump of the
needle to the magnet and the decision of the chess-player
or the labours of the politician, for to the Divine Wisdom
or Logos is due everything that makes for order, right,
truth and rationality. The Self subsists, first and last,
in an actual or potential relationship with the God who
maintains it in this real world of ours; and the Self lives
amid a hierarchy of processes from the physical to the
ideological, all of which have a meaning, through the
processes that give sufficient coherence and stability to both
the observer, the subject, and to the objects presented to
him.[2]

Instead of thinking of fundamental processes in terms of
wooden models, cylinders and other sense-data, the mental
world—it may be suggested—supplies more flexible illustrations, metaphors and parallels. We may think of ourselves as historical events, cycles of action, small units in
larger ones, fundamentally part of an ultimate "history"
and fundamentally in contact with the God of the Universe.
In the continuous flux of events the constituents are always
undergoing change, yet there are relatively stable patterns
and cycles. As we survey things historically our mind

[1] Cf. Watkin, *Philosophy of Form*, p. 14f.: "a concrete object is a
particular arrangement of physical units; the atom is an arrangement
of electrical energy, the concept one of intelligent energy."

[2] See Watkin, *Philosophy of Form*, p. 254 (cf. p. 46), on the correspondence between the subject and the object, both manifesting in
their structure the Divine Logos. On the question of the relation
between the structure of a presented fact and the (subject's) expression
of it, cf. Wittgenstein, *Tractatus Logico-Philosophicus* (1922), pp.
39ff.; cited by J. W. N. Sullivan in *The Nation and Athenaeum*,
27th January, 1923, p. 675f., cf. also 3rd February, p. 684.

passes from A to B, from B to C, and so forth, and we
ignore the intervening data. Thus we can speak of the
"Dark" or "Middle Ages" (p. 218), or pass naturally from
the Old Testament to the New, or follow the progressive
development of some branch of research, attending as it
were only to the crests of the successive waves and ignoring,
if not ignorant of, the troughs.   In this manner we are
really making jumps or leaps; and when we do turn to the
intervening data—for example, in the case of the Bible,
the apocryphal and apocalyptical literature—we may have
to supplement or modify the line we had hitherto traced.
To put it otherwise, our historical survey will give us a
certain melody which, when we consider the material anew
or more carefully, may be amplified or changed into another.

We constantly find we have material that falls outside
our patterns, lines or melodies.   Constantly, too, there is a
certain indeterminacy because we have passed beyond one
system and have not yet found the one that shall replace it;
possibilities abound until we reach the right one that
thenceforth excludes all others.   Thus it is possible to
suggest illustrations of or analogies to the "quanta."[1]
Again, when we consider "bodies" of thought, such as the
growth and history of Science or Religion, our mental
world has a space-time of its own; time being the length of
the duration of a process in its field,[2] and space the extent
of the field at any given moment.   And when we consider
the fluctuating boundaries of these bodies, their overlapping
and interpenetration, and the way in which each can retain
its own individuality and grow (e.g. Art and Religion), we
may even speak of our mental world as multi-dimensional.
In general, if only it were possible to give an adequate
account of the ideological processes in the growing mind,
and of the vicissitudes of thought in history, we should
surely possess an organon more valuable than the use of

[1] Cf. also C. S. Myers, on the "all or none" reactions in psychology
("Psychological conceptions in other Sciences," p. 18f.; see p. 198, n. 2).

[2] Various attempts have been made to correlate similar processes
such as the rise and fall of cultures.   Spengler's is well-known, cf.
also Sir Flinders Petrie, *Revolutions of Civilisation* (1911).

sense-data; for further discovery and progress turn upon what the mind can apprehend.

Characteristic of the evolution of thought has been the tendency to purify the cruder anthropism, if not to banish it altogether. At the same time there has been an increasing tendency to emphasise the significance of Thought, Mind, Reason, Wisdom, and Logos,[1] if not to work towards an absolute idealism. There will always be contradictions in our thinking, and one might almost say that "there are as many Gods as there are philosophers."[2] "The modern God of evolution," says the same writer, "is nothing but the transfer, without correction, of biological categories to the spiritual world."[3] *Un dieu défini c'est un dieu fini*; but the conception of an immanent God that infuses and transfigures the whole personality has a transcendent worth not possessed by any conception that is essentially intellectual and answers to mental and not to personal needs as a whole. It is equally difficult to believe that human nature can be satisfied with mere numinousness or mysticism, or with what is sometimes called "metabiology."[4] There is a Self which knows of its ultimate apartness from this world in which it has to live; and the more it learns of the processes operating in this, God's Universe, the more conscious does it become of the gulf between it and God, a gulf which God alone bridges. "The fear of the Lord is the beginning of Wisdom."

Were we to take a thorough-going crudely rationalistic and materialistic view of evolution, we could say that the Universe at long last produced Man who, with slowly developing ideas of the good, the beautiful and the true, becomes increasingly conscious of the nature of his environment. We see him maintaining sundry religious and

---

[1] Breasted finds in Egypt almost prehistoric testimony to the conception of thought and speech as the source of everything (*The Dawn of Conscience* [1934], p. 37f.; the date is round about 3500 B.C.).

[2] F. J. Sheen, *op. cit.*, p. 196.

[3] *Op. cit.*, p. 261.

[4] Cf. J. Middleton Murry, *God ; being an Introduction to the Science of Metabiology* (1929), also Watkin, *Philosophy of Form*, p. 415.

mystical beliefs and practices to which he attaches supreme importance.   They undergo change, but are never for long renounced; they are replaced, but there is a certain continuity throughout; and in spite of repeated opportunity for varying choice, it is made along typically similar lines. Characteristic is the transition from the primitive and religious view of the world to one that is scientific.   At first, the world is essentially that of Man's animistic and related beliefs; and his outlook, though it is intensely realist, is yet dominantly spiritual.   Then, through the growth and development of the scientific outlook the world becomes essentially external, and the duality of the seen and the unseen realms is felt to be more self-evident.   To synthesise these two views of the Universe is the task of this age.

In and behind the Bible are special interrelated ideas and beliefs, such as are familiar elsewhere, but in a form that distinguishes Biblical religion and its place in history from all other religions.   In the course of a few centuries some remarkable, historical developments led to Christianity, and to a Christendom culminating in our day when life and thought are on trial, and "the age in which we live—it is commonly agreed—is an age of confusion."[1]

The Bible is the Book of the broken relationship between God and Man.   It tells of the creation of the Universe and of Man, Man's persistent shortcomings, the occasions of forgiveness and reconciliation, and finally the vision of a new world.   It goes full circle (p. 129); and although the fundamental ideas extend over centuries, writers, compilers, editors and canonists have succeeded in enabling us to view the Bible as one single whole, to see in it one absolute idea.   The Bible is an Oriental book, and to the Ancient Near East we turn for the finest language of devotion and worship, and the immediacy of man and his gods.   Here, e.g., are words addressed to the Babylonian goddess Ishtar: "let my prayer and my supplication come unto thee, and let thy great mercy be upon me."   And here is a passage from the prayer of Nebuchadrezzar II (605 B.C.) to Marduk:

[1] Viscount Samuel, *Belief and Action* (1937), p. 8.

"without Thee, O Lord, what would happen unto the
king whom thou lovest and whose name thou dost call . . .
grant (unto me) that which may seem good unto thee."
Especially noteworthy is the language of the so-called
"heretic" king, Amenhotep IV, Ikhnaton, to the Sun-god
Re, for of all "divine kings" a more human, if not thoroughly
domesticated monarch, it would be difficult to find: "There
is no other that knoweth thee save thy son Ikhnaton; thou
hast made him wise in thy designs and in thy might.". .

Israel inherited and developed earlier beliefs which it
focussed upon its god Yahweh, his people, and a land which
was possessed by both god and people: we have a special
germinal form of our ideas of God, Man and the Universe.
Whereas some Asiatic religions are apt to be dangerously
tolerant, Yahwism was typically nationalist and intolerant;
and, as monotheistic idealism grew, it was continually
necessary for Israel to think out her convictions of Yahweh
and his purpose with his people.   The profound ideas that
Israel felt to be true have a general validity, and what now
inspires us surely also inspired the early writers, though we
view the ideas in a light other than theirs.   It is to be
observed that the great events in Israelite tradition are placed
at the beginning of the national career in the Pentateuch,
so that the division between Judaeans, or Jews, and the
rival people to their north, the Samaritans, is not accentuated.
But a religious imperialism and universalism give Jerusalem
the supremacy over all lands.

The "history"—the historical books are called the
"Former Prophets"—is essentially the religious "form"
impressed upon the material, so that the record has a
religious, one might say, a "sacramental" value. Criticism
does not destroy the material, but aims at giving the whole
a new sacramental value; and it may be said that misguided
criticism hurts only the critic himself. Frequently an
artistry is displayed in both the Old Testament and the New
which bespeaks a genius which is without equal.   To ask
in such cases if we have "truth"—in the narrower sense—
is to lose their beauty and take a really materialistic view.
The leading ideas are embodied in narrative form; they are

acted or exhibited before they become explicitly articulated; hence the Book of the Old Israel is largely symbolical, while the New Testament may be said to envisage a New Israel, the Body of Christ, in which shall be embodied the new religious idealism.

Especially remarkable is the delineation of various types, each of which is composite in its own way.   Consider, for example, how tribal, national and personal *motifs* are fused together in the great ancestor Jacob or Israel.   David, the first king, is the dynastic ideal, founder of the temple-organisation and Psalmist; Job is the type of innocent suffering, perplexed and protesting.   No less noteworthy is the overlapping of the "natural" and the "supernatural," and the mingling of the terrestrial and the celestial.[1]   The usage is particularly important for our interpretation of the eschatology and the belief in a Kingdom of Heaven (i.e. God).   Of God Himself there are extraordinarily realistic and even exceedingly anthropic conceptions.[2]   On the other hand, the prince of Tyre in Ezek. xxviii. is at once the spirit of the famous commercial city, a semi-mythical being, and, like the divine kings, a representative of the gods or a god in human form.   The "Son of Man" in Daniel vii. 13, is Israel's counterpart or representative, the guardian angel, and a personal and symbolical conception. As for the Messianic ideas, "we may doubt whether Isaiah, if he had been asked whether the ideal King of his vision was human or Divine, could have answered the question at all."[3]   A completely consistent monotheism was not maintained in Israel; and one might almost say that already the problem of the unity of the Godhead was making itself felt.

The "Servant Songs" of the Second Isaiah undoubtedly take us to the profoundest part of the Old Testament.

[1] SeeR. H. Kennett, *The Church of Israel* (1933), pp. 176ff., 185f.

[2] Note the scene on the summit of Mt. Sinai (Ex. xxiv. 9–11), and with God's attack upon Job (xvi. 12–14) compare the story of Jacob's wrestling (Gen. xxxii. 24–32) and the encounter with Moses (Ex. iv. 24).

[3] W. E. Barnes in *Cambridge Theological Essays*, *p.* 356.

Dating from a time of upheaval, they are the highest contribution of pre-Christian religion on the subject of atonement and redemption. The Servant stands at the end of one age and anticipates another. His is a composite picture, a conception incarnated, but with real historical foundation; it is both individual and collective, it is actual, ideal and spiritual. Hence it was capable of growth.[1] The Servant, says the writer to whom I am constantly indebted, is "an intellectual creation of surprising brilliancy, a piece of literature to which there is nothing equal perhaps in any other writings that exist . . . The Scriptures, besides being the word of God, are splended creations of mind."[2]

The Servant is a figure easier to appreciate on the religious plane than to set within a historical frame. But he is not quite unique. The "pierced one" in Zech. xii. 10 is also a complete mystery, whether it refers to an individual, a martyr, or to a type. Again, in the Book of Wisdom there is the unknown "righteous" one, who calls himself the Lord's child; God is his father, and He will uphold the righteous even when insulted, tortured and killed.[3] In this connection it is helpful to refer to Asiatic religion where "the Buddhist genius for compassion" has invented or constructed a benignant goddess of Mercy, Kuan-Yin or (in Japan) Kwannon, the Madonna of the East.[4] As for Amitābha (Amida), the saviour of all who call upon his name, Streeter observes that he "had no historical existence,

---

[1] A. B. Davidson, *Old Testament Prophecy* (posthumous, 1903) treats Christ, the Spirit of Christ and the Church as parallel to the idea of the Servant (p. 441, cf. pp. 258, 467). But the parallelism extends beyond ideas to history.

[2] *Op. cit.*, p. 445.

[3] ii. 13 ff., iv. 7 ff.   In v. 5 he is reckoned among the sons of God, and in iv. 7–14 the Enoch of tradition is evidently in the writer's mind, but the righteous in general are meant.

[4] Streeter, *The Buddha and the Christ*, p. 89.   The definite article is important, it distinguishes the Buddha idea from the Buddha of history.   Streeter's book is especially valuable for its discussion of the parallels between Christianity and Mahāyāna Buddhism, for in the latter greater emphasis is laid upon the ideas that men can realise than on the Buddha of history (viz. Sakyamuni).

but is a personification of the spirit of saving renunciation expressed in Sakyamuni's great consent to live. To the student of the content of religious intuition and of the history of its expression in philosophy and myth, there is no figure of greater interest than that of Amida."[1] But while Buddhism is an escape from the world,[2] Christianity is a return.

Approaching the New Testament from the Old we are struck by the "Jewishness" of Christianity. Think of the confidence and assurance of the prophets, men who like Moses stood in the council of Yahweh and met him face to face (Ex. xxxiii. 11, Num. xii. 6–8). Note Israel's conviction of her function: spouse of Yahweh and his first-born, a prophetic and a priestly people, a covenant people and an intermediary; it was the function of Israel to organise the relationship between God and Man. Christianity, first Jewish and then Gentile, was a true heir of Israel; but in spite of the continuity it was a new phenomenon, a stumbling-block to the Jews and foolishness to the Greeks. More clearly than the contemporaries we can perceive what a stupendous event it was, although we can hardly recapture the experience of freshness and timelessness that it gave the early Christians. Palestine and the Jews had come into contact with the Greek world: the world of Homer, the philosophers and the tragedians. The religion of the Old Testament among the Alexandrian Jews underwent a subtle change, and their translation, the Septuagint, with its Greek religious phraseology became a stepping stone between it and Christianity.[3] Besides the influence of Greek thought upon Jewish ideas of Wisdom, there was a trend towards personification, and the feeling that a new age was imminent.[4] It was the new era of Apollo, and Apolline types of god

[1] *Op. cit.*, p. 91.

[2] On the exception, see below, p. 327.

[3] See esp. the chapters by Oesterley in *Judaism and Christianity*, Vol. I (1937), and that by W. L. Knox in Vol. II.

[4] The IVth Eclogue of Virgil (40 B.C.) is famous. The new age (Aeon) was even personified; see Rankin, in *The Labyrinth* (ed. S. H. Hooke, 1935), pp. 198 ff.

were current by the side of the earlier Adonis, Attis and Osiris.[1] Old religious systems were being undermined.

We must not look at the scene through Old Testament eyes and assume that there were already well-defined conceptions of a God of Righteousness. The existence of religious beliefs and religious literature is not enough in itself to effect a new change in religious development. An age of conflicting policies, it was an age that stood in need of a purification of the current ideas of God, His Messiah and His Kingdom. Loyalty to Rome—for one aspect of Judaism and one of the best of its traits is political loyalty (Jer. xxix. 7)—was faced by vehement anti-Roman intrigue, and bitter dissensions were inflaming the Jews at home and abroad, and disintegrating the Jewish State. There were men who were upsetting the whole civilised world (Acts xvii. 6); but there is no reason to suppose that either Jesus or St. Paul was a revolutionary in any political sense, although social and political conflict was in the air (cf. the spirit of the Magnificat, Luke i. 51 ff). Nevertheless, Jesus came "to cast fire upon the earth" (Luke xii. 49, cf. Matt. x. 34), and the internal domestic conflicts which are envisaged (Matt. x. 35 ff) are of the sort that arise when a new religious movement arises and chooses its adherents independently of all social and economic classes.[2] The presence of a general revolutionary background is most clearly seen in the Fourth Gospel, where Jesus is confronted by fierce religious opposition and by men who wished to make him the centre of revolt.[3] After the endeavour to make him king, shortly

---

[1] *The Religion of Palestine in the Light of Archaeology*, pp. 157, 180, 204.   There was also a special deity, the face or presence of Baal; see above, p. 68f.

[2] Cf. the rise of the Levites (Ex. xxxii. 27, Deut. xxxiii. 9), and the purged Israel in Deut. xiii, 6 ff.

[3] Cf. C. H. Dodd, *The Expositor*, XXII (1921), 289f.   They were of the patriots who "believed in the Apocalyptic vision of Israel's future, but also believed that it was their duty to assist God, so to speak, to make the Apocalyptic vision a reality by political activity" (S. H. Hooke, in *Judaism and Christianity*, I. p. 268).   It is worth adding that it has been said of Lenin and Stalin that they felt that "history must be given a shove," and "forced" (in the horticultural sense); Viscount Samuel, *Belief and Action*, p. 203.

before the Passover (John vi. 4, 15), he became a marked
man, and, when the next Passover came round, the "King
of the Jews" was crucified with two "robbers," Barabbas,
a notable rebel, being released.[1]   But his kingdom was not
of this external world (John xviii. 36) ; and after a few decades
the civil war and the war against the Romans brought the
utter ruin of those who had sought to inaugurate their own
kingdom by violence.   It was the final fall of a house divided
against itself; it was contemporary with the rise of a new
spiritual unifying force.

The personality of Jesus of Nazareth must have been
such as to account for what He became to His followers:
"Never man so spake" (John vii. 46).   The absolute value
that the Cross had from the first testifies to the profound
impression made by what otherwise might have seemed to
be merely one of the many tragic incidents during the days
of civil and political strife.   Ideas do not float in the air,
nor are they borne along on the stream of history save in
human vessels.   On the most naturalistic and secular
grounds, we have to understand—in the light of our knowledge of our kind—the rise and persistence of Christianity
and the convictions it has ever inspired.   Just as the
chequered history of Israel, the Exile, and finally the fall of
Jerusalem and the Jewish state plunged men into despair,
but also gave a new form to their faith, so the life of Jesus
and the culmination on Calvary led, not to the belief in a
helpless God Who had forsaken His Servant, but to the final
conviction that the tragic loss of a life devoted to His
service meant His supremacy.   God, as the old Israel, the
firstborn of Yahweh, had come to know, was supreme over
all His servants and instruments; and the life and death
of Jesus, in showing what Man could do, enhanced the convictions, not of some ruthless historical necessity, but of a
God Who must have loved the whole world that He could
even give His Son for others (John iii. 16).   Either men
could see in history God's powerlessness to save His own, or,
rising on the wings of faith, above the clouds, they found a

[1] The Passover was a time of disturbance; see Josephus Wars II, i,
3, xii, 1 and contrast the special reference to the quiet in xii, 6.

Living God and a Loving Father Who could transmute what to them was the greatest of tragedies into the greatest of saving acts.

Faith in a God above and behind history turned events in the world of flesh and blood into a supreme event in the spiritual development of Man. A new complex of ideas was inaugurated. That all sin was an offence against the gods was an old Oriental belief; but when God is the All-Father, sin is more than an affair between a man and his god, it has a wider repercussion. To injure others is to injure God's own;[1] and although every individual is precious in His eyes, he has no value in his own right, being at the best an "unprofitable servant" (Luke xvii. 10). The very highest ideals are set forth; one may win the world but lose one's soul (Mark viii. 36), and the simplest human relation-ships in God's Universe outweigh all that the world can bestow upon us in our three-score years and ten (1 Cor. xiii). Through Jesus Christ the course of history took a new direction. Old questions were answered by raising new ones; and present despair and anxiety were blotted out by the new and confident hopes for the future, based upon foundations than which no surer could be conceived.

Christianity arose, not as a people's choice of a new god, but as God's choice of a new people; it was not a new stage in an old body, but a transformation into a new body with a new spirit.[2] Christ is not to be made the function of our instinctive desires.[3] Men may capture the Jesus of the Gospels for a party, a class or a state; but the Christ of spiritual history cannot be so handled. The aberrations of the Christ-idea have made men conscious of what He is *not*, even as the old Israel of the past was from time to time led to realise that their Yahweh was *not* as the gods of the nations.[4] The idea of God must not be a "blank cheque"; and the Messiah, the Christ, became the *eikōn*, the repre-sentative of the invisible God (Col. i. 15, cf. 2 Cor. iv. 6): not

---

[1] Similarly in the case of Israel, Gen. xii. 3.

[2] *O.T.R.*. p. 210. Cf. above p. 168.

[3] Cf. Keller, *Religion and the European Mind*, p. 61 f.

[4] Cf. *O.T.R.*, p. 158.

that He was God, but God was like Him.[1]   The new Israel,
like the old, had to exclude the idea of a God wholly immanent in His Anointed or in the body of worshippers.   Christo-
centricism was therefore to be avoided.   But the whole world
of thought has changed so profoundly in nineteen centuries
that "the time has come for a fuller apprehension of His
[God's] nature, His character and His relationship with men."[2]

Through the Christ men have gained a deeper knowledge
of themselves and of their nature: a knowledge both
"religious" and "secular."   He does not intoxicate the
emotions, like the Indian Krishna.[3]   He has given men
their convictions of the contact between Man and God;
and they have found that there is an Ultimate Reality in
the Universe that responds to the highest that they have
sought in Him.   God operates "naturally"; current Messianic ideas were transformed and spiritualised.   Indeed
Christianity became a mixture of not wholly reconcilable
elements; and had the Logos-idea been fully developed, it
might have transposed the Faith into a system of episte-
mology or a cosmological speculation, and neither Religion,
nor Philosophy, nor Science would have gained.[4]

There is a tendency to isolate unduly the Incarnation and
the Cross; but from the Biblical point of view the incarna-
nation is "the culmination of the theophanies in the Old
Testament.[5]   There must have been many lesser Calvaries
in history.[6]   Yet, like the Sinaitic Covenant and the
"Servant of the Lord," they inaugurate eras; and from
being events in human history they become stages in
religious development.[7]   Historical events may be of

[1] Streeter, op. cit., pp. 127, 182f.; cf. above, p. 305.

[2] Report of the Lambeth Conference (1930), p. 76. Cf. W. R.
Matthews, The New Learning (ed. Raby, 1933), pp. 324, 331f.

[3] R. G. Milburn, The Logic of Religious Thought (1929), p. 140.

[4] L. W. Grensted, The Philosophical Implications of Christianity
(1930), p. 15.

[5] Davidson, Old Testament Prophecy, p. 412.

[6] Raven, op. cit., p. 20f.

[7] Cf. Davidson, op. cit., p. 454: "it is the practice of Scripture in
general to deal with concrete cases and apply its principles to them—
principles which, though not applied by it further, are capable of
further application."

permanent significance in changing once and for all the
course of life and thought. To-day is the outcome of all
that has gone before, and what in our minds is now more or
less a contemporary whole could doubtless be analysed and
dates found for the first appearance of various constituent
elements or stages. What is real and true for us now may
have been realised for the first time at some given point in
the past; although, on the other hand, much may have
atrophied or fallen away which was once felt to be vital,
true and full of promise.

It is often easier to outline the past growth of ideas
than to present our own to-day as an integrated structure.
Accordingly, as regards Biblical religion, we can point
to some great epoch-making steps in the past; but although
they have made history what it is, we do not necessarily
feel that they concern our history to-day. The great
religious ideas of the past which we can single out and
isolate had their context, their body; but to-day there are
isolated "true" ideas which need a body in order that their
truth may be manifest, even as there are "bodies" sorely in
need of a truly animating "spirit." Any account of what
the Bible has to say is incomplete until it points us towards
what we can affirm as true for ourselves to-day; but
repeatedly, like Israel of old, men find they can speak only
of the God of the past (cf. Hab. iii), and not of One still
working in their midst. Israel was able to give a religious
form to its traditions of the past only because of its living
religious faith; whereas it is because of the lack of such a
faith that history to us scarcely seems to be part of a Divine
creative process. It took the harshness of history to bring
to the front the ultimate truths by which men have lived;
and it takes history, again, to turn into actual life what have
become abstract ideas and doctrines.

It can be said that in reality there is a continuous process
of creation, incarnation and atonement.[1] But only the
interpretation of the historical development of past life
and thought enables us to justify this statement, and turn
what in the Bible is one great cosmic process spread over

[1] Cf. also Raven, *op. cit.*, pp. 29ff.

centuries into actual principles of the Universe. In like manner, the fact of an ever-present God, or rather that Man is ever in God's presence (p. 193), is justified by all that we can cull from the history of religious and other thought, it is part of the "Theory of Religion"; but as an Absolute Truth only history can actualise it. "Lo, I am with you alway" (Matt. xxviii. 20), and the Second Coming are complementary, belonging to Religion and History respectively; and if we would reinterpret for ourselves the early Christian anticipation of a Parousia, we may understand how the latter, not as a cosmic spectacle, but as an inward revelation, a genuine experience in the lives of individuals, substantiates the former. That "God is Love" was felt and enunciated in the most explicit manner only nineteen hundred years ago; but that this has always been true is forced upon us by the combination of religious experience and the only reasonable explanation of the history of the Universe of Nature and Man.

Similar occasions interpret each other, and the real significance of the past epoch-making stages in Religion will be best understood by individuals and communities only as they experience for themselves what such changes can mean. Past and present history will then be mutually illustrative, and the dialectic process will have completed another cycle: the supernatural within the natural, the reality of both the spiritual world and of the world of space and time, and the Creation of the Universe by an unseen spiritual Power and the drawing of it to Him in the Christ.

Profound genuine experiences of the relationship between God and Man are world-wide. A Mohamedan mystic tells how Moses once rebuked a shepherd for praying to Allah in language so naïve, familiar and gross as to be almost blasphemous. But Allah rebuked the prophet, "I look not at the tongue and the speech, but at the inward spirit and feeling; I gaze into the heart of the worshipper and regard not the mode of expression."[1] Yet the fact of the abiding presence of God everywhere must not obscure the essential

[1] R. A. Nicholson, *Mathnawi* (1926), ii. 310ff.; cf. Sir Thomas Arnold, *The Islamic Faith* (1928), p. 62.

facts of the evolution of religious thought and expression
and of all else that goes to make Human Culture. The
development of Religion in and behind the Bible and the
difference between Biblical religion and religion elsewhere
in history are stern warnings of a process in the Universe
which cannot be ignored with impunity. The future of a
progressive religion is a cultural and not solely a religious
concern, requiring hard thought not less than sincere
prayer; and in promoting the further development of
Human Culture—in the best sense of the term—Man is
co-operating with a Divine Power that is waiting to help
him.

Meanwhile, a world that is building bigger and better
barns is experiencing malaise, unrest, fear and a sense of
frustration. Yet there is also a hunger and thirst after
Righteousness; and it is a right and honest intuition that
rejects the religion of a past age until it has become the
religion of the present. If, in a sense, we seem to know too
much, and the immensity of the Universe overwhelms us,
the right sort of knowledge has always been better than
knowledge as such. If there is a reaching forward and the
anticipation of some new stage of development, the course
of history cannot be forced. In the field of life as in that
of research attention to the minor issues will often prepare
the way for the major, and the successful forward step is
taken only when the path has been prepared by humbler toil.

To-day the truth of Religion often does not seem con-
vincing because of the gulf between the sphere of the
"religious" and that of the "non-religious." Religion is out
of touch with ideas that seem to us to have a greater validity.
On the other hand, if there is a tendency—especially in
Biblical Criticism—to "secularise" the Bible, and—especially
in psychology—to treat Religion as a "natural" phenomenon,
this, however, does not destroy Religion, nor—so to speak—
"cheapen" it; on the contrary, the result of the tendency
is ultimately to restore to Religion the effective realism that
properly belongs to it, by demonstrating the absolute interpenetration of the two spheres, and the reality of each for the
normal individual. Indeed, the essential truths of Religion

are "every-day" ones: the interpenetration of God (and all that He stands for) and Man in everything; and they are so tremendous that His creatures can feel overwhelmed, and yet so "natural" that they may come to hold them loosely and cease to reverence Him.   In fine, if the complete course of the history of the Universe is "supernatural," it lies wholly outside human hands; if it is "natural," can Man co-operate with its processes unaided?

The only absolutely and ultimately inevitable processes are those of a Righteous God Who does not force his creatures, but gives them a measure of freedom and creativeness.   He leads them step by step; and by this we mean that there is, in spite of appearances, an intelligible continuity in life. Men may be too far "outside," and not "ahead" of their environment; they are said to "run past themselves"; too one-sided, extreme or specialistic a development can be harmful to the healthy progress of life and of thought alike. There are things in Christianity which could not conceivably have found a place in the less developed religion of Israel; and Jesus Himself could not tell all that was in his heart (John xvi. 12).   There can be—or are—religious and other truths for which the environment is not ready; and although it is here and now that we have to live we are conscious that there is vastly more waiting to be known.

Can one reconcile this existence of ours with the intuitions of a vaster one?   India had its four stages: the student, the householder, the hermit, and finally the ascetic meditating on the relation between his soul and that of the Universe. Buddhism sought an escape from earthly existence and the chain of human cause and effect; but the beautiful conception of the Bodhisattva is that of the man who will forego bliss and remain in the cycle of birth, death and rebirth in order to save others.   Plato, in turn, tells the wise man to descend from the heavenly places and return to the cave and live with his less enlightened comrades.   It seems that at times there must be a self-emptying, a *kenōsis* (p. 274 n.), if men would carry others along with them.   And if this calls for patience, to strive after God's own patience is surely to co-operate with Him.   If one recalls the fine

Israelite conception of the "Remnant," or the "Salt of the earth," who, in times of uncertainity and decay, maintain higher principles and history-making ideals, spanning the years from one stage of equilibrium to another, one must in any event avoid that caricature of the conception, the notion that true Religion is only for our coterie, and that we alone are God's elect.

It takes an age of crisis and change for men to re-discover that the Bible is the Book of the Prophet's Path; and when the Kingdom of Heaven seems to delay its coming, it may need the completest faith in the God of the Universe and His Righteousness. But Hope is still one of the three great Christian virtues. Although in Him we already live and move and have our being, it is a relationship to be besought, and humbly striven for.   There is a path to be trodden; and, like the man in *Pilgrim's Progress*, if we cannot see the wicket-gate on the other side of our field, there is—or rather, there *seems* to be—a shining light, of which we can only say, with him, that we *think* we see it.   We walk by faith and not by sight (2 Cor. v. 7); but faith has moved men in all their religious and non-religious ventures: *possunt quia posse videntur*.   Alone the highest faith offers the completest answer to all the quests of life.

The religions have had their symbols[1]: the Swastika as a symbol of good fortune, the Caduceus, the Solar-wheel, and others.   In Egypt the Winged-Sun suggested light, life and protection.   The symbol popularised by Ikhnaton displayed the Sun, the god of all lands and peoples, offering life and a helping hand wherever its rays fell: the reform failed, but the symbol deepened personal religion.   But of all the symbols the Cross stands on a hill, apart.   It is the crowning symbol of all who testify and bear witness to their ultimate truth; it speaks also of seeming failure, disappointment and disillusion; it tells of daily burdens, not known to others, but not borne alone; and it is the assurance that it is not men alone whose concern is with the history and conditions of men, but that behind and above all is the Divine Love.

[1] See Count Goblet d'Alviella, *The Migration of Symbols* (1894).

Chronological Notes

These notes provide merely a rough survey of some of the events and dates in the development of the great historical religions. Reference may be made to *O.T.R.*, pp. 225–232, and to the books mentioned below, viz.—B. (J. H. Breasted, *The Dawn of Conscience*, 1934); M. (G. F. Moore, *History of Religions*, I, 1914, II, 1920); and S.S. (Sydney Smith, *Early History of Assyria*, 1928).

The *geological* history of Palestine is particularly interesting; it is enough to refer to the great rift of the Jordan Valley, and the broken country of Judaea (p. 149). For *prehistoric* man there is abundant evidence, and definite advances can probably be dated round about 5000 B.C.[1] There is reason to believe that there was a united Egypt not later than 4000 B.C. (B., 10ff.). A second and more enduring union is dated for the thirty-fifth to the twenty-fifth centuries B.C., during which the foundations of culture are being laid over the whole of the Ancient Near East (Egypt, Crete, Asia Minor, Babylonia, etc.). Lands come into constant contact with each other, and literary forms become fixed. Babylonian culture begins to exercise a very wide influence, and in spite of the differences in language there is a very general similarity of life and thought throughout Egypt and south-west Asia (S.S., 165f., 202; cf. B., 120ff.).

c. 2000 B.C. *First great Biblical epoch.* The Twelfth Dynasty of Egypt. The First Dynasty of Babylon, with whose royal law-giver, Hammurabi, the Hebrew writers evidently identified Amraphel of the days of Abraham (Gen. xiv). The age of the prime of Crete. Impending prominence of the Ḥatti (Hittites). Suggested date of the earliest elements of the Rig-Veda.

A period of disturbance follows, due to Indo-Iranian Ḥurri and other tribes. Fall of Babylonia. Hyksos invasion of Egypt; the Palestine of this period is clearly marked.

Fourteenth century, B.C. *Second great Biblical epoch.* Egypt recovers independence (Eighteenth Dynasty); far-reaching conquests in south-west Asia. The "Amarna" age is one of close international intercourse. Note the importance of the Ḥatti of Asia Minor and the land of Mitanni and their Indo-Iranian connections (p. 140); like Ras Shamra (in North Phoenicia), they form a bridge between Babylonia, etc., and Greece. The reform of Ikhnaton, the naturalism in art, and the prominence of certain fundamental ideas distinguish an age that is presumably that of Moses.

c. 1200 B.C. A period of disturbance follows. The older cultures decay. Movements of Philistines and other Levantine peoples by sea and also of Aramaeans from the desert. Rise of ecclesiasticism in Egypt. Decline of the great powers; and the rise of small states. Palestine's fight for independence, the disturbances round about 1200 B.C., the repulse of the Philistine occupation of the highlands and the rise of Israel make a definite landmark.

[1] See Eduard Meyer, *Geschichte des Altertums* i (1909), §§ 592, 597.

A virtually "Dark Age" follows (especially for Greece, Egypt and Babylonia). The "Epic" age of Greece. In India the Rig-Veda period is followed by the priestly Brahmanism and the Upanishads. In Israel the fall of the Omri Dynasty and the rise of that of Jehu (841) mark a new stage (cf. the figures of Elijah and Elisha).

Eighth century B.C. A new age opens. Greek expansion. First Olympiad 776 B.C., also the first real date in Chinese history.[1] Foundation of Rome, 754. The first of the great line of prophets, Amos and Hosea; later, Isaiah and Micah. Hesiod, Homer's principal successor; the Greek pantheon becomes fixed (C.A.H., III, 610 f). The fall of Samaria (722–1) leads to a change in population in (North) Israel.

Seventh century B.C. Keen interest in ancient Babylonian literature by Ashurbanipal (699–); fall of Nineveh (612). Rise of New Babylonian empire under Nebuchadrezzar II (605). Saite restoration in Egypt (Twenty-sixth Dynasty; Psammetichus, 663), antiquarian return to the old Egypt. Activity of Medes, Lydia, Cimmerians and Scythians. Probable date of Zoroaster (c. 660), or at least of some revival in the Iranian religion.

Sixth century B.C. *Third great Biblical epoch. The Age of the Exile.* Internal changes in Palestine (p. 136). The fall of Jerusalem (597, 586) and the Exile. The Second Temple of Jerusalem rebuilt under Zerubbabel (520–16). Period of the Second Isaiah. Contemporary is the marked antiquarianism in Egypt and in Babylonia (Nabonidus, 556). Rise of Persian or Achaemenid Empire under Cyrus (539). In the West: Orphic movements, Solon (638–538), Thales (643–546), and the Ionian school of thinkers; in S. Italy the Pythagorean school. Parting of the ways between West and East (see Chap. VIII).

In India two great "heresies" arise, Jainism, under Mahavira (d. 484) and Buddhism, under Sakyamuni Gautama, the Buddha (560–480). In China rise of Tao-ism under Lao-tse (b. 604), and Confucianism under Kong-fu-tse (551–478).

Fifth century B.C. Greece repels the Persian invasion. Age of Pindar (d. 443, the purifying of the old ancestral religion), Aeschylus (d. 456, the idea of a divine order in the Universe); Sophocles (495–406) and Euripides (480–406), Socrates (c. 470–399) and Plato (see below). The inauguration of post-exilic Judaism, associated with the names of Nehemiah (445) and, later, Ezra (? 397). Conquests of Alexander the Great (333–2), who reaches India (327). Seleucid era begins (312): spread of Greek influence to the East (Hellenism).

Fourth century B.C. Plato (427–347) and Aristotle (384–22). In China, Mencius (Meng-tse, 372–289) and his contemporary Chuang-tsze, representatives of Confucianism and Taoism.

Third century B.C. Strength of Iranism (Old Persian culture) and spread of Oriental cults to the west (the Egyptian Isis, the Phrygian Cybele). Oriental reaction against Hellenism. Antiochus Soter I (280–261), patron of Berosus, the Babylonian historian.

[1] E. W. Hopkins *The History of Religion* (1918), pp. 226, 233. The date for Japan is 660 B.C. (*ib.* p. 276, M i. 100).

Revival of Babylonian literature, popularity of "Chaldaean" priests, etc. Zeno (d. 261), founder of the Cosmopolitan School. In India Buddhism is state religion under King Asoka; missionary enterprise, even to Egypt.

Second century B.C. Antiochus IV Epiphanes; his forceful Hellenising measures (175) provoke Jewish reaction (book of Daniel, probably 166); rise of the Maccabees. Hasmonaean power and revival of the old Davidic Idea. Ben Sira (Ecclesiasticus). Panaetius introduces Stoicism into Rome (c. 140).

First century B.C. Palestine between Rome and Parthia (Pompey enters Jerusalem, 63); Parthian invasions. Herod the Great, 37–4 B.C. The Fourth Eclogue of Virgil and the anticipated inauguration of the Golden Age (40 B.C., see C.A.H., X, 472). Augustus (63 B.C.–A.D. 14) and the new page in history (C.A.H., X, 583). The cult of Apollo elevated; revival of the old Roman religion in opposition to Oriental cults.

First century A.D. The fourth great Biblical epoch. The Foundation of Christianity. Its separation from Judaism, and its spread (facilitated by the Dispersion of the Jews and their Synagogues and by the unity of the Roman Empire). Pontius Pilate procurator, 26–36; probable date of the Crucifixion of Jesus, 33; death of St. Paul, 64 (?). Philo, the climax of Jewish–Hellenistic syncretism, prior to the bifurcation. The Jewish War (66–70), capture of Jerusalem by Titus (70). The New Testament writings (?50–100). Josephus writes the War (75–79) and the Antiquities (93–4). Oriental cults strong in the West. In China, Wang Ch'ung (towards A.D. 100) has been compared to Epicurus and Lucretius (98–55 B.C.).

Second century A.D. Text and Canon of Old Testament fixed. Rabbinical Judaism establishing itself. Serious Jewish disturbances in the Levant; 132–5 the Second Jewish Revolt (Bar Kokhba), followed by Hadrian's reorganisation of Palestine. Jerusalem becomes Aelia Capitolina. Persistence of old Palestinian motifs on coins, etc. Christianity confronts Gnosticism. The Indian Bhagavad-gita, according to some authorities, is of this period.

Third century A.D. Origen (d. 254). Rise of Neo-platonism (with its exceptional influence upon Christian theology) under the non-Christian mystic Plotinus (205–70) and the anti-Christian Porphyry (233–304). Mani (215–76), founder of Manichaeism, which became a world-religion, rival to Christianity, and lasted about ten centuries. Spread of Oriental cults (the Syrian emperor-priest Elagabalus at Rome, 218–222), and in particular of Mithraism (carried by the Roman army to the West). Sassanian (late Persian) national revival, A.D. 226–650.

Fourth century A.D. Christianity, persecuted by Diocletian, the patron of Mithraism (303–4); but recognised by Constantine (324). Councils of Nicaea (325) and, later, of Constantinople (381). Julian "the Apostate" reopens temples of Baalbek, etc. (361–3); but paganism is put down by Theodosius (392). The century in which "Christian saints gradually usurped the position of pagan gods and demigods" (A. B. Cook, Zeus, I, 167).

Fifth century A.D. St. Augustine (350–430). Council of Chalcedon (451). The heresy of Nestorius denounced (431). The Nestorian school at Edessa (the "Athens of Syria"), closed by Zeno (489), moves to Nisibis, its missionaries later reach China (by 630). Sack of Rome by Alaric and the Goths (410), prelude to the destruction of Rome (466) and the severance into Eastern (Byzantine) and Western Christianity. Proclus (411–85), a bridge between Plato (and Aristotle) and mediaeval learning. Death of Hypatia (415) and of Alexandrian philosophy.

Sixth century A.D. At Athens, the school of philosophy, after a career of 900 years, closed by Justinian (529). Neo-platonism, represented by the so-called "Dionysius the Areopagite" (c. 500). The old South Arabian culture (closely related to the ancient Oriental culture of Babylonia, etc.) has by now disappeared; a traditional great deluge (the Bursting of the Dyke) and the "Age of Ignorance" precede the Mohammedan age.

Seventh century A.D. Mohammed (570–632); his flight to Medina (the Hejra, Hegira), 15 July, 622. The Koran is fixed (c. 650). Rapid conquests of Islam (634–44), extending in the early eighth century to Sind in the east and Spain in the west (Battle of Tours in 732 saves Gaul).

Eighth century A.D. Noteworthy decline of Buddhism in India, before the more attractive types of Hinduism (M., I, 312 ff.); its increasing strength in East Asia. Çankara, Indian Monist (c. 800).

Ninth-Eleventh century A.D. *Rise of Jewish-Arabian Philosophy.* Translations of Aristotle, etc., reach Arabs and Jews through the Syrians. Their influence upon Europeans (e.g. John Scotus Eriugena, 800–877). "Scholasticism" gaining strength.

Twelfth century A.D. In the East, Ramanuja (c. 1100), Indian theologian and philosopher. In China, Chu Hsi (1130–1200), one of the best known interpreters of Confucianism. In Japan the rise of new Buddhist sects has been compared with the rise of new monastic orders in Europe (M., I, 122, II, 279), e.g. St. Francis of Assisi (1182–1216) and the Franciscans. In this, the great century of scholasticism, Paris was "the Athens of the Middle Ages," and Jewish scholars began to exercise influence on Christendom.

Thirteenth century A.D. *The Golden Age of Scholasticism.* Futile attempt to prohibit Aristotelian philosophy (M., II, 271); the fusion of Christian, Oriental and Greek thought culminates in St. Thomas Aquinas (1225–74).

Forerunners of the Reformation: Wycliffe (1350–1384), Hus (1369–1415) and Savonarola (1452–98). Active printing of the Bible (1450–1520, see M., II, 295). The Fall of Constantinople (1453) to the Moslems sends Greeks and Greek MSS. westwards, opening up a new world and inaugurating "a new untheological kind of international culture" (M., II, 292). The rediscovery of antiquity, the revival of learning, and humanism constitute the Renaissance, and sever the Modern World from the Middle Ages. In India new religious movements under Kabir and Nanak (1469–1539), the religion of the Sikhs. In China, the Neo-Confucian school of Wang-Yang-Min (1472–1528).

Sixteenth century A.D. *The Reformation.* Erasmus (c. 1466–1536); Luther (1483–1546); his 95 theses at Wittenberg, 1517. Zwingli (1484–1531), Calvin (1509–64), and Melancthon (1497–1560).

The Act of Supremacy, 1535, makes a decisive breach between England and the Papacy. 1538 a copy of the Bible ordered to be placed in every church. Publication of the "Copernican theory," 1543 (condemned by the Inquisition in 1615). The Council of Trent (1545–63) and the "Society of Jesus" (founded by Ignatius de Loyola [d. 1556]), are the reply to the Protestant Reformation. Latter sixteenth century, brief revival of Scholasticism in Spain. 1549, Xavier takes Christianity to Japan, and finds a sort of Buddhist native Lutheranism, with earlier parallels in India (M., I, 136, cf. pp. 328, 337, and 135f.). In India the Emperor Akbar (1542–1605) attempts to found a new eclectic religion.

Seventeenth century A.D. The Authorised Version, 1611. Active work at the Biblical languages: *Clerus Anglicanus Stupor Mundi*.[1] The Westminster Confession of Faith, 1645; Bunyan's Pilgrim's Progress, 1678; George Fox (d. 1691). Descartes (1596–1650) and Spinoza (1632–77). Galileo (1564–1642) and Isaac Newton (1642–1727). Close of century, Shabbetai Zebi (1626–76), followed by other mystics and Messianic pretenders; Baal Shem founder of Hasidism.

Eighteenth century A.D. The "Methodists" (John Wesley, d. 1791; George Whitefield, d. 1770). Moses Mendelssohn (1729–1786), the "Luther" of the Jews, the removal of "the ignominy of a thousand years." Lessing (1729–81), Kant (1724–1804), Hegel (1770–1831); the change from Authority to Reason, and the rise of the Historical Method. Mohammed ibn Abd al-Wahhab founder of the Arab puritan movement.

Nineteenth century A.D. The main factors are Romanticism, social-economic movements, immense advances in science, rediscovery of the Ancient Near East, progress in new fields (e.g. anthropology, comparative religion), and the closer critical study of the Bible and other Sacred Books. Among special landmarks are the works of Darwin (1859 and 1871), Herbert Spencer (1860), Marx (*Das Kapital*, 1867), and Wellhausen (1878, see p. 17). In the sphere of religion may be mentioned the Oxford Movement, 1833; and a series of papal Encyclicals: the Syllabus of Errors, 1864; the revival of Scholasticism (*Aeterni Patris*), 1879; the condemnation of Modernism, 1907; also the proceedings of the Biblical Commission at Rome, 1906, 1908, etc. Revival of national religion in India and Japan, the religion of the Bāb (Mirza Ali Mohammed, d. 1850), and Bahaism (Baha Allah, d. 1892); and the Mohammedan Ahmed movement (1889).

Twentieth century A.D. Of special interest are—outside social and political events—the newer movements in science; the "rediscovery" of the work of Mendel (1822–82); and, as regards the Bible, the greater interest in its place in history and religion.

[1] Cited by G. H. Box in *the Legacy of Israel*, p. 368.

Index of Biblical and other Passages

All references are made to the R.V. The references to the Apocrypha and other sources are placed at the end.

General Index

References are often made to the footnotes in order to facilitate the identification of the portion of the page in question. Attention is drawn to the key entries: Spirit; Environment; Quantitative and Qualitative Changes; Differentiation; Dualism; Isolate; Patterns; Revelation; Right. The index also includes a few abbreviations (e.g. *C.A.H.*).

337

Davids, T. W. Rhys, 146.
Davids, Mrs. Rhys, 245n.
Davidson, A. B., 89n., 91n., 93,
97n., 123n., 271n., 307n., 318n.,
323n.
Dawson, Christopher, 116n., 156n.,
250n., 252n.
Death and the Dead, 93, 123f., 184,
192, 268ff., 288f.
Democratic note in the Bible, 38,
42, 45f., 165.
Desert, the, as a factor, 63, 155,
168ff.
De-spiritualising and Re-spiritualis-
ing processes, 225, 227, 229ff., 249,
254, 257. See Religion (creative
stages).
Deuteronomy, book of, 42f., 45, 95,
118, 153, 212.
Dialectical Materialism, 220, 225,
258, 261n., 283ff., 291, 298n.
See Marxism.
Differentiation, processes of: ideas
of right and order, 11, 34f., 110,
131, 144, 244; ideas of spirit, 267;
less differentiated stages, 150f.,
228, 231.
Dilthey, W., 135n., 216n.
Discontinuity. See Continuity.
Disintegration. See Redintegration.
Dodd, C. H., 320n.
Drummond, Henry, 262, 273n.
Dualisms, some familiar: Mind and
matter, 265, 308; Thought and
action, 303f.; God and Satan,
265; this world and the beyond,
11, 183, 282; the "natural" and
the "supernatural," 96, 99, 125,
159ff., 199, 282, 317, 327; "this"
world and the "beyond," 11, 99,
183, 282; the "religious" and the
"non-religious," 1f., 4, 7, 11f.,
14, 77f., 117, 185, 230, 233, 286,
289, 326. See Spirit.

Ecclus. = Ecclesiasticus (Ben Sira).
Eckhart, Meister, 195.
"Ecology," 293.
Eddington, Sir A. S., 262n.
Edwards, D. M., 253.
Egypt, ideas of sin, 126. See
Ikhnaton, *Maat*.

Einstein, 8n., 185n.
Eldad and Medad, 42.
Elephantine, 137.
Elijah, 169f., 247n.
Embodiment of a god, 252. See
Spirit and Body.
"Emergence" of the new, 184, 298f.
See New.
Emerson, 183, 254.
Ency. Bib. = *Encyclopaedia Biblica*.
England, T. E., 198n.
Environment, the, protects, 163,
232, 258, 267, 272, 297, cf. 302,
and see Change. See Field, Out-
side.
Epictetus, 193n.
Eschatology, 124f., 156, 238.
Evolution, applies to "isolates,"
283f. (see Isolation); not to God,
191; does not exclude "leaps" and
"revolutions," 259, 268 (see Dia-
lectical Materialism, Quantita-
tive); may be sectarian, and a
devolution, 225, 243, 295, 300;
in Biblical history and religion,
4ff., 18f., 55f., Chap. V, 72n., 74,
85f., 214, 224. See also New.
Events, 265, 309, 311.
Exile, Age of, Chap. VIII, illustrated by the Pentateuch, 236f.; a
second Exodus, 26f., 47f., 127.
Exodus. See above.
Ezekiel, 270.

Farquhar, J., 144n.
Fascism, 284.
Feibleman, J., 157n.
Field or environment, 90, 107,
195n., 232, 254, 296, 298f. See
Environment, Outside.
Forgiveness, reconciliation and
atonement, 116, 120ff., 222.
"Forms," 263, 265, 307, 316. See
Patterns.
Fowler, W. W., 189n.
Freedom and liberty, 114, 116, 119,
124, 130, 230, 259, 289, 327.
Fulfilment, 56, 58, 130.
"Fullness of Time," 160.

Galloway, G., 135n., 254n., 300n.
Gautama. See Buddha.

Saul   c.   1025 B.C.
David   c.   1000
Solomon   c.   970.
The Disruption   933

Amos 760-746. } temp.
Hosea 746-34 } Jeroboam II

Micah   } about 739-700
Isaiah (1-39)   } Uzziah Jotham
                 } Ahaz Hezekiah

Fall of Samaria 721.

Finding of Law-book } 621
Josiah's reforms   }

First deportation to Babylon 596.

Fall of Jerusalem 586.   Isaiah 40-55 prob 549-538

                                Leviticus (before close of Exile)

Cyrus captures Babylon 538.
Return of Zerubbabel & Joshua 537.
Dedication of 2nd Temple 516.   ← Isaiah 56-66 prob. c. 450
Return of Nehemiah 445
2nd visit of Nehemiah 433.